Human Trafficking and Human Rights

Kay Firth-Butterfield

Kendall Hunt
publishing company

Cover image © Shutterstock, Inc.

All chapter opener images © Shutterstock, Inc.

Kendall Hunt
publishing company

www.kendallhunt.com
Send all inquiries to:
4050 Westmark Drive
Dubuque, IA 52004-1840

ISBN 978-1-4652-4112-2

Printed in the United States of America
10 9 8 7 6 5 4 3 2 1

Dedicated

To my fabulous family: Rohaise, Audrey and Walter. Also, to all of those victims who suffer, and have suffered, the hideous crime of human trafficking. May this book bring awareness of their lives and help to bring an end to their suffering.

Slavery of all kinds is innocence lost.

Contents

Acknowledgments

I could not have written this book without the support and help of my family and many colleagues. Also, I want to say thanks to William England from Kendall Hunt who believed I would deliver the script even when I was being pressed by other concerns and who supported me throughout.

There are many influences which lie behind a book like this one. My mother for one. She supported the need to educate a girl and my need to qualify at the Bar, unusual for a women in those days. Also, I want to acknowledge the late Colonel Professor Draper, my Professor at the University of Sussex, who inspired me to care about the legal rights of human beings.

With my colleague, Dr. Myhr, I led workshops on Human Trafficking in 2010. As we taught them we saw that most of our 900 students had little or no knowledge of human trafficking and I decided this book needed to be written. In 2013, we repeated the workshop and were gratified to see that the courses at our University dedicated to Human Rights and Human Trafficking had reached many of our students who came to the Workshops with a baseline of knowledge upon which we could discuss modern slavery, social justice and possible solutions. Dr. Myhr has been a huge support for the project and to me personally.

Children and young people across the globe are particularly vulnerable to human trafficking, and awareness will help to protect them. Some of the most vulnerable are street children – those children for whom the street is a central reference point and plays a significant part in their everyday lives and identities. I am proud to help them through my work as the U.S. Ambassador for the Consortium for Street Children.

I am fortunate to know many people dedicated to bringing an end to human trafficking, but two of the most dedicated are David Walding and Dottie Laster. They work tirelessly to help those who cannot help themselves, to recognize those who the world has forgotten, shunned or simply not noticed. In acknowledging them I acknowledge the many people who work to support victims despite the many obstacles placed in their way.

A special thanks to my editor: Walter Burrough.

About the Author

Kay Firth-Butterfield is a lawyer and academic. In the United Kingdom she practiced law as both a Barrister and Solicitor. Also, she holds a part-time judicial appointment and is a Member of the Inner Temple, London. She is a Fellow of the Royal Society for the Encouragement of the Arts and Manufactures and a Liveryman of the City of London. In the United States she has held a number of adjunct and full-time academic appointments in Communication, Global Studies and Law. She has taught Human Trafficking to undergraduates, Judges and Prosecutors and, in the U.S. has served in the development of public policy and legislation on the topic.

For many years she has been an advocate for the rights of children and human trafficking victims, especially street children who are intensely vulnerable to all forms of trafficking and other social injustices. In this capacity she has worked with USAID and represented the Consortium for Street Children at the 2010 U.N. General Assembly meetings.

She holds a B.A. (Hons.) in English Law, an LLM from St Mary's School of Law, San Antonio, and, currently pursuing an M.A. in International Relations and a PhD in History.

"One of the best means of fighting against the crime of human trafficking is to educate ourselves and our students. This book helps students understand modern slavery and the human rights issues it raises and empowers them to think creatively about what we can do to end it."

Mity Myhr, Ph.D. Associate Professor of History : Course Coordinator, Cultural Foundations 3331, St. Edward's University, Austin, USA

Introduction

Human Trafficking IS Modern Slavery. The use of the expression Human Trafficking can lead to misunderstandings, for example that victims must be 'moved' because the idea of 'trafficking' suggests movement as in arms and drugs. Whilst that movement often occurs, it need not. Likewise the words suggest that only foreign born victims can be trafficked. That, too, is incorrect. Victims are trafficked within their own countries and across borders. Whilst sex slavery is the form of human trafficking most often portrayed by the media there are many other variations including labor, babies and organ trafficking. As will be seen there are also quasi-trafficking offences of forced marriage and mail order brides.

It is the purpose of this book to synthesize work on this subject into a format which will enable students new to the subject to earn about modern slavery and invite them into further investigation of the subject. No book on the topic can be complete because the subject itself is so wide ranging and complex. Accordingly aspects of the problem have been considered together with some international and national laws and case examples. Finding solutions to the problem is extremely difficult because of the multiple types of actors who are involved in the enslavement of innocent victims. The motivations of traffickers are considered in an attempt to engage readers in thinking deeply about how to eradicate this modern scourge.

The book is designed to help the reader think not only about modern slavery but also the answers to questions commonly asked about the subject and the global social injustices which lead to trafficking in human beings. Thus, the book begins with an overview of modern slavery, why slavery continues to exist in the 21st century and some definitions with which readers need to become familiar.

The work contains references to international, U.S. and U.K. law and some other legal systems. It is important for scholars of human trafficking to understand how the various laws which have been enacted to assist victims work not only in and of themselves but also within a national and international structure. The reader is also required to understand some of the overarching Human Rights Conventions because reference will be made to them throughout the book. Therefore, these aspects are introduced in Chapters One, Two, Three and Four of the book. There is specific information on the way in which various countries adhere to the international human rights Treaties in Chapter Four, "Beauty is in the Eye of the Beholder".

Chapter Five deals with the history of slavery in so far as it is important to learn that slavery exists today despite vigorous attempts to break it by both the British and Americans in the 19th century. This chapter is particularly important for the lessons which its teaches about the way in which a solution must be structured to involve many national governments in concerted efforts to end slavery and work against the international criminals who evade capture and trial whilst peddling in misery. In particular, the fight against slavery which cost the British so much time and money is considered in detail to highlight a number of responses which are required. These include concerted government action, international diplomacy, media support and awareness, popular campaigns and politicians who are determined to change the situation whatever the personal cost. The first example of a human rights movement can be seen in the campaign to abolish the slave trade and, then, slavery throughout the British Empire.

Children are most vulnerable to trafficking because they often lack most of the even most basic requirements to keep them safe. Chapter Six examines some of those vulnerabilities and introduces the reader to the complex issues of human rights and children and the sort of work in which children are enslaved. One such vulnerability is statelessness which has been described as the single most dangerous thing which affects children. The Convention on the Rights of the Child is examined at length because of the role it should, if properly followed in nations, play in the protection of the human rights of children. In Chapter Seven, the work of children in the cocoa industry is examined along with the efficacy of a voluntary protocol to prevent children being enslaved in this work.

In Chapters Eight and Nine, other forms of slavery are considered and another protocol, the Kimberley Process, examined. These forms of slavery affect both adults and children and are an important study for readers to see how their own purchasing behavior affects those vulnerable to being enslaved and those already enslaved. Specifically, the link between slavery in the Democratic Republic of the Congo and the electronic devises so necessary to the daily life of a student in the Global North is examined as well as the work of the Coalition of Immokolee Workers who spend their time trying to ensure slave free production of food in America.

Chapters Ten, Eleven and Twelve deal with sex slavery in a variety of forms, including sex tourism. Here readers are encouraged to address their attitudes towards prostitution and its counterpoint, human trafficking. Likewise, the impact of tourists from the Global North on sex slaves in countries known as sex tourism destinations is discussed to show that demand fuels supply and that demand comes from the countries most readers call home. The discussion of the Validity of various statutes aimed at curbing sex tourism is then used to show the extent of the problem.

In Chapter Thirteen the reader is introduced to what could be termed, quasi-trafficking issues. These are certainly human rights issues and, the readers earlier acquired knowledge of the Human Rights Conventions is used to help to explain some of the challenges which surround mail order brides, forced marriage, female genital cutting and breast ironing. Readers are asked to consider these issues within their cultural and religious contexts and read widely by using the footnotes for further research. Again the reader is brought back to the way in which many of these problems manifest themselves in the Global North.

Chapter Fourteen takes the reader back to children but the specific issues of street children. This leads into a chapter which asks how people become slaves. The purpose of this chapter is to show readers just how easy it is for people to fall victim to human trafficking even when they have education and, comparative wealth. The reader is encouraged to see that whilst some victims are particularly vulnerable, like street children, everyone remains vulnerable, even college students. The next chapter looks at immigration and the xenophobic concerns of various Western governments. This is done to encourage deeper thought about how public policy on one subject affects that of another and how a concerted public policy initiative is required to deal with the many legal issues which create vulnerability to human trafficking.

Chapter Seventeen addresses the risks which human trafficking victims face during their enslavement. This is done to encourage readers to consider the way in which greed, desire and common brutality feed into the enslavement and abuse of all slaves, men, women and children. It challenges readers to think about how a solution can be found when some users of slaves are prepared to take such obvious risks to their own health let alone the health of another. The chapter on organ trafficking takes such thinking a stage further and invites the reader to ask themselves what would they be willing to do to save their life or the life of a loved one in such circumstances, both as done and donor.

No book on modern slavery could be complete without consideration of the place of the internet. Whilst it is undoubtedly a force for good it also enables the easy, and relatively risk free, sale of human beings for sexual services, and into other forms of slavery. Likewise, the internet has done much to 'normalize' the viewing of pornography and the access to it by young people as the report of the U.K. Children's Commissioner makes clear. Here the tensions between for example, the right to free speech and artistic content are seen in relief to the rights of children to live safe and secure lives.

In conclusion, the reader is encouraged to reflect upon the information provided in the book and sourced from reading the footnoted references and further study and to consider some questions which might lead to solutions. A book about human trafficking needs some happy stories and so some accounts of rescues of victims are included here in the hope that it will encourage the reader to a lifelong commitment to work to prevent human trafficking, think about their consumer habits and raise awareness of the issue.

Chapter 1

Modern Day Slavery

Why should I care?

"I have looked into the eyes of the victims, I have seen their terror, I have seen the scars which will never heal". [1]

Billy Sifuentes is an extraordinary man. He cares passionately about the fate of men and women in Austin, Texas who have been trafficked into modern-day slavery. Acting as liaison officer for the Austin Police Department Human Trafficking Department, in February 2010 he spoke to students at a local University. He spoke with emotion about his job and the terrible conditions in which his officers find modern day slaves. On that day he created understanding in the minds of one hundred students. His words inspire them still and, hopefully, will continue to inspire those who read them to take action and do what they can to help stop human trafficking.

So why should you care?

This book is dedicated to answering this question but here are some possible reasons:

a. You thought slavery was abolished in most of the world in the nineteenth century but it flourishes around the globe today.
b. You may have encountered a slave but, because of lack of knowledge, you didn't see him or her and therefore you didn't help them.
c. Slaves produce some of the products which you use.
d. You would prefer not to live in a world where young children are raped on a daily basis, sometimes forty times a day, to make money for their slave-owner.
e. You don't want to live in a world where one person owns the life of another.
f. You believe in universal human rights and equality of human beings.
g. Now you know about 21st century slavery.
h. Social injustices endemic in the modern world enable slavers to prey on the vulnerable and disadvantaged.
i. It is estimated that some 28.3-31.3 million people are enslaved today.[2] In 2012, the ILO estimated that the number was 20.9million.[3]

---

[1] William J. Sifuentes, "Human Trafficking in Austin, Texas," 2010.

j. Estimates of the income derived from the trade in human beings are as high as thirty two billion U.S. dollars.[4] However, this figure dates from an ILO report in 2005 when it estimated that some 12.3million people, about one half t their 2011 estimate, were enslaved. It can be safely assumed that the annual profit has increased with the increase in numbers of people enslaved.
k. It is estimated that 1.8m children are engaged in the sex industry (porn and selling sex).
l. Modern slavery is the second largest and the fastest growing criminal activity in the world.[5] Drug trafficking is the world's largest criminal activity by income but, unlike drugs, human beings or their services can be re-sold many times. Slavery can be an accident of birth, some are enslaved simply because their parents are slaves. Peonage (debt-bonded labor) continues to exist in the world today. It is most common in S.E. Asia but can be found around the developing world.[6]

Of course, it is difficult to count slaves who are invisible and disposable people.[7] They may be enslaved for a few days, months, years or a lifetime.[8]

What Does 21st Century Slavery Look Like?

Slaves today are the same as slaves in history. They are children and adults making things and collecting things for us and providing their bodies to be abused by some of us.[9]

Here are some examples:

Palatka Camp, Florida, USA was used as a base for foreign slaves brought into the USA to pick fruit on Florida farms. There was no escape for the workers who labored

---

[2] "Overview," *Global Slavery Index*, accessed October 27, 2013, http://www.globalslaveryindex.org/findings/#overview. Kevin Bales is one of the leading scholars on modern day slavery/human trafficking. Together with a team of scholars he produced the data on this website.

[3] International Labour Organisation, "Questions and Answers on Forced Labour," *Forced Labour*, accessed October 28, 2013, http://www.ilo.org/global/about-the-ilo/newsroom/comment-analysis/WCMS_181922/lang--en/index.htm.

[4] Ibid.

[5] "Slavery Today," *Free the Slaves*, accessed October 29, 2013, http://www.freetheslaves.net/page.aspx?pid=301.

[6] Kara, Siddhartha. *Bonded Labor: Tackling the System of Slavery in South Asia*. New York, NY: Columbia University Press, 2012.

[7] Kevin Bales, *Disposable People, New Slavery in the Global Economy*, 1st ed. (Berkeley, CA: University of California Press, 1999).

[8] David W. Salmon, "A New System of Peonage--A Challenge to Industrial Relations.," *Labor Law Journal* 24, no. 8 (August 1973): 558–564.

[9] Edward D. Melillo, "The First Green Revolution: Debt Peonage and the Making of the Nitrogen Fertilizer Trade, 1840–1930.," *American Historical Review* 117, no. 4 (October 2012): 1028–1060.

long days for no money until they were rescued by Federal Agents in 2005.[10] In the USA and Europe slaves are used to pick crops. Typically, slaves tell of being required to fill buckets which when full weigh thirty two pounds (fourteen and a half kilograms). They are not paid, housed in cramped conditions and worked seven days a week. Escape is discouraged by armed guard.

Many people are unaware of the extent of twenty first century slavery in the Western World. Often when asked about slavery people say it happens "in the third world" if they think it happens anywhere at all. Sadly that is not true. To illustrate, consider the case of Cindy. On 4 April 2011, Cindy had a baby, nothing unusual about that except that, Cindy had been a slave up until a few days before her confinement. All she had for herself and the baby was supplied by donations. She was a sex slave and the baby was born in Austin, Texas, USA.

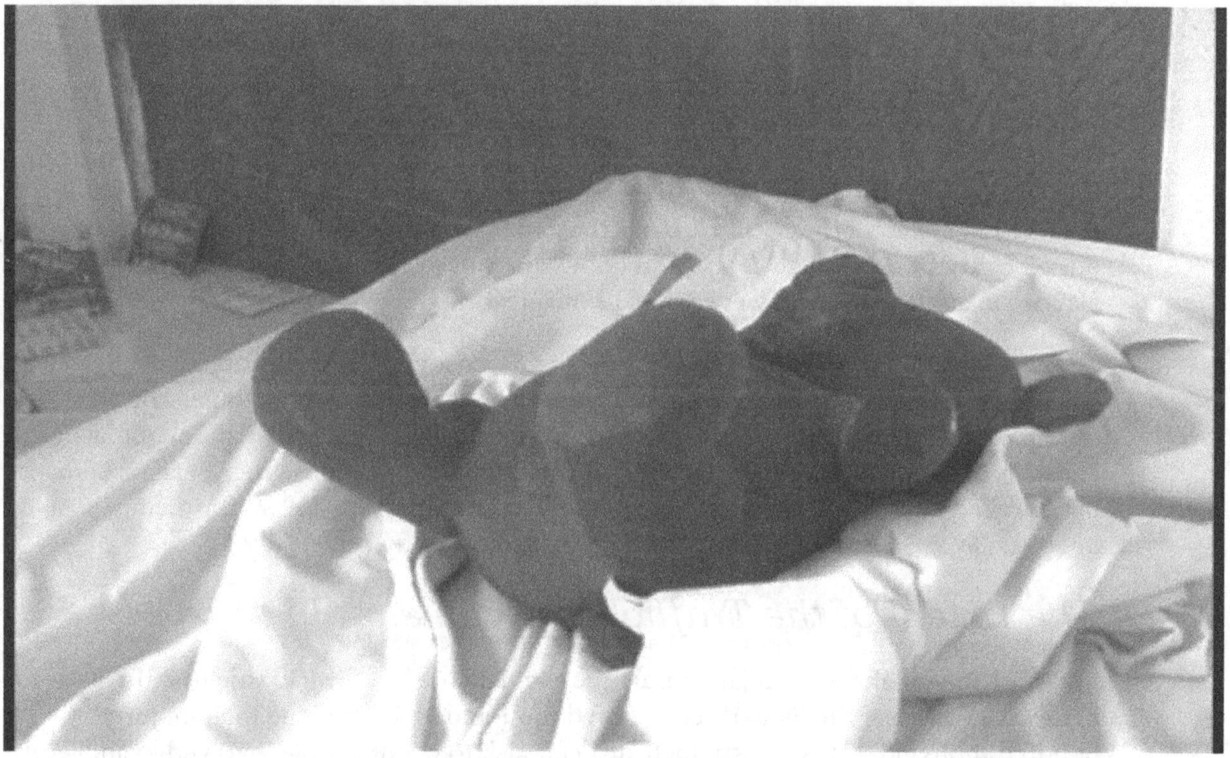

This photograph shows the teddy bear left behind by a 12 year old sex slave in Austin, Texas after a raid by the Austin Police Department Human Trafficking Division.[11] Where was this brothel? In town, in an up-market neighborhood, unnoticed by the neighbors.

[10] The Associated Press, "Slave Labor Camp Raided in East Palatka," *The Gainsville Sun*, June 7, 2005.
[11] William J. Sifuentes Austin Police Department, Human Trafficking Division, *Teddy Bear - Human Trafficking Evidence*, 2010.

International Treaties

Slavery has been outlawed by the international community in many international treaties, of which the foundational human rights treaty of the twentieth century is:

Article 4 of the Universal Declaration of Human Rights states:

"No one shall be held in slavery or servitude; slavery and the slave trade shall be prohibited in all their forms." [12]

"Invisible and Disposable"

Kevin Bales was the first to call modern slaves invisible and disposable.[13] They are invisible because in most countries slavery is illegal. They are also invisible because we either do not know about them or are in denial that they exist. Also, often, we are frightened to call the authorities to report a possible slave. Many of us just don't want to make a fuss. But slave markets and well-organized slave trade networks still exist. The slave trade routes on which just women and children are brought into the USA are multiple.[14] Modern slavery is complex. It is not just a case of slaves being brought from the developing world to the developed world. Slaves are traded within their countries, across local country borders and around the globe. As a huge global business it thrives in our globalized world where capital and goods are moved faster and easier than ever before. Slaves too are transported by every means imaginable.

Modern slaves are disposable because they cost very little, or nothing at all, and when they are worn out, they are ejected from the system as broken people. By way of example, at slave markets in Thailand girls are viewed like cattle and then bought like cattle. How much for? That depends, child virgins fetch the most because the users, or perhaps better called rapists, will pay up to seven hundred and fifty U.S. dollars for them; interestingly the next user will pay two U.S. dollars and fifty cents.[15]

The Extent of the Trafficking Problem

The Walk Free Foundation puts the estimate of slaves worldwide in 2013 at between twenty eight million, three hundred thousand and thirty one million, three hundred thousand.[16] It is an extremely difficult task to count people involved in an illegal industry and different people count different things as trafficking, for example, forced marriage. Various governments put various figures on their own trafficking problems. The US State Department estimates that one hundred and fifty thousand American teenagers

---

[12] United Nations, "Universal Declaration of Human Rights." United Nations. Accessed October 27, 2013. http://un.org/en/documents/udhr/.

[13] Bales, *Disposable People, New Slavery in the Global Economy.*

[14] "Trafficking of Persons Especially Women and Children: USA Route" (The Future Group, 2002), http://www.thefuturegroup.org/id20.html.

[15] Bales, Trodd, and Wilkinson. *Modern Slavery*

[16] "Overview."

are trafficked for sex but Stop Child Trafficking Now put the figure at three hundred thousand.[17] In 2011, the UK Home Office revealed that up to 15 September, there were two hundred and two suspected child trafficking victims which extrapolated to two hundred and eighty five per annum.[18] This was an increase on the one hundred and ninety five victims reported in the previous year. This may be a result of better training and identification or it may be part of an overall increase in trafficking of children. The US State Department estimates only 0.04% of victims in the USA are rescued. If that is so of the UK then the government's figures are simply the tip of the iceberg. In the UK report, supply countries include Vietnam (forty eight victims), Nigeria (twenty nine victims) and Romania (twenty three victims). Fifty four children were working on farms and construction sites, in restaurants and nail bars.

The Elements of Human Trafficking – Force Fraud and Coercion

Human Trafficking does not need the physical movement of people but it does require the use of one or more of the following[19]

Force

- Beating
- "Seasoning"
- Torture
- Sexual Assault
- Burning
- Drug Addiction
- Branding / Tattooing
- Confinement
- Intimidation / Humiliation
- Threats to Family Members

Fraud

- False Promises, Marriages, Employment
- Deceitful, Enticing, Affectionate Behavior, "The Boyfriend"
- Withholding Wages
- Lying about Working Conditions
- Misrepresenting The Promise of A "Better Life"

[17] "Stop Child Trafficking Now," *Stop Child Trafficking Now*, accessed November 2, 2013, http://www.sctnow.org.
[18] *Child Trafficking Update* (U.K. Home Office), accessed November 7, 2013, http://ceop.police.uk/Documents/ceopdocs/child_trafficking_update_2011.pdf.
[19] *United Nations Convention Against Transnational Organized Crime and Protocols Thereto (Palermo Protocol)* (United Nations), accessed October 26, 2013, http://www.unodc.org/documents/treaties/UNTOC/Publications/TOC%20Convention/TOCebook-e.pdf.

- Threats of Serious Harm or Restraint
- Emotional Abuse
- Control of Daily Lives, Brainwashing
- Deportation Threats
- Confiscation of Documents

These are known as the 'means' element of the crime which also required an 'act' and 'purpose'.

Vulnerable Populations

What makes a person vulnerable to human trafficking? There are a myriad of causes, many interlinked but these are some:-

- Poverty and low paying jobs
- Lack of self-esteem
- Large bills which cannot be paid by daily income, for example: medical
- Lack of education
- Lack of day to day parental support
- Moving to a new place
- Being used to being abused
- Not knowing where their friends come from or who they can trust. As has been seen Somaly Mam is a good example of this problem. She was living on the streets and had lost her mother. As a child of 10 years old she was approached by a man who claimed to be her grandfather. As she said on the Tyra Banks Show and in her autobiography, she wanted to be loved and so she believed him.[20] Unfortunately, he enslaved her, beat & raped her and then sold her to a brothel in which she suffered for about 10 years.

Students often fail to see that they share some of these characteristics, notably moving to new places where they don't know the people around them. This gives traffickers a carte blanche opportunity to befriend and enslave. In 2010, that happened to a young student in Austin, Texas. Her friends reported that her new boyfriend seemed like a nice guy but within three weeks she had disappeared. Over a year later she was found during a raid on a slave brothel in Houston, Texas. The 'boyfriend' had seen her vulnerability, befriended her and enslaved her. This process of 'grooming' and enslaving is well illustrated in the documentaries "Cargo : Innocence Lost" and "Flesh".[21] Perhaps the

[20] *Somaly Mam on the Tyra Banks Show (1 of 3)*, 2008, http://www.youtube.com/watch?v=YlpjTc8iJqo&feature=youtube_gdata_player; Somaly Mam and Ruth Marshall, *The Road of Lost Innocence* (New York: Spiegel & Grau, 2009).

[21] Kristin, Ross Lauterbach, *Flesh*, 2010, http://www.fleshthemovie.org/; Michael Davis C., *Cargo: Innocence Lost* (The Journey Film Group, 2008), http://http://www.cargoinnocencelost.com/.

most vulnerable human beings in the world are "Street children", children who are stateless and children displaced by war.[22]

Of course, slave traders cannot prosper without the customers to purchase the slaves. These may be outright purchases for business or personal use or may be purchases of a slave's services for minutes, hours, days and more. Men in USA, Europe, Australia, or Japan are vulnerable to enabling this criminal system by supporting it with their money. In Austin, Texas, the police have collected examples of how sex slaves can be sold. The author taught a male student who had been handed one of these cards as he was going about his shopping in town. The lady who gave it him did so with this comment "If you want an underage girl call this number". Unsurprisingly he threw the card away and thought it was a prank. Sadly, he should have phoned the police who might have been able to rescue the 'underage' girl. This picture shows cards collected by Austin Police Department: Human Trafficking Division.[23]

Definitions

Kidnap

In this book the word kidnap can be used to describe number of scenarios:

[22] Street Children is 'shorthand' for children who are better described as 'in and of the street'. See below at Chapter "Street Children"

[23] William J. Sifuentes Austin Police Department Human Trafficking Division, *Business Cards - Human Trafficking*, n.d.

a. Taking a victim from a private or public space by force[24]
b. Preventing a victim from leaving the trafficker
c. Turning a smuggling situation into a trafficking incident
d. A job offer which is spurious

There are many different definitions of kidnapping in the laws of nations but most amount to the same thing. In the United States each state has a different set of criminal laws and the national government (Federal law) another set.[25]

In the UK, kidnapping comprises four elements (1) the taking or carrying away of one person by another; (2) by force or fraud; (3) without the consent of the person so taken or carried away; and (4) without lawful excuse. It is a different crime to kidnap a child/children.[26]

Pimp

Often the media mistakenly, or for shorthand, call traffickers "pimps". Certainly they are acting as pimps forcing men and women and children to work as sex slaves but the use of this term, as opposed to slavers or slave traders or traffickers has an unfortunate tendency to alter the public, and untrained law enforcement, perception of the problem. As Kevin Bales and Ron Soodalter point out:

> *"..from Hollywood, to the major record companies, to the front-stoop stories of wide-eyed school children, pimps have acquired a glitzy, dangerous "outlaw" persona."*[27]

The 2006 Oscar for best song was awarded to "It's hard out here for a Pimp". This sort of glamorization of the role prevents the victims from being seen. It is difficult to see how it is hard to be a pimp but it is very easy to see how it is hard to be a sex slave.

Pimps and Hos parties can be found in 'ordinary neighborhoods' diluting the reality of sex slavery and diluting the sense of risk for potential victims and each year the 'Players Ball' attracts celebrities and pimps alike. As part of the glitz and flamboyance there are awards for:

> *'"No. 1 International Pimp of the Year" and No 1 Super Player'*[28]

---

[24] See Toldelo case – post

[25] Kay Firth-Butterfield, Tina Miranda, *Laws on Human Trafficking.* ([S.l.]: Kendall Hunt, 2012).

[26] "Kidnapping - False Imprisonment:Offences against the Person: Sentencing Manual: Legal Guidance: The Crown Prosecution Service," accessed October 27, 2013, http://www.cps.gov.uk/legal/s_to_u/sentencing_manual/kidnapping_false_imprisonment/.

[27] Kevin Bales and Ron Soodalter, *The Slave next Door Human Trafficking and Slavery in America Today* (Berkeley: University of California Press, 2009).

[28] Ibid.

Bales and Sooldalter go on to say that, Kevin O'Connor, U.S. Attorney for Connecticut, told them in an interview in June 2007 that, although club owners hosting the Balls deny any connection to trafficking:

> *"...the pimps who attend are often facing indictments for sex trafficking, involuntary servitude, sexual abuse of a minor, kidnapping, assault with a deadly weapon, and racketeering."* [29]

Smuggling/Illegal Immigrant

A person who wishes to avoid the boundary controls imposed by a sovereign state when she migrates there is an illegal immigrant. That person is often helped to enter the country of immigration by a criminal who helps illegal immigrants. The 'helper' is a smuggler of people who WISH to enter the country illegally. In the Mexico/United States border area these smugglers are colloquially known as 'coyotes'. The person who WISHES to enter illegally is an illegal immigrant and, usually, a criminal.

Foreign Born Human Trafficking Victim

In contrast to the illegal immigrant the human trafficking victim DOES NOT WISH to become a slave even though they may have tried to enter the country illegally to become an illegal immigrant. As Krista Melton says "No one wakes up one morning and thinks 'I would like to be a slave'."[30]

Prostitute

A prostitute is a person who voluntarily enters into a contract with a client who pays money for the act of sex with the prostitute. In many countries of the world prostitution is illegal. There is much debate about whether the majority of women and men involved in prostitution have a choice about their work.[31] They may be controlled by pimps, addicted to drugs or be desperate for money and the are scholars who fear that anti-trafficking agencies do a general disservice to sex workers by leading the public to think that all sex workers are coerced into the job.[32] However, only adults consenting to commercial sex are prostitutes not human trafficking victims.

Child Prostitute

The media, and even the USA government, often uses this easy descriptive moniker for the forced labor which is endured by children when they are coerced to sell their bodies.[33] Whilst it is true that in certain states the age of consent to sex is 16 (whereas

---

[29] Ibid.

[30] *Truckers Against Trafficking Training Video* (Truckers Against Trafficking), accessed October 27, 2013, http://truckersagainsttrafficking.org/.

[31] Anthony M DeStefano, *The War on Human Trafficking: U.S. Policy Assessed* (New Brunswick, N.J.: Rutgers University Press, 2008).

[32] Editorial, "Unpacking the Sex Trafficking Panic," *Contemporary Sexuality* 47, no. 2 (. Mar2013): 1–6.

[33] Ron Sooldalter, "In Our Own Backyard: Child Prostitution and Sex Trafficking in the United States" (presented at the Human Trafficking Workshop, Austin: Kozmetsky Center, 2010).

majority is 18) the essential point is that a child cannot consent to sex until the age specified in a state statute and that is, throughout the USA, no younger than 16 or, in many cases, older. As this is the case a child cannot be a prostitute because s/he cannot consent to sell his/her body, although, arguably nor can adults because prostitution is illegal in all but a few counties in the USA. By way of example see the case of In re: B.W.[34] Of course, it could be properly argued that not all sexual services involve the act of sex and thus children can consent to supplying those services. As examples in this book and the majority of research shows it seems that few, if any, children consent to performing such acts. This is recognized in most human trafficking legislation around the world.[35] Thus they should properly be considered to be human trafficking victims and not child prostitutes and correctly called victims of sex slavery.

Migrant Worker

A migrant worker enters the foreign country willingly and legally. In the United States, the migrant worker will have a H-2A or H-2B temporary visa for seasonal work and is welcomed into the country for the work that they will do and the resulting boost to the economy.

John

Just as "ho" is a colloquial term for a prostitute; so too is "John" used to denote a user of prostitutes. It is "Johns" who fuel the demand for sex-slaves and, in many countries, the ever increasing demand for young girls who are virgins.

John School

This is a training course which has been set up in various states in America.[36] Traditionally the school brings the users of prostitutes face to face with a representative of the women they have hurt. In the San Francisco First Offender Program the participants have opted to take the one-day school and pay $1000 to avoid prosecution. Offenders learn that not all sexual encounters, even with prostitutes who are considered to be freely consenting, are in fact consensual or desired.[37]

Child Pornography

> *"It can be argued that the term child pornography does not accurately reflect its content, and implicitly implies consensual activity,"*[38]

---

[34] In Re: B.W. (Supreme Court of Texas 2010).

[35] Virginia Kendall, *Child Exploitation and Trafficking: Examining the Global Challenges and U.S. Responses* (Lanham: Rowman & Littlefield Publishers, 2012).

[36] Amy Gurd and Erin O'Brien, "Californian 'John Schools' and the Social Construction of Prostitution.," *Sexuality Research & Social Policy: Journal of NSRC* 10, no. 2 (June 2013): 149–158.

[37] "John Schools," *John Schools* (PBS, May 30, 2008), http://www.pbs.org/now/shows/422/prostitution.html.

[38] M Aiken, R.M. Moran, and M.J. Berry, "Child Abuse Material and the Internet: Cyberpsychology of Online Child Related Sex Offending" (presented at the INTERPOL Specialists Group on Crimes Against

Whilst this is undoubtedly true the term "child pornography" is used throughout the book to describe children being used in the porn industry. As has been seen, children cannot consent to being used in this way and the sexual acts in which they are forced to engage are by law, and in the main in practice, non-consensual.

Children, Lyons, France, 2011), http://www.interpol.int/Crime-areas/Crimes-against-children/Internet-crimes.

002846-85107721-87210-3940

Chapter 2

Why Don't Slaves Run Away?

It has been seen that human trafficking is accompanied by force fraud and coercion. To understand why slaves do not run away very often, we need to look at that definition in more detail. Of course, this minimizes the fact that slaves start out as the most vulnerable people in their population and so, often, do not have the personal resources necessary for escape. The real world is not like "Taken" and most slaves die enslaved.[39]

Disorientation

A slave taken to a new place/country where s/he does not speak the language is inevitably disorientated. When traveling willingly in a country which is foreign and in which a different language is spoken a traveler is disorientated; it is one of the pleasures of travel. When travelling in China in1989, the author was given cards by the owners of places where she stayed which, it was said, carried the message "Please take me to…" Of course, not speaking Chinese not only could she not ask the way home but also couldn't tell if that is actually what was written on the card! To whom does a slave turn for help in a place where s/he doesn't understand the language, or cannot even understand the writing on the signs?

An Example:

We will call her Kiki,

Kiki who was rescued by the Bernardo Kohler Center (BKC) came from Thailand.[40] She was enslaved in the sex industry and moved around America. She saw signs as she was moved from town to town but couldn't read English and so had no idea where she was or even what language they were written in.

The movement from place to place not only disorientates, but in the case of the sex industry, ensures a steady supply of new girls for customers. It also prevents customers getting too close to girls who might find enough courage to ask for help.

Of course, had she stayed in Thailand and been victimized there the trade is also illegal but widely ignored by law enforcement agencies. There it may have been possible for her to be sold on to a former client or another slave

[39] Pierre Morel, *Taken*, 2009.
[40] "Trafficking," *Bernardo Kohler Center*, accessed October 26, 2013, http://www.bernardokohler.org/Trafficking.htm.

brothel but she would very likely have stayed in one slave brothel until her 'career' ended. Most often through the contraction of AIDS.[41]

Not knowing who to turn to for help

Slaves are told that the person to whom you turn may think you are just another illegal immigrant and turn you in to the authorities who, because of limited training, manpower, or funds hand you on, in the United States to Immigrations and Customs (ICE). You are deported and, in many cases, the traffickers are waiting for you. After all they know where they acquired you in the first place.[42]

Honor

Fear of reprisals to their families at home is also a powerful tool to keep victims in line. It also ensures that people who believe that they incurred a debt to the traffickers feel bound to keep working even though their promised 'job' turns out to be a slavery or semi-slavery situation[43]. See also Honor killings.[44]

Tattooing and Other Marking in the Sex Industry

Just as the holocaust victims had their humanity reduced to the numbers they had tattooed upon them so too do sex traffickers mark their victims.

2009

S.M. met Epps on "My Space". She was 16years old and he was 22. His self-ascribed job was pimp. Within three weeks he had her turning tricks at cheap motels. She had a tattoo which covered most of her lower arm with bundles of cash and Epps street name in 71 point cursive.[45]

---

[41] *Truckers Against Trafficking Training Video*.

[42] See Katya's story, post.

[43] Pete Patterson, "Revealed: Qatar's World Cup 'Slaves,'" *The Guardian*, September 25, 2013, http://www.theguardian.com/world/2013/sep/25/revealed-qatars-world-cup-slaves.

[44] Preeti Malik, "HONOUR-BASED VIOLENCE WITH SPECIAL REFERENCE TO 'KHAP PANCHAYAT' IN HARYANA AND THE INDIAN PANEL CODE.," *Indian Streams Research Journal* 3, no. 5 (June 2013): 1–4; Preeti Malik, "KILLING IN THE NAME OF HONOUR AND TRADITION.," *Golden Research Thoughts* 2, no. 12 (June 2013): 1–3.

[45] Nicholas D. Kristof, "She Has a Pimp's Name Etched on Her," *The New York Times*, May 23, 2012, sec. Opinion, http://www.nytimes.com/2012/05/24/opinion/kristof-she-has-a-pimps-name-etched-on-her.html.

2012 – New York

A father and son ran a 'prostitution' ring in Manhattan. Both had their own street names tattooed on the girls, the father "Vee" and the son "King Koby". One woman was tattooed with a bar code.[46]

2012 – Barcelona

The Spanish National Police rescued a human trafficking victim who had been held captive. The 19-year-old woman was tattooed with a barcode on her wrist after she had tried to escape from the ring. The bar code was used to dehumanize her and to show ownership of her. Beneath the bar code was tattooed the amount of money she owed the traffickers.[47]

[46] "Manhattan DA: Father, Son's Prostitution Business Busted; Men Branded Victims With Tattoos," *Huffington Post*, April 24, 1920, http://www.huffingtonpost.com/2012/04/24/manhattan-da-father-sons-prostitution-ring-busted_n_1449107.html.

[47] Suzanne Daley, "Women Enslaved by Spain's Brothel Tourism Boom," *The New York Times*, April 6, 2012, sec. World / Europe, http://www.nytimes.com/2012/04/07/world/europe/young-men-flock-to-spain-for-sex-with-trafficked-prostitutes.html.

Chapter 3

United States Federal Laws and International Treaties

The US was a prime mover in creating international treaties for the suppression of modern day slavery. In the 1990s it came together with Argentina to call for global action against human trafficking. Human trafficking has many definitions, however, the one enunciated in the Palermo Protocol requires an act, means and a purpose.[48] The purpose, or intent, (mens rea) must be exploitation. The actus reus has two elements, the 'act' and the 'means'. The Act (trafficking) is established when a person transfers, transports, receives, harbors or recruits another person with the purpose of exploiting them. The means which are used can be any of the following: threat or use of force, abduction, coercion, fraud, deception, abuse of power and/or the giving payments or benefits.

As part of its obligations to the Palermo Protocols, which are included in the United Nations Convention against Transnational Organized Crime 2000, the USA Congress passed the following laws, because the Convention is not self-executing: [49]

- Victims of Trafficking and Violence Protection Act of 2000 (passed on 10.28.00)[50]
- U.S. Leadership on HIV/AIDS, Tuberculosis, and Malaria Act of 2003 (passed on 01.07.03)
- Trafficking Victims Protection Reauthorization Act of 2003 (passed on 01.07.03)
- Prosecutorial Remedies and Other Tools To End the Exploitation of Children Today Act of 2003 (Protect Act) (passed on 01.07.03) – This Act deals with the victimization of children by American citizens travelling to their home country to victimize them sexually.
- Trafficking Victims Protection Reauthorization Act of 2005 (passed 01.10.06)

---

[48] *Palermo Protocol* (United Nations, October 27, 2013), http://www.unodc.org/documents/treaties/UNTOC/Publications/TOC%20Convention/TOCebook-e.pdf.
[49] United Nations Convention against Transnational Organized Crime and its Protocols, 2000. http://www.unodc.org/unodc/treaties/CTOC/index.html
[50] *Victims of Trafficking and Violence Protection Act of 2000*, 2000, http://www.state.gov/documents/organization/10492.pdf.

- William Wilberforce Trafficking Victims Protection Reauthorization Act of 2008 (passed 12.10.08)
- The Violence Against Women Reauthorization Act 2013 (passed 03.07.13)
- National Organ Transplant Act 1984 (this criminalized buying and selling of organs and made the crime punishable by up to 5yrs in prison and a $50,000 fine per offence.
- Violence Against Women and Department of Justice Reauthorization Act of 2005, which incorporates the International Marriage Broker Act of 2005[51]
- Violence Against Women Act 2013 (includes re-authorization of the TVPA)

To add to the arsenal of provisions to protect victims and apprehend traffickers the U.S. developed a standard against which other countries are to be measured. The Trafficking in Persons Report (TIP Report) is produced annually.[52] It enables the State Department to 'rank' the laws and prosecutions against Human Traffickers of each country and place the countries in Tiers.[53] Counties all around the world are placed in one of three tiers, based on their compliance with the required standards. Countries that are placed in Tier 1 are those which demonstrate the strongest compliance with these standards. Countries placed in Tier 2 are those which are not fully complying but are making significant efforts to bring themselves into compliance. These countries are placed on a "watch list". Countries in Tier 3 are not fully complying nor making an effort to do so. As a result of the various anti-trafficking laws that the United States has created, it has placed itself in Tier 1.[54] As will be seen, not all States within the U.S. are at Tier One. The information in the TIP report is used for making decisions upon the distribution of foreign aid and other considerations.[55]

The laws which, since 2000, Congress has passed also contain a budget for the rehabilitation of trafficked foreign victims and the provision, annually, of 5000 "T" visas for victims to be able to stay in the US if they meet certain conditions, for example, co-operation in the trial of their trafficker. The T-Visa is specifically for foreign born victims of Human Trafficking and the resources available to victims include health care, housing, clothing etc.

---

[51] *Violence Against Women and Department of Justice Reauthorization Act of 2005*, accessed October 25, 2013, http://usaimmigrationattorney.com/images/IMBRA2005.pdf.

[52] Ashley Feasley, "TIME FOR A TUNE-UP: RETOOLING THE 2012 TIP REPORT IN ORDER TO BETTER MEET INTERNATIONAL LEGAL RESEARCH STANDARDS," *Florida Journal of International Law* 25, no. 1 (April 2013): 5–26.

[53] U.S. Dept. of State, "Trafficking in Persons," *State Government Trafficking in Persons*, accessed October 30, 2013, http://www.state.gov/j/tip/laws/.

[54] U.S. Dept of State, "Tier Placements," accessed October 23, 2013, http://www.state.gov/j/tip/rls/tiprpt/2012/192363.htm.

[55] Anne Gallagher, "Improving the Effectiveness of the International Law of Human Trafficking: A Vision for the Future of the US Trafficking in Persons Reports," *Human Rights Review* 12, no. 3 (September 2011): 381–400.

Additionally, foreign born victims of criminal activity have been able to obtain a U-Visa (10,000 available annually), provided under the Violence Against Women Act (as re-authorized) (VAWA).[56] These visas do not provide as many resources to victims as are provided by the T-Visa. Another form of protection to foreign born victims is "continued presence".[57] This allows victims to stay in the U.S. during the pendency of the case but provides no assistance to remain beyond trial. The ability to remain is the incentive for victims to feel sufficiently empowered to testify. It should be noted that many foreign born victims will give birth whilst in the US and their children will, of course, be US citizens. Between 2011 and 2013, foreign born victims of trafficking and criminal activity were affected by the inability of Congress to agree upon a re-authorization of the TVPA and VAWA. As can be seen above by the dates on which other re-authorizations took place previous re-authorizations had passed on a bi-partisan basis. In 2012, President Obama referred to the re-authorization of the TVPA as a "no-brainer".[58] Representatives Smith and Berman introduced the TVPA re-authorization bill on August 30, 2011, which soon had bi-partisan support. However, in September 2011, the Department of Health and Human Services, which holds the trafficking grant money for various reasons connected with the sexual health of victims, decided not to award any grant money to the U.S. Conference of Catholic Bishops.[59] The Conference had refused to fund organizations which referred victims for contraceptives, condoms, abortion or other reproductive health services. The bi-partisan support for the TVPA fell away and, in December 2011, Representative Smith, introduced an amended Bill. This Bill included a "conscience clause" to stop the federal government denying a grant to an organization based on its moral or religious objections to providing particular services, such as abortion.

The clause prevented the federal government from denying '*assistance under any specified federal laws* or *discriminated against in the solicitation or issuance of grants, contracts, cooperative agreements, or other federal funding under such laws'* to any organization, including religious ones, or requiring "*as a condition of receiving such assistance,* (the organization) *to endorse, utilize, provide, make a referral to, become integrated with, or otherwise participate in any program, project, or activity to which the organization has a religious or moral objection; or for refusing to meet any such requirements.'*[60]

Additionally, Representative Smith's amended Bill sought to remove the victim assistance program from the Department of Health and Human Services altogether. It provided for the budget to pass to the Department of Justice which had no mandate to distribute funds for services for victims. This is because its mandate is to prosecute traffickers. The new House Bill did not authorize any exceptions to a total ban on abortion, save in cases of rape and incest; the original bill contained alternative options for pregnant

---

[56] *Violence Against Women and Department of Justice Reauthorization Act of 2005.*

[57] Heather J. Clawson et al., *Study of HHS Programs Serving Human Trafficking Victims: Final Report,* December 2009, http://aspe.hhs.gov/hsp/07/humantrafficking/final/index.shtml.

[58] President Obama, "Remarks" (presented at the Clinton Global Initiative, New York, 2012), http://www.whitehouse.gov/the-press-office/2012/09/25/remarks-president-clinton-global-initiative.

[59] Yasmin Vafa, "Bishops and House Republicans Seeking to Deny Essential Services to Victims of Sex Trafficking," *Human Rights Project for Girls*, accessed April 18, 2012, http://www.rights4girls.org/.

[60] Christopher Smith, *Trafficking Victims Protection Reauthorization Act of 2011. HR 3589*, n.d.

victims. Additionally, Representative Smith's new Bill took the Head of HHS off the Interagency Task Force to Monitor and Combat Trafficking. This political maneuvering undermined the protection and funding of victim services and left the United States, the country which had led the fight against human trafficking, at a disadvantage (reduced to a Tier 2 country) as it tried to help other countries in their fight against human trafficking and abuse of women. Then, quite suddenly, in March 2013, the House agreed the Senate bill on the Violence Against Women Act with no amendment. The Act had been amended in the Senate to include the re-authorization of the various Trafficking in Persons Acts.

The effect of the loss of 'T' and 'U' Visas on victims can be enormous. It may be the difference between testifying safely against their traffickers or not doing so. One such example is Cindy whose story is told in the introduction to this book. Cindy was a 15 year old child trafficked into the U.S. from her home country in Africa. For 2 years Cindy was exploited by her slavers and used by U.S. citizens in cities around the U.S.A. One of those users made her pregnant. It is easy to guess that she had no suitable clothing for herself and the baby, but also she had a need for housing, medical care, food, counseling and the ability to pay utility bills whilst she couldn't work, not only because of the baby but because, as an illegal alien, she could not work in the U.S. until she received the "T" Visa for helping in the prosecution of her traffickers. During her captivity Cindy had endured between 10-40 rapes daily. When her baby was born Cindy became the mother of an American citizen. The TVPA provides for her to live for one year or until the grant of the T Visa. But during that period 2011-2013 Cindy stepped into the tangled web of law and politics which bedevils the help given to human trafficking victims. With the failure to re-authorize the TVPA funds for victims like Cindy were drying up and she had to look to non-profits for help. The sad reality is that sometimes victims feel that the only way they can survive is by going back on the street to ply the trade in which they have suffered such gross harms. Of course, if the victims are then caught they become 'prostitutes' and, thus, criminals and lose their right to the T visa. The result is usually that they are deported to the place where they first met with the traffickers. At that time a mother like Cindy has to decide whether to leave her American child in the U.S. foster/adoption system to enjoy 'a better life'.[61] If Cindy had co-operated with law enforcement prior to her deportation it is very likely that the traffickers will extract revenge on her when she returns to her home country.[62] Furthermore, depending upon the circumstances she finds at home she may be immediately re-sold into trafficking, sometimes by relatives.[63]

Human Trafficking as a Transnational Crime

The global reach of traffickers is long. Adults and children are trafficked into the U.S. from all parts of the globe, often by transnational criminal gangs who are also engaged in trafficking of drugs, arms, counterfeit drugs and money laundering; to name but a few.

---

[61] Cindy's story is true. She was rescued in Central Texas and helped by local anti-slavery organizations.

[62] See Katya's story, post

[63] The Bernardo Kohler Center obtained a T Visa for a young man who had been deported as a Juvenile from the US and re-sold by his family to traffickers which brought him back to the US. Whilst he was still a minor.

Houston, in Texas, has the sad distinction of being known as the sex slavery capital of the U.S.[64] The divisions between the various criminal gangs holding 'territory' in the city are clear; Mexican Cartels, Chinese Triads and American Mafia. Other gangs involved in human trafficking include the Yakusas of Japan and those emanating from the former Soviet bloc. The Albanian and Moldovian gangs have been particularly involved in human trafficking.[65] By way of example, this is the case of Katya "*When they assessed her case, British immigration officials knew that Katya, a vulnerable 18-year-old from Moldova, had been trafficked and forced into prostitution, but ruled that she would face no real danger if she was sent back.*"[66] This ignored the fact that she had been kidnapped by traffickers when 14 years old and spent the previous several years in sex slavery variously in Italy, Turkey, Hungary, Romania, Israel and the U.K. Moreover, within days of her return the traffickers had found her. They gang raped her, pulled out one of her front teeth using pliers and then forced her to dig her own grave before stringing her up from a tree. After this warning not to cause trouble again she was trafficked into Israel and then back to the U.K. When freed in the U.K. she said, "*Just look around you - see how many girls there are like me. They are coming all the time. I see them every day - in tube stations, …*" She pointed out that it was possible to see victims like her "*all made up, early in the morning. Maybe for you it is difficult to see them, but I see them,…I think the police should work better to stop this. Why don't you shut down saunas and brothels? Then there would be no prostitutes, no pimps.*" The slavers sold her in London for £150 an hour but she received no money.

This case reveals a number of issues common to human trafficking around the world:

a. The unwillingness of immigration officials to accept that a victims is a victim and not an illegal immigrant
b. The unwillingness, or lack of education, amongst individuals working in the area to truly understand the threat
c. The supply and demand quotient
d. The fact that these victims are often 'hidden in plain sight'[67]
e. There is a considerable amount of re-trafficking of victims.[68] Sally Montier, of the Poppy Project, said the charity was still regularly helping women who were wrongly sent home and re-trafficked. She warned that twenty one per cent of the women who came to the charity seeking help had already been sent home and re-trafficked at least once."[69]

---

[64] Mimi Swartz, "The Lost Girls," *Texas Monthly*, April 2010.
[65] Nicole Smith Kendal, "HUMAN TRAFFICKING AND RICO: A NEW PROSECUTORIAL HAMMER IN THE WAR ON MODERN DAY SLAVERY," *George Mason Law Review* 18 (April 1, 2011): 759.
[66] Amelia Gentleman, "Katya's Story: Trafficked to the UK, Sent Home to Torture," *The Guardian*, April 18, 2011, http://www.guardian.co.uk/law/2011/apr/19/sex-trafficking-uk-legal-reform.
[67] Kevin Bales and Ron Soodalter, *The Slave next Door Human Trafficking and Slavery in America Today* (Berkeley: University of California Press, 2009).
[68] Cherish Adams, "RE-TRAFFICKED VICTIMS: HOW A HUMAN RIGHTS APPROACH CAN STOP THE CYCLE OF RE-VICTIMIZATION OF SEX TRAFFICKING VICTIMS," *George Washington International Law Review* 43, no. 1 (2011): 201–234.
[69] Gentleman, "Katya's Story: Trafficked to the UK, Sent Home to Torture."

f. The level of inhumanity involved in the trafficking of human beings

In Katya's case she was rendered unconscious, whilst on a Birthday picnic and kidnapped. Her traffickers blindfolded her and took her on the long drive to Romania where she was placed in a dinghy to cross into Hungary. From there she had to walk "through the forest across the border during the night" and after going through Slovenia she was trafficked in Italy.[70]

What happened next was typical of the experience of an Eastern European sex slave. Sold in Italy she worked out of a flat in a coastal city and then on the streets of metropolitan Milan. Eventually she managed to escape to the Moldovan embassy. Discovering that she was pregnant she returned to her family to have the child, "but her traffickers found her, beat and raped her brother and killed the family dog as punishment."[71] Katya had been kidnapped with a friend who, she found out "had been murdered by traffickers in Israel who had drugged her and thrown her off a seven-story building."[72] Following the birth of her daughter she returned to Turkey 'willingly' working in a nightclub whilst her aunt kept her child safe. Later she was smuggled, by truck to a London brothel. "*During her time working as a prostitute, she was given no money for her work and was not allowed to go anywhere unaccompanied in case she tried to escape.*"[73] Of her clients in London Katya said that they didn't ask about her or why she was doing the work, but, had they done so she would have been too afraid to answer. "*The clients, they're drunk, and just come and say, 'Give me this, that'.*"[74]

When the brothel was raided Katya was arrested, but she did not tell the Police about her status, she knew too well what happened to those who the traffickers wished to punish. Her trafficker visited her nine times in the detention center to further intimidate and ensure she didn't cooperate with the authorities. Eventually, this second time, she was identified as a trafficking victim and received help from the authorities. For a different perspective on the moral panic which is believed to be driving the policy and publicity in the area of sex-trafficking see: Appropriating the rights of women: Moral panics, victims and exclusionary agendas in domestic and cross-borders sex crimes.[75]

Human Trafficking and Drug Trafficking

As has been seen a deported victim can usually be found and punished by these traffickers, and it is that fear, or fear of punishment being inflicted upon their family, which helps to stop the victims leaving their servitude, or co-operating with law enforcement once rescued. A fully funded TVPA makes a great difference to whether a rescue is truly a

---

[70] Ibid.
[71] Ibid.
[72] Ibid.
[73] Ibid.
[74] Ibid
[75] Selda Dagistanil and Sanja Milivojevic, "Appropriating the Rights of Women: Moral Panics, Victims and Exclusionary Agendas in Domestic and Cross-Borders Sex Crimes.," *Womens Studies International Forum* 40 (October 2013): 230–242.

rescue. In the effort to stop drug trafficking U.S. governments at both State and Federal level have devoted huge resources in terms of money and law enforcement. To combat any crime there has to be a willingness to do so but, more, there has to be a recognition that this is a crime which is undesirable in the Nation and does harm to its citizens. Therefore, it becomes necessary to examine whether human trafficking is viewed in a way which affects the willingness of law enforcement to act and governments to legislate and fund. A simple contrast can be seen between drug trafficking enforcement and human trafficking enforcement. In 2012, the White House requested $26.2 billion to spend on the war against drugs.[76] In the same year, the Trafficking in Persons Office had one hundred and fifty six open and active projects in sixty six countries totaling $60.2 million.[77]

> *"...last November, the office's [Human Trafficking Department] $21.2 million annual budget to fight the war on slavery was already microscopic. At the time, it was barely equal to the U.S. government's daily budget to fight the war on drugs. For fiscal year 2012, Congress sliced away nearly a quarter of those antislavery funds, as part of its broader $8 billion State Department budget cuts."*[78]

The prosecution rate in 2012 was at 0.04% of the estimated number of crimes against foreign victims. Many U.S. teenagers who are victims of sex slavery are brought before the Courts as offenders rather than victims because, in part, departments which are set up to care for them are overloaded and, often, under-funded. Prosecutions are, occasionally, of traffickers and, more frequently of 'prostitutes' (the victims) and, rarely, of users because of the way the human trafficking laws are drafted. However, it is more than arguable that it is the demand which fuels the supply.

Who is harmed by modern slavery?

Obviously, the victim but does the American public see itself as harmed by slavery in the way that it is harmed by drugs or arms trafficking? In the case of drugs U.S. citizen children are having their lives ruined by addiction to drugs. In 2010 it was estimated that more than twenty two million Americans aged over twelve (nearly nine per cent of the US population) use illegal drugs.[79] In the case of arms or counterfeit drug trafficking the economy is being harmed and, some people are killed by illegal guns.[80] What harm is done

[76] EXECUTIVE OFFICE OF THE PRESIDENT, OFFICE OF NATIONAL DRUG CONTROL POLICY, *National Drug Control Budget - FY 2012 Funding Highlights* (Washington D.C., 2012), http://www.whitehouse.gov/sites/default/files/ondcp/policy-and-research/fy12highlight_exec_sum.pdf.

[77] Office To Monitor and Combat Trafficking in Persons, *Obama Administration Accomplishments on Combating Trafficking in Persons as of February 2012*, President's Interagency Task Force & Senior Policy Operating Group, March 15, 2012, http://www.state.gov/j/tip/rls/reports/2012/184881.htm.

[78] Benjamin E. Skinner, "How U.S. Budget Cuts Prolong Global Slavery," *Time*, June 28, 2011.

[79] U.S. Dept. of Health and Human Services, *Results from the 2010 National Survey on Drug Use and Health: Summary of National Findings*, 2010, http://www.oas.samhsa.gov/NSDUH/2k10NSDUH/2k10Results.htm.

[80] Andrew F. Sunter, "The Harm of Drug Trafficking: Is There Room for Serious Debate?," *The Manitoba Law Journal* 32 (January 1, 2007): 174.

to the American people by sex trafficking. Some US citizens, who do not wear condoms, may contract AIDs which may be passed to their partners but this is a small number. At first blush the harm is to the victims and, by extension, to the moral fiber of society. An estimated three hundred thousand U.S. minors are victimized in this trade and there are no figures for the adult women and men involved, although in 2010 an estimate was made of one million.[81] Clearly, not all of these adults are in the business against their will and it can be deduced that the problem is much smaller than the drug problem amongst U.S. citizens. However, if the total number of U.S. citizens involved in sex trafficking is reduced to seven hundred thousand the budget of $15.9 million provides not only for these victims but also all the work done in the international fight against human trafficking by the U.S. By way of reminder, nationally the U.S. spends, $26.2 billion on law enforcement etcetera for twenty two million drug addicts.

What harm is done to the American people by labor trafficking? Possibly these victims take the jobs of U.S. citizens but the jobs which they are doing are commonly also done by immigrants, illegally or otherwise. These jobs are rewarded with low incomes and are careers which are not desirable to Americans. Thus, it could be argued that the harm which the anti-trafficking legislation seeks to address is actually to foreign-born victims of exploitation and has nothing to do with the American citizen who, in fact, profits from the crime through cheap goods, cheap sex, cheap porn and cheap domestic help. In sex slavery cases there are two sets of citizens who profit, those who use the slaves for sexual pleasure and those who are not exploited for sex because the demand is met by slaves from abroad. In labor slavery cases, from agriculture through construction to sweat shops, the 'employers' benefit from free labor and the U.S. citizen benefits from cheaper goods. The question arises, therefore, why should the U.S. citizen spend money on protecting these victims who are often mistaken for illegal immigrants? One immediate answer will be because it is morally right to do so.[82] The U.S. is a nation which fought a horribly bloody war over slavery and only emerged from the after effects of the African slave trade in the 1960s and so it is of importance to the nation to rid itself of modern day slaves and slave masters. If that is the case why, then, are so few being prosecuted and so few resources allocated and why was the TVPA 'stuck' in Congress for over a year?

Federal Agencies and State Laws

Having set out some of the problems faced by victims in the U.S. it can be seen that the problems securing help for victims are complex as becomes even more obvious by an examination of the US Federal and State law on the subject.[83] First, the States of

---

[81] Foundation Scelle, "La Prostitution par pays," accessed November 4, 2013, http://www.fondationscelles.org/index.php?option=com_content&view=article&id=2&Itemid=140.
[82] Alexandrra Pierce, "American Indian Adolescent Girls: Vulnerability to Sex Trafficking, Intervention Strategies," *American Indian and Alaska Native Mental Health Research: The Journal of the National Center* 9 (2012): 37–56.
[83] Pricilla A. Rocha, "OUR BACKYARD SLAVE TRADE: THE RESULT OF OHIO'S FAILURE TO ENACT COMPREHENSIVE STATE-LEVEL HUMAN-SEX-TRAFFICKING LEGISLATION," *Journal of Law & Health* 25, no. 2 (2012): 381–417.

Massachusetts, West Virginia, Maine and Wyoming do not have specific human trafficking legislation. In those States prosecutors must rely upon charging traffickers with existing crimes. For example, a case of rape might be made out against a trafficker, but only if he, and not others, had raped his victim to 'season' her for the assaults she would endure as a sex slave.[84] An inchoate crime may, of course, have been committed if he had been involved in the rape in some way even not as rapist. This may or may not carry the same penalty as if the State had enacted Human Trafficking legislation.[85] The State must rely upon federal prosecution of traffickers. In Wyoming the crime of kidnapping is a Class 2 felony. In the case of US v. Jacobo Dominguez Vazquez and Others in 2007 Wyoming gave jurisdiction to Arizona because of its own lack of Human Trafficking laws. [86] The defendants, three Mexican nationals were found guilty of using a 13 year old in sex slavery in Cheyenne but, despite the possibility of a life sentence, they were only sentenced to a maximum of eight years in jail.

In regard to labor slavery it is more difficult to find a crime which would result in the conviction of the trafficker and a sentence commensurate with the gravity of the crime.[87] For example, the crime of kidnapping may not fit in a case where the victim was tricked into coming to the U.S. voluntarily. Even if it did the sentences for kidnapping are generally not as long as those for Human Trafficking. For example in Texas kidnapping of an adult is a Class 3 Felony whereas trafficking is a Class 1 felony. In Mississippi sentences range from one year to life imprisonment and in Tennessee it is a Class C felony.

Secondly, the sheer number Federal agencies which are mandated with the prevention of human trafficking, the rescue of victims and the prosecution of traffickers leads to crossed-wires and silos.[88] On the Federal government level there are six government departments which carry this mandate. The Federal Bureau of Investigation works to investigate potential crimes, arrest criminals and rescue victims. It has over 88 human trafficking task forces which work with "local, state, and federal law enforcement agencies and national victim-based advocacy groups" to "combine resources and expertise on the issue."[89] This creates a further layer for victims because, whilst the FBI works with victims during rescue and prosecution of the traffickers it is grant funding from the U.S. Department of

[84] Seasoning is a process used by traffickers to terrify slaves into accepting their fate and not running away. In sex slavery it will include multiple beatings and gang/individual rapes. In other forms of slavery it will include starvation rations and beatings.

[85] Carrie N. Baker, "CRIME & PUNISHMENT: THE MODERN DEVELOPMENT OF HOMEGROWN CREATIVE JUSTICE: THE INFLUENCE OF INTERNATIONAL HUMAN TRAFFICKING ON UNITED STATES PROSTITUTION LAWS: THE CASE OF EXPUNGEMENT LAWS," *Syracuse Law Review* 62 (January 1, 2012): 171.

[86] US v. Jacobo Dominguez Vazquez and Others (District Court Wyoming 2007).

[87] Notes, "COUNTERACTING THE BIAS: THE DEPARTMENT OF LABOR'S UNIQUE OPPORTUNITY TO COMBAT HUMAN TRAFFICKING.," *Harvard Law Review* 126, no. 4 (January 1, 2013): 1012–1033.

[88] Allison Cross, "Slipping Through the Cracks: The Dual Victimization of Human-Trafficking Survivors.," *McGeorge Law Review* 44, no. 2 (January 2013): 395–422.

[89] "Federal Bureau of Investigation," *Federal Bureau of Investigation*, accessed November 4, 2013, http://www.fbi.gov/about-us/investigate/civilrights/human_trafficking/initiatives.

Health and Human Services which helps the victims to survive after their rescue by providing assistance to victims to help restore their lives and achieve self-sufficiency.[90] This is done by funding local stakeholders who can work directly with the victims. In the case of the U.S. Department of Homeland Security it, like the U.K. immigration service involved in Katya's case can find itself on the horns of a dilemma. This Department has two branches:

a. U.S. Immigration and Customs Enforcement (ICE), which has it's own victim assistance programs and investigative programs. The victims rescued by ICE will be treated as victims of human trafficking and not illegal immigrants. Unfortunately, there are multiple instances where a mistake is made and the victim is deported. One example is that of a young West African boy who was rescued from slavery as a domestic. As has been seen he was deported by ICE to his home where his family sold him back to human traffickers who smuggled him back into the U.S.A. where he was, again enslaved. Subsequently, he was rescued, again, by ICE and a friend, in the Detention center where he was awaiting a second deportation, gave him the number of a legal advocacy organization which were able to prevent his second deportation and, eventually, obtain a T Visa for him.[91] Of course, ICE deports immigrants on various bases but being a repeat 'immigration violator' placed this child towards the top of the list for swift deportation.
b. Working in tandem with the section of ICE which deports illegal immigrants and/or which saves victims is another department, U.S. Citizenship and Immigration Services, which provides T visas and U Visa to victims once they have cleared the necessary hurdles to be awarded either visa. This department also processes refugee applications. In this department overlaps between human trafficking and refugees can be seen. For example, a human trafficking victim may be fearful of being returned to his or her country of origin because he or she knows that the people who originally enslaved them will be waiting for them when they return.

The U.S. Department of Labor offers employment services for certified victims of trafficking and investigates any labor law violations. As most labor laws violations involve the employment of illegal immigrants victims of Human Trafficking are often caught up in deportations. The U.S. Department of State coordinates global efforts against trafficking, provides assessments of trafficking and employs an Ambassador at Large "to coordinate U.S. government activities in the global fight against contemporary forms of slavery."[92]

---

[90] Tessa L. Dysart, "THE PROTECTED INNOCENCE INITIATIVE: BUILDING PROTECTIVE STATE LAW REGIMES FOR AMERICA'S SEX-TRAFFICKED CHILDREN.," *Columbia Human Rights Review* 44, no. 3 (Spring 2013): 619–695.

[91] See: Nigerian Boy case. As told to the author by a Representative of the Bernardo Kohler center, Austin. http://www.bernardokohler.org/index.htm

[92] "L CdeBaca," *U.S. Department of State*, accessed October 20, 2013, http://www.state.gov/r/pa/ei/biog/124083.htm.

Since 2009 this office has been held by a former distinguished Federal prosecutor, Luis CdeBaca. It is Mr. CdeBaca's task to serve

> *"as Senior Advisor to the Secretary and directs the State Department's Office to Monitor and Combat Trafficking in Persons, which assesses global trends, provides training and technical assistance, and advocates for an end to modern slavery."*

In this role he oversees the creation of the 'Trafficking in Persons Report' and compliance with the international Treaties regarding Human Trafficking, most notably, the Palermo Protocol.[93] Additional to the work of the Department of Health and Human Services, the Department of State provides victim outreach services and, in 2004, assisted in the creation of the Human Smuggling Trafficking Center. Based in Washington, this Center was set up by the Secretary of State, the Secretary of Homeland Security, and the Attorney General to try to bring together the various government bodies which have individual and different mandates to address human trafficking.

> *'The Center will achieve greater integration and overall effectiveness in the U.S. Government's enforcement and other response efforts, and work with other governments to address the separate but related issues of alien smuggling, trafficking in persons, and criminal support of clandestine terrorist travel. The Center provides a mechanism to bring together federal agency representatives from the policy, law enforcement, intelligence, and diplomatic areas to work together on a full time basis to achieve increased effectiveness, and to convert intelligence into effective law enforcement and other action.'*[94]

Undoubtedly all these efforts are laudable, however, they are not working well enough to ensure a high level of prosecutions and rescue of victims. Therefore, they are not serving as a deterrent to the gangs which run this criminal industry. The Department of Justice is mandated to prosecute federal offences of human trafficking and help the victims.[95]

A third level of help to trafficking victims is provided by the States.[96] Confusingly, many States felt it necessary to invent their own trafficking legislation rather than adopt the

[93] United Nations, *Protocol to Prevent, Suppress and Punish Trafficking in Persons Especially Women and Children, Supplementing the United Nations Convention against Transnational Organized Crime*, 2000, http://www2.ohchr.org/english/law/protocoltraffic.htm; Bureau of Public Affairs Department Of State. The Office of Website Management, "Trafficking in Persons Report 2007," June 12, 2007, http://www.state.gov/j/tip/rls/tiprpt/2007/; Laura L. Shoaps, "ROOM FOR IMPROVEMENT: PALERMO PROTOCOL AND THE TRAFFICKING VICTIMS PROTECTION ACT.," *Lewis & Clark Law Review* 17, no. 3 (2013): 931–972.

[94] *Intelligence Reform and Terrorism Prevention Act*, 2004.

[95] Samantha Healy Vardaman and Christine Raino, "Prosecuting Demand as a Crime of Human Trafficking: The Eighth Circuit Decision in United States v. Jungers.," *University of Memphis Law Review* 43, no. 4 (summer 2013): 917–967.

[96] Vance Carole S., "States of Contradiction: Twelve Ways to Do Nothing about Trafficking While Pretending To.," *Social Research* 78, no. 3 (Fall 2011): 933–948.

Federal statute which came from the worldwide agreements at Palermo. The negative effect of creating new law is multi-layered; first it leaves room for clever lawyers to challenge the law, secondly, it is difficult for Prosecutors to feel confident in bringing prosecution and, thirdly, it requires prosecutors and law enforcement officers to undergo considerable training and, in some cases, a change of mindset.[97] In the case of victims of sexual slavery law enforcement officers are required to see women who they have always thought of prostitutes as potential victims of trafficking. Likewise, as has been seen, the federal work of finding victims has been left, in part, to the Immigration and Customs Enforcement Agency (ICE). The principal function of this agency is the finding and deporting of illegal immigrants. Again, asking them to find and rescue victims of trafficking who also happen to look like illegal immigrants involved in criminal activity requires operatives to have training and make significant changes in their operating regime. An examination of the laws against human trafficking which have been enacted by the various States show lacunae in the way in which this criminal activity is treated.

Comparison of State Laws

As has been seen there are no human trafficking laws in the States of West Virginia, Massachusetts, Wyoming and Maine.[98] One of the duties for the Federal Bureau of Investigation is to present an annual report on crime statistics in the United States. When crime analysts consider these statistics, they often compare crime throughout various regions. Some of the comparisons they make include: where do certain crimes occur more frequently; what are the laws in a particular region; how are they contributing to the prevention of certain crimes? According to statistics released, in 2011, in the *Huffington Post*, the top ten least peaceful states in so far as violent crime in the United States are: Louisiana, Tennessee, Nevada, Florida, Alabama, Texas, Arkansas, Oklahoma, South Carolina, and Maryland.[99] Human trafficking falls within the list of violent crimes committed in these states. In this comparison States have been chosen across the continent and across the political spectrum; the laws of New York, Washington, Washington D.C., Montana Wisconsin, Pennsylvania, Michigan, California will be considered and, then, in depth, the law in Texas.[100] According to the United States Department of Justice, over 2,500 cases were under investigation in 2010, with more than 1,000 cases involving children.[101] These numbers only represent reported cases and so it is estimated that the figures are higher, indeed thousands more cases probably go unreported every year.

---

[97] Babb Lenora C., "UTAH'S MISGUIDED APPROACH TO THE PROBLEM OF SEX TRAFFICKING: A CALL FOR REFORM.," *Journal of Law & Family Studies.* 14, no. 2 (2012): 277–298.

[98] Firth-Butterfield and Miranda, *Laws on Human Trafficking.*

[99] Henry Bradford, "10 Most Viiolent States in the US: The Institute for Economics and Peace," *The Huffington Post*, April 13, 2011.

[100] Melissa Dess, "WALKING THE FREEDOM TRAIL: AN ANALYSIS OF THE MASSACHUSETTS HUMAN TRAFFICKING STATUTE AND ITS POTENTIAL TO COMBAT CHILD SEX TRAFFICKING.," *Boston College Journal of Law & Social Justice* 33, no. 1 (Winter 2013): 147–182.

[101] "Bureau of Justice Statistics," *Bureau of Justice Statistics*, September 16, 2011, http://www.state.gov/r/pa/ei/biog/124083.htm.

However, there is insufficient data about victims.[102] Looking first at similarities, all the laws against human trafficking enacted in these states provide definitions of both the crimes and the methods of coercion used in these crimes.[103] Another similarity is that all states prosecute those who force or coerce others to provide labor and services against their will. Likewise, the human trafficking laws in all of these states prosecute those who force others to engage in either "commercial sex acts" or "sexually explicit performances". Another similarity between the human trafficking laws of these states is that they all list the means that traffickers use to make others provide forced labor and services. For example, the laws of all eight states cite the threat of physical harm as a felony violation. Additionally, many states punish individuals who destroy, conceal, remove, or confiscate another person's passport or individuals who physically restrain another. Finally, all eight states prosecute the act of one person causing or the threat to cause financial harm to another, and penalize the crime of blackmail.

Amongst the many differences amongst the States human trafficking laws first, the states have different severity levels for trafficking crimes. For example, Washington classifies trafficking in both the first and second degree as a class A felony. However, New York ranks labor trafficking as a class D felony and sex trafficking as a class B felony. Another difference in the human trafficking laws of these states is the level of detail which is involved in the definition of the crime. Also, each State has a different law using different material and definitions.

New York

New York, only defines the terms "labor trafficking" and "sex trafficking", but the law has considerable detail. According to New York's penal code, "a person is guilty of labor trafficking if he or she compels or induces another to engage in labor or recruits, entices, harbors, or transports such other person..."; "a person is also guilty of sex trafficking if he or she intentionally advances or profits from prostitution..." New York serves as "both an entry point for people who are trafficked into the United States, and a destination for it."[104] In 2005, over six hundred and forty five thousand illegal immigrants were estimated to be in New York. These immigrants alone made up over twenty percent of New York's population.[105] In 2006, the United States Department of Justice identified New York as one of the regions where human trafficking is constantly growing. This was also the year when New York City established their anti-human trafficking task force. This task force shares human trafficking information between agencies and provides services for victims. New York enacted anti-trafficking law in 2007 and has also dedicated itself to providing services for victims of human trafficking by launching an awareness campaign

[102] Ibid.

[103] Kelly Heinrich and Kavitha Sreeharsha, "The State of State Human-Trafficking Laws.," *Judge's Journal* 52, no. 1 (Winter 2013): 28–31.

[104] *New York Penal Code*, accessed November 4, 2013, http://codes.lp.findlaw.com/nycode/PEN.

[105] Gideon Belmaker, "New York City: Point of Entry for Human Trafficking in US," *Epoch Times*, March 23, 2011, http://www.theepochtimes.com/n2/united-states/new-york-city-point-of-entry-for-human-trafficking-in-us-53388.html.

and community based organizations such as Safe Horizon and GEMS.[106] Despite being recognized as the largest service on the east coast, Safe Horizons has only managed to help three hundred and sixty victims.[107] In 2010, New York prosecuted forty human trafficking cases involving the crimes of either labor trafficking or sex trafficking.[108] Not all states see human trafficking in the same way. Therefore, laws created by some states are ignored by others.[109] For example, Washington is the only state with a law that mentions the crime of illegally harvesting or selling of human organs; organ trafficking. Although, as will be seen later, New York prosecuted someone for organ trafficking. In October 2013, New York opened a new Court specifically designed to help victims of human trafficking.[110]

Washington DC

Is categorized by the Polaris Project as a Tier 2 State.[111] In 2009, Jermaine Moore pled guilty to transporting fifteen and seventeen year-old girls across state lines for the purpose of prostitution. He was sentenced to seventeen and a half years in prison. In the same year, Shelby Lewis, pled guilty to prostituting four girls who were ages twelve to sixteen; he was sentenced to twenty years in prison. In 2007, Sunni Ham was sentenced to nine years in prison for forcing two underage girls to wear revealing clothing while performing sexual acts. Washington DC, also, has a crime of 2nd Degree Sexual Abuse which has the same punishment as human trafficking; up to twenty years in prison and two hundred thousand U.S. dollar fine. The actus reus requires the victim to be: (A) Incapable of appraising the nature of the conduct; or (B) Incapable of declining participation in that sexual act; or (C) Incapable of communicating unwillingness to engage in that sexual act. As discussed above, in some states kidnapping offences may be sufficient to deal with human trafficking. This is the case in Washington DC where punishment, at up to 30 years in prison is actually greater than human trafficking.

Montana

This State relies on Title 45 Montana Code Annotated in order to prosecute trafficking crimes. Section 45-5-305 deals with subjecting another to involuntary servitude which incorporates the mens rea of "purposefully or knowingly" obtaining or maintaining "forced labor or services" by issuing threats. Punishment includes a fine of up to fifty

---

[106] Rachel Lloyd, *Girls Like Us: Fighting for a World Where Girls Are Not for Sale: A Memoi* (Harper Perennial, 2012).

[107] "Safe Horizon," accessed November 4, 2013, http://www.safehorizon.org/.

[108] All of the information about prosecutions can be found on the Human Trafficking Law Project (HTLP) database. University of Michigan Law School http://www.law.umich.edu/clinical/HuTrafficCases/Pages/searchdatabase.aspx>

[109] Marisa Nack, "THE NEXT STEP: THE FUTURE OF NEW YORK STATE'S HUMAN TRAFFICKING LAW," *Journal of Law & Policy* 18, no. 2 (2010): 817–853.

[110] Sadhbh Walshe, "New Court Helps New York's Human Trafficking Victims," *Al Jazeera*, October 31, 2013, http://america.aljazeera.com/articles/2013/10/31/new-court-systemhelpsvictimsofhumantraffickinginnewyork.html.

[111] "For a World Without Slavery," *Polaris Project*, accessed November 2, 2013, http://www.polarisproject.org/.

thousand U.S. dollars and/or up to ten years in a state prison. In this code we see the common mistake represented in the Human Trafficking laws repeated by many states that some human trafficking involves rape and torture of the victims which, in turn, deserves much higher punishment. Also, Montana created its own statute instead of following the federal lead. A couple of cases arising in Montana were prosecuted in a federal court, for example:

United States v. Kendal Ray Williams.[112] In this case the defendant was found guilty of interstate commerce to engage in prostitution as well as interstate commerce in minors engaging in prostitution. In another example of the problems seen in rescuing human trafficking victims the victims were charged with the crime of prostitution, even though they were forced to prostitute themselves and were minors. The Appellate court reconsidered the sentencing because it found the victims were 'vulnerable'.

Wisconsin

Has introduced a specific section into its Criminal Code. Section 940.302 criminalizes human trafficking for 'commercial sex act' and 'debt bondage'. What is interesting about this law is that it is a hybrid with section 1(a-c) being written by the state but section 1(d), which deals with the meaning of 'trafficking', coming straight from the Federal legislation. What is surprising is that human trafficking is categorized as a Class D Felony. This carries a penalty of a fine of up to ten thousand U.S. dollars, or imprisonment of up to twelve years, or both which is more than Montana but less than Texas. The mens rea (guilty mind) is "knowingly engaging". A victim may bring a civil suit which includes the option for the jury to award punitive damages not to exceed treble the actual damages incurred and reasonable attorney's fees. This is interesting because many sex slaves are raped multiple times and some have children to support from those rapes. Of course, they have lost the possibilities of careers during their enslavement too. One can only imagine that the potential for damages is very high indeed.

United States v. Elnora Calimlim.[113] In this case Elnora, Jefferson and Jefferson M. Calimlim were found guilty of Obtaining and Conspiring to Obtain Forced labor along with Harboring and Conspiring to Harbor an Alien for private financial gain. The victim was Irma Martinez, who was from the Philippines had been forced to work for the family, who lived in a spacious home with a private tennis court and worked as physicians, for nineteen years during which they paid her nineteen thousand U.S. dollars. The Court of first instance sentenced the Defendants to forty eight months in prison. On appeal the Court remanded the sentence for further consideration. In 2009, Irma Martinez sued Jefferson Calimlim for violation of violating RICO, WOCCA, and the 13th Amendment.

United States v. Eric A. Olson; this case involved the production of child pornography.[114] When the FBI raided the defendant's home they found more than one hundred and twenty thousand graphic images and two hundred and seventy four videos on

[112] United States v. Kendal Ray Williams, 291 F.3d 1180 (9th Cir. 2002).
[113] United States v. Elnora Calimlim, 129 S. Ct. 2237 2244 (Supreme Court 2009).
[114] United States v. Eric A. Olson (7th Cir. 2008).

his hard drive. Of these seven hundred and fifty were unknown victims but one hundred and thirty three were known victims. He was charged with possession of child pornography. Additionally, he was charged with manufacturing pornography based upon a twenty minute video which was discovered. It depicted Olson having sexual contact with a minor female who was about three or four years old. The agents found a further sixty eight images on Olson's hard drive showing him involved in sexual contact with the same minor. He was sentenced to twenty years in jail on the count of manufacturing and a further ten years for possession of which only twenty months of the second sentence was to run consecutively to the first sentence.

Pennsylvania

Chapter 30 of Title 18 on the Consolidated Statutes of Pennsylvania defines human trafficking as 'forced labor or services" and uses part of the federal definition of trafficking. The trafficking must be done 'knowingly' and included the inchoate crime of attempt. If the victim is a minor or suffers bodily harm the crime is a 1st degree felony (punishable with up to twenty years in prison), otherwise a 2nd degree felony (punishable with up to ten years in prison). The criminal court may order restitution and a civil court is then also allowed to award damages. The criminal court may also order forfeiture of property acquired from the trafficking.

In United States v. Michael Wayne Thomas the defendant pled guilty to transportation of a minor across state lines for the commercial purpose of prostitution and interstate transportation in aid of racketeering and intestate.[115] He was sentenced to seventeen and a half years and four years of supervised release.

Michigan

The Complied Laws include human trafficking in Chapter 750, Michigan Penal Code Act 328 of 1931 at Chapter LXVIIA. The definitions include 'forced labor or services' taking a victim's passport in various ways, using a minor in sexual activity and kidnapping. It uses part of the federal definition of 'trafficking' and expands the same. There have been thirteen federal prosecutions of human trafficking offences in the State.

California

In its Penal Code California adheres to the federal definition of human trafficking; "sex trafficking in which a commercial sex act is induced by force, fraud, or coercion, or in which the person induced to perform such act has not attained eighteen years of age; or "the recruitment, harboring, transportation, provision, or obtaining of a person for labor or services, through the use of force, fraud, or coercion for the purpose of subjection to involuntary servitude, peonage, debt bondage, or slavery." However, penalties for violation of the human trafficking provisions are low: punishable by imprisonment in state prison for three, four or five years. But if the victim is under eighteen at time of offense, imprisonment cane be for four, six or eight years. Human Trafficking involving a

[115] United States v. Michael Wayne Thomas (10th Cir. 2005).

commercial sex act can be punished by imprisonment and/or a fine of no more than one hundred thousand U.S. dollars. This money must be deposited in the Victim-Witness Assistance Fund which fund services for victims of human trafficking. Fifty percent of this money goes to community-based organizations that serve victims of human trafficking. California defines rape as nonconsensual intercourse accomplished by means of threats, force, or fraud and provides penalties for the offences of formal probation or three, six or eight years in state prison (three to five years more if victim sustains significant physical injury), a maximum fine of ten thousand U.S. dolars, registration as sex offender and a possible strike on the record.

Nevada

Is the only state in the country where prostitution is legal in eight counties. As a result law enforcement have the difficult job of identifying when providers are victims or voluntary. The code refers to sex trafficking as 'involuntary servitude' and includes a separate classification for child trafficking. Solicitation of a minor for prostitution is a class E felony which carries only a one to four year sentence which can be suspended, with a maximum fine of five thousand U.S. dollars. (s. 201.354(3)). Offering or agreeing to engage in prostitution is a misdemeanor punishable by six months (max) in prison and up to a one thousand U.S. dollar fine (s. 207.030(1)). Possession of child pornography of under sixteen year olds is a class B felony punishable by one to six years in jail, asset forfeiture and up to a five thousand U.S. dollar fine. (s. 200.730) Using the internet with intent to view child pornography is a class C felony punishable by one to five years in prison, up to ten thousand U.S. dollar fine and forfeiture of assets.(s. 200.727). It seems odd that the legislature decided that prostituting minors warrants a lesser penalty than viewing them online.[116]

It will have been noted that the cases included in this section have been federal prosecutions and not state prosecutions. The problem is that there are few state prosecutions.

Texas, Human Trafficking Law in detail.

The Texas penal code states that, "a person commits an offense if the person knowingly traffics another person with the intent that the trafficked person engage in forced labor or services etc..." Like New York, Texas is a 'gateway' for human trafficking and illegal immigration. Victims coming from Latin and Central America are very likely to enter through Texas. In 2006, over one million, seven hundred thousand illegal immigrants were believed to be in Texas.[117] According to the United States Department of Justice, more than two thousand five hundred human trafficking cases were investigated between 2008 and 2010. A quarter of all calls to the US National Trafficking Hotline came from Texas in 2010. This may be because Texas includes one of the main human trafficking hubs, Houston, or because the state has been at the forefront of raising awareness and

---

[116] Alicia W. Peters, "'Things That Involve Sex Are Just Different': US Anti-Trafficking Law and Policy on the Books, in Their Minds, and in Action.," *Anthropological Quarterly* 86, no. 1 (Winter 2013): 221–256.
[117] "Immigration to Texas," accessed April 20, 2013, http://www.usimmigrationsupport.org/texas.html.

developing anti-trafficking laws. It is common to see notices in gas stations, restaurants and other places where victims may be brought advertising the Hotline number. In 2011, in another type of outreach campaign public workers in Houston were educated on how to detect signs of human trafficking activities. Law enforcement officers have also been required to receive at least four hours of human trafficking training.[118] Likewise, the author taught the Municipal Judges of Texas about human trafficking at various conferences across the state in 2011/2012. This was of particular importance because Municipal Judges are often the people who see minor victims who may be brought before them as delinquents. The Judges are often confronted, without them knowing it, by pimps posing as guardians and children who have legal representation from the lawyers hired by the traffickers to ensure that nothing untoward is said in Court.

Despite the estimated numbers of victims the prosecution of traffickers is very low. The Bureau of Justice Administration Human Trafficking Task Force reported five hundred and fifty four investigations in 2010 which led to only one hundred and thirteen indictments. The victims saved included two hundred and sixty under eighteens, one hundred and eighty eight domestic victims and twenty six foreign born victims. Two 'Innocence Lost Task Forces worked in Texas in 2010 but only rescued one hundred and nine minor victims.[119]

Like many other states Texas devised its own law which led Prosecutors to doubt whether convictions could be obtained and, therefore, few prosecutions resulted. In 2010, the legislature changed the wording of the statute to bring it in line with the federal provisions and, thus, increase the understanding of the evidence and elements required to prove this crime. A look at some of the legislation shows how comprehensive this revision has been. Despite the Texas problems with the law before 2010 Texas prosecuted, and won, some notable human trafficking cases. For example the Mondragon case freed one hundred and twenty women from slavery in the "Wagon Wheel" cantina in Houston. They had been enslaved drinking with clients and providing sexual favors until a raid, organized by federal, state and local law enforcement officers in 2005 resulted in the arrest of the owner, his wife, Walter Corea, the chief smuggler and others. Although this was one of the largest human trafficking rings discovered in the US, Mondragon only went to prison for thirteen years and Corea for fifteen. This case is an example which shows just how much money is made in such rings; Mondragon was ordered to pay one million, seven hundred thousand U.S. dollars in compensation to victims. This case enabled legislators to see the need to increase penalties.

The legislature reorganized the Texas Penal Code (Section 20A) to clearly define types of criminal conduct according to the victim's age and type of abuse. It criminalizes trafficking of adults and children for labor or sex and simplifies the law in relation to evidence for child trafficking cases. Additionally, in all cases protection is given to victims

---

[118] "Texas Attorney General," *Texas Attorney General*, July 21, 2011, https://www.oag.state.tx.us/oagnews/release.php?id=3807.

[119] Polaris Project, *National Human Trafficking Resource Center Call Data 2009 Executive Summary*, 2009.

by allowing the testimony of a victim to be accepted without corroboration. Also, following the case of Re B.W., a child's involvement in prostitution is reclassified as conduct in need of supervision provision, not delinquent conduct. [120] In the dissenting opinion of the Court it was argued that "the language of the prostitution statute includes thirteen-year-olds, and the Juvenile Justice Code makes them subject to juvenile delinquency proceedings for committing that offense" but the majority of the Court found that, as a matter of law, a thirteen year old should be considered a victim and not a criminal. It is interesting to note that the U.S. Trafficking Victims Protection Act (TVPA) provides that any child (defined as under 18) who is arrested or apprehended in a commercial sex act is legally defined as having been trafficked.[121] A commercial sex act requires a payment to pass between user and slave, even thought that money will not, ultimately, end up in the hands of the slave.

Addressing one of the chief problems of achieving a conviction the Legislature added sex trafficking offenses to the list where bail may be denied when victim is a child (under fourteen years of age) and original bond conditions are violated.[122] Likewise they added child sex trafficking-related offenses to the list of offenses requiring a child safety zone.[123] These offences became '3G' offences which require a reasonable notice of a proposed bail reduction to be provided to the State. Bail was often set at a sum which was so low that the offender could easily meet bail and fail to return to Court. This usually left the victims unprotected and unwilling to co-operate with law enforcement. As has been seen failing to cooperate with law enforcement will lead to a denial of a T Visa and often deportation thereafter.[124]

Turning to penalties the legislature increase penalties for soliciting a child for prostitution making it a 3rd degree felony where the child is between 14 and 18 and a second degree felony where the child is under fourteen.[125] Under HB 2014 Sec. 25.08 of the Texas Penal Code there are enhanced penalties for the sale or purchase of a child for human trafficking, or a related offence. Sale or purchase is a third degree felony if it is an adoption or merely selling for remuneration or profit with no sex involved. Where the accused is proved to have intended to engage in child human trafficking, compelling prostitution, or promotion of prostitution a second degree felony is committed and HB 290 and HB 2014) Sec. 43.251 Texas Penal Code provides for enhanced penalties against persons who employ, authorize or induce a child to work in a sexually oriented business; second degree felony if child between 14 to 18 and first degree felony if child under

---

[120] Texas, *Family Code*, 2010.

[121] Rebecca Carroll Sager, "An Anomaly of the Law: Insufficient State Laws Fail to Protect Minor Victims of Sex Trafficking," *New England Journal on Criminal & Civil Confinement* 38, no. 2 (Summer 2012): 359–378.

[122] Texas, *Code of Criminal Procedure*, 2010.

[123] Ibid.

[124] It is estimated by Austin Police Department Human Trafficking Division that a sex slave in Austin will make his/her trafficker around $120,000 per annum. Interview by author of Officer Sifuentes, former Head of liaison at the Austin Human Trafficking Department.

[125] *Texas Penal Code*, 2010.

fourteen. The intent is to make it less easy for a pimp to use others to recruit children for sexual slavery. Prior to this new law the offence was classified as a Class A Misdemeanor. Penalties for adult prostitution were also revised in relation to human trafficking. It is a Class B misdemeanor to solicit a prostitute and a Class A misdemeanor to solicit a prostitute with a prior conviction. In some cases there is no requirement for mens rea on the part of the accused and the phase "regardless if the actor knew" is used to clearly indicate knowledge is NOT required. There are also increased protections for victims of human trafficking. Sec. 7A.01 allows persons to apply for Protective orders whatever their relationship with the child, which will be granted where there is "an applicant in clear and present danger of sexual assault, stalking, or other harm."[126]

The extension of venue jurisdiction means that cases are based upon the entirety of the criminal episode, similar to kidnapping, and Prosecutors to a single jurisdiction where the crime was actually committed. Venue can be in any county where, through or into the person was trafficked. Adult sex and labor trafficking, Compelling Prostitution (adult) can be prosecuted for up to 10 years after the offence but Child Labor Trafficking and Compelling Prostitution (child) has a limitation of 10 years after the 18th birthday of the victim.

Often traffickers violate other state laws such as, Kidnapping, Unlawful Restraint (PC 20.01); Murder (PC 19.02); Assault Offenses (PC 22.01); Aggravated Sexual Assault (PC 22.021); Sexual Assault (PC 22.11); Aggravated Kidnapping (PC 20.04); Compelling Prostitution (PC 43.05); Organized Criminal Activity (PC 71.02). Under CCP 59, the Texas Courts can order the seizure and forfeiture of assets. Contraband is defined as property of any nature, including real, personal, tangible, or intangible, that is:

(A) used in the commission of:

(i) any first or second degree felony under the Penal Code

In addition to this raft of laws the Attorney General of Texas maintains a Task Force of experts to advise on changes to the law, enforcement education and other issues relevant to criminalizing and catching human traffickers. He also employs a Prosecutor dedicated to human trafficking cases.

Local Police

Lastly, some local Police Departments maintain human trafficking departments. Some of these are effective in arresting traffickers and freeing victims but again the tangle of laws and agencies can impede their work. Such an example can be found in local jails. In most local jails there is no screening process for trafficking victims. For example, in the Travis County jail victims are brought into the jail by the Police and then, often, handed over to ICE for consideration of their immigrant status. The ICE questionnaire which is used includes a question which asks the victim if she or he wished to come to the U.S. In the case of victims who originally did want to come to the U.S. to do a job which they

[126] Ibid. 7A.02

believed was genuine they will often say yes. Once they say 'yes' regardless of whether they then became a trafficking victim they are, most often, assigned to the deportation track.

A final layer is that of the interaction between the various agencies already mentioned and international, national and local nonprofits acting in the rescue and assistance of trafficking victims.

Beauty is in the Eye of the Beholder

***"...recognition of the inherent dignity and of the equal and inalienable rights of all members of the human family is the foundation of freedom, justice and peace in the world"*[127]**

Although human rights were defined in the Universal Declaration of Human Rights they are interpreted in many different ways in the various nations in the world.[128] Indeed, the Islamic nations, although they have ratified the Universal Declaration of Human Rights, have their own declaration of Human Rights which post-dates the Universal Declaration and reflects modern statehood rather than the colonial boundaries of 1948.[129]

Amongst most of the peoples of the globe there are some human rights which are usually agreed to be the most basic which should attach to every human being just because of their being human.

Tip
Take a moment to think of the rights you think are basic to the human condition and then check the Universal Declaration of Human Rights.

But as people and their governments often see Human Rights through a specific lens which gives more emphasis to one right than another or one set of rights than others or to rights of one type of human being over another the enforcement of Human Rights across the world vary widely.[130]

These are a few of the lenses through which human rights are viewed:

- Age

[127] "The Universal Declarartion on Human Rights," UN Treaty, 1948, http://www.un.org/en/documents/udhr/.
[128] Ibid.
[129] "Cairo Declaration on Human Rights in Islam," United Nations document (U.N. GAOR, World Conf. on Hum. Rts., 4th Sess., August 5, 1990), http://www1.umn.edu/humanrts/instree/cairodeclaration.html.
[130] Leslie Holmes, *Trafficking and Human Rights: European and Asia-Pacific Perspectives* (Cheltenham: Edward Elgar Publishing, 2010).

- Gender[131]
- Culture
- Religion
- Nationality
- Position of Influence
- Economic Circumstance

Tip:
As you read keep a record of the ways in which human rights depend upon their interpretation by specific groups.

Convention on the Elimination of All Forms of Discrimination against Women [132]

This treaty, which has had international force since September 3, 1981, seeks to protect women. Women were protected as 'human beings' in the 1948 Universal Declaration of Human Rights. However, the members of the United Nations had established the United Nations Commission on the Status of Women, in 1946, to monitor the situation of women and to promote women's rights. The members of the United Nations were worried that in numerous countries the rights of women were seen as inferior to those of men and, it is true that excessive discrimination continues to exists today. This is true despite the fact that the Convention on the Elimination of All Forms of Discrimination against Women (CEDAW) has been ratified by every country except the United States and Palau both of which have signed but not ratified it.

> *"The spirit of the Convention is rooted in the goals of the United Nations: to reaffirm faith in fundamental human rights, in the dignity, and worth of the human person, in the equal rights of men and women…The Convention gives positive affirmation to the principle of equality by requiring States parties to take 'all appropriate measures, including legislation, to ensure the full development and advancement of women, for the purpose of guaranteeing them the exercise and enjoyment of human rights and fundamental freedoms on a basis of equality with men'(article 3)".*[133]

This Treaty is different from other human rights Treaties in that as well as dealing with civil rights and legal status it is also concerned with human reproduction and the impact of cultural factors on relations between the sexes. The provisions of the Convention on the Political Rights of Women 1952 are restated in article 7.[134] These

[131] Julietta Hua, *Trafficking Women's Human Rights* (Minneapolis: University of Minnesota Press, n.d.).
[132] "Convention on the Elimination of All Forms of Discrimination against Women" (Copenhagen, July 17, 1980), http://www.un.org/womenwatch/daw/cedaw/text/econvention.htm.
[133] Ibid.
[134] United Nations, *Convention on the Political Rights of Women*, 1952.

guarantee women the right to vote, take part in government and represent their country. The Convention on the Nationality of Married Women1957 is also integrated.[135] This Convention provides for statehood of women, irrespective of their marital status; in many cases they are dependent on their husband's nationality rather than being individuals in their own right.

It is widely acknowledged within the International community that if women could be educated and protected then great benefits would ensue for the economy of their country and their children. Indeed Millennium Development Goal 3 is to achieve gender equality.[136] The Millennium Development Goals also address maternal health. In many countries women have little control over their reproductive rights and many die as a result (one every 60 seconds).[137] CEDAW is the only human rights legislation to mention family planning which in some countries and communities has made it extremely controversial. In fact there is only 'encouragement' to states to educate children about family planning and "to develop family codes that guarantee women's rights

> *"to decide freely and responsibly on the number and spacing of their children and to have access to the information, education and means to enable them to exercise these rights."*[138]

It is not possible to address human rights issues for women without looking at the cultural and traditional contexts that deny them. The treaty asserts

> *"that a change in the traditional role of men as well as the role of women in society and in the family is needed to achieve full equality of men and women".*[139]

The express affirmation of equality between male and female and the rejection of a man's role being public and a woman's domestic has lead to controversy in many areas of the world. It was a major thrust of Allied work in Afghanistan which ratified CEDAW in March 2003.

Convention on the Rights of the Child 1989[140]

This document gives legal status to the rights of children (from birth to 18 years of age). Out of all U.N. treaties it was the fastest to be signed and ratified. It has now been

---

[135] "Convention on the Nationality of Married Women" (1957, n.d.), http://treaties.un.org/doc/Treaties/1958/08/19580811%2001-34%20AM/Ch_XVI_2p.pdf.

[136] "Target 3.A: Eliminate Gender Disparity in Primary and Secondary Education, Preferably by 2005, and in All Levels of Education No Later than 2015" (United Nations), accessed October 25, 2013, http://www.un.org/millenniumgoals/gender.shtml.

[137] WHO, "Why Do so Many Women Still Die in Pregnancy or Childbirth?," August 21, 2013, http://www.who.int/features/qa/12/en/.

[138] "Convention on the Elimination of All Forms of Discrimination against Women."

[139] Ibid.

[140] UN, "Convention on the Rights of the Child," 1989, http://www.ohchr.org/en/professionalinterest/pages/crc.aspx.

ratified by all the countries of the world except Somalia, which doesn't have a government, and the United States.

Convention on the Rights of Persons with Disabilities[141]

This treaty and its optional protocol were adopted on December 13, 2006. It has been ratified by one hundred and seventeen countries and signed by one hundred and fifty three.

Of course, as will be seen, agreeing to an international law does not mean that a government will follow it. Thus, it is necessary to look at the enforcement mechanisms. Essentially there are no enforcement mechanisms for these human rights laws. The United Nations relies upon bringing pressure to bear upon the countries abusing human rights through its mechanisms of the General Assembly, United Nations bodies and departments and the Secretary General. The Security Council can, if all five nations which have a veto agree, vote for military action but this is rare. For example, the United Nations stood by and did not send a military force to Rwanda during the 1994 massacre and Russia held out for years against a Security Council resolution to allow military action against human rights abuses in Syria.[142] The CEDAW Convention is typical of the type of provisions inserted to help keep states to their obligations.

> *"At least every four years, the States parties are expected to submit a national report to the Committee, indicating the measures they have adopted to give effect to the provisions of the Convention. During its annual session, the Committee members discuss these reports with the Government representatives and explore with them areas for further action by the specific country. The Committee also makes general recommendations to the States parties on matters concerning the elimination of discrimination against women."*[143]

The Convention for the Suppression of the Traffic in Persons and of the Exploitation of the Prostitution of Others was created in 1949.[144] The world next revisited the matter of trafficking in a global treaty in 2000 by which time it had become very apparent that slavery was again on the rise. This is interesting because slavery is outlawed in all countries and also prohibited within signatory states of the 1948 Universal Declaration of Human Rights. The treaty which covers human trafficking is, in fact, an anti-transnational crime treaty with significant challenges.[145] The United Nations Convention

[141] United Nations, "Convention on the Rights of Persons with Disabilities," 2006, http://www.un.org/disabilities/convention/conventionfull.shtml.

[142] For further information on international Human Rights Law see: Michael K. Addo, *The Legal Nature of International Human Rights*, !st (Leiden, The Netherlands: Martinus Nijhoff Publishers, 2010), http://www.brill.com/legal-nature-international-human-rights.

[143] "Convention on the Elimination of All Forms of Discrimination against Women."

[144] United Nations, "Convention for the Suppression of the Traffic in Persons and of the Exploitation of the Prostitution of Others," 1949, http://treaties.un.org/Pages/ViewDetails.aspx?src=IND&mtdsg_no=VII-11-a&chapter=7&lang=en.

[145] Heather Smith, "Sex Trafficking: Trends, Challenges, and the Limitations of International Law," *Human Rights Review* 12, no. 3 (September 2012): 271–286.

Against Transnational Organized Crime[146] started life as a treaty designed to combat drug smuggling and the arms trade. It has now been ratified by one hundred and forty nations.[147]

Some countries have their own human rights law. For example, this can be seen in the U.S. and South Africa in their Constitutions. The U.K. has an unwritten constitution which means that it adapts over time but also has the Human Rights Act 1998.[148] Additionally many of the countries in Europe have signed and ratified the European Convention on Human Rights (ECHR).[149] This convention established the European Court of Human Rights which tries cases brought before it by citizens of the member countries who believe that their human rights have been breached by their home government. The effect of this treaty is far reaching because it requires all domestic legislation to be considered for its compliance with the treaty and, if a citizen has exhausted all the levels of the domestic court they may seek redress in this regional Court. This means that nations have bound themselves to accept the decisions of the regional court and, where necessary amend their domestic legislation accordingly. There are politicians around Europe who oppose such a Court but the majority accept the Convention.

Essay : What is the effect of European and Domestic Human Rights Legislation on cases heard in the UK

European Court of Human Rights (ECHR)

Britain pays twenty million British pounds a year to the Council of Europe which funds the court. In 2012 the court asked for more money because it has a backlog of one hundred and fifty thousand cases. In making the request the court said that states can choose to have their extra contribution spent on dealing with cases against them.

In 2011, the majority in a poll of voters in the U.K. wished to pull out of the ECHR. A decision which gave prisoners a right to vote precipitated this ill feeling.[150] On

[146] *United Nations Convention Against Transnational Organized Crime and Protocols Thereto (Palermo Protocol).*

[147] Ibid.

[148] United Kingdom, "Human Rights Act," 1998, http://www.legislation.gov.uk/ukpga/1998/42/contents.

[149] Council of Europe, "European Convention on Human Rights" (Strasbourg, 1950), http://www.echr.coe.int/Documents/Convention_ENG.pdf.

[150] Clive Coleman, *UK Inmates Lose Right to Vote Ruling*, Journal Article (London: BBC, October 16, 2013), http://www.bbc.co.uk/news/uk-24545294.

19 and 20 April 2012 the members of the ECHR signed up to the 'Brighton Declaration' which limits the power of the Court.[151]

In the case of Re: J (A Child) [2012] EWCA Civ 720 the Court of Appeal in England decided against allowing contact (visitation rights) for a Pakistani husband with his child living in the United Kingdom.[152] It based its decision upon the fact that he had been extremely violent towards the mother and had not taken the therapeutic help offered. The Court was cognizant of his right to a family life under Article 8 of the European Convention on Human Rights but put the best interests of the child first. The result led to the deportation of the father to Pakistan. In this case the tension between the rights of the child and the rights of the father can be seen. In English law the rights of the child will always triumph.[153]

In another case, tried by Charles J (Judge Charles) he allowed a mother's application to have a prohibited steps order set aside because it breached her human rights. Following her separation from the father of her children the lower court had issued a prohibited steps order which stopped her from moving home, requiring her to stay near her estranged husband. As a result she lost her job and subsequently another. Charles J had to balance the right of the father to see his children (right to family life) with that of the mother to be able to earn a living and support the family. The mother and family were in danger of losing their home as she could not pay the mortgage, (right to family life).[154]

In 2012 the United States of America sought the extradition from the United Kingdom of an alleged pedophile, Shawn Sullivan, who had been on Interpol's most wanted list. He was wanted in Minnesota for raping a fourteen year old and sexually assaulting two eleven year olds in 1993/1994. The Court was told that if he was convicted in Minnesota and sentenced to jail at the end of his imprisonment he would go onto a treatment program (known as civil commitment) which keeps people in jail past their prison term because they are sexually dangerous. The Court was also told that no one had been released under the program since it started in 1988. The English High Court Judges decided that civil commitment would breach his right not to suffer loss of liberty without due process, which is protected by the ECHR. The Justices – Lord Justice Moses and Mr. Justice Eady gave the Federal government of the United States of America the opportunity to say that civil containment wouldn't be used but it declined to do so (because it couldn't bind Minnesota). Mr. Justice Moses said "It is clear to me that were an order of civil commitment to be made, it would be a flagrant denial of this appellant's rights under

---

[151] Council of Europe, "High Level Conference on the Future of the European Court of Human Rights: Brighton Declaration" (Brighton U.K., 2012), http://www.echr.coe.int/Documents/2012_Brighton_FinalDeclaration_ENG.pdf.

[152] Re: J (A Child) [2012] EWCA Civ 720, Samantha Bangham, accessed October 20, 2013.

[153] United Kingdom, "Children Act 1989," 1989, http://www.legislation.gov.uk/ukpga/1989/41/contents.

[154] Christopher Booler, "Legal Miracle Then Business as Usual," *The Telegraph*, June 23, 2012, http://www.telegraph.co.uk/comment/9350679/A-legal-miracle-then-business-as-usual.html.

Article 5.1."[155] Shawn Sullivan is the tenth person to have their extradition to the United States of America blocked by the Courts or Home Secretary in the United Kingdom in recent years.

Many United Nations agencies tackle human trafficking because it persists across many areas. Some of these are :

- United Nations Children's Fund (UNICEF) for children
- International Labor Organization (ILO) for adults and children in work
- Office of the High Commissioner for Human Rights for human rights
- United Nations Office for Drugs and Crime (UNODC) relating to transnational crime
- International Organization for Migration (IOM)
- Organization for Security and Cooperation in Europe (OSCE)[156]
- United Nations High Commission for Refuges (UNHCR) which protects the interests of external and internal refugees and
- United Nations Global Initiative to Fight Human Trafficking (UNGIFT) which is dedicated to the fight against human trafficking.[157] UNGIFT was effectively created because the United Arab Emirates made a gift of fifteen million U.S. dollars to help combat trafficking. Launched in March 2007 it is a collaboration of the ILO, OHCHR, UNICEF, UNODC, IOM and OSCE. Since 2007, other governments and UN bodies have made donations but compared to the thirty two billion U.S. dollars annual profit believed to be made out of trafficking each year it is sorely underfunded. Indeed this figure of annual profit was estimated by the ILO in 2005 when the number of victims of trafficking was estimated at about one third of the 2013 estimate.

Essay: The USA had not ratified three of the five treaties mentioned in this Chapter, discuss the reluctance to do so.

Essay: The UN describes CEDAW as "an agenda for action by countries to guarantee the enjoyment of those rights." Given that the UN does not have an enforcement mechanism and populations might be highly resistant to change, can the existence of the legislation bring about change?

[155] Martin Beckford, "Pedophile Spared Extradition to US on Human Rights Grounds," *The Telegraph*, June 28, 2012, http://www.telegraph.co.uk/news/uknews/crime/9362298/Paedophile-spared-extradition-to-US-on-human-rights-grounds.html.

[156] Sarah H. Krieg, "Trafficking in Human Beings: The EU Approach between Border Control, Law Enforcement and Human Rights," *European Law Journal* 15, no. 6 (November 2009): 775–790.

[157] UNGIFT, *About* (UNGIFT), accessed October 20, 2013, http://www.ungift.org/.

BRITONS
Strengthen the hands of your
GOVERNMENT!
AFRICA
ABOLITION OF THE SLAVE TRADE 1807
WILLIAM WILBERFORCE
1st

Chapter 4

Slavery as Old as Time

"I am naturally anti-slavery. If slavery is not wrong, nothing is wrong. I cannot remember when I did not so think, and feel."[158]

This is not a book about historical slavery, the information in this chapter is set out to draw parallels with modern slavery and give background information which assists in the understanding of the modern trade. The in-depth review of the law of Britain and the history of the British Anti-Slavery movement is set out to show how the most powerful country in the world at that time set about conquering the scourge of slavery which may help readers to formulate ideas for eradicating modern slavery.

The Origins of slavery

Slavery has existed since the dawn of time. Although written records of slave holding do not start until 1760BCE it is likely that slaves would have been used in agriculture from its beginning in the Neolithic Age, some 11000 years ago. Trades routes for goods were also used to trade slaves, who were seen as goods. It will be seen that this definition of people as goods (chattels) will endure well into the late 18th century in Europe and beyond that date in other areas of the world. Equally, once human beings started to own territory and defend it against others, or fight to take over the territory of others there has been war. In war when early humans won the options for dealing with the conquered were generally slavery or death.Slavery depended then, and, in many ways continues to do so today, on multiple factors of social injustice but also two factors explored below – prejudice and greed.[159]

Prejudice: Color of Skin and Ethnicity

Originally slaves were the citizens of conquered peoples, quite literally "not us". This is part of the concept of citizenship. In historical Athens Aristotle extolled the virtues of the active citizen who took part in the running of the state. Of course these active participants in democracy were male citizens. The politics of Athens was run by them but

---

[158] Roy P. Basler, ed., *Letter to Albert G. Hodges (April 4. 1864*, vol. VII, The Collected Works of Abraham Lincoln (New Brunswick, NJ: Rutgers University Press, 1953).

[159] Job Elom Ngwe and O Oko Elechi, "HUMAN TRAFFICKING: THE MODERN DAY SLAVERY OF THE 21ST CENTURY.," *African Journal of Criminology & Justice Studies; Nov2012, Vol. 6 Issue 1/2, p103-119* 6, no. 1/2 (November 2012): 103–119.

the work was done by slaves, foreigners and non-citizen labourers all of whom were not citizens and "not one of us". Women were also excluded from citizenship.[160]

The nation of Mauritania is a lingering example of this notion. The ethnic Africans were enslaved by the Arabian Moors coming from the north in the early part of the Common Era.[161] Since that time the Moor has been the political elite in Mauritania and the African, the slave. Society is divided into three groups

- The 'white Moor'
- Harantines, slaves who were freed generations ago
- Afro-Mauritanians.

Slavery was abolished in Mauritania in1980; however "everywhere you look, on every street corner and shop, in every field and pasture, you see slaves".[162] These are the ethnically different people (Afro-Mauritanians) who have been enslaved for generations. Because of interpretation, the introduction of Sharia law, the abolition of slavery in 1980 appears to have made the situation of the slaves worse despite containing provisions about the care of slaves. Adam Nossiter's article about the continued presences of slavery in the country in 2013 demonstrates just how difficult it is to eradicate such a system. As will be seen this is also applicable to debt bonded and other forms of forced and slave labor.[163]

When European's started the West African Slave trade they believed that the African human being was of less value than they were. In his original thinking Bishop Bartlome de Las Casas even thought that the African slaves were of less worth than the enslaved indigenous peoples of South America.[164] The slave owning classes justified their ownership by religion and color. Despite the work of Darwin and our knowledge of the descent of man from Africa those prejudices remain key players in modern day slavery.

Greed

Greed was probably the silent, but greater, player in the slave trading and holding business. Slave Traders earned huge fortunes, the colonies needed strong workers and there was no other supply of labor. The slave trade differed from the traditional way of procuring slaves through war and featured the trade in human beings as cargo/chattels along with supplemental slave markets where slaves could be viewed prior to purchase. The Arabian slave trade was first documented in the first century CE in which the trade in Africans from East Africa was described. Later slaves traders added cargo from the Mediterranean and then from Asia. Although there are much older records of slave

[160] Aristotle and Benjamin Jowett, *Politics* (Mineola, NY: Dover Publications, 2000).

[161] Although some scholars assert that Moors were originally black Africans who had migrated northwards.

[162] Bales, *Disposable People, New Slavery in the Global Economy*.

[163] Adam Nossiter, "Mauritania Confronts Long Legacy of Slavery," *New York Times*, November 11, 2013, http://www.nytimes.com/2013/11/12/world/africa/mauritania-confronts-long-legacy-of-slavery.html?_r=0.

[164] Bartolomé de las Casas, *History of the Indies* (New York: Harper Torchbooks, Harper & Row, 1971).

trading, the Arabian trade was by far the most extensive, even including the later Atlantic trade. In the Atlantic trade, if the colonies were to survive, prosper and send money back to Europe they needed labor. Slave labor was cheap because, after the initial investment it was, all but, free. It is said that the reason for the delay in abolition in the U.S. was because of fear that the new country would divide over the issue of slavery. However, there was an important economic problem underlying the noble fears for the country – slaves were needed to power the economy. It is often said that the United Kingdom did itself untold financial damage by banning the slave trade and working to ensure the ban was complete throughout the world and it was only the extension of Empire that enabled it to continue as a major player in the world.[165]

Today, we see that slavery is simply a means to make the slave traders and holders wealthy. Across the world there is little slavery directly related to color or religion but those things still play a part in the way slaves are treated. For example, sex slaves in the Far East have a value based upon their ethnicity. In Thailand, Thai girls cost more and their services are sold for more than girls imported from neighboring countries. In the United States of America the social conventions which enable people to 'look down' upon prostitutes enable domestic sex slavery to continue unnoticed. The notion that those girls are just bad, or enjoy the work which 'good girls' wouldn't do places them below the rest and into that no-man's land which allows exploitation.

The first written evidence we have of slavery is in The Code of Hammurabi. The Prologue and Rules (1760BCE).

> *Rule 7 : "If any one buy from the son or the slave of another man, without witnesses or a contract, silver or gold, a male or female slave, an ox or a sheep, an ass or anything, or if he take it in charge, he is considered a thief and shall be put to death."*[166]

The taking of slaves and the ill-treatment of slaves abounds in the Old Testament. Written at a time when slaveholding was normal it gives us evidence of the taking of slaves after battle, the treatment of slaves because they were 'not like us' and the many ways in which slaves enabled societies to exist in biblical times.

The taking and holding of slaves can also be found in the Qur'an. The prophet Mohammed kept, bought and sold slaves as was commonplace at the time. Of course, problems can arise from both the Bible and the Qur'an when modern day believers seek to follow the letter of these religious documents. Slavery abounded throughout the Ancient World, the Egyptians, Greeks, Romans and Chinese all kept slaves. Both Socrates and Plato justify slavery in their writings. It was quite simply a norm which was not questioned.

---

165 Chaim D. Kaufmann and Robert A. Pape, "Explaining Costly International Moral Action: Britain's Sixty-Year Campaign Against the Atlantic Slave Trade," *International Organization* 53, no. 4 (Autumn 1999): 631–668.

166 L.W. King, trans., "The Code of Hammurabi. The Prologue and Rules (1760BCE)," accessed October 20, 2013, http://avalon.law.yale.edu/ancient/hamframe.asp.

Slavery as Old as Time

Arguably, the first state code which referred to slaveholding is the first Justinian Code, completed in 529BCE but revised in 534BCE.[167] Book One Article VIII had this to say:

> *"We now come to another division relative to the rights of persons; for some persons are independent, some are subject to the power of others. Of those, again, who are subject to others, some are in the power of parents, others in that of masters. Let us first treat of those who are subject to others; for, when we have ascertained who these are, we shall at the same time discover who are independent.*
>
> *First let us consider those who are in the power of masters.*
>
> *1. Slaves are in the power of masters, a power derived from the law of nations: for among all nations it may be remarked that masters have the power of life and death over their slaves, and that everything acquired by the slave is acquired for the master.*
>
> *2. But at the present day none of our subjects may use unrestrained violence towards their slaves, except for a reason recognized by law. For, by a constitutio of the Emperor Antoninus Pius, he who without any reason kills his own slave is to be punished equally with one who has killed the slave of another. The excessive severity of masters is also restrained by another constitutio of the same emperor. For, when consulted by certain governors of provinces on the subject of slaves, who fly for sanctuary either to temples, or to the statues of the emperors, he decided that if the severity of masters should appear excessive, they might be compelled to make sale of their slaves upon equitable terms, so that the masters might receive the value; and this was a very wise decision, as it concerns the public good, that no one should misuse his own property. The following are the terms of this rescript of Antoninus, which was sent to Laelius Marcianus: The power of masters over their slaves ought to be preserved unimpaired, nor ought any man to be deprived of his just right. But it is for the interest of all masters themselves, that relief prayed on good grounds against cruelty, the denial of sustenance, or any other intolerable injury, should not be refused. Examine, therefore, into the complaints of the slaves who have fled from the house of Julius Sabinus, and taken refuge at the statue of the emperor; and, if you find that they have been too harshly treated, or wantonly disgraced, order them to be sold, so that they may not fall again under the power of their master; and, if Sabinus attempt to evade my constitutio, I would have him know, that I shall severely punish his disobedience." (2)*
>
> *Cato, as we learn from the ancients, has with good reason written that slaves, when adopted by their masters, are thereby made free. In accordance with which opinion, we have decided by one of our constitutiones that a slave to whom his master by a solemn deed gives the title of son is thereby made free, although he does not require thereby the rights of a son.*
>
> *A slave whilst freed by adoption by a free man does not obtain the rights of a son."*[168]

---

[167] "Justinian Code," 534, http://www.fordham.edu/halsall/basis/535institutes.asp.

The act of manumission (freeing slaves) has had different definitions throughout history. The effect of manumission is also different according to the laws of the country.

Early European Slavery

Following the Classical period slavery probably died out in Europe until about the eighth century when the Arab slave traders started to supply African slaves to southern Europe. Of course, during this period most medieval citizens were tied to a Lord through the Feudal systems and so were little better than slaves. Those feudal systems persisted in Eastern Europe until the Bolshevik revolution in Russia, and later in other Slavic nations.

The Arab Slave Trade

Whilst the American slave trade in the sixteenth to nineteenth centuries was important, and some ten to twelve million human beings were enslaved, it was not the only slave system. It is estimated, for example that four times that number were taken from Sub-Saharan Africa to North Africa and the Middle East during the same time period. Indeed one of the reasons that African tribes were willing to engage in the slave trade with Europeans was because they had been doing so for many years with the Arabs. Arab slave trade routes ran from West Africa across the Sahara overland and by sea from East Africa.

It took the Royal Navy far longer to control the Arab slave traders of East Africa than to enforce the ending of the West African trade to the Americas. Indeed, Britain entered into the Treaty of Heligoland with the Germans for both strategic purposes and to forward its campaign to stamp out slavery. In this Treaty it obtained Zanibar Island and Pemba, which helped the Royal Navy take successful enforcement measures against Arab slave traders.

The suffering of slaves at the hands of their Arab captors was less well known than the suffering of slaves on the Middle passage which was revealed by the drawings of the "Brookes" in 1788.[169] In fact, the seamen of the Royal Navy, who stopped the ships setting off on the middle passage, reported even worse overcrowding than shown on the Brookes. Nevertheless, in this passage, Captain Fairfax Moresby describes the terrible sufferings of slaves travelling by dhow:

> *"In these vessels temporary platforms of bamboos are erected leaving a narrow passage in the centre. The Negroes are then stowed, in the literal sense of the word, in bulk, the first along the floor of the vessel, two adults side by side, with a boy or girl resting between them or on them, until the tier is complete. Over them the first platform is laid, supported and inch or two clear of their bodies, when a second tier is stowed and so on until they reach above the gunwale of the vessel. The voyage, they expect will not exceed 24 or 48hrs: but it often happens that a*

---

[168] Ibid.

[169] Societ for Effecting the Abolition of the Slave Trade, *Stowage of the British Slave Ship "Brookes" under the Regulated Slave Trade of 1788*, 1788, Library of Congress, http://www.loc.gov/rr/rarebook/guide/ra023002.html.

> *calm or unexpected breeze delays their progress. In this case a few hours are sufficient to decide the fate of the cargo. Those of the lower portion of the cargo that die cannot be removed. They remain under the upper part are dead and thrown over. And from a cargo of 200-400 stowed in this way, it has been known that not a dozen at the expiration of ten days have reached Zanzibar."*[170]

Africa to Americas Slave Trade

In 1348 the Black Death had arrived in Europe. In Southern Europe it killed up to eighty percent of some populations; in the North less. Overall it is estimated that forty to fifty percent of Europeans died in the period 1348-1352. The Arab countries suffered similar loses, some forty percent of the Egyptian population died. The effects of this destruction of life were still being felt in the next century. The economies were still largely agrarian and needed many laborers to keep them going. Those who didn't die of the Plague went hungry. The areas needed new labor.

Henry the Navigator, King of Portugal, was born in 1394. He was a keen explorer and created a navigation school in the Algarve, Portugal, to encourage exploration of the West Coast of Africa. At that time European sailors believed that the water boiled in the region of Cape Bojador and anyone who sailed there would burn and die. Additionally, the ships which they had at the time were not built for sailing oceans. Henry invited the cleverest scholars of navigation, mathematics, boat building, map-making, astronomy and sailing to work for him. The result of this effort was that, in 1433, Gil Eannes, rounded Cape Bojador and proved that the water didn't boil. Thereafter the Portuguese started to make regular trading journeys to West Africa. In 1441, a Portuguese merchant, Antao Goncalves, traveling in Africa met an Arabian slave-trader who gave him ten African slaves to take back to King Henry as a present.[171]

The Europeans are considered to have started their trade in African slaves on 8th August 1444. Lançarote de Freitas was a Portuguese entrepreneur. He started kidnapping and enslaving people in the areas now known as Lagos, Nigeria, and Senegal. The first of these two hundred and thirty five victims arrived in Europe in August 1444.[172] Many believed that the trade was given religious backing when on 18 June,1452 Pope Nicholas V issued *Dum Diversas*, a Papal Bull authorizing the Spanish to reduce any non-Christians to the status of slaves. However, one translation seems to suggest that the Bull was specific in its purposes and authorization and did not allow the wholesale commencement of slavery.[173] In 1516, more religious support was given to the African slave trade in the "*Memorial de Remedios para Las Indias*" written by the well-meaning Bishop Bartlome de Las Casas. In this document, he supported the African slave trade as a way of protecting the indigenous people of central and south America from enslavement by the western

---

[170] Bernard Edwards, *Royal Navy versus the Slave Traders: Enforcing Abolition at Sea 1808-1898* (Barnsley: Pen & Sword Maritime, 2007).
[171] Ibid.
[172] Ibid.
[173] "Unam Sanctum Catholicam," accessed October 23, 2013, http://unamsanctamcatholicam.blogspot.com/2011/02/dum-diversas-english-translation.htm.

colonizers. However, once he had witnessed the inhumanity of the Atlantic slave trade he changed his mind and was an early advocate for the human rights of all peoples, not just the 'civilized Christian' ones from whom he witnessed such barbarity.[174]

The lives of slaves and people in developing countries are often subject to the whim of powerful and developed countries. It was no different in the sixteenth century. In the mid sixteenth century, Queen Elizabeth I ascended the throne of England bringing with her the Protestant religion. The conflict between her and her Catholic, former brother-in-law, Phillip II of Spain escalated until 1588 when he sent an Armada to invade England. The English defeat of that maritime attack was led by the nephew of Sir John Hawkins, Sir Francis Drake. The Armada was the final push by Philip II of Spain, to bring England back into the Catholic fold and secure her for himself. He had tried through marriage to Mary I and then, through what he had hoped to be marriage, to Elizabeth I. However, it was also an act of revenge against the privateering of the English whose attacks on the galleons of Spain which were transporting gold from the New World helped them to amass huge fortunes, whilst also putting money into the English royal coffers. The Catholic countries of Spain and Portugal held the central and South American colonies and Elizabeth I wanted the gold being brought out of those colonies. She commissioned 'privateers' to whose piratical exploits she turned a blind eye. Sir Francis Drake was one of the most successful and became the wealthiest man in England.

But, before the Amada of 1588, his uncle, Sir John Hawkins, enjoyed a working relationship with the Spanish and it was he who was the first Englishman to transport slaves from Africa to the New World so claiming the dubious fame of starting the English slave trade. Indeed his coat of arms features an enslaved African girl in chains. Hawkins came from a nautical family and his father, William, sailing a ship called the "Pole" had seen slaves being taken from Guinea as part of the Portuguese slave trade.[175] His trading journeys (not in slaves) to the New World made him wealthy and in 1562 his son followed in his footsteps. The backers for his first of three slave trading voyages were interesting bed-fellows. Investors in London included Benjamin Gonson, the treasurer of the Royal Navy, together with wealthy influential Spaniards from the Ponce family of the Canary Islands who provided a Spanish pilot and intelligence.[176]

The ships of this flotilla were, Hawkins ship the Solomon, the Jonas and the Swallow. They travelled to Africa and then bought or kidnapped slaves before taking them to the Caribbean and selling them to Spanish colonists. Needless to say the Spanish King was not pleased and for his next two journeys Hawkins knew that if he was caught he would be hanged. Further, more elaborate plotting with his Spanish partners had to be undertaken to ensure that no harm, only the riches of a slave trader, came to them. To this end Hawkins put on a public show of force so that colonists could claim that they were not willing to trade with him but had been forced to do so.

---

[174] Casas, *History of the Indies*.
[175] Todd Gray, *Devon and the Slave Trade: Documents on African Enslavement, Abolition and Emancipation from 1562 to 1867* (Exeter: Mint Press, 2007).
[176] Ibid.

On his first voyage he took three hundred (at least) slaves to Hispaniola. Hawkins second voyage took 11months and was fraught with difficulties in capturing slaves, waging war in some parts of Africa to capture the slaves, poor winds, lack of water and difficult selling conditions (some islands in the Caribbean were more diligent in following orders from Spain than others). Nevertheless enough money was made for Hawkins to make a third slave trading trip. This was a long journey too, 1567-68. Hawkins was enormously annoyed by the difficulties he encountered when trying to sell the slaves and felt betrayed by his Spanish 'partners'. Some two hundred slaves of the four to five hundred collected in Africa had to be sold in the dead of night.

The fates of great powers change and by the eighteenth century it was the British who owned much of the West Indies and had one thousand five hundred sugar plantations there. The need for labor in the colonies was enormous. The slave traders brought slaves from West Africa making huge profits on each trip. The average profit per trip was two million U.K. pounds at today's value.[177] This dreadful trade was made worse by the fact that a twenty percent loss of 'cargo' was considered 'acceptable'.

By the 19th century good field-hand slaves were selling in America for the modern day equivalent of four hundred thousand U.S. dollars each.[178] In contrast Nicholas Kristoff paid one hundred and fifty U.S. dollars for a slave in Cambodia in 2009.[179] It could be said that this is not a direct comparison because his slave was a sex worker and they have less value than agricultural workers but, whereas that might be correct in the nineteenth century, today that is not true. What is true is that the capital value of slaves has plummeted; they have become disposable.

Some Early English Case Law

Cartwright 1569 Mr. Cartwright bought a slave in Russia who he brought back to England. He was accused of flogging the slave. It is believed that the Court ruled that the power to punish slaves was limited and that slaves could not be kept in England. The court found that "the air of England was too pure for a slave to breathe".[180]

Chamberlain v Harvey or Chamberlaine v Harvey 1667 1 Ld. Raym. 146., In this case the Lord Keeper, Sir John Somers, held that trespass did not lie for taking a slave.

However, the Navigation Acts 1650-1696 brought a conflict with case and statute law which would only be fully resolved with the abolition of the slave trade in 1807. The Navigation Acts required that all trade between Britain and its colonies should be carried in British ships. In 1677 the Solicitor-General declared 'negroes ought to be esteemed goods and commodities within the Acts of Trade and Navigation'.

---

177 Edwards, *Royal Navy versus the Slave Traders.*

178 Kevin Bales, Zoe Trodd, and Alex Kent Williamson, *Modern Slavery: The Secret World of 27 Million People* (Oxford: Oneworld, 2009).

179 Nicholas D. Kristof and Sheryl Wudunn, *Half the Sky*, 1 edition (Vintage, 2009).

180 Cartwright 1569, Historical Collections J. Rushworth 468 (n.d.).

Butts v. Penny (1677) 2 Lev 201, 3 Keb 785.

In an action brought to recover possession of 100 slaves the court held that slavery was legal in England in relation to infidels. Thus, they were the property of the slave holder. Therefore an action for damages for wrongfully taking a person's property could be pursued.

Two years later the Habeas Corpus Act 1679 gave everyone in England protection against illegal arrest, imprisonment or removal to a foreign country. This included slaves thereby producing the interesting anomaly which allowed slaves in England to be protected by the Habeas Corpus Act 1679 even though the Navigation Acts reduced slaves to mere commodities.

Smith v Gould, 1705 2 Salk. 411 Chief Justice Holt (who was the Chief Justice of the Court of King's Bench) held, in a judgement directly contrary to that of Butts v Penny, that damages could not be claimed for taking slaves. He observed: "By the common law no man can have a property in another" and he added: "there is no such thing as a slave by the law of England".[181]

The tide changed again for slaves in 1729 when both the Attorney General and Solicitor General of England signed the Yorke–Talbot slavery. As representatives of the government their opinion shows the prevailing view in government circles that slavery was lawful in England and her colonies. On the 7 September, 1730, *Boston Gazette* contained the following "advertisement":

> *"In Order to rectify a Mistake, that Slaves become free, by their being in England, or Ireland or being Baptized, it has been thought proper to consult the King's Attorney and Solicitor General in England thereupon, who have given the following Opinion, subscribed with their own Hands.*
>
> *We are of Opinion, that a Slave, by coming from the West-Indies to Great Britain or Ireland, either with or without his Master, doth not become free, and that his Master's Property, or Right in him, is not thereby determined or varied. And that Baptism doth not bestow Freedom on him, nor make any alteration in his temporal Condition in these Kingdoms. We are also of Opinion, that his Master may legally compel him to return again to the Plantations.*
>
> *P. Yorke and C. Talbot. Jan. 14. 1729*[182]

But less than 40 years later Lord Henley LC held in *Shanley v. Harvey* (1763) 2 Eden 126, 127 that

> *"as soon as a man sets foot on English ground he is free."*[183]

[181] Horace Greeley, *a History of the Struggle for Slavery Extension or Restriction in the United States from the Declaration of Independence to the Present Day*, 1856.
[182] Sir John Macdonell and Sir John Edward Power Wallis, *Reports of State Trials: New Series... 1820 to [1858]...* (H.M. Stationery Office, 1889).

> *In 1765 the great British jurist, Blackstone said*
>
> *"I have formerly observed that pure and proper slavery does not, nay cannot, subsist in England; such I mean, whereby an absolute and unlimited power is given to the master over the life and fortune of the slave. And indeed it is repugnant to reason, and the principles of natural law, that such a state should subsist anywhere".*[184]

Thus, a slave is freed by coming to the UK. For this statement of the common law Blackstone relied upon natural law. In natural law theory no person could be enslaved. This meant that people were enslaved only by the laws of nations. He referred back to Cartwright, the Elizabethan case.[185]

In 1771 Lord Mansfield led the Court in a decision in the case of R v Stapylton.[186] This was a criminal case in which Stapylton, the slave owner, attempted to forcibly remove Lewis, the slave, from Britain. The jury found the slave owner guilty and Lord Mansfield allowed the slave to testify on his own account. This is important because it recognized Lewis as having a legal identity as a human being rather than being mere a chattel (which, of course, had no right to speak).

The subject of slavery in England was eventually settled in the case of James Somersett 1772.[187] James Somersett was the slave of Charles Stewart. In 1769 Stewart had brought him to England from the West Indies. After arrival he became ill and was discarded by Stewart but once he was well again Stewart took him back as his slave; other accounts say that Somersett was an escapee. He was to be transported back to Jamaica and was held in irons on the ship "Ann and Mary" which was moored in the River Thames when, at the behest of anti-slave campaigners, the Court intervened.[188] The case was tried by Lord Mansfield and took a very long time, December 1771 to June 1772. He was represented by William "Bull" Davy and Francis Hargrave. It is in his closing statement of this case, on 14th May 1772, that Davy repeats the phrase from Cartwight's case.

> *"However, it has been asserted, and is now repeated by me this air is too pure for a slave to breathe in. I trust I shall not quit this court without certain convictions of the truth of that assertion."*[189]

Earlier, Davy, had put forward his fundamental theory against slavery:

---

[183] H. E. B, *Free England: Or, Old Stories of the English Parliament, by H.E.B.*, 1884.

[184] William Blackstone, *Blackstone's Commentaries on the Laws of England*, accessed October 20, 2013, http://avalon.law.yale.edu/subject_menus/blackstone.asp.

[185] Cartwright 1569, Historical Collections J. Rushworth 468 (n.d.).

[186] R v Stapleton, 8 Cox, C.C. 69 (n.d.).

[187] Francis Hargrave et al., *An Argument in the Case of James Sommersett, a Negro, Lately Determined by the Court of King's Bench: Wherein It Is Attempted to Demonstrate the Present Unlawfulness of Domestic Slavery in England: To Which Is Prefixed a State of the Case* (London: Printed for the author: And sold by W. Otridge ..., 1772), http://archive.org/details/anargumentincas00harggoog.

[188] Granville Sharpe, who was the principle instigator of this case coming before the Court.

[189] Somersett v Sharpe, Lofft 1 (English Court of Appeal 1772).

Slavery as Old as Time

> *"To punish not even a criminal for offences against the laws of another country: to set free a galley-slave; who is a slave by his crime: and make a slave of a Negro, who is one, by his complexion: is a cruel and absurdity that I trust will never take place here: such as if promulgated, would make England a disgrace to all nations on earth: for the reducing of a man, guiltless of any offence against the laws, to the condition of slavery: the worst and most abject state."*[190]

The argument which the defense team for Somersett had crafted was based upon natural law sources.[191] Davy said that it mattered not what the law was in the Thirteen colonies, or in Barbados or in lands "unluckier than England" because if Parliament had not legislated in favor of slavery then whatever the laws in those countries they could have no "more influence, power or authority in this country [England] than the laws of Japan."[192]

Francis Hargrave, argued that slavery exists in so many places and forms that it was difficult to define. He referred to the Justinian code to describe slavery only as a construct of the laws of nations. Thus, it was up to a nation whether or not it chose to have slavery because, in the 'natural law' state no slavery existed. In this period the *Digest of Justinian* was used by most early scholars about the law of nations and it is from this that they obtained their understanding of natural right. The *Digest* described slavery as man-made or a construct of nations rather than nature. Grotius said it is a law which is based on the will of nations which can change and adapt over time however, the law of nations is universal and unchangeable.[193]

James Somersett was released and slavery in England came to an end. This had the instant effect of freeing the approximately fifteen thousand African slaves in the UK who had no way of looking after themselves, many could not find work and, though free, became homeless and hungry. With the backing of the government, Granville Sharpe and some abolitionist friends created the Sierra Leone Plan in 1786which allowed slaves to repatriate to Sierra Leone.[194] Of course, no-one knew where they had actually come from but it was generally felt by the well-meaning people of the abolitionist movement that a return to Africa would be good for the freed slaves. Of course, this showed a huge lack of understanding of African culture but they thought they were helping. Sharpe hired two ships to take slaves who wished to return to Africa. By January 1787, only two hundred and fifty nine ex-slaves had volunteered for repatriation. Setting sail from Gravesend the ships made it as far as Plymouth. There they were joined by three hundred and eighty four more people of whom sixty were prostitutes who were included to clean up the streets of London and provide breeding females for the new colony. It is an interesting vignette about how prostitutes were seen then and the history which lingers in the treatment of sex

---

[190] Gray, *Devon and the Slave Trade*.
[191] Ibid.
[192] Steven Condie, *Simon Schama's Rough Crossings* (BBC Home Entertainment, 2009).
[193] Hugo Grotius and A. C. Campbell, *The Rights of War and Peace* (Evergreen Review, Inc., 2009).
[194] Glanville Sharpe, "The Plan for Sierra Leone 1786," 1786, http://assets.cambridge.org/97805216/62345/excerpt/9780521662345_excerpt.pdf.

slaves nowadays. Effectively, these women were being transported to Africa against their will and with no payment to be forced 'brides' for the freed slaves.

Whilst the position of slaves in Britain had been settled in 1772 their position in the colonies remained as terrible as ever and the trade in slaves continued unabated. In 1783 Lord Mansfield, who retired in 1788, was called upon to provide the leading Judgment in an insurance case about a ship "The Zong". "The Zong" was a slave trading ship. She was owned by two wealthy merchants from Liverpool. Both held high office in that City. They insured their vessel against loss, including loss of cargo, at sea. The Zong set sail from Africa with four hundred and fifty eight slaves. The Zong was caught in the doldrums for six months and then some sixty slaves and seven crew members met their end from tropical diseases incubated in the dreadful holds. On 27th November, the Captain, Luke Collingwood sealed the fate of many by making a simple error. He mistook Jamaica for Hispaniola. Had he gone on to Jamaica he could have landed the slaves safely but instead he 'ran', not only from Hispaniola (as he believed) but also from a budding hurricane. Now Collingwood had another problem; he decided that they would run out of supplies, particularly fresh water, before they reached harbor. This meant that the cargo (the slaves) would be decimated, there were fresh deaths each day, and the sick slaves who did reach land would not fetch as much money as healthy slaves. The Captains of slave ships shared in the profits of voyages with the ship owners. Collingwood could see his profit and that of his employers diminishing. What should he do? He talked to the crew about his idea. English insurance law was settled that if a ship or its crew was at risk then cargo could be jettisoned. The owner of the ship would then be entitled to be reimbursed for the lost cargo by the insurers. What Collingwood proposed was that some of his ship's cargo, African slaves, should be thrown overboard to ensure the safety of the ship. On 29th November, he and the crew threw fifty-two slaves overboard and the following day a further forty-two. It then rained and so the shortage of clean drinking water was ameliorated, nevertheless, on 1st December they discarded twenty-six more slaves and ten jumped overboard in order, they thought, to save themselves.

One might expect that Collingwood and his crew would have been hanged for mass murder but such was the sentiment towards slaves at the time that when the ship owners learned of their lost 'cargo' they claimed against the insurers. Eventually the case was heard with Lord Mansfield as the senior Judge.[195] Given that he was the leading Judge in the Somersett case, it could have been expected that he would have been sympathetic to the murdered slaves and would seek to stop future occurrences of such crimes. In fact, the Court decided that the slaves had been rightly classified as cargo and ordered the insurers to compensate the ship owners for the jettisoned "cargo".[196] Lord Mansfield held that there was "no doubt, though it shocks one very much, that the case of the slaves was the same as if horses had been thrown overboard."[197] Apparently, a difference was perceived between the slave on English soil and the slave who would be used as labor in the colonies. The ship-owners received thirty G.B. pounds each for the slaves thrown overboard. By way of

[195] Gregson v. Gilbert, 3 Doug 232 (Court of Appeal, England and Wales 1783).
[196] Edwards, *Royal Navy versus the Slave Traders*.
[197] Gregson v. Gilbert, 3 Doug 232 (Court of Appeal, Engand and Wales 1783).

post-script, after the case it came to light that in fact there had been enough water for the slaves throughout, Collingwood was actually throwing slaves overboard who, being sickly, would not have commanded a good enough profit at sale.

Granville Sharpe led a group of horrified abolitionists and, in July 1783, he wrote a lengthy letter to the Prime Minister and Lords of the Admiralty as part of the campaign against slavery which was given the impetus of public opinion against the case. Arguably, in 1787, the first human rights organization, Committee for the Abolition of the Slave Trade was formed by Thomas Clarkson, Josiah Wedgewood, and Granville Sharpe and others, and shortly thereafter, joined by William Wilberforce.[198]

By 1788 the Abolitionist movement was gaining steam amongst public and media but in Parliament it was known that there was too much money at stake! The Times newspaper declared – "For Englishmen to chain their innocent fellow-creatures together, and keep them in bondage for life, is much more repugnant to Christianity, than cutting off the ears of the enemy in barbarity, in the followers of Mahomet".[199] The abolitionists used a number of marketing 'firsts' to get their message across. They wanted the complete emancipation of slaves throughout the empire and they organized grass-root support to spread the message. By 1791, the organization had 1300 branches throughout Britain working to raise awareness of the trade and to arrange a boycott of goods coming to Britain from colonies which used slave labor. They used Petitions, pamphlets and speeches to raise awareness and persuade the government to change the law.[200]

In May 1788, William Dolben asked the House to consider measures to reduce the overloading of slave ships. As a result the Slave Trade Regulation Act was passed limiting ships to no more than two fifths children and one point six seven men per ton up to two hundred and seven tons and thereafter one man per ton.[201] It is worth noting that the stowage pictures of the Brookes post date this attempt to help the slaves but her 1782 voyage had been undertaken with six hundred and nine slaves (three hundred and fifty one men, one hundred and twenty seven women, ninety boys, and forty one girls).[202] Following the Slave Trade Regulation Act her cargo dropped to four hundred and fifty four slaves. The Act required yearly renewals until the Slave Trade Act 1799 was passed. This permanent law was eventually subsumed in the Act for the Abolition of the Slave Trade

---

198 "Minutes of the First Meeting of the Committee for the Abolition of the Slave Trade," accessed October 20, 2013, http://www.bl.uk/onlinegallery/takingliberties/staritems/66minutesofcommitteeabolition.html.

199 Anthony Sattin, *The Gates of Africa: Death, Discovery and the Search for Timbuktu* (London: Harper Perennial, 2004).

200 David Brion Davis, *DAVIS PROB SLAVERY REV 1770-1823 C* (Oxford University Press, 1999).

201 James W. LoGerfo, "Sir William Dolben and 'The Cause of Humanity': The Passage of the Slave Trade Regulations Act of 1788," *Eighteenth-Century Studies* 6, no. 4 (Summer 1973): 431–451.

202 Society for Effecting the Abolition of the Slave Trade, *Stowage of the British Slave Ship "Brookes" Under the Regulated Slave Trade of 1788*, 1788, Library of Congress, http://www.loc.gov/rr/rarebook/guide/ra023002.html.

1807.[203] It is a good lesson for modern abolitionists. For example, as part of the "African well fund" George Clooney paid for the digging of a well in Africa after a visit there. Unfortunately, the neighboring village was envious of the well and sought to take the water by force. Clooney's kind deed had very unintended consequences.[204]

The abolitionists worked to recruit the most influential and wealthy members of the small but powerful London community. Members of the Anti-Slavery Society could be found in Gentlemen's Clubs and Associations and Parliament. A good example of this interconnectedness which ultimately helped to secure the abolition of slavery can be found in the person of Henry Beaufoy who spoke in the debate about the Slave Trade Regulation Act 1788. Henry Beaufoy was a founder and secretary of the African Association, a Quaker and a member of Parliament. He was the author of "The Effects of Civilization on the Real Improvement and Happiness of Mankind" and delivered thunderous speeches against slavery "the stigma of everlasting dishonor" and against the captains of the slave ships. Also wealthy, he had owned a first folio edition of Shakespeare and Draft C of the "*Essay concerning human understanding*" (1685) by John Locke.

The African Association was created in 1788 by a group of friends, all of whom were prominent members of London society to map the interior of Africa.[205] Why – because it needed mapping!

> *'That as no species of information is more ardently desired, or more generally useful, than that which improves the science of Geography; and as the vast continent of Africa, notwithstanding the effects of the ancients, and the wishes of the moderns, is still in great measure unexplored, the members of this Club do form themselves into an Association for promoting the discovery of the inland parts of that quarter of the world.'*[206]

But the rich, influential and powerful members of the Association, almost to a man, supported the abolition of slavery. Both Conway and Rawdon backed the printing of the

---

203 "An Act for the Abolition of the Slave Trade 1807" (London, U.K., March 25, 1807), http://www.pdavis.nl/Legis_06.htm.

204 Nicholas D. Kristof, "'Stories of Survival and Courage from the Fight to End Human Trafficking'," Speech (Austin, Texas, February 13, 2012), http://ddce.utexas.edu/news/2012/02/09/feb-13-pulitzer-prize-winning-columnist-to-speak-about-human-trafficking/.

205 Lord Francis Rawdon, later to be Gov Gen of India, but recently acquitted himself well in the Am War of Independence; General Conway – former Secretary of State; William Pulteney – one of the richest men in the country – wanted to better the condition of slaves but spoke against the abolition of slavery because of the ruin, as he saw it, which would come to the West Indies; Sir William Fordyce – doctor – works from venereal disease to medical properties of rhubarb; The Earl of Galloway – twin passions – agriculture and the abolition of slavery; Sir Adam Ferguson – Commissioner for Trade and Plantations; Andrew Stuart – lawyer and MP; Sir John Sinclair – to become a Privy Councilor; Earl of Craysfort – scholarly evangelist; Richard Watson, Bishop of Llandaf and Chair of Divinity and Chemistry at Cambridge. Seven of them are members of the Royal Society and 8 are MPs. Most own substantial estates. From - Anthony Sattin. *"The Gates of Africa"*

206 Robin {Ed } Hallett, *Records of the African Association 1788-1831*, 1St Edition edition (Thomas Nelson & Sons,Ltd., n.d.).

book by Olaudeh Equiano.[207] Up until this point exploration had been the domain of rulers and the very wealthy now a group of friends with ideals gathered together without political or economic purpose – they just want to explore. Sir John Sinclair's son wrote that

'Hitherto Europeans had visited Africa to plunder, to oppress and to enslave;- the object of this society was to promote the cause of science and humanity; to explore the mysterious geography, to ascertain the resources, and to improve the condition of that ill-fated continent.'[208]

An underlying concern of these gentlemen was the slave trade. Between 1720 and 1772 the trade between Britain and W Africa grew from sixty five ships (trade valued at one hundred and thirty G.B. pounds - now six and a half million G.B. pounds) to one hundred and seventy five ships (valued at eight hundred and sixty six thousand G.B. pounds - now forty three million three hundred thousand G.B. pounds. However, the trade was limited by what the Africans could pay for the imports from Britain. Europeans wanted gold dust, ivory, animal skins and senna but, of course, the vast bulk of payment was in slaves. Whether it was Banks, who objected to the trade for economic reasons, or Beaufoy, who objected on moral grounds, these men saw exploration as a way of helping to stop the trade.[209]

As scholars of their time, they knew the stories of the 1324 pilgrimage of Mansa Kankan Musa, the idea of West Africa and Mali being another El Dorado, the tales of Al-Idrissi, twelfth century cartographer, of the riches of Kaugha, Kuku and Ghana (the King was reported as wearing a thirty pound lump of gold) and the accounts of Leo Africanus, in the sixteenth century, which spoke of the wealth of Tibuktu.[210]

This led Beaufoy to predict

> *"Their mines of gold (the improvable provision of many of the island states) will furnish, to an unknown, and probably boundless extent, an article that commands, in all the markets of the civilized, world a constant and unlimited scale".*[211]

Of course they were not to know that the Arab march across Northern Africa had left these riches and trades a thing of the past. The Association decided to send two expeditions in the hope of these mapping the interior and finding legendary places, including the goldfields. Therefore, although John Ledyard crossed the Sahara from Cairo to the west and Simon Lucas went south from Tripoli, no trace of the gold was heard of or found. They did, however, map the interior of Africa and the Association went on to be

---

[207] Olaudah Equiano, *The Life of Olaudah Equiano*, Dover Thrift Editions (Dover Publications, 2012).

[208] Robin Hallett, *The Penetration of Africa: European Enterprise and Exploration Principally in Northern and Western Africa Up to 1830* (Routledge & Kegan Paul, 1965).

[209] Sattin, *The Gates of Africa*.

[210] Leo Africanus, *The History and Description of Africa: And of the Notable Things Therein Contained*, ed. Robert Brown, trans. John Pory, Cambridge Library Collection Hakluyt First Series (Cambridge University Press, 2010).

[211] Sattin, *The Gates of Africa*.

re-named, the Royal Geographical Society, sending explorers around the world, particularly throughout Africa.

It is surprising that the Anti-Slavery Society made as much headway as it did. Many in the United Kingdom had other things on their mind, not least the effect on commerce of the abolition of slavery, the French Revolution, which many feared might cross the Channel and, later, the rise of Napoleon and the pan-European war he created. The success of the movement lay in clever, tenacious politicians – notably Clarkson, William Pitt the Younger (Prime Minister in 1801 and from 1804-06) and William Wilberforce together with the mobilization of public sentiment. Credit for ensuring the passage of the two Acts of Parliament required to abolish slavery and the slave trade is generally given to Wilberforce who had been inspired not just by his fellow MPs and public sentiment but also the 'poacher turned gamekeeper', John Newton.[212] John Newton had been a slave trader. Indeed he wrote his famous hymn 'Amazing Grace' when in fear of shipwreck. However, after his return to Britain he became a Minister of Religion and it was he who preached the anti-slavery message to Wilberforce, who was one of his parishioners, and who became leader of the Parliamentary abolition movement in 1787.

During 1787-88 Wilberforce and Clarkson worked together to gather evidence which they placed before the Committee of the Privy Council. On May 12, 1789 Wilberforce introduced his Anti-slavery Bill, giving his first anti-slavery speech in the House of Commons. The scene was reported in the newspaper "The Star"

> *"ᵃthe gallery of the House of Commons on Tuesday was crowded with Liverpool Merchants; who hung their heads in sorrow - for the African occupation of bolts and chains is no more'".*[213]
>
> *But those Liverpool Merchants had powerful friends in the House of Commons and they filibustered and maneuvered until on June 23, 1789 the further hearing of the Bill was adjourned until after the summer recess. Further delays hit the Bill in fall of 1789 and in January 1790 it was sent to a Select Committee. Evidence in favor of abolition was given until April and evidence against the Bill followed until the Parliamentary session was abruptly ended by a General Election in June and July 1790. As so often happens in the history of human rights campaign an event occurred to set back the efforts of the abolitionists – the Haitian slave rebellion in 1791. This gave the politicians pause and the despite Wilberforce's speech in the debate on the floor of the House on April 18, 1791 the vote on the following evening was won by those who stood against abolition with a majority of seventy five votes. In the context of ships, the old quote 'rats leaving a sinking ship' comes to mind. By the time of the vote, more than*

---

212 Michael Apted, *Amazing Grace* (20th Century Fox, 2007); William Hague, *William Wilberforce: The Life of the Great Anti-Slave Trade Campaigner* (Orlando: Harcourt, 2007).

213 Stephen Tomkins, *William Wilberforce: A Biography* (Michigan: William B. Eerdmans Publishing Company, 2007).

> *half of the MPs had already left and didn't take part in that important vote.*

Nevertheless, the abolitionist movement had strong popular support and went back to basics with more petitions, meetings, pamphlets and the boycott of sugar. Again they were hindered in their campaigns by the successful slave revolt in Haiti and the all-encompassing revolution in France.

On April 22, 1792 Wilberforce spoke in support of the abolition of the slave trade. By now he had considerable popular support for the campaign and seemed to have won over many of his fellow MPs. There was one vocal opponent, however, Henry Dundas. His amendment provided for the 'gradual' abolition of the slave trade, simply by adding the word 'gradual' to the text of the Bill.[214] Thus, the amended Bill was passed (two hundred and thiry votes to eighty five) but the date for the abolition of the slave trade was to be 1796. In fact, Henry Dundas had scored a victory for the West India Interest (slave traders and holders). Every possible delaying tactic was used and abused and although Wilberforce introduced a Bill for abolition of the slave trade every year during the 1790s, none was passed and the abolition, promised for 1796, never occurred.

By 1804 the situation had improved. Napoleon was known to be against abolition and this seemed to help the British to support it. MPs of both parties moved towards support of the abolition of the slave trade and their ranks were swelled by many of the new Irish MPs. Coincidentally, Thorpe CJ who later dispensed justice to slave traders in Sierra Leone was born and brought up in a liberal Irish home.[215] In both 1804 and 1805 Wilberforce introduced bills to abolish the slave trade. In 1806, he wrote an influential public piece in support of abolition which was followed, in June, by resolutions in parliament which supported the ban on slave trading.[216] As the new year approached, the auguries came into alignment with a powerful public campaign and a supportive Whig (liberal) government.

At last, Wilberforce introduced an Abolition Bill (January 1807) which would be passed without amendment. On January 23, 1807 his fellow MPs voted overwhelmingly to end the slave trade. The many good speeches included tributes to Wilberforce but none more so than that of the Solicitor General Sir Samuel Romilly who used the opportunity to happily contrast the nobility of mind and cause of Wilberforce with the failures of Napoleon, Britain's enemy. The Morning Chronicle reported that Wilberforce, who wept for part of the proceedings was given 'three distinct and universal cheers'.[217] In a letter to his old friend, William Hey, the Yorkshire surgeon, evangelist, and former Mayor of Leeds, Wilberforce said that

---

[214] Judith Jennings, *The Business of Abolishing the British Slave Trade: 1783 - 1807* (London [u.a.: Cass, 1997).

[215] "Biography – THORPE, ROBERT – Volume VII (1836-1850) – Dictionary of Canadian Biography," accessed October 27, 2013, http://www.biographi.ca/en/bio.php?id_nbr=3696.

[216] Robert Isaac Wilberforce and Samuel Wilberforce, *The Life of William Wilberforce* (John Murray, 1838).

[217] "Abolition of Slavery," *Morning Chronicle*, January 24, 2013.

'I was myself so completely overpowered by my feelings [...] that I was insensible to all that was passing around me'.[218]

The Royal Assent, needed to make the Bill a lawful Act, was given on March 25, 1807. It would take another twenty six years of hard fighting for slaves to be emancipated in the British colonies because, unfortunately, this did not abolish slavery in the British Empire (at that time comprising a large section of the known world) nor did it affect the trade of other slave trading nations. However, the British wanted the slave trade to stop and were prepared to put money and resources into preventing it. Enter the Royal Navy's African Squadron.[219] *In 1807 the British Navy had seven hundred and ninety five ships in commission but they were spread across the globe and particularly focused on France. The Act of Abolition of the Slave Trade 1807 came into force in January 1808 but it was not until later in the spring of 1808 when the Royal Navy sent two ships – The Solebay (twenty three years old) a frigate with thirty two guns, two hundred and fifty crew and the Derwent (a new sloop) with only eighteen guns and one hundred and ninety five crew to look for slave ships breaking the Act. The admiralty felt this was all they could spare and this sparked a long-running dispute between the politicians and the Admiralty about the extent of the task and the number of ships required to achieve it.*[220] *Eventually, political will overcame and the patrols of the Royal Navy in West and East Africa were important instruments in breaking the slave trade. At this juncture, though, the two ships had to patrol three thousand miles of West African coastline. This was made an even more gargantuan effort by two factors:*

a. The West African coastline is notorious for its small creeks, bays and estuaries which were perfect hiding places for slavers.
b. The West coast of Africa is rightly known as 'the white man's grave'. The men of the Royal Navy died of tropical disease in great numbers, especially due to Malaria.

Add to this the fact that the Solebay and Derwent were slow whilst the slave ships were the fastest of ocean going vessels and it is surprising that any ships were arrested and any slaves freed.

The British Government was prepared to put money into the abolition of the trade and, later slavery. Indeed, the cost to the Treasury of stopping the trade and slavery in its colonies and in Europe and elsewhere was enormous. Not just in funding the war against slaver traders (estimated at two billion G.B. pounds in today's money) but also in lost revenue from the slave trade itself which had brought considerable wealth to Britain. Royal Navy crews were given sizable incentives – sixty G.B. pounds for every male slave freed, thirty G.B. pounds for every women and ten G.B. pounds for every child. By Prize

[218] John Stoughton, *William Wilberforce* (London : Hodder and Stoughton, 1880), http://archive.org/details/williamwilberfor00stou.
[219] Edwards, *Royal Navy versus the Slave Traders.*
[220] Ibid.

regulations these sums were distributed between the officers and crew.[221] They were authorized to seize any pirate vessel or any ships with false or suspected false papers. This was a clear breach of international law because the British had territorial waters only off Sierra Leone, which became a British colony in 1808, but elsewhere either the land was owned by African tribes or other European powers. Add to this the fact that the British had no right to stop ships of different nations in international waters and the stage is set for much diplomatic bickering (and a war with the United States of America).[222] It is a measure of the determination of Parliament, pushed on by the public, that the Navy continued on post in West Africa until the 1860s and in East Africa until the late 1890s to counter the slave trade. The development of Sierra Leone as a colony provided secure anchorage for the Royal Navy and enabled it to take captured slavers, ships and slaves to Freetown.

By June 15,1809 the Derwent and Solebay had not caught any slave ships. They were travelling back to Britain and had been joined for the homeward journey by three other ships. Tigress, Agincourt and George when, to the excitement of Major Maxwell, the garrison commander, all put into Goree Island which had been suffering from the actions of French privateers. He was able to persuade the Navy to help him attack the bases of those privateers and so, on July 13, the French surrendered, allowing the Commodore of the Solebay to take possession of St Louis and its dependencies for the British Crown. Unfortunately the Solebay was lost and no slaves had been rescued at all during this first assignment. However, the prize of St Louis and dependencies would have an effect upon the abolition through Thorpe C.J. in Sierra Leone and the provision of more territorial waters.[223]

By 1809, reports of more Spanish slave traders were received in London. Also, it was reported that the Americans were re-flagging their slave traders under Spanish flag. The British government and people were increasingly annoyed. To the credit of the governments, in 1810, the British and Portuguese signed a treaty allowing the British Navy to stop Portuguese ships in their territories waters. On 18 July 1811 Wilberforce wrote to Charles Yorke, First Lord of the Admiralty. He requested that a ship be sent to catch Portuguese slave ships in the Calabar River, where under Treaty they had no right to be trading. As a result, despite the fighting in Europe and the mounting threat of war with the USA, the admiralty sent another force, the ships Amelia, Ganymede, Trinculo and Kangaroo to police two thousand six hundred miles of the West African coastline. They found British ships flying false flags and, in contravention of any understanding of international law, the squadron was specifically told to stop Spanish, American and Portuguese ships. Within weeks the squadron was arresting and freeing slaves.[224]

---

[221] "An Act for the Abolition of the Slave Trade 1807."
[222] Matthew Mason, "Keeping Up Appearances: The International Politics of Slave Trade Abolition in the Nineteenth-Century Atlantic World," *William & Mary Quarterly* 66, no. 4 (October 2009): 809–832.
[223] Edwards, *Royal Navy versus the Slave Traders.*
[224] Ibid.

In 1814 the British Government persuaded the Dutch to enter into a treaty which banned the slave trade using Dutch ships.[225] The British then moved on to conclude the Anglo-Portuguese Treaty 1815.[226] This gave the Portuguese a compensation package in the amount of three hundred thousand G.B. pounds. In return, the Portuguese agreed not to engage in the African slave trade north of the Equator. In 1818, Spain and the United Kingdom concluded a treaty under which Spain agreed that the Spanish slave trade would be illegal as of May 30, 1820. In return for this concession, the British Treasury paid four hundred thousand G.B. pounds to the Spanish government as compensation for injuries committed against her nationals by the West Africa Squadron of the Royal Navy and British privateers.[227]

The Court of Vice Admiralty existed in Freetown, Sierra Leone from 1807 to 1817 and, in the main, was presided over by Thorpe C.J.. The Navy would bring the captured ships into Freetown. The slaves would be freed and the ships auctioned off. The slave traders were tried. One such trader was Samuel Samo. Samo was a wealthy slave trader with good connections to local African chiefs. It should be remembered that the trade largely depended on the ability of West African Chiefs to deliver slaves to the traders. The slaves who were sold to the slave traders were usually

a. prisoners of war
b. criminals from the Chief's tribes
c. if no one else could be found, unfortunates chosen by the Chief from his tribe

In this case Thorpe C.J. feared that the trial would be a breach of international law because although Samo was British the raid to capture him had been into sovereign African territory. Therefore, once Samo had been convicted Thorpe gave him time to collect references from the local chiefs and others so that his sentence could be commuted, thus lessening the impact on the growing unrest amongst African chiefs about their loss of trade. Also, he had to agree to help the authorities in eliminating the slave trade in the area where he lived. Two other slave traders, William Tufft and Joseph Peters, were tried at the same time. They were convicted and transported to Botany Bay in Australia.[228]

On 18 May 1811, a British slave trader, in the British Virgin Islands, called Arthur William Hodge was tried for the murder of one of his slaves.[229] He was known to be

---

[225] Edward Keene, "A Case Study of the Construction of International Hierarchy: British Treaty-Making Against the Slave Trade in the Early Nineteenth Century," *International Organization* 61, no. 2 (Spring 2007): 311–339.

[226] Keith Hamilton and Patrick Salmon, *Slavery, Diplomacy and Empire: Britain and the Suppression of the Slave Trade, 1807-1975* (Sussex Academic Press, 2009).

[227] Edwards, *Royal Navy versus the Slave Traders*.

[228] "R v Samo and Others, Two Letters of the Slave Trade" (Sierra Leone, 1812), http://www.recoveredhistories.org/pamphlet1.php?page=1&orderby=MaxID&catid=50.

[229] House of Commons, "Papers Relating to the West Indies, Viz. Correspondence Between the Earl of Liverpool and Governor Elliot: In Reference to the Trial and Execution of Arthur Hodge, for the Murder of A Negro Slave, Ordered to Be Printed. No. 254" (London, U.K., June 26, 1811).

particularly cruel in the treatment of his slaves. For example, he would hold the heads of children, he had fathered with his female slaves, underwater until they passed out. In 1804, Hodge had killed his slave, the unfortunately named Prosper. Prosper was supposed to stop mangos from falling and was fined six shillings by his master when he missed one. Able to borrow only three shillings Prosper received a hundred lashes. The next day he received one hundred more lashes, having been unable to find the extra money. Prosper was then tied to two other slaves for five days at the end of which he went home and was subsequently found dead. The post-mortem examination found that he had little skin on his back and had been eaten by maggots from inside.

In 1809 Hugh Elliot became Governor of the Leeward Islands which include the British Virgin Islands. He was the Brother-in-Law of Lord Auckland a famous anti-slavery campaigner who presented the Abolition of the Slave Trade Bill to Parliament. Elliot oversaw the prosecution of Hodge. Hodge used the defense that

> *'A Negro being property, it was no greater offense (sic) for his master to kill him than it would be to kill his dog.'*

But he did not persuade the jury which convicted him and he was hanged for the murder of Prosper. In doing so he became the first slave owner to be so punished. The news of this case gave added impetus to the anti-slavery campaign when it reached England. Wilberforce and the anti-slavery campaigners had remained hard at work throughout this period. He knew that there was little political support for outright emancipation and that the West Indies Interest (the name given to supporters of the continuation of slavery for the benefit of the West Indies) would fight hard to protect what they saw as their slaves and the fortunes made off the backs of these unfortunates. Although he was unwell, he started to work on the Slave Registration Bill in 1812. He felt that without the registration it would be easy for slave traders to circumvent the Abolition of the Slave Trade Act. He reasoned that if slaves were registered it could be proved when they had come from Africa and thus illegal imports of slaves could be stopped. Although he had some governmental support that waned and by 1815 Wilberforce was so disillusioned that he refused to accept the Whip on matters concerning the emancipation of slaves.[230]

However, by 1815, Major Maxwell, the Royal Navy and Thorpe C.J. were wreaking havoc with the slave trade off the coast of West Africa. Perhaps not because of the number of slavers caught but by the latitude taken with the law. In that year their activities came to wider notice, appalled by the loss of their ship and others the Spanish merchants in Havana paid a gentleman called Page to present a memorial on their behalf in Britain.[231] The government and judiciary in Britain could no longer ignore what was happening in Sierra Leone. It acted to agree Treaties with Spain, Portugal and the Netherlands set out above. As has been seen earlier, the British government supported the abolition of the

---

[230] A MP who belongs to a political party must vote as required by the Party "Whip" unless a 'free vote' is allowed. To refuse the "whip" can be grounds for expulsion from the Party.

[231] Tara Helfman, "Court of Vice Admiralty at Sierra Leone and the Abolition of the West African Slave Trade, The," *Yale LJ* 115 (2005): 1122.

slave trade, just not the emancipation of slaves. Thus, Thorpe's judicial experiment at Freetown helped to bring the slave-trading powers of Europe to the negotiating table with Britain. Following the Congress of Vienna1815, which ended the Napoleonic Wars, the Vice Admiralty Court at Sierra Leone was abolished and the Mixed Prize Commissions set up.[232]

> *"These were international tribunals constituted by treaty for the adjudication and condemnation of ships involved in the slave trade. They provided a foretaste of other international committees to come."*[233]

In the, proposed, Treaty of Ghent 1824 the United States of America and Britain agreed to co-operate in the abolition of the slave trade but this treaty was never signed because, the British said, amendments in Congress radically changed the effect of the treaty. Wilberforce continued his campaign for the emancipation of slaves both in Parliament and by garnering the support of the public. In 1823, he published another anti-slavery tract but, in failing health, he handed the leadership of the Parliamentary anti-slavery MPs to Thomas Fowell Buxton. Two years later, in 1825, Wilberforce resigned from Parliament but continued to participate in the Anti-Slavery Society when he could. It was fitting that his last public appearance, in 1830, was to chair a meeting of that Society. Finally, in 1833, the Emancipation Bill received Royal Assent to become The Abolition of Slavery Act 1833. Parliament agreed to abolish slavery throughout the British Empire.[234] Wilberforce died 3 days later, on 29 July 1833, having seen his labors succeed. He is buried, alongside other British heroes, in Westminster Abbey, London.

The Act compensated the slave-holders who had to free their slaves but not, of course, the slaves themselves for having been uprooted, transported and enslaved. Even today there is little or no government provision for rescued slaves in most of the world. Some countries do better than others. For example: the T-Visa. Sadly, for many victims the effects of being a trafficked victim and practical problems such as learning to speak English leave them extremely vulnerable for years after the resources from the government have ceased. Of course, American born victims do not get even this much help.[235] The United Kingdom seems to have left behind its previous good work in abolition and there victims are only allowed resources for forty five days. In extremely enlightened legislation the government of the United Arab Emirates agreed to compensate children who had been

---

[232] Eugene Kontorovich, "THE CONSTITUTIONALITY OF INTERNATIONAL COURTS: THE FORGOTTEN PRECEDENT OF SLAVE-TRADE TRIBUNALS.," *University of Pennsylvania Law Review* 158, no. 1 (December 2009): 39–115.

[233] Edwards, *Royal Navy versus the Slave Traders.*

[234] United Kingdom, "An Act for the Abolition of Slavery throughout the British Colonies; for Promoting the Industry of the Manumitted Slaves; and for Compensating the Persons Hitherto Entitled to the Services of Such Slaves. 1833," Act of Parliament (London, U.K., 1833), http://www.pdavis.nl/Legis_07.htm.

[235] *Victims of Trafficking and Violence Protection Act of 2000.*

working in the camel racing business for their labor and injuries when it outlawed the use of children in that sport in 2005.[236]

As has been seen many historians have commented that, because other nations were still trading and holding slaves, the costs to the British economy and the money paid out to former slave owners under the Act dealt a death blow to British economy. At a time when the wealth of America was growing hugely through the use of slave labor, the British had 'shot themselves in the foot'. However, economies are never made up of one action and Britain was certainly leading the way in the agrarian and industrial revolutions and held on to its Empire until after World War II. Whatever the correct interpretation, for scholars of the way to abolish modern slavery, it is useful to look at the possible consequences for the developing economies of those nations where slavery is still used (notably China and India).

The United States and the Alien Tort Claims Act 1789

In an action utterly unrelated to slavery, in 1789, Congress passed the Alien's Action for tort.[237] This Act proved valuable to slaves and oppressed people around the world and, until 2013 when the US Supreme Court decided that the Act did not aply outside the United States, was one of the few ways in which a few people could take on the might of a multi-national company.[238] In 2005, the International Labor Rights Fund filed a claim under the Alien's Action for tort 1789 in the US District Court in California against Bridgestone, alleging "forced labor, the modern equivalent of slavery" on a Firestone Plantation in Harbel, Liberia.[239] The lawsuit states:

> *"The Plantation workers allege, among other things, that they remain trapped by poverty and coercion on a frozen-in-time Plantation operated by Firestone in a manner identical to how the Plantation was operated when it was first opened by Firestone in 1926."* [240]

The Firestone plantations started to attract notice early on. In 1930 the Christy report, named after the Committee's chairman, was published.[241] The Committee concluded that:

---

[236] See child slavery below

[237] *Alien's Action For Tort, 28 USC 1350,* accessed October 20, 2013, http://www.law.cornell.edu/uscode/text/28/1350.

[238] "Kiobel v Royal Dutch Petroleum," *SCOTUSblog*, accessed October 20, 2013, http://www.scotusblog.com/case-files/cases/kiobel-v-royal-dutch-petroleum/?wpmp_switcher=desktop.

[239] *Alien's Action For Tort.*

[240] Flomo v. Firestone Natural Rubber Co LLC, Boimah FLOMO, et al., Plaintiffs–Appellants, v. Firestone Natural Rubber Co., LLC (United States Court of Appeals, Seventh Circuit 2011).

[241] International Commission of Inquiry into the Existence of Slavery and Forced Labor in the Republic of Liberia and Cuthbert Christy, *Report of the International Commission of Inquiry into the Existence of*

- Slavery as defined by the Anti-Slavery Convention, in fact, does not exist in Liberia.
- Shipment to Fernando Po and Gabon is associated with slavery because the method of recruiting carries compulsion with it.
- Persons holding official positions have illegally misused their office in recruiting with the aid of the Liberian Frontier Force.
- Labor for private purposes is forcibly impressed by the Government, and used in the Firestone Plantations.

This company employed more than ten thousand laborers on its plantations in 1930. However, according to official government sources more than eight and a half thousand had not come to work for Firestone voluntarily.

In August 1961, the Government of Portugal – in retaliation to Liberia's staunch anti-colonial position – filed a complaint with the International Labour Organisation (ILO) concerning the observance of the Liberian Government of the Forced Labour Convention 1950.[242] Before the Commission, which had been appointed by the ILO to investigate the complaint, published its findings in 1963, the Liberian Legislature hastily enacted a law regulating the recruitment of labor in Liberia (1962).[243] This ended a system of recruitment of laborers for the Firestone plantation which had been in place since 1926 and made that system unlawful. Bridgestone is a Japanese company but it's subsidiary, Firestone, has headquarters in Indianapolis which allowed the case to be brought against Bridgestone under the Alien Tort Claims Act 1789.

In the 1990s the multi-national oil company Royal Dutch Shell discovered oil on the land of the indigenous Oguni People in Nigeria. The military government which was running Nigeria at the time supported the exploitation of those oil reserves by Shell. The individuals in government profited tidily from the deal. However, the Oguni people did not consent to this exploitation of their homeland and the activist Ken Saro Wiwa brought the troubles of his people to the attention of the world's press.[244] He alleged that Shell had conspired with the Nigerian government to send government troops to clear the historic homelands of his people of the people themselves, their homes and, in the event of trouble, to terrorize, maim and kill them. Certainly the Oguni give evidence of the violence Nigerian government troops metered out to them, they say, to protect the oilfields run by

---

Slavery and Forced Labor in the Republic of Liberia. Monrovia, Liberia, September 8, 1930 (U.S. Govt. print. off., 1931).

[242] International Labour Organization, *Report of the Commission Appointed under Article 26 of the Constitution of the International Labour Organisation to Examme the Complaint Filed by the Government of Portugal Concerning the Observance by the Government of Liberia of the Forced Labour Convention, 1930* (International Labour Organisation, April 1963), https://www.ilo.org/dyn/normlex/en/f?p=1000:50012:0::NO:50012:P50012_COMPLAINT_PROCEDURE_ID,P50012_LANG_CODE:2508364,en:NO.

[243] Liberia, *An Act to Amend the Labor Practices Law in Relation to the Rights and Duties of Labor Organizations and the Members There Of.*, 1962, http://dlxs.library.cornell.edu/l/liberian/.

[244] *In Rememberance - Ken Saro-Wiwa, Part I*, 2009, http://www.youtube.com/watch?v=qkFEhnnwfWI&feature=youtube_gdata_player.

Shell. Stories of people losing their limbs, homes and having loved ones killed by the government troops abound. However, if there is a link to Shell that still needs to be proved. In 1995, it is alleged that Shell conspired with the government to get take Ken off the scene. Whether linked or not, Government troops came onto the Oguni lands and rounded up a number of the people, Ken Saro Wiwa included. They accused Wiwa and some of his activist colleagues of killing another activist. After a military trial, Wiwa was convicted of the charge and hanged on October 10, 1995.[245] The Oguni continued their struggle against Shell and sought redress against Shell in America using the Alien's action for Tort Act of 1789. It fell in the judgment of Kiobel.[246]

Essay: Compare and contrast the success of the special interest lobbyists and the fear of foreigners (the war with France had started) in Britain in the 1790s to 1830s with the obstacles encountered in 2012 in the re-authorisation, in the USA, of the Violence Against Women Act and the TVPA[247]

Development of Human Rights During the First Abolitionist Era

> *"'Human Rights' is perhaps the most discussed and least understood of political terms in the late twentieth century."*[248]

The development of the campaign against slavery grew in tandem with idea of human beings having rights simply because they are human. In the Eighteenth and Nineteenth century discussion was of civil and political rights but during the twentieth century these distinctions became blurred as discussion became simply of human rights allotted because of birth as a human being.

Writing in 1690 John Locke said:

> *"Man being, born, as has been provided, with a Title to perfect Freedom, and an uncontrolled enjoyment of all the Rights and Privileges of the Law of Nature, equally with any other Man, or Number of Men in the World, hath by Nature a Power, not only to preserve his Property, that is, his Life, Liberty and Estate, against the Injuries and Attempts of other Men; but to judge of, and punish the breaches of that Law in others."*[249]

---

[245] Chuks Iloegbunam, "The Death of a Writer," *The Guardian*, November 10, 2006, http://www.theguardian.com/theguardian/1995/nov/11/fromthearchive.

[246] "Kiobel v Royal Dutch Petroleum."

[247] *Victims of Trafficking and Violence Protection Act of 2000.*

[248] Lynn Hunt, *The French Revolution and Human Rights: A Brief Documentary History* (Boston: Bedford Books of St. Martin's Press, 1996).

[249] John Locke, *Two Treatises of Government* ([Whitefish, Mont.]: Kessinger Publishing, 1988).

It was, he believed, the duty of government to protect these rights. However, by the end of the century he had corrected himself. The word "Man" did not include any of the following:

a. Women
b. Poor/penniless men
c. Slaves

In fact, Locke invested in the slave trade and his notion of equality was limited to free property-owning, probably European/American men, who fell into this category.

The French philosopher, Jean Jacques Rousseau, wanted to widen the scope of "Man". Together with other French thinkers of the period, he believed that government should rest upon rational principles and these principles should belong to everyone. Only a few, however, believed that women and slaves fell into the "everyone" category. No one considered that children had rights of their own. Unfortunately, although they spoke of reason revealing "self-evident truths", one of which was the natural rights of all peoples, these thinkers never went beyond the right of all men to participate in the social contract; and as has been seen the word 'men' meant different things to different people.[250]

Duke Mathieu De Montmorency was one of a group of 'reforming nobles'. He fought in the American War of Independence and had this to say in a four day debate on the Declaration of the Rights of Man and Citizen:

> *"The rights of man in society are eternal; no sanction is needed to recognize them…The rights of man are invariable like justice, eternal, like reason; they apply to all times and all countries."*[251]

With so much discussion and violence surrounding human rights and government in France it is surprising to find that the first 'human rights society' is to be found in Britain which had so much to lose by espousing the idea. Certainly, Britain had ended the absolutist monarchy in 1649 when the government had chopped the head off King Charles I and the restored monarchy was constrained by Parliament but it still had little genuine democracy. Furthermore, it had been the notion of human rights and equality that had caused such problems for the British government in the Thirteen Colonies, resulting, of course, in the loss of America, and, through the French Revolution would ignite war across Europe when Napoleon came to power.

Abolition in France

During 1789-1794 the French engaged in a wide ranging discussion as to the human rights of various sections of society, for example, women, Jews and executioners. Also, they discussed the rights of "free blacks and slaves." In 1738, Jean Boucaux v

---

[250] D. Diderot and J d'Alembert, ed., "Natural Law," *French Encyclopedia*, 1755, http://quod.lib.umich.edu/d/did/.
[251] Mathieu De Montmorency, "The Rights of Man and Citizen" (Paris, France, 1789).

Verdelin was a case brought by a slave against his Master. The applicant was a slave brought back to France from the colonies. He sued his Master for back wages and his freedom. He won the case but the government subsequently passed the Declaration of 1738 designed to prevent slaves from entering France. The *Police des Noirs* went even further seeking to prevent people on the basis of race rather than nationality from entering France. The commander of shipping in Bordeaux, Le Moyne, expressed concern that this act was essentially racist and excluded people of property and their descendents and not just slaves from the colonies. His protests fell on deaf ears.[252]

On 4 February 1794, the First Republic (Convention) voted for the abolition of slavery in all French colonies. The abolition decree stated that

"the Convention declares the slavery of the Blacks abolished in all the colonies; consequently, all men, irrespective of color, living in the colonies are French citizens and will enjoy all the rights provided by the Constitution."[253]

In 1802, Napoleon restored slavery but abolished it again in 1815. It was fully abolished in 1848 by the work of Victor Schoelcher in the Second Republic.[254] An interesting by-product of the restoration of slavery by Napoleon was the alternative effect it had in England. The English abolitionist cause was spurred on by the fact that the enemy of Britain, Napoleon, was in favor of slavery, therefore Britain should be against it! Many scholars have suggested that modern human rights law has it roots in the enlightenment but starts in the post-World War II period. In her book, Martinez looks back to the Abolition of the slave trade in Britain and the Courts of Mixed Commission as the source of modern law.[255]

---

[252] Sue Peabody, *There Are No Slaves in France: The Political Culture of Race and Slavery in the Ancien Régime* (New York: Oxford University Press, 1996).
[253] Hunt, *The French Revolution and Human Rights*.
[254] Government of France, "Victor Schoelcher (1804-1893), A Life, a Century, Slavery Past and Present," *Senat*, accessed October 23, 2013, http://translate.google.com/translate?hl=en&ie=UTF8&prev=_t&sl=fr&tl=en&u=http://www.senat.fr/evenement/victor_schoelcher/abolitions.html&sandbox=0&usg=ALkJrhg_szTHJcaTzukJqjc_hB6OgVkFcg.
[255] Jenny S. Martinez, *The Slave Trade and the Origins of International Human Rights Law.* (Oxford: Oxford University Press, 2011).

SAY NO TO CHILD LABOUR
NO CHILD LABOUR
SAY NO TO CHILD LABOUR

Chapter 5

Child Slavery

"Considering that the child should be fully prepared to live an individual life in society, and brought up in the spirit of the ideals proclaimed in the Charter of the United Nations, and in particular in the spirit of peace, dignity, tolerance, freedom, equality and solidarity,"[256]

In many places, the underlying problem with trying to eliminate child labor and slavery is poverty. This is true be it in the brick kilns of India, the streets of Mexico, the favelas of Rio, the brothels of S.E. Asia, the runaways of the USA or the cocoa farms of West Africa. If poverty is not tackled and alleviated, children will continue to work. The economies of those countries in which children work rather than receive education are handicapped by having an illiterate or semi-literate population which cements the cycle of poverty. This cycle of poverty also affects the rest of the world and is very similar to the problems considered by the African Association.[257] They hoped to find other items with which African tribes could trade apart from slaves. This, they believed would empower the tribes in their trading with Britain and other Western nations. The same is true now. Although child slavery (labor) provides cheap goods to the markets of developed countries, those developed countries lose because the poverty of the developing country means that there is no market for goods from the developed world. The developed world needs to make a decision about whether it wishes to go on plundering the less developed world or fight child labor and slavery to produce a fairer and more competitive world for itself and others. Fair trade products may help but it is only one of a number of measures which need to be put into place.[258]

Children labor in many different industries around the world. Not all children are slaves but many work in hazardous occupations. The ILO estimates that two hundred and fifteen million children work, of whom, one hundred and fifty eight million work in hazardous jobs.[259] In 2011, UNICEF estimated that about one hundred and fifty million

---

[256] UN, "Convention on the Rights of the Child."

[257] Sattin, *The Gates of Africa*.

[258] *Chocolate The Bitter Truth 1 of 5 Child Trafficking BBC Panorama Investigation*, 2011, http://www.youtube.com/watch?v=LD85fPzLUjo&feature=youtube_gdata_player.

[259] International Programme on the Elimination of Child Labour and International Labour Organization, *Children in Hazardous Work What We Know, What We Need to Do* (Geneva: International Labour Office, 2011), http://site.ebrary.com/id/10512167.

children aged five to fourteen in developing countries were involved in child labor.[260] In Sub Saharan African, one in four children aged five to seventeen work, in the Asia Pacific area one in eight children work and one in ten children work in Latin America.[261] The number of working children is decreasing worldwide with the exception of sub-Saharan Africa where children are working more, often because they have been orphaned by AIDS and have to take on the responsibility of caring for their young siblings. On the face of these numbers it seems that there are more working girls than boys even though the jobs girls do often hide them from sight, for example domestic servants and sex workers. It is estimated that roughly ninety percent of children involved in domestic labor are girls.[262] Child labor accounts for twenty two percent of the workforce in Asia, thirty two percent in Africa, seventeen percent in Latin America and one percent in US, Canada, Europe and other wealthy nations.[263]

What Jobs are Children Doing?[264]

Many jobs for child slaves are common to the globe, driven by the global market:

In the UK: sex work, benefit fraud, cannabis farming, farms, restaurants, nail bars, building sites, factories and in the fields.

In the USA: sex work, farms, restaurants, nail bars, building sites, factories and in the fields.

In Asia: child soldiers, sex work, farms, restaurants, factories building sites and as 'organ donors'. In India many children are in debt bondage. Girls are trafficked within the sex industry within India and from neighboring countries, such as Nepal.[265] Additionally, girls can be found in forced marriage, including being married to the Temple or Goddess and then used as if she were the vessel of the Goddess in sexual activity (Devadasi). These girls use to have a high status but since the practice was made illegal the girls have no protection.[266] In China there is evidence of the human trafficking of babies for adoption.[267]

---

260 UNICEF, *Executive Summary." The State of the World's Children 2011.* (UNICEF, 2011), http://www.unicef.org/publications/files/SOWC_2011_Executive_Summary_EN_01122011.pdf.

261 UNICEF, "Child Protection from Violence, Exploitation and abuse - Child Labour," *UNICEF*, accessed October 27, 2013, http://www.unicef.org/protection/57929_58009.html.

262 UNICEF, *Executive Summary." The State of the World's Children 2011.*

263 International Labour Organisation, "State of Child Labour 2000," accessed October 20, 2013, http://www.childlaborphotoproject.org/childlabor.html.

264 Emily Camastra, "Hazardous Child Labor as a Crime against Humanity: An Investigation into the Potential Role of the International Criminal Court in Prosecuting Hazardous Child Labor as Slavery," *Georgetown Journal on Poverty Law & Policy* 15 (July 1, 2008): 335.

265 Tameshnie Deane, "Cross-Border Trafficking in Nepal and India-Violating Women's Rights," *Human Rights Review* 11, no. 4 (December 2010): 491–513.

266 Beeban Kidron, "Devadasi Practice in India," *Every Child*, accessed October 27, 2013, http://www.everychild.org.uk/devadasi.

In Africa: child soldiers, sex work, farms, restaurants, factories building sites. In the DRC and Zimbabwe, mining is a big employer; in West Africa coffee and cocoa growing, and girls can be found in forced marriage and the sale of babies.

In South America and the Caribbean: child soldiers, sex work, farms, organ 'donors', restaurants, factories building sites. In Brazil, charcoal burning creates slaves of teenage men.[268]

In Japan: sex work, farms, restaurants, factories building sites.

In Eastern Europe: sex work, 'organ donors', farms, restaurants, factories building sites and domestics.

The Middle East: sex work, farms, restaurants, factories building sites, camel jockeys, domestics.

Children are not simply enslaved in their home country; some one million two hundred thousand are trafficked each year internationally and crossing borders.[269] The population of child slaves is, of course, unknown. If the children could be identified they might, given the will to do so, be saved. It is estimated that one in six children in the world is in labor or slavery.[270] World Vision has a number of campaigns against child trafficking and produces annual data.[271] Child slaves and child workers have much in common. They do not receive education, do not have time to play or enjoy their childhood, have little or no chance of a better life, suffer from poverty and have a high susceptibility to injury, illness and death. It is estimated that one out of every six children in the world are child laborers and some of them are enslaved.

Article 31 the Convention on the Rights of the Child,

> "children have the right to rest and leisure, to engage in play and recreational activity, and to participate freely in cultural life and the arts. It also states that children have the right to participate in cultural and artistic life and be provided appropriate and equal opportunities for cultural, artistic, recreational, and leisure activity."[272]

---

[267] Custer, "Kidnapped and Sold: Inside the Dark World of Child Trafficking in China," *The Atlantic*, July 25, 2913, http://www.theatlantic.com/china/archive/2013/07/kidnapped-and-sold-inside-the-dark-world-of-child-trafficking-in-china/278107/.
[268] Bales, *Disposable People, New Slavery in the Global Economy.*
[269] UNGIFT, "Human Trafficking - The Fact," 2007, http://www.unglobalcompact.org/docs/issues_doc/labour/Forced_labour/HUMAN_TRAFFICKING_-_THE_FACTS_-_final.pdf.
[270] Toko Tomita, "Fighting Slavery Today" (Anti-Slavery Campaign), accessed October 28, 2013, http://www.anti-slaverysociety.addr.com/media.htm.
[271] "World Vision Child Slavery," *Orld Vision*, accessed October 23, 2013, http://www.worldvision.org/our-impact/child-protection?campaign=11935146&gclid=CLP41byLvLoCFenm7AoduVwAVA.
[272] UN, "Convention on the Rights of the Child."

Of course, being a slave is worse because you are not laboring for your family or yourself (although some may believe that they are doing so) and there is no one to help or care.[273] Once a child slave is past being useful to their slave-owner, they are often unable to go back to their families, especially if they were sexually enslaved.[274] They are disposed of by their owners by being turned out onto the street to fend for themselves. This is regardless of their ability to keep themselves and their state of health.

Example: USA

In 2005, the Innocence Lost task force in Florida (FBI, Department of Justice, and the National Center for Missing and Exploited Children) successfully prosecuted Justin Evans, a pimp based in Florida, for inciting a minor to engage in prostitution.[275] Behind this bland legal definition is the suffering of a 14 year old with AIDS. In February 2005, the girl was hospitalized for two weeks and diagnosed with AIDS. Soon after leaving hospital, Evans had her working again, despite his never identified associate telling him:

"She's in her last stages, dog. You fucked that girl up, man… When I told you she was sick man don't put her on the street…you were like, fuck it. I need the money…That whore was too sick, dog."

From the rest of the conversation it is known that Evans had stripped and beaten the child even though he knew she was seriously ill. In response to CW he said:

"That's part of being a pimp[,]man. In the pimp rulebook it says when you beat 'em like that. You strip them down naked and beat them. They respect you more…You're supposed to strip 'em butt naked …and beat her ass."

CW then expresses his sympathy for the girl (of course he did nothing to help) and Evans responds:

"Listen. Even though you're sick, you can still get out there and pull tricks. If you're so sick you can't walk that's one thing. But if you're still physically able to walk.. she should be able to go get that money."[276]

---

[273] See sex trafficking post

[274] "What Is the Red Thread Movement," *The Red Thread Movement*, accessed October 26, 2013, http://www.gogirlsmusic.com/rtm_band.pdf; Andrew Levine, *The Day My God Died* (Independent Lens, 2004), http://www.pbs.org/independentlens/daymygoddied/film.html.

[275] United States v Justin Evans, 476 F.3d 1176 (11th Cir. 2007), 1177-78, Justia (11th Cir. 2007).

[276] U.S. Government, United States v Justin Evans, Government Notice of Filing,, accessed October 20, 2013.

> In May 2005, the girl was hospitalized again, her body covered in sores and blisters. She had been forced to work up until that hospitalization.
>
> In "The Slave Next Door" Bales and Soodalter note: "There is nothing glamorous or romantic here. Behind the flashy clothes and expensive cars, these [pimps] are bad guys. They degrade, exploit, and brutalize the girls and women they control."[277]

The above example occurred in the United States of America but the same businesslike callous disregard for the victim can be seen in every sex trafficking situation around the world. But sex continues to sell and innocent people are degraded because of it. In June 2012, even the National Trust (a venerable British institution dedicated to the preservation of historic houses and landscape) released a mobile phone app to guide visitors through the streets of the London sex industry. The R-rated (X-rated) app is marketed to help visitors understand the "long love affair with sex, drugs and rock 'n' roll" in London.[278] Nothing is made of the suffering of those for whom the sex, drugs and rock 'n' roll culture made their lives a misery.

Looking back to the Evans case there are a number of lessons which should be being learned:

a. The general health of the population suffers if men are using sex slaves who have HIV/AIDS . They are liable to pass the disease to other sexual partners who may or may not be prostitutes or sex slaves.

b. The general economy of the country suffers when the men and women afflicted by HIV/AIDS have to be treated for their illness and related healthcare problems, not just from direct health costs but also from the loss of jobs etc by the user of the girl and any other women infected.

c. The loss of family members, the father who used the girl or the mother who was infected by his use. This consequent poverty and possible orphaning of the children can start the cycle of enslavement over again in these children.

d. The lifelong sorrow of the victim's relations.

e. The use of a sex slave is achieved only because she has been tortured and degraded.

In addition to suffering the general health problems of all slaves, and the fact that they are not free to lead their lives, children suffer particularly from fatigue, and beatings. Children are often mal-nourished which impairs both physical and mental development. These children often suffer from a lack of Vitamins A and C. These cause night blindness

277 Bales and Soodalter, *The Slave next Door Human Trafficking and Slavery in America Today*, 2009.
278 National Trust, "Get Your Free Soho Stories Here," accessed October 20, 2013, http://www.nationaltrust.org.uk/article-1356398419972/.

and, the old sailors' disease, scurvy. Children with scurvy experience bleeding, poor healing, fatigue and gum disease

In agricultural slavery, children work with dangerous implements and chemicals. It is well-known that organophosphates cause nerve and mental health problems, in many cases, child slaves work with them entirely unprotected. Building sites are dangerous places for all. Un-regulated construction sites are particularly dangerous. If fatigue and malnutrition are added then the child working in construction is placed in a very dangerous position. Amputations, cuts, muscle injuries and lifelong crippling injuries are commonplace. As has been seen a particular example can be found in the alleged building contracts for stadia for the World Cup in 2022.[279]

Children working as slaves in the manufacturing industry fare little better than those in the construction industry. Many are housed in dangerous, cramped, and often, locked factories. There is no suggestion that a fire which occurred on December 14, 2010 in the Hameem factory in Dhaka affected slaves, but it does show the risks which are experienced by child slaves and child laborers working in garment sweat shops which are often fire hazards, containing as they do flammable clothes and unsafe equipment.[280] If children who are tired and locked or blocked exits are added into the mix a lethal cocktail can ensue. In this case Gap, one of the companies being supplied by the factory, agreed to pay compensation to the families of victims.[281] Even worse problems in the garment factories of Bangladesh were seen in 2012.[282] Yin, a child slave in China sums up her lot succinctly when she said

> *'We were allowed very little sleep each day; we were forced to start working the moment we opened our eyes [and] I often worked until midnight.'*[283]

In some factories child slaves are kept awake by electrical current in tables to shock them if they sleep or they are forced to work at gunpoint.[284] Children are in much demand in the sex industry and their fate is similar to adults also trapped in sex slavery.[285] The porn industry has grown exponentially since the development of the internet. Of concern is the fact that child pornography commands much higher profits than adult pornography. The demand seems to be unlimited and the children involved are abused in a similar way as in

---

[279] Patterson, "Revealed: Qatar's World Cup 'Slaves.'"
[280] "Bangladesh Factory Fire Kills at Least 20," *N.Y. Times*, December 14, 2010, http://www.nytimes.com/2010/12/15/world/asia/15bangladesh.html?_r=0.
[281] Saad Hammadi and Matthew Taylor, "At Least 27 Die and More than 100 Are Injured in Blaze at Bangladesh Manufacturing Plant," *The Guardian*, December 14, 2010, http://www.theguardian.com/world/2010/dec/14/bangladesh-clothes-factory-workers-jump-to-death.
[282] Dave Jamieson and Emran Hossain, "Bangladesh Factory Fire Victim Calls O Walmart to Pay Compensation," *The Huffington Post*, April 12, 2013, http://www.huffingtonpost.com/2013/04/12/bangladesh-factory-fire-walmart_n_3071974.html.
[283] Bales, Trodd, and Williamson, *Modern Slavery*.
[284] Ibid.
[285] See sex slavery post

the sex slavery business. Children are also involved in seeing sex online through chat rooms and made to enact sexual scenes for webcam sessions.

Before 2005 children, as young as five, from East Africa and the Indian sub-continent, were in great demand to be camel jockeys in the United Arab Emirates and elsewhere in the Middle East. Betting on camel racing is big business and the fate of thousands of dollars used to rest on the work of one small boy. These children were small, generally malnourished and losing a race could result in severe penalties which ranged from sleep deprivation to beatings; sometimes death. They suffered many injuries from being around and riding the camels. The children would have been velcroed onto the back of the camel and when they fell the average drop would be two meters at speeds of between thirty to forty kph. Typically, races involves up to two hundred and fifty camels.[286] In 2005, the United Arab Emirates took the lead in the area and made it illegal to use child camel jockeys who have been replaced by robot jockeys.[287] Therefore, child camel jockeys would be being used illegally in that country. As mentioned earlier the United Arab Emirates has led the way on this matter, in particular it has compensated the children for their injuries, but the tradition continues elsewhere in the Middle East.

Street begging is common in most countries. Street beggars and street children are often seen as blots on the community. The local police will often beat, sometimes, kill children on the street. Local citizens will abuse them both physically and mentally. The report by Sarah Thomas de Benitez "State of the World's Street Children – violence" lists examples and illustrates the sort of problems which beset this sub category of working or enslaved child.[288] Another example comes from the 1993 Candelaria Massacre in Rio in which an off-duty police officer shot eight street children in cold blood. But perhaps the most haunting statistic comes from the outcomes of those who were not killed on that day. Of the sixty two children who survived, forty four had died by 2000 most of them never seeing their twentieth birthday.[289]

Children working down mines or in the opencast mining business are liable to suffer physical injuries similar to those in agricultural, manufacturing or construction slavery. However, they are also exposed to noxious chemicals such as carbon monoxide and, in open caste mining for rare earth materials and gold, mercury. Below ground workers can get lung disease. In this enclosed environment the noise of machinery is even more likely to cause deafness to them than to their above surface working brethren.

---

[286] Dr Fikri M Abu-Zidan, "Prevention of Child Camel Jockey Injuries: A Success Story From The UAE," *Clin J Sport Med.* 22(6) (2012): 467.

[287] *Robot Replace Children as Camel Jockeys in the UAE* (IRINFILMS, 2007), https://www.youtube.com/watch?v=b0aEtNH1NyY.

[288] Sarah Thomas De Benitez, *State of the World's Street Children – Violence* (Consortium for Street Children, October 20, 2007), http://www.amazon.com/State-Worlds-Street-Children-Violence/dp/0954788656.

[289] Nicole Veash, "Violent Death Claims Survivors of Brazils Child Massacres," *The Guardian*, September 9, 2000.

In forced marriage children suffer as domestic and sex slaves and often have to work to support their families as well. Many of these child brides will have no control over their reproductive health and many will die from early pregnancy. It has been seen that one woman dies in child-birth every sixty seconds but that statistic goes up if the mother is a teenager. Teenage mothers are five times more likely to die in child-birth than women in their twenties. The risk for girls in Africa is even higher.[290]

Fishing Industry

Children sold into fishing are often at sea for many years, transferred from one boat to another rather than at a dock.[291] The dangers of fishing boats are many including crushing and amputation injuries. Some children are unable to obtain quality, or any, medical care for these injuries. They are at risk of sexual and physical violence from the other members of the crew.

Rug-making

> *"the owner and his brother shut my eyes and put my finger in boiling oil and said: 'Now it's all right, now you get back to work'"*[292]

The quote comes from a young man called Rambho Kumar, he is a former slave who worked in the rug-making industry. He is describing 'medical attention' he received for a cut. This small quotation illustrates a number of the evils of child labor

a. Lack of proper medical attention
b. Fatigue
c. Cruelty of slave masters
d. Unsafe industrial practices

It is known that children around the world can suffer extreme levels of violence whether they are in the care of their parents or not; child slaves are infinitely more vulnerable.[293] Only physical injuries have been listed above but, perhaps, more damaging is the level of psychological damage done to children who are enslaved. Feelings of worthlessness, abandonment, lack of trust, lack of an appropriate role model all combine to make an adjustment to life outside slavery even more difficult. Even where children are

---

[290] Kristof and Wudunn, *Half the Sky*; Robert E. Black et al., *Maternal and Child Undernutrition: Global and Regional Exposures and Health Consequences*, Maternal and Child Undernutrition (John Hopkins University and World Health Organization, January 17, 2010), http://www.who.int/nutrition/topics/Lancetseries_Undernutrition1.pdf.

[291] Cari B. Jenson, "Child Slavery and the Fish Processing Industry in Bangladesh," *American Geographical Society's Focus on Geography* 56, no. 2 (Summr 2013): 54–65.

[292] Bales, Trodd, and Williamson, *Modern Slavery*.

[293] United Nations, *Violence Against Children* (United Nations, Office of the Secretary General, 2006), http://www.unviolencestudy.org.

enslaved with their parents, Bales et al suggest that, they come to feel distrust of their parents who are unable to help them in this situation.[294]

Should Any Class of Person Have a Priority in Human Rights?

It has been seen that thinking about human rights originally did not include, for example, women, slaves, and poor men in the minds of some thinkers.[295] Whilst there was considerable improvement in the lot of children during the nineteenth century in Western countries, internationally the rights of children were not considered until the early part of the twentieth century. In 1919, Eglantine Jebb was moved to help the children of Germany and Eastern Europe whose lives had been decimated by World War I and were suffering enormously.[296] She founded a non-profit which has had lasting influence and is now the seventh largest NGO in the World. It is Save the Children.[297] In 1923, she went on to look at the legal rights of children who, she believed, needed protection against similar awful incidents. As a result she drafted the Declaration of the Rights of the Child which was endorsed by the League of Nations Assembly on 26 November 1924 as the World Child Welfare Charter and, on 20 November 1959 became part of the United Nations Declaration of the Rights of the Child in expanded form. Thus, children have had their human rights protected for nearly 100 years. However, around the world children continue to lack basic access to legal remedies. This is compounded by the fact that, without the help of an adult, the child has no legal standing.

A child without legal remedies is ripe to be abused by whosoever chooses. Even in societies where the rights of the child are recognized there is a blurring of boundaries. This is strongly evidenced in the news media, where, as has been seen, children who are the victims of rape by men paying the child's pimps for sex are referred to as "child prostitutes". In a world where parents 'own' their children, some subject to control of their parenting by the state it can be expected that children are prepared to be owned by someone, even if that someone denies their human rights. This is especially important where street children are concerned. Simply put, they have no access to justice. They are too young to advocate for themselves and, without an adult protector, unable to access the system. Only through NGOs can street children be heard. Likewise child slaves have rights but no way to enforce them. Who is there when a five year old has her human rights violated by a man raping her, and paying her 'owner' for the pleasure? It can be postulated that a child can only have human rights if there is an adult or organization to represent them. In such a case, can it be said that "all human beings are born free and equal in dignity and rights"?[298]

---

[294] Bales, Trodd, and Williamson, *Modern Slavery*.
[295] French Revolution and John Locke supra
[296] Nicole Dorothy, *Eglantine Jebb Saves the Children* (London, U.K.: Blue Hills, 2010).
[297] "Save the Children," accessed October 20, 2013, http://www.savethechildren.org/site/c.8rKLIXMGIpI4E/b.6115947/k.8D6E/Official_Site.htm.
[298] "The Universal Declarartion on Human Rights."

Child Slavery

Migrants, refugees and undocumented children swell the numbers of children vulnerable to being trafficked. Take, for example, the case of a young man, we will call him, Dean, escaping from the Democratic Republic of the Congo (DRC).[299] Dean had been forcibly recruited as a child soldier in the DRC. At the age of thirteen he was able to escape from captivity and he began a long trek to freedom. He found that freedom in Cape Town, South Africa where, through the amazing dedication of the staff at the Cape Town Multi-Service Centre, he was able to find a career.[300] Unfortunately, he didn't have any papers to prove that he came from the DRC or anywhere else for that matter. This proved to be a major handicap because if you are not a registered citizen of a country, in most cases, you are not allowed to work legally. Thus, when Dean proved to be highly talented and an employer wanted to give him a job Dean couldn't take the job because of his lack of citizenship. Fortunately for Dean his potential employer valued him so highly that negotiations took place with the South African government and eventually Dean was not only able to stay, but also work. Without that employer Dean would have been just one of millions who, at 18 years old, can no longer stay in the care system but cannot work legally and would have to make his home on the streets or worse. A child without citizenship loses many things and there are millions of them. This can be because their parents do not register them because of ignorance or expense or it can be because, in war torn areas, they move a great deal. Whatever the reason for lack of registration Susan Bissell, Head of Child Protection at UNICEF told a meeting in December 2011 that the most important child protection work which could be done was to get every child a birth certificate.[301]

The advantages of a birth certificate are many because citizenship brings access to whatever welfare system is available in the country be it:

a. education;
b. health care;
c. legal job market; or
d. benefits such as housing and food.

It enables a child to have something to work for – if you know that you will be forever consigned to a life in the black-market economy, your life will remain half lived and hopeless forever. For more details see the Report to United Nations OHCHR.[302]

---

[299] Interviewed by author June 2011

[300] H. B. Kruger and H Oosthuizen, "SOUTH AFRICA - SAFE HAVEN FOR HUMAN TRAFFICKERS? EMPLOYING THE ARSENAL OF EXISTING LAW TO COMBAT HUMAN TRAFFICKING.," *Potchefstroom Electronic Law Journal* 15, no. 1 (2012): 282–343.

[301] Susan Bissell, "Children in Adversity" (presented at the Children in Adversity, USAID, Washington D.C., 2011).

[302] Human Rights Council, *Report of the Independent Expert on Minority Rights. Mission to Bulgaria* (United Nations General Assembly, July 11, 2013), <http://www2.ohchr.org/english/bodies/hrcouncil/19session/reports.htm.

Being Stateless

It leaves a child open to traffickers offering to make its life better with a job offer that may seem too good to be real but that child will take a chance from sheer desperation.[303] Of course, without education the child might not even notice that the offer is too good to be true. Some children, like Dean, obtain housing and education through the good offices of a NGO. This keeps them safe as children but once they become 18 many NGOs can no longer care. This is true, also, of many foster care systems around the world. Thus, the most vulnerable, find themselves living on the streets or with friends. Without citizenship they are destined for a life of poverty. Where children have parents they were never thought of as having rights of their own. Their rights were always subsumed by the rights of their parents and rulers/governments. In many countries parents still believe that they have the right to exploit their children for their own ends; for some unfortunate souls that includes being sold into a life of slavery.

Example

Nigerian boy sold by family - Bernardo Kohler Center rescue

We will call this young boy Tim. He was trafficked by members of his family to the US as a 10year old domestic slave. ICE found him and deported him as an illegal immigrant. On his return to Nigeria he was again sold into slavery in the United States. This time he was rescued by the Bernardo Kohler Center and has since obtained his T-visa. He has also been reunited with some of his sisters who were also enslaved in the United States.[304]

In the 1980s, discussion amongst human rights groups, lawyers and child care professionals grew surrounding the fact that the rights of children were still being ignored or marginalized. These groups started to talk about increasing the empowerment of children through domestic and international legislation. For example, the Children Act 1989 was passed in the UK giving children of 'sufficient age and understanding the right to be consulted in legal proceedings concerning their lives.[305] Where there was insufficient age and understanding, a guardian system was set up and a guardian was required to be appointed and represent the child in all cases where he or she might be separated from one or both parents in care proceedings (in cases brought by child protection services). During this time-frame the United Nations, specifically, UNICEF, was creating a document which would become the Convention on the Rights of the Child 1990 (CRC).[306]

The Convention recognizes children as having equal rights to those of other human beings rather than being under the ownership of their parents or guardians. As equal

[303] *Somaly Mam on the Tyra Banks Show (1 of 3)*, 2008, http://www.youtube.com/watch?v=YlpjTc8iJqo&feature=youtube_gdata_player.
[304] Interview by author with staff at BKC 2013
[305] United Kingdom, "Children Act 1989." S.1
[306] UN, "Convention on the Rights of the Child."

human beings they have their own natural rights but, by the CRC, they also have added protection due to their vulnerability. As we have see the Convention on the Rights of the Child has been ratified by every country in the world, although not by the United States of America.

Here are some possible reasons why the United States has not ratified the CRC:

a. The U.S.A. is not at ease with international law.
b. What is the point – Children are adequately protected in the U.S.
c. It gives children rights which are apart from the parents, for example choice of religion.
d. It would make seventeen year old military personnel child soldiers.

In the context of human trafficking, Article 9 of the CRC provides that children shall be protected from all forms of abuse, physical, sexual and emotional, as well as receive protection from negligence. Children should also have access to programs that can aid a child experiencing these abuses. The effect of this is that in any country where the trafficking of child occurs, there is a breach of international law as well as, if any exists, national law.

The CRC set international standards for the protection of children but without governments at national and local level providing care of children, protection from trafficking and appropriate law enforcement children are left just as vulnerable as they were before the CRC. Fortunately, the very existence of the CRC has brought about a change of attitude and law in many countries so far as children are concerned. Unfortunately this is not true in every country and one of the problems endemic to UN Treaties is that countries sign up to Conventions (a Treaty by another name) but do not fulfill their obligations under it. We can go back to the DRC for an example of this problem. There, despite having signed and ratified the CRC, child soldiers are being recruited, sometimes forcibly, by government and rebels alike.[307]

Violation of the CRC in developing countries

It is not just developing countries which apparently violate the CRC. In Canada the passing of An Act to amend the Immigration and Refugee Protection Act, the Balanced Refugee Reform Act, the Marine Transportation Security Act and the Department of Citizenship and Immigration Act 2013 permits the detention of children under 18 and certain other migrant groups for up to a year.[308]

In the United States, it was alleged that children were detained without representation or access to representation which would be a breach of Article 37.d, although as we have seen the United States has not ratified the CRC. In June 2012, children

[307] Bryan Mealer, *All Things Must Fight to Liv* (New York, NY: Bloomsbury, 01/08/20111).
[308] Government of Canada, *An Act to Amend the Immigration and Refugee Protection Act, the Balanced Refugee Reform Act, the Marine Transportation Security Act and the Department of Citizenship and Immigration Act*, 2013, https://openparliament.ca/bills/41-1/C-31/.

were detained in BCFS-International Children's Shelter (Lackland Air Force base) San Antonio . In May 2012, it was understood that only ten out of sixty nine young people at the facility had representation and it was alleged that the authorities had been denying the children access to representation. RAICES, a government funded organization rather than an independent Non-Profit, represented the ten children. It was further alleged that RAICES was the only free representation agency which was allowed contact with the children which seemed contrary to the decision in the Flores Settlement, the Homeland Security Act, the Homeland Security Act of 2002, 6 U.S.C. § 279 ("HSA"), or the William Wilberforce Trafficking Victims Protection Reauthorization Act of 2008, Pub. L. 110-457, (TVPRA).[309]

Specifically § 235(c)(5) of the TVPRA provides:

> The Secretary of Health and Human Services shall ensure, to the greatest extent practicable ... that all unaccompanied alien children who are or have been in the custody of the Secretary or the Secretary of Homeland Security, ... have counsel to represent them in legal proceedings or matters .... To the greatest extent practicable, the Secretary of Health and Human Services shall make every effort to utilize the services of pro bono counsel who agree to provide representation to such children without charge.

Whilst the HSA, 6 U.S.C. § 279, provides:

> [T]he Director of the Office of Refugee Resettlement shall be responsible for ... developing a plan to be submitted to Congress on how to ensure that qualified and independent legal counsel is timely appointed to represent the interests of each such child ...

The *Flores* settlement provides:

> No minor who is represented by counsel shall be transferred without advance notice to such counsel, except in unusual and compelling circumstances such as where the safety of the minor or others is threatened or the minor has been determined to be an escape-risk, or where counsel has waived such notice, in which cases notice shall be provided to counsel within 24 hours following transfer.

Also the *Flores* settlement states that, ORR must "promptly provide each minor not released with ... the list of free legal services providers compiled pursuant to INS regulation ..." and the *Flores* settlement guarantees detained class members the right to —

> [l]legal services information regarding the availability of free legal assistance, the right to be represented by counsel at no expense to the

[309] *Homeland Security Act 2002, USC*, 2002, http://www.law.cornell.edu/uscode/text/6/111; *William Wilberforce Trafficking Victims Protection Reauthorization Act of 2008, USC*, 2013; "'Flores Settlement' Flores v. Meece Agreement," January 1, 1997, http://www.aclu.org/files/pdfs/immigrants/flores_v_meese_agreement.pdf.

government, the right to a deportation or exclusion hearing before an immigration judge, the right to apply for political asylum or to request voluntary departure in lieu of deportation."

Therefore, it seems clear that BCFS cannot stop unrepresented minors having access to available free legal services, regardless of whether a given representative is affiliated with RAICES or not. Indeed, BCFS is under an affirmative obligation to maximize detained minors' access to representation and legal information.

Thus, if that is not happening in a center where children are detained it is in breach of national law and, clearly, both the CRC and the UDHR (which the United States has ratified) as to representation and the choice of representation.[310] In 2012, the Latino Policy Coalition complained to the United Nations about the policy of the U.S. government which removed large numbers of children from the care of their immigrant parents, often, they alleged, on wrongful allegations of abuse or neglect.[311] As a result, it is alleged, many of these children were placed in the foster care system and some disappeared.

In the United Kingdom the age of criminal responsibility is 10years; this means that a child can be charged, convicted and imprisoned for a crime for which she is responsible.[312] The Commissioner of the European Council for Human Rights, Thomas Hammarberg, disapproves of this law and contends that imprisonment at such an early age creates criminals rather than assisting in the rehabilitation of such child offenders. [313]In 2010, Paul Mendelle QC, the chairman of the Criminal Bar Association, and Maggie Atkinson, the Children's Commissioner for England agreed, with Mr Hammarberg and called for the age to be raised to fourteen.[314]

Example:

Jamie Bulger was nearly three when he was murdered in 1993. Robert Thompson and Jon Venables abducted him at a shopping mall in Liverpool, his mutilated body some 2 ½ miles away two days later. These boys, who were both 10 years old, became the youngest defendants in

---

[310] Women's Refugees Center, *Forced from Home: The Lost Boys and Girls of Central America* (New York, NY, October 2012), http://www.youthtoday.org/hotdocs/Forced%20From%20Home1.pdf.

[311] Latino Policy Coalition, "Latino Policy Coalition Files United Nations Human Rights Complaint Against the United States of America for Removal of Children From Undocumented Immigrant Parents," *PRneswire*, accessed October 27, 2013, http://www.prnewswire.com/news-releases/latino-policy-coalition-files-united-nations-human-rights-complaint-against-the-united-states-of-america-for-removal-of-children-from-undocumented-immigrant-parents-147840825.html.

[312] *Children and Young Persons Act 1963*, 1963, http://www.legislation.gov.uk/ukpga/1963/37.

[313] "UK 'Breaches Human Rights Laws' over Youth Sentencing," *Channel 4 News*, March 15, 2012, http://www.channel4.com/news/uk-breaches-human-rights-laws-over-youth-sentencing.

[314] Tom Whitegead, "Age of Criminal Responsibility Should Be Raised, Says Leading Barrister," *The Telegraph*, October 7, 2010, http://www.telegraph.co.uk/news/uknews/law-and-order/7804238/Age-of-criminal-responsibility-should-be-raised-says-leading-barrister.html.

British legal history. They went to detention until they were 18 years old and were then released on lifelong parole.

It has been seen how the United Kingdom passed the Children Act 1989 following the thinking of the CRC which was being discussed at the same time.[315] However, the United States has failed to act on this issue because of powerful interest groups. An example of these can be found on "parentalrights.org" the authors of this website have a commonly held believe amongst Americans that the CRC takes away a parent's right to their child.[316] The views of this group reflect a wider view of the role of government in American society. They do not want the US government to ratify a Treaty which would give someone else the right to tell them how to bring up their children. A wider example of this parenting view can be found in the withdrawal of children from certain classes at school; for example, not allowing a child to read Romeo and Juliet because it is bawdy.

Essay question
Should a child be prevented from learning with his/her peers and kept from one of the greatest plays in the world because of the parent's views or should it be allowed to choose for itself by a certain age?

Despite the CRC, children continue to suffer breaches of their rights in every country in the world. The systems which exist to help them are woefully inadequate. What example does this set for children to take forward into adulthood? Research shows that those who are physically and sexually abused as children often repeat that abuse in their adult life. Could it be that children who have had their rights ignored continue to do that to the next generation when adults?

Why are certain societies afraid of valuing their children?

a. Working children are generally paid less than adults and so, if a short-term view is taken, it suits entrepreneurs and the governments chasing economic growth to allow children to work when they should be at school.[317]
b. Generally, children have no idea about health and safety concerns and generally make more compliant workers.
c. Dictators fear an educated population which is aware of its rights.
d. Some religious groups oppose the education of girls.

---

[315] United Kingdom, "Children Act 1989."

[316] Michael Farris, "Protecting Children By Empowering Parents," *Parental Rights.org*, accessed October 27, 2013, http://www.parentalrights.org/index.asp?SEC={CE4F4C7A-F6ED-4732-8FA5-677F0649AF8D}&Type=B_BASIC.

[317] "International Labour Standards on Forced Labour," *International Labour Organization*, October 27, 2013, http://www.ilo.org/global/standards/subjects-covered-by-international-labour-standards/forced-labour/lang--en/index.htm.

Examples:

In Afghanistan and Pakistan there have been attacks on schools which take girls as pupils. Girls have had acid thrown in their faces when walking to school. In one incident, in Kunduz, poison was put into water being drunk by girls at school. These girls experienced nausea and vomiting.[318]

In the Swat Province of Pakistan, in 2012, Malala Yousafzai was shot in the head because of her insistence that education should be available to girls on an equal footing to men.[319]

It may be that for children to enjoy their rights, parents and employers and governments have to come to see children as individuals who can contribute during their lifetime and not just as a resource for eighteen years. An appreciation that one person can have rights and those do not violate the rights of another person is required to make the whole human rights system work but never is it required so much as in the child/adult situation. Nor can adults abrogate their duty to care for children in the best interests of the child rather than in the best interest of themselves. Children are not bargaining chips. They are, when young, in want of adult care and support and, as adolescents, in want of care which allows them to become individuals. In the nineteenth century, in many western societies children were working in hazardous conditions. In many parts of the world that continues; take for example, the Indian children working in a firework factory or the rug makers of Pakistan or the children living in brothels in India.[320]

An Example:

In Nigeria, children were poisoned by lead over a two year period because their homes were near mining areas. This problem is ongoing but the government has not taken action to protect them. Doctors are unable to provide care for these children who are constantly exposed to lead until the exposure is halted. Lead poisoning is extremely dangerous and can kill people who are exposed at high levels.[321]

---

[318] Garath Dirrian, "150 Afghan Schoolgirls Seriously Ill after Being Poisoned in Anti-Education Attack by Muslim Extremists," *The Mail*, April 18, 2013, http://www.dailymail.co.uk/news/article-2131526/Afghan-schoolgirls-poisoned-contaminated-water--Radicals-blamed.html#ixzz1uDMtawjx http://www.malala-yousafzai.com/.

[319] "Malala Yousafzai," *Malala Yousafzai*, accessed October 27, 2013, http://www.malala-yousafzai.com/.

[320] Zana Briski and Ross Kauffman, *Born into Brothels*, 2004, http://www.imdb.com/title/tt0388789/.

[321] "Nigeria: Country Urged to Show Commitment On Child Lead Poisoning," *All Africa*, May 6, 2012, http://allafrica.com/stories/201205071058.html.

In 2012, the Committee of Ministers of the Council of Europe to set out recommendations concerning the protection rights of children.[322] The recommendations call for educating and informing children of their rights and the creation of programs and organizations that will teach children about democracy and their roles as citizens. The object is to create well-informed citizens in the upcoming generation who will bring about a sea change in thinking about children when they reach adulthood. In Wales, the government has created a Flying Start program to provide care and protection for children from low income families which follows the recommendations of the Committee of Ministers.[323] In England and Wales, a Children's Commissioner was appointed in 2004. The role of the commissioner is:

> *"to promote the views of children and young people from birth to 18 (up to 21 for young people in care or with learning difficulties)... Our mission. We will use our powers and independence to ensure that the views of children and young people are routinely asked for, listened to and that outcomes for children improve over time. We will do this in partnership with others, by bringing children and young people into the heart of the decision-making process to increase understanding of their best interests."*[324]

In accordance with that mandate the Office of the Children's Commissioner considers the impact of laws and society on children.

An Example:

On June 12, 2012, Sue Berelowitz, the Deputy Children's Commissioner gave evidence to the Home Office Select Committee that children are being exploited in every "town, village and hamlet". She said that the problem is exacerbated by "social networking sites and easy access to pornography".[325] "In one case, boys aged fourteen and fifteen were 'summoned' via Blackberry messenger to the gang rape of a 'very, very young girl' which lasted several days," she told the Home Affairs committee.[326]

---

[322] The Committee of Ministers, *Recommendation CM/Rec(2012)2 of the Committee of Ministers to Member States on the Participation of Children and Young People under the Age of 18*, Human Rights and Rule of Law (Council of Europe, March 28, 2012), http://www.coe.int/t/dg3/children/participation/Newdefault_en.asp.

[323] Gwenda Thomas, "Welsh Government Makes Children's Rights a Priority," *Western Mail, Wales Online*, May 7, 2012, http://www.walesonline.co.uk/news/health-news/2012/05/07/welsh-government-makes-children-s-rights-a-priority-91466-30914333/.

[324] "The Children's Commissioner," *The Children's Commissioner*, accessed October 20, 2013, http://www.childrenscommissioner.gov.uk/info/about_us.

[325] *Child Sexual Exploitation and the Response to Localised Grooming*, House of Commons Home Affairs Committee (London, U.K., 2014 2013), http://www.publications.parliament.uk/pa/cm201314/cmselect/cmhaff/68/68ii.pdf.

[326] Ibid.

Peter Davies, chief executive of Child Exploitation and Online Protection (CEOP), believes that group and gang related child sexual exploitation is far more widespread than people like to imagine.[327]

Examples – United Kingdom and United States:

The Manchester case

Shabir Ahmed was a fifty nine year old takeaway delivery driver. He was jailed for nineteen years at Liverpool Crown Court in June 2012. He had been raping and trafficking white English girls. The indictment accused him of thirty separate counts of child rape.

In a separate trial at Manchester Crown Court, Ahmed was accused of raping an Asian child. The jury found that for over a decade he had raped an Asian victim almost weekly, dominating her by the use of extreme violence. The Judge extended his sentence to twenty years.

His victim gave evidence that after her first rape by Ahmed she was so small that she had to stand on a wooden chair to wash herself in the sink. Detectives gave evidence that the girl was three or four at the time. The young woman said that her experience had put her off having sexual intercourse altogether, even with a boyfriend, although she had never wanted to have one because of her ordeal. She told of the fact that she was isolated from friends who had married and have children; both of which she didn't feel would ever be an option for her."[328]

In Georgia, USA, the Court heard the case of Kenny A. v Perdue . In this case children had been the victims of abuse and neglect. "Kenny A. filed a class action lawsuit in the District Court for the Northern District of Georgia in 2002 against the Georgia Department of Human Resources and the Governor of Georgia, among others (collectively "Georgia"), under 42 U.S.C. § 1983 for "systemic deficiencies" in Georgia's foster care program that allegedly resulted in violations of their rights to substantive due process, liberty, privacy, and association under the First, Ninth, and Fourteenth Amendments. Kenny A. also brought claims under the Adoption Assistance and Child Welfare Act of 1980, the Multiethnic Placement Act of 1994, the Medicaid Act, and Georgia law". Two counties in Georgia were involved in the suit and the court found that the representation of the child victims had been poor and not in their best interests. As a result of this judgment the law now entitles children to their own legal counsel and ensures that

---

327 Ibid.

328 Press Association, "Rochdale Paedophile Ringleader Is Named," *The Guardian*, June 21, 2013, http://www.guardian.co.uk/uk/2012/jun/21/ringleader-rochdale-paedophiles-named.

sufficient legal counsel should be employed for all children to be adequately represented.[329]

What Can be Done to Improve Adherence to the CRC?

As in all cases if the person who has the rights do not know about them then they cannot exercise them. Thus, education on the rights of children, as recommended by the Council of Ministers in Europe, is required in schools around the world. UNICEF has a major campaign to educate children about the CRC which is part of the mandate of the Children's Commissioner also. Where children are empowered they can use their rights to keep themselves safe and access services.

An Example:

See the case of Nujeed, a child bride who obtained a divorce having heard that it was possible for her to petition.[330]

Furthermore, children who know their rights can be protected against human trafficking because they have a better opportunity of recognizing traffickers trying to take advantage of their youth and vulnerability. Where children are aware of their rights governments are more likely to uphold them, thus access to education, democracy and health care begins to occur. This can be seen in South Africa where the general population has been growing in awareness of their rights since the election of Nelson Mandela in 1995 and the coming to power of the first Black government of South Africa.

How Does the CRC Work?

Governments which sign up to the CRC are required to report to a committee of independent experts on a regular basis. These experts examine the laws, policy and practice of each country and consider them against the standards of the CRC. The committee makes recommendations to the individual states. Of course, if the states are unwilling to follow those recommendations there is nothing that the UN can do to force cooperation. However, the U.N. acts through diplomacy and can bring pressure to bear on states which don't comply.[331]

Why Do Children Work?

a. poverty, need of basic necessities like shelter, food, and clothing drives children to begin working
b. lack of education,

[329] Kenny A v Sonny Perdue (UNITED STATES DISTRICT COURT FOR THE NORTHERN DISTRICT OF GEORGIA ATLANTA DIVISION 2006).
[330] See post: Child Brides
[331] K. Addo, *The Legal Nature of International Human Rights*.

c. parental illiteracy,
d. exploitation of cheap labor.
e. overpopulation
f. children choose or are forced by their parents to work
g. factory owners often find it more profitable to employ children at cheap rates rather than adults.
h. They can be sold into work by their parents[332]

What can be done?

President Obama said in his 'Cairo speech' in 2009 "it is no coincidence that countries where women are well-educated are far more likely to be prosperous".[333] The Child Labor Deterrence Act was considered in the USA during the 1990s. It banned the import of goods manufactured using child labor. However, in an example of the doctrine of unintended consequences, it had detrimental effects on the children making these products, especially those working in the garment industry in Bangladesh. According to Michael Nielsen, over sixty percent of children working in the garment factories were girls. This allowed females to play a greater role and gain more independence in a patriarchal society. But after this Act was introduced to Congress, thousands of children in Bangladesh were dismissed from the garment industry and forced to take more strenuous jobs such as stone crushing or sex work.[334] An example of an industry which employs children and child slaves is the Cocoa industry.

[332] Siddharth Kara, *Bonded Labor: Tackling the System of Slavery in South Asia*, 1st ed. (Columbia University Press, 2012). See also supra: Story of a Nigerian Boy
[333] President Obama, "REMARKS BY THE PRESIDENT ON A NEW BEGINNING," *The White House*, June 4, 2099, http://www.whitehouse.gov/the_press_office/Remarks-by-the-President-at-Cairo-University-6-04-09.
[334] Michael Nielsen, "The Politics of Corporate Responsibility and Child Labour in the Bangladeshi Garment Industry.," *International Affairs* no. 81.3 (2005): 559–580.

Chapter 6

The Cocoa Industry

"I would tell them that they are eating my body"[335]

In 1791, during the abolition campaign in the United Kingdom, William Fox said of sugar

> *"If we purchase the commodity we participate in the crime. The slave dealer, the slave holder, and the slave driver, are virtually agents of the consumer, and may be considered as employed and hired by him to procure the commodity." He went on to point out that for every pound eaten "we may be considered as consuming two ounces of human flesh."*[336]

Plus ça change. The quote which starts this chapter is from a child slave who was asked what he would like to say to those of us who eat the product of his labor; chocolate. Slavery in the production of chocolate is not new but now the worldwide value of the product is huge.[337] The global chocolate market was worth eighty three billion three hundred million U.S. dollars in 2010 and is expected to rise in value to ninety eight billion three million U.S. dollars by 2016.[338] Most of the cocoa produced is grown in the Ivory Coast (Cote d'Ivoire) and Ghana. Many cocoa growing farmers rely upon child labor but yet others on slavery, mostly of young boys. Although the chocolate producers, anti-slavery movements and governments have been aware of the problem since the 1990s progress for these enslaved children has been a long time in coming.

The key to change is to

- raise awareness amongst the chocolate buying public.
- raise awareness amongst the families in Mali and Burkina Faso whose children are used to supply the slave farms.
- encourage enforcement of existing protocols.[339]

---

[335] *Chocolate The Bitter Truth 1 of 5 Child Trafficking BBC Panorama Investigation*.

[336] William Fox, *Address to the People of Great Britain on the Utility of Refraining from the Use of West India Sugar and Rum* (London, U.K.: M. Gurney and W. Darton and Co, 1791), https://ia600508.us.archive.org/6/items/addresstopeopleo1791foxw/addresstopeopleo1791foxw.pdf.

[337] Lowell J. Satre, *Chocolate on Trial: Slavery, Politics, and the Ethics of Business* (Athens, OH: Ohio University Press, 2005).

[338] "Global Chocolate, Cocoa Beans, Lecithin, Sugar and Vanilla Market By Market Share, Trade, Prices, Geography Trend and Forecast (2011-2016)," *MarketsandMarkets.com*, September 2011, http://www.marketsandmarkets.com/Market-Reports/global-chocolate-market-164.html.

[339] "Harkin-Engel Protocol" (Responsible Chocloate), accessed October 20, 2013, < http://responsiblecocoa.com/about-us/the-harkin-engel-protocol/.

- Change management thinking in this area, this is true of all slavery involving international business[340]

The Harkin-Engel protocol was signed in 2001 by members of the chocolate industry. It was developed in partnership with United States Senators Harkin and Engel. The intent of the protocol was to bring about the end of slave labor, particularly child slave labor, in the cocoa industry in West Africa; and if not end it then reduce it substantially. This industry partnership now includes ADM, Barry Callebaut, Cargill, Ferrero, The Hershey Company, Kraft Foods, Mars Incorporated, and Nestlé. On September 13, 2001, the industry stakeholders, together with the governments of Cote de Ivoire, Ghana and the USA (and Senators Harkin and Engel) signed a Joint Declaration and accompanying Framework of Action to Support the Implementation of the Harkin–Engel Protocol. Now, the deadline is to reduce child labor, as defined in the ILO Convention 182 in the cocoa industry by seventy percent by 2020.[341] In 2012, some progress was made when Ferrero Rocher, an Italian chocolatier which sells its produce throughout Europe, agreed to stop using slave produced cocoa from the Ivory Coast by 2020 with an aim "to create a growing, sustainable supply chain improving social, economic and environmental conditions while preventing and combating the worst form of child labor".[342] It has been suggested that they should start labeling chocolate wrappers with the amount of child labor which it has taken to produce the product until they can certify the product slave free.[343] Whilst Hershey and Nestle have said that they will eradicate child/slave labor from their cocoa production by 2020; Ferrero and Mars have gone a step further and intend to ensure that no child or slave labor appear in the entire production line.

Despite these high profile promises and agreements, the use of child slaves is endemic in the West African cocoa industry. Gilbert Kone Kafana is the minister of labor and social affairs in the Ivory Coast. He is trying to make the chocolate companies accept their moral obligation to change their policies and work with the government to eradicate child labor and slavery in the industry.[344] However, global chocolate makers are transnational companies and owe a duty of care not to the workers who supply their company, nor to their families or the government in which raw materials are grown but to their shareholders. Thus, although Kafana would like to feel that

---

[340] Andrew Crane, "MODERN SLAVERY AS A MANAGEMENT PRACTICE: EXPLORING THE CONDITIONS AND CAPABILITIES FOR HUMAN EXPLOITATION.," *Academy of Management Review.* 38, no. 1 (January 2013): 49–69.

[341] International Labour Organisation, "CONVENTION CONCERNING THE PROHIBITION AND IMMEDIATE ACTION FOR THE ELIMINATION OF THE WORST FORMS OF CHILD LABOUR (Convention 182)" (International Labour Organization, June 17, 1999), http://www.ilo.org/public/english/standards/relm/ilc/ilc87/com-chic.htm.

[342] "Ferrero Sets Date to End Cocoa Slavery," *CNN Freedom Project Ending Modern Slavery*, April 20, 2012, http://thecnnfreedomproject.blogs.cnn.com/2012/04/20/ferrero-sets-date-to-end-cocoa.

[343] "Eat Traffick Free Chocolate," *Stop the Traffick*, accessed October 25, 2013, http://www.stopthetraffik.org/campaign/chocolate.

[344] Humphrey Hawksley, "Ivory Coast Cocoa Farms Child Labour: Little Change," October 20, 2011, http://www.bbc.co.uk/news/world-africa-15681986.

The Cocoa Industry

> *"the chocolate companies have a duty to engage with [the government]. [The Government] needs to build roads, schools, hospitals and social centres; anything that would allow Ivory Coast to progress",*[345]

it will take continued pressure from the world community, particularly pressure which will affect their bottom line.[346] This was seen with Nike and Gap in the 1990s and the work that Apple felt it necessary to do in 2012 following revelations about the working conditions at Foxconn in China.[347] Furthermore, the government itself is partly to blame for the use of child and slave labor in this industry. The government has set a rate of 40% tax on cocoa. Dale found that "the total amount of tax on cocoa, from nine different taxes, is almost three times the price that farmers receive for the cocoa they sell to middlemen."[348]

So far as the impact on the industry of Protocols are concerned, a study done in the United States of America shows that there has been little progress since 2001.[349] Less than 4% of people have been helped by the programs in an industry which is estimated to include around 250,000 children, some of whom are slaves and others who are working in harsh and hazardous conditions.

In order to put pressure on chocolate companies there needs to be a campaign of raising awareness. If consumers started to ask where the chocolate came from and whether chocolate was free of slave labor or child labor it would force the companies to make a difference. One student taught by the author telephoned the helpline of a multinational chocolate company to ask just that question. He reported that the individual to whom he spoke "had no idea what I was talking about". It is clearly a conversation which needs to be started and had around the world but particularly in the chocolate buying West. If the label is not "Fair Trade" child labor is likely to have been an ingredient although Romano and Mistrati suggest in their film that even this may not be a guarantee.[350]

---

[345] Ibid.

[346] Robin T. Byerly, "Combating Modern Slavery: What Can Business Do?," *Journal of Leadership, Accountability & Ethics.* 9, no. 5 (November 2012): 25–34.

[347] Jim Armitage, "Even worse than Foxconn': Apple rocked by child labour claims, *The Independent*, July 30, 2013, http://www.independent.co.uk/life-style/gadgets-and-tech/even-worse-than-foxconn-apple-rocked-by-child-labour-claims-8736504.html.

[348] Dale Youngbee, "Cote D'Ivoire and Ivorian Government: Leader in Child Labor, Abuse and Trafficking.," *The Washington Post*, March 18, 2012, http://communities.washingtontimes.com/neighborhood/rights-so-divine/2012/mar/18/real-trafficker-chocolate-slavery/.

[349] *Oversight of Public and Private Incentives to Eliminate the Worst Forms of Child Labor in the Cocoa Sector in the Cote De Ivoire and Ghana* (Tulane University), accessed October 15, 2013, http://www.childlabor-payson.org/Tulane%20Final%20Report.pdf.

[350] Laura Burke, "Ivory Coast's Child Labor behind Chocolate," *Global Post*, January 28, 2012, http://www.globalpost.com/dispatch/news/regions/africa/120116/ivory-coast-child-labor-chocolate; Miki Mistrati and Robin Romano, *The Shady Side of Chocolate*, 2012.

Chapter 7

Agricultural Slavery

"Debt bondage in South Asia is implemented with varying degrees of subtlety and coercion. In the Sindh Province in Pakistan, agricultural workers and sharecroppers, most of whom are from indigenous Indian communities, often work under constant watch from guards, and are kept locked up at night."[351]

Agricultural slavery can be found all over the globe, from the plains of northern India, to the cannabis farms of London and the citrus fields of Florida. Such slaves work in all kinds of weather. Sometimes they work inside, for example the children growing cannabis in residential buildings in the United Kingdom. Agricultural slaves have the common problem of carrying heavy weights and laboring long hours without much food. They are often kept in fear of their lives and that of their families. Agricultural slaves can be debt-bonded or simply first generation slaves picking fruits and vegetables because they have been lured into a contract in the hope of a better life.[352]

Example

Miguel told his story in a film made by "Free the Slaves". He told of how he was living in Mexico and needed money for his sick child. He took a job to work in the USA picking fruit in Florida. His passport was taken from him and he began working as a slave on a farm in Florida. The slaves were guarded by armed men and he overheard them talking about killing difficult workers and throwing them to the alligators. He feared for his life and could not escape his servitude.[353]

---

[351] Justin Campbell, "A Growing Concern: Modern Slavery and Agricultural Production in Brazil and South Asia," *Topical Research Digest: Human Rights and Contemporary Slavery. University of Denver, Colorado, USA* (2008): 131–141.

[352] Kara, *Bonded Labor: Tackling the System of Slavery in South Asia*.

[353] "Free the Slaves," *Free the Slaves*, accessed November 5, 2013, www.freetheslaves.net/.

Debt bondage

> *"Entire families kept like cattle on farms in India, Pakistan and Nepal; migrant agricultural workers forced to remain on ranches in Brazil; and the organised export of women into domestic and sexual slavery in Europe."*[354]

What might it be like to be an agricultural slave in Northern India today? In "Disposable People, New Slavery in a Global Economy" Kevin Bales give a sample diet for a slave.

> *"Fill up a coffee mug four times with rice or wheat. Now feed a family of five for one day with the grain you have measured out. For every meal you'll need to give each person only one-third of a coffee mug of grain so that it will last all day…Repeat this recipe every day for the rest of your life.*

There are some possible variations. Once every two weeks replace half the grains or rice with beans and lentils. From your backyard find some dandelions or clover and add the greens to the rice when you boil it…and while you have some strength, grow some peppers or onions or some more beans. Then work even harder so that you'll have enough onions to trade for some cooking oil and salt."[355]

These slaves, according to Bales live in a mud hut of one room, and carry their cooking water at least half a mile. Of course, there is nothing spare to sell for medicine or other essentials.

> *"This slow starvation, a cruelly balanced way to get the most work from the bonded laborers for the least input."*[356]

In exchange for such food and living conditions these slaves work as agricultural laborers from dawn to dusk seven days a week in the blistering sun of Northern India.

Ask yourself:

- would you be hungry?
- would you be immensely tired?
- would you have any pleasure from tasting your food? Something those of us who have a choice of food find it difficult to comprehend. In the developed world we are inundated with food programs on the television and the tastes of multiple varieties of food

In summer 2010, the author tried the diet of an Indian slave for about 3 weeks.[357] She was

---

[354] Anti-Slavery Campaign, "Bonded Labour," *Anti-Slavery Campaign*, accessed November 5, 2013, http://www.antislavery.org/includes/documents/cm_docs/2009/b/bonded_labour.pdf.
[355] Bales, *Disposable People, New Slavery in the Global Economy.*
[356] Ibid.

- hungry morning, noon and night,
- tired, and
- hated having breakfast, lunch and dinner which tasted the same.

After three weeks she had to give up. She had lost 10lbs and was feeling very unwell. She felt dizzy and faint.

And yet she had not

- labored in the fields from dawn to dusk;
- carried water from a well for a quarter of a mile; or
- cooked on a fire for which she had collected cow dung.

Nor was she mal-nourished from birth. But best of all for her, she had undertaken the diet as a way of understanding in the hope of being able to teach the subject more clearly and she was able to STOP.

Debt bondage, also known as peonage, can be found most notably in S.E. Asia.[358] However, also, it is found in smaller pockets around the world, for example, as Le Breton explains, the cattle ranching areas of Brazil.[359]

Cannabis Farms

> *'The children, generally aged between 14 and 16, are smuggled into the country before being locked in the houses to water cannabis plants. They have been found sleeping in cupboards or attics to make more space for plants, and are at constant risk of fire or electrocution due to illegal rewiring of electricity supplies.'*[360]

Children are widely enslaved to grow cannabis. However, this business is not one where the slavery exists only in the developing world. The Metropolitan police estimate that, in the UK, there are more than seven thousand cannabis farms, of which four thousand are in the Greater London area. Children are commonly brought to the UK from Afghanistan, West Africa, Vietnam, Algeria, Morocco, India, Albania and Palestine to work on these farms. The slave traders buy ordinary homes which they then strip of their contents. Often they are stealing electricity from the local area to give enough light and heat to the plants growing within. The boy slaves are then used for manual labor to keep the plants in good condition until harvest.

---

[357] "Professor Goes on 'Slave Diet,'" *Free the Slaves BLOG*, October 29, 2013, http://ftsblog.net/2010/08/06/professor-goes-on-slave-diet/.

[358] Kara, *Bonded Labor: Tackling the System of Slavery in South Asia*.

[359] Binka Le Breton, *Trapped: Modern-Day Slavery in the Brazilian Amazon* (Bloomfield, CT: Kumarian Press, 2003).

[360] Samira Schackle, "Slavery on Britain's Cannabis Farms," *New Statesman*, November 26, 2008, http://www.newstatesman.com/law-and-reform/2008/11/cannabis-farms-children.

In March 2007, *Druglink* magazine revealed that on average, UK police were raiding three cannabis farms a day. In just two years, one thousand five hundred cannabis farms were shut down in London alone. An analysis of nationwide police raids revealed that around two-thirds to three-quarters of UK cannabis farms were run by Vietnamese criminal gangs.[361] The figures shown in the Independent newspaper in 2012 make interesting reading, presenting, as they do a picture of huge increases in cannabis farming in the UK. Not all cannabis farms employ slave or foreign labor but where there is money criminal trafficking gangs will usually be involved, cannabis farming is no different.

> ***"7,865*** *Cannabis farms were discovered in 2011/12 compared with 3,032 in 2007/8.*
>
> ***936*** *Farms found in West Yorkshire, the area of the country with the highest production rates – the equivalent of 42 factories per 100,000 people.*
>
> ***10 million*** *The number of adults aged 16-59 who have used cannabis, making it the most widely consumed narcotic.*
>
> ***16,464*** *The number of cannabis production offences last year compared with 14,982 in 2010/11.*[362]

The article continues that in a two year period police seized one million, ninety six thousand, seven hundred and ninety seven plants which had a street value of two hundred and seven million three hundred and sixty eight thousand, four hundred and forty seven G.B. pounds. .

Heroin

> *"Two-year-old Nilab sits on the floor, drawing with a stick. She is wearing a red dress and black shoes, her unruly curls falling in her eyes. Shy around strangers, she hides her face behind her big sister from time to time. The toddler has no idea what awaits her: she has been traded away in baad, to make up for the sexual misconduct of her uncle."*[363]

Heroin is produced from the opium poppy which is principally grown in Afghanistan.[364] The Afghan government, at the behest of the western powers has been

---

[361] "DrugScope Reveals Child Victims of UK Cannabis Farm Boom," *Drugscope*, September 6, 2007, http://www.drugscope.org.uk/Media/Press+office/pressreleases/Cannabis-farms-trafficked-children.

[362] Jerome Taylor and Paul Peachey, "Cannabis: Britain's Growth Industry," *The Independent*, October 29, 2013, http://www.independent.co.uk/news/uk/crime/cannabis-britains-growth-industry-7704330.html.

[363] "Refworld | Afghan Girls Suffer for Sins of Male Relatives," *Refworld*, October 29, 2013, http://www.refworld.org/cgi-bin/texis/vtx/rwmain?docid=49dc4b201c.

[364] Sherard Cowper-Coles, *Cables from Kabul: The inside Story of the West's Afghanistan Campaign* (London: HarperPress, 2012).

pursuing a campaign of eradication of the poppy crops.[365] In 2012, PBS/Frontline journalist, Najibullah Quraishi, found that an unfortunate side effect of this practice was the enslavement of young children. In far flung places in Afghanistan, an old custom called "baad" has resurfaced.[366] Poppies are primarily grown by small poor farmers. They supply the land and the drug lords provide the poppy seed. When the crop is harvested the drug lords come back to collect it and pay the farmers. Farmers say that growing heroin is much more profitable than any other crop and that the incentives provided by the allies to grow other crops do not reach them but are kept by officials.

Indeed, the poppy sustains many poor farmers in Afghanistan.[367] Whatever the correct facts, entering into a contract with a drug lord can be very costly to farmers who cannot provide their opium harvest. When the authorities destroy the poppy crop nothing is left behind. Thus, when the drug lords come for their harvest the farmer cannot provide the product and nor can s/he repay the drug lord for the seed. The drug lord has to be compensated or they will threaten to kill members of the family. What Quraishi found is that the drug lords demand a child, or two, in compensation for the lost seed. What happens to these children varies. Some are kept as hostages until the family can raise the money due. Others are forced to work for the drug lords and one girl in the film talks of being forced into marriage with a drug lord. Other children are exported to Iran and Pakistan and a life of slavery. These children are quite literally paying their parents debt with their lives.

Fruit and Vegetables

Antonio Martinez found himself a labor slave at the age of twenty one. Like many he had been lured to the US by the promise of well-paid work, for him, it was in the construction industry in California. Instead he ended up being sold for five hundred U.S. dollars in Florida.

> *"I realized I had been sold like an animal without any compassion,' ...He was right. In modern times, in the United States, Antonio had been sold into slavery in Florida's tomato fields."*[368]

The enslavement of people growing and harvesting the food which we eat around the globe is extensive. However, it is not necessary to look outside the developed world

---

[365] Harry Shapiro and David Guttenfelder, *Politics of the Poppy* (Druglink, November 2011), http://www.drugscope.org.uk/Resources/Drugscope/Documents/PDF/Publications/politics_of_the_poppy.pdf.
[366] "Opium Brides," *FRONTLINE*, October 29, 2013, http://www.pbs.org/wgbh/pages/frontline/opium-brides/.
[367] Robert Draper, "Opium Wars," *National Geographic Magazine*, February 2011, http://ngm.nationalgeographic.com/2011/02/opium-wars/draper-text.
[368] Amanda Kloer, "Your Tomato's Possible Ties to Slavery," *CNN Freedom Project*, accessed November 28, 2013, http://thecnnfreedomproject.blogs.cnn.com/2011/04/21/your-tomato-possible-ties-to-slavery/.

for examples. Both Europe and the USA have a thriving trafficking system to provide agricultural slaves.

Example

In the USA, the Coalition of Immokalee Workers has been at the forefront of the rescue and prosecution of slaves and slave traders in Florida. This extract from their website shows the cases which they have helped to bring to Court and through which they have been able to draw attention to the plight of the slaves who pick produce for the U.S. table.

"In one of the most recent cases to be brought to court, a Federal grand jury indicted six people in Immokalee on January 17th, 2008, for their part in what U.S. Attorney Doug Molloy called "slavery, plain and simple" (Ft. Myers News-Press, *"Group accused of keeping, beating, stealing from Immokalee laborers,"* 1/18/08). The employers were charged with beating workers who were unwilling to work or who attempted to leave their employ picking tomatoes, holding their workers in debt, and chaining and locking workers inside u-haul trucks as punishment (*"How about a side order of human rights,"* Miami Herald, 12/16/07).

This case became the seventh such farm labor operation to be prosecuted for servitude in Florida -- involving well over 1,000 workers and more than a dozen employers -- in the past decade. Since 2008, the federal government has initiated two more prosecutions, bringing the total to nine as of 2010. Here below is a list of the nine cases, in chronological order:

U.S. vs. Flores -- In 1997, Miguel Flores and Sebastian Gomez were sentenced to 15 years each in federal prison on slavery, extortion, and firearms charges, amongst others. Flores and Gomez had a workforce of over 400 men and women in Florida and South Carolina, harvesting vegetables and citrus. The workers, mostly indigenous Mexicans and Guatemalans, were forced to work 10-12 hour days, 6 days per week, for as little as $20 per week, under the watch of armed guards. Those who attempted escape were assaulted, pistol-whipped, and even shot. The case was brought to federal authorities after five years of investigation by escaped workers and CIW members.

U.S. vs. Cuello -- In 1999, Abel Cuello was sentenced to 33 months in federal prison on slavery charges. He had held more than 30 tomato pickers in two trailers in the isolated swampland west of Immokalee, keeping them under constant watch. Three workers escaped the camp, only to have their boss track them down a few weeks later. The employer ran one of them down with his car, stating that he owned them. The workers sought help from the CIW and the police, and the CIW worked with the DOJ on the ensuing investigation. Cuello worked for Manley Farms North Inc., a major

Bonita Springs tomato supplier. Once out of prison, Cuello supplied labor to Ag-Mart Farms, a tomato company operating in Florida and North Carolina.

U.S. vs. Tecum -- In 2001, Jose Tecum was sentenced to 9 years in federal prison on slavery and kidnapping charges. He forced a young woman to work against her will both in the tomato fields around Immokalee, and in his home. The CIW assisted the DOJ with the prosecution, including victim and witness assistance.

U.S. vs. Lee -- In 2001, Michael Lee was sentenced to 4 years in federal prison and 3 years supervised release on a slavery conspiracy charge. He pled guilty to using crack cocaine, threats, and violence to enslave his workers. Lee held his workers in forced labor, recruiting homeless U.S. citizens for his operation, creating a "company store" debt through loans for rent, food, cigarettes, and cocaine. He abducted and beat one of his workers to prevent him from leaving his employ. Lee harvested for orange growers in the Fort Pierce, FL area.

U.S. vs. Ramos -- In 2004, Ramiro and Juan Ramos were sentenced to 15 years each in federal prison on slavery and firearms charges, and the forfeiture of over $3 million in assets. The men had a workforce of over 700 farm workers in the citrus groves of Florida, as well as the fields of North Carolina. They threatened workers with death if they were to try to leave, and pistol-whipped and assaulted -- at gunpoint -- passenger van service drivers who gave rides to farm workers leaving the area. The case was brought to trial by the DOJ after two years of investigation by the CIW. The Ramoses harvested for Consolidated Citrus and Lykes Brothers, among others.

U.S. vs. Ronald Evans -- In 2007, Florida employer Ron Evans was sentenced to 30 years in federal prison on drug conspiracy, financial re-structuring, and witness tampering charges, among others. Jequita Evans was also sentenced to 20 years, and Ron Evans Jr. to 10 years. Operating in Florida and North Carolina, Ron Evans recruited homeless U.S. citizens from shelters across the Southeast, including New Orleans, Tampa, and Miami, with promises of good jobs and housing. At Palatka, FL and Newton Grove, NC area labor camps, the Evans' deducted rent, food, crack cocaine and alcohol from workers' pay, holding them "perpetually indebted" in what the DOJ called "a form of servitude morally and legally reprehensible." The Palatka labor camp was surrounded by a chain link fence topped with barbed wire, with a No Trespassing sign. The CIW and a Miami-based homeless outreach organization (Touching Miami with Love) began the investigation and reported the case to federal authorities in 2003. In Florida, Ron Evans worked for grower Frank Johns. Johns was 2004

Chairman of the Florida Fruit and Vegetable Association, the powerful lobbying arm of the Florida agricultural industry. As of 2007, he remained the Chairman of the FFVA's Budget and Finance Committee.

U.S. vs. Navarrete -- In December 2008, employers Cesar and Geovanni Navarrete were sentenced to 12 years each in federal prison on charges of conspiracy, holding workers in involuntary servitude, and peonage. They had employed dozens of tomato pickers in Florida and South Carolina. As stated in the DOJ press release on their sentencing, "[the employers] pleaded guilty to beating, threatening, restraining, and locking workers in trucks to force them to work as agricultural laborers... [They] were accused of paying the workers minimal wages and driving the workers into debt, while simultaneously threatening physical harm if the workers left their employment before their debts had been repaid to the Navarrete family." Workers first reported the abuse to Collier County police, and additional workers sought help from the CIW. The CIW collaborated with the DOJ and the police on the year-long investigation and prosecution.

U.S. vs. Bontemps -- In July 2010, Cabioch Bontemps, Carline Ceneus, and Willy Edouard were indicted by a federal grand jury on charges of conspiracy to commit forced labor. DOJ officials accuse the three of holding over 50 guest workers from Haiti against their will in the bean fields of Alachua County, Florida. The indictment states that Bontemps raped one of the workers in his employ and threatened her if she were to report it. The employers held the workers' passports and visas, and forced them to work in fields recently sprayed with harsh pesticides, causing permanent scarring. The grower, Steven Davis, asked the judge during the court hearing to release Bontemps since he was key to the harvesting operation. "All these people [the workers] look up to him," Davis said. "All these people respect him. All these people worship him." As of September 2010, the prosecution is ongoing. The CIW trained local law enforcement and church groups shortly before the workers were rescued, and assisted in referring the case to the DOJ.

U.S. vs. Global Horizons -- In September 2010, staff of guest worker recruiting giant Global Horizons were charged with operating a forced labor ring active in 13 states, including Florida. Global Horizons President Mordechai Orian and six others are accused of holding hundreds of guest workers from Thailand against their will, in what prosecutors call "the largest human trafficking case in U.S. history." FBI Special Agent Tom Simon described the latest case as "a classic bait-and-switch what they were doing. They were telling the Thai workers one thing to lure them here. Then when they got here, their passports were taken away and they were held in forced servitude working in these farms." The prosecution is ongoing, with more details to emerge about the various states workers lived in and what crops they picked."[369]

In 2010, the Bernardo Kohler Center (BKC) became involved in helping nineteen victims of agricultural trafficking. Like many victims, found themselves travelling around the USA, from Texas to Louisiana and on to New Jersey and then back again, following the crops. In 2011 they received T Visas after being release from their enslavement.

Fishing Slaves

As was seen in the chapter on child slavery the fishing industry uses slaves both in the catching process and the packaging process. The S. E. Asian fishing industry is responsible for enslaving many young men and keeping them perpetually at sea so that they cannot flee. This report on slavery in the fishing industry shows one aspect of the health risks run by the victims:

> *'When Ruslan, 36, snapped two bones in his left hand in a winch, it took three weeks before he was allowed to go to a hospital. The morning after his discharge he was ordered back to work but could not carry out his duties. The company removed him before any follow-up medical appointments. He said, 'I was a slave, but then I became useless to the Koreans, so they sent me home with nothing,...Today, back in his home village in Central Java, Ruslan has a deformed hand. While IMS, the recruiting agency, finally paid him $335 for three months of work, it has blacklisted him, according to Ruslan, because he spoke to investigators, and it has refused to help with medical bills.'*[370]

Cutting tools, hooks, the sea, nets, ships, long hours, tiredness, and exhaustion are all regular hazards for the slave at sea. Slavery is not only present in Indonesia, where the government has passed laws to try to stop it but slavery is an 'invisible' enterprise. Thailand, too, has a huge fishing fleet and uses many slaves to labor aboard the boats.[371]

[369] Coalition of Immokalee Workers, "About," accessed November 4, 2013, http://ciw-online.org/.
[370] E. Benjamin Skinner, "Slaves Put Squid on Dining Tables From South Pacific," *Bloomberg*, October 29, 2013, http://www.bloomberg.com/news/2012-02-23/slaves-put-squid-on-u-s-dining-tables-from-south-pacific-catch.html.
[371] Kate Bollinger and Kim McQuay, "Human Trafficking Rampant in Thailand's Deep-Sea Fishing Industry," *The Asia Foundation*, October 27, 2013, http://asiafoundation.org/in-asia/2012/02/08/human-trafficking-rampant-in-thailands-deep-sea-fishing-industry/.

Chapter 8

Environment

"Justice is what love looks like in public." Where is the justice for all of the victims? Where is their love? [372]

In Brazil there exists a type of slavery which could be regarded as doubly destructive. Not just Brazil is affected, however, illegal charcoal production can be found destroying the habitat of the mountain gorilla in Virunga National Park in the DRC to finance the predations of the FDLR Rwandan militia and in other locations around the world.[373] In 2010, President Lula da Silva committed Brazil to the production of green steel. This involves the growth of eucalyptus trees to fuel the smelting of charcoal and, it is claimed, green steel removes a ton of gas from the atmosphere instead of polluting it by the use of fossil fuels for charcoal production.

The eucalyptus plantations in Brazil have a troubled past. In the 1970s, the then military government offered incentives to clear the Amazon and plant eucalyptus trees which would, eventually, be turned into paper. By the 1990's there were few paper mills and the trees started to be used for charcoal production. Thus, whilst President da Silva's idea is a laudable, it is by no means new and carries the ability to enslave with it. This form of production involves the enslavement of young male teenagers. There are two principal elements needed to make steel: pig-iron and carbon which comes from charcoal. Charcoal is made from burning trees. The trees are burned in the absence of oxygen, a process called 'pyrolysis'. According to the ILO, Department of Labor and Greenpeace the steel created is used by car manufacturers.[374] Unfortunately, the plantations are located many miles from villages and so, laborers to make the charcoal have to be brought into the area by slave traders, known as Gatos. Most of the charcoal camps are many miles from habitation and the workers are brought in vans on journeys which are many hours, sometimes days, long.

The workers are generally drawn from towns in the poor north-east of Brazil. There is much unemployment and they are promised good wages which will enable them to send money back to their families. They go willingly with the Gatos and, along the way hand over their "labor' card. This card is the key to legal employment and is used as an

---

[372] Justin Dillon, *Call and Response*, 2010, http://www.callandresponse.com/cast_detail.php?e=west.
[373] "Anti-Charcoal Operation Needs Funding!," *Gorilla CD. Virunga National Park, D.R.C*, accessed November 7, 2013, http://gorillacd.org/2011/07/19/anti-charcoal-operation-needs-funding/.
[374] Greenpeace, *Driving Destruction in the Amazon*, 2012, http://www.greenpeace.org/international/Global/international/publications/forests/2012/Amazon/423-Driving-Destruction-in-the-Amazon.pdf.

identity card for other state officials and business. Just as traffickers of international slaves keep the passports of their victims so the Gatos keep the labor cards; effectively the workers are trapped. "From this moment the worker is dead as a citizen and born as a slave."[375] Once they get to the camps, the accommodation is rudimentary, often tents or shanty built huts and the work day is long and hard. The heat is terrific, not just from the sun but also from the smelting kilns which require temperatures of six hundred and sixty – eight hundred and fifty Fahrenheit (three hundred and fifty-four hundred and fifty centigrade) These temperatures carbonize the wood with volatile organic compounds disappearing in the hot blue acrid smoke. This acrid smoke is a particular problem for workers burning eucalyptus because it is extremely foul. The workers have to be trained and be extremely careful because if the temperature gets too high the carbon will burn and turn to ash which is then not usable in the smelting process. They get enough food to allow the greatest extraction of labor and little clothing. Just like the 'seasoning' of girls in the sex slavery trade these slaves are subject to beatings and humiliation to ensure compliance and the maximum work.

Escape is difficult; the Gatos and their henchmen are armed and the jungle dense with wildlife and plants. Escape is really not possible without a camp wide uprising but the workers are too hungry and tired to take on the armed guards. Of course, should they evade the guards they face a walk of many miles through the rainforest because the one road in and out of the camp is used by the traffickers. The chances of making it out without good knowledge of the jungle are minimal; these workers don't have that knowledge because, as has been seen, they are immigrants to the area. Some workers are taken to chop down and transport the trees. Others feed the trees into the charcoal kilns. This is a difficult and dangerous process. Yet others load the charcoal for transportation to the steel works. There are many deaths and injuries amongst the slaves and whole-scale destruction of the environment around the camps. Fortunately this type of slavery is short-term. Camps move on to the next stand of trees and slaves are often not taken on to the new camp. The duration of slavery then is estimated at three months to two years.[376]

Many people in the West recycle their thrown away items in the hope of preserving the environment and sustainable living. There are plants in the United States of America which recycle but much of our waste, particularly e-waste, ends up in China, the far-east and Africa. Greenpeace is a non-governmental environment group which fights for responsible recycling.[377] Guiya is a town in China with an environment which has all but been destroyed by the influx of e-waste.[378]

[375] Bales, *Disposable People, New Slavery in the Global Economy*.
[376] Ibid.
[377] "VICTORY! Philips Accepts Recycling Responsibility," *Greenpeace*, February 26, 2009, http://www.greenpeace.org/international/en/news/features/victory-philips260209/.
[378] K.C. Cheung et al., "Heavy Metals Concentrations of Surface Dust from e-Waste Recycling and Its Human Health Implications in Southeast China," *Environmental Science and Technology*, American Chemical Society (2008).

Mining Slavery

Diamonds

"Tiny diamonds that make a wash sparkle."[379]

The quote comes from an article about research conducted at the Universities of Warwick and Ashton in the United Kingdom. They have found that nanodiamonds remove stains, grease and fat in washes as cold as fifty nine Fahrenheit (fifteen centigrade). The research was partly funded by the multi-national company Proctor and Gamble. For an increase in cost of about seven cents washes could be done at these lower temperatures saving electricity.

But where do diamonds come from? There is a distinction between gem diamonds – those we wear – and industrial diamonds. Millions of industrial diamonds are needed each year for precision cutting and other manufacturing. Gem diamonds come mainly from Australia and industrial diamonds come mainly from the Democratic Republic of the Congo.

Slavery and Human Rights abuses have been endemic in the production of diamonds, particularly in Sierra Leone, Namibia, DRC and Zimbabwe. Many will have seen the dramatization of the horror of 'blood diamond' mining in the 2006 movie, Blood Diamond, staring Leonardo Di Caprio.[380] Despite attempts to clean up the industry widespread use of slave labor continues.

Example:

Zimbabwe: A huge find of diamonds were discovered at Marange. The Marange mining field is sixty six thousand hectares and some experts believe that it is the largest diamond find in the last century. It has been alleged that when the scale of the diamonds was discovered the Zimbabwean army moved into the area to claim it for the government. A massacre of miners working on the field is alleged to have taken place.[381] Certainly, since the government moved in there have been many allegations of human rights violations. On August 9, 2011 the BBC reported that "torture camps" existed in the Marange mining field.[382] It reported that men had been beaten with logs and rocks until they were unable to walk and

---

379 Cecilia Jamasmie, "Diamonds Are Now Your Washings Best Friend," *Mining*, June 26, 2012, www.mining.com.

380 Edward Zwick, *Blood Diamond* (Warner Bros., 2006).

381 "Zimbabwe: End Repression in Marange Diamond Fields," *Human Rights Watch*, June 26, 2009, http://www.hrw.org/news/2009/06/26/zimbabwe-end-repression-marange-diamond-fields.

382 Hilary Andersson, "Marange Diamond Field: Zimbabwe Torture Camp Discovered," *BBC; Panorama*, August 8, 2011, http://www.bbc.co.uk/news/world-africa-14377215.

> women were beaten and raped in the camps where both sexes work in extremely harsh conditions for little or no pay. A former member of a paramilitary police unit who worked in the main camp told the BBC that he had tortured workers by mock-drowning and other methods if necessary.
>
> On November 2, 2011 the World Diamond Council, which has representatives from the United States, the EU and participating African nations, announced that it "welcomed" the decision to lift the ban on the exportation of diamond from Zimbabwe's Marange ward. Diamond mining is controlled by an international body which ensures that diamonds mined in a particular area are not used to fuel conflict in the region. The Kimberley Process meeting, held in the DRC, lifted the ban after the US and EU stopped blocking the move. They had been against lifting the ban because of concerns that high level military and civilian Zimbabweans had stakes in the diamond industry. Specifically, it had been alleged that the Marange field was controlled by the Zimbabwean military and funds from the diamonds were used to underpin President Mugabe's Zanu-PF party. The leaders appeared to have accepted Zimbabwe's frequent and loud denials of all allegations, including those of torture camps.

The opening up of the market to Marange will certainly be excellent for the failed Zimbabwean economy because it is thought that the diamonds from there have an annual value of three billion U.S. dollars (one billion one million G.B. pounds). After years of economic reverses brought about by the government of Robert Mugabe this could be the move necessary to restore prosperity to the beleaguered Zimbabwean people.

If the money does go to the Zanu-PF party then Zimbabweans can look forward to more of the same. Zanu-PF members have tortured and raped their political opponents and used rape as a tool to control the voting public. Zimbabwe has high levels of levels of maternal mortality, displaced people – especially children – and poverty; it has to be hoped that the money from the diamonds will be used to help them.

WDC President Eli Izhakoff said,

> *"[It] demonstrates categorically that the Kimberley Process provides the framework through which the integrity of the rough diamond chain of distribution can be protected, while at the same time enabling producing counties to gain benefit from their natural resources."*

Human Rights groups do not agree. Global Witness, one of the founding members as well as the driving force behind the Kimberley Process, decided to leave the Kimberley Process because of the Zimbabwe decision; effective December 5, 2011. In 1998, Global Witness was one of the NGOs which brought to the attention of the world the use of "blood" diamonds to fuel armed militia groups and opposition movements to democratic governments in Sub-Sahara Africa.

However, lamenting the fact that some nine years after the Kimberley Process came into force most buyers of diamonds still couldn't tell if they were financing violent or abusive regimes, the founding Director and Chairman of Global Witness, said

> *"the scheme failed to deal with the trade of conflict diamonds in Cote d'Ivoire, was unwilling to take serious action of the blatant breaches of the rules over a number of years by Venezuela and has proved unwilling to stop the diamonds fuelling corruption and violence in Zimbabwe."*[383]

Enforcement of the Kimberley Process has been left up to the military of Zimbabwe which is the only group in the region assembled and large enough to patrol the mining field.

The workers are believed to be enslaved in this mining operation or be paid a very small sum. They risk injury from carbon monoxide, physical injury (crushing, back problems, deafness from loud machinery) and emphysema.

Rare Earth Minerals

Children and adults are also enslaved in the production of rare earth minerals in the Democratic Republic of the Congo (DRC) which has a long and bloody history. Officially five million four hundred thousand people died in the ten years of war which was believed to have ended in 2008 although a study conducted in 2012 puts the figure at under three million.[384] In actuality the DRC war continues today with four factions fighting over the territory, these include the Government army and the Lord's Resistance Army, led by the infamous Joseph Kony.

The riches of the DRC are many, including its rich flora and fauna but also rare earth minerals and industrial diamonds. It is rare earth minerals that power our electronics and, currently, cannot be substituted because whilst there are other metals available tantalum is 'king'

> *"...with enough time and money, engineers could probably construct tantalum free phones...chunkier, pricier handsets... Is Jo Consumer ready to swap his $199 Droid for a $3000 phone that looks like a prop from Miami Vice?"*[385]

Perhaps if "Jo Consumer" knew the price other people were paying for his cell phone and computer s/he would be prepared to make that change.

---

[383] "Press Release: Kimberley Process," *Global Witness*, December 5, 2011, http://www.globalwitness.org/library/global-witness-leaves-kimberley-process-calls-diamond-trade-be-held-accountable.

[384] "D.R. Congo War Deaths Exaggerated," *BBC News*, accessed November 3, 2013, http://news.bbc.co.uk/2/hi/africa/8471147.stm.

[385] Brendan I. KOERNER, "How Do I Figure out How Many Non-Bot Twitter Followers I Have?," June 22, 2012, http://www.wired.com/opinion/2012/06/st_kia_twitter_followers/.

For more information consider "The Enough Project", Kony 2012, Invisible Children, Regulating Information Flows, Regulating Conflict : An Analysis of United States Conflict Minerals Legislation. : Ochoa, Christiana; Keenan, Patrick J. Gottingen Journal of International Law. 2011, Vol. 3 Issue 2, p129-154., Sexual Violence in African Conflicts; Alexis Arieff, Analyst in African Affairs; 2011-02-23; 29. The Democratic Republic of Congo: Background and Current Developments; Ted Dagne, Specialist in African Affairs; 2011-10-17; 16, Consuming the Congo [electronic resource] : War and Conflict Minerals in the World's Deadliest Place. Eichstaedt, Peter : Chicago : Lawrence Hill Books, 2011.

Chapter 9

Sex Sells

"American youth are being sold the concept that women and girls' value lies in their youth, beauty and sexuality"[386]

As noted earlier, many communities have major inconsistencies with the way in which they view sex. The novel series "Fifty Shades of Grey" is a best seller and being made into a movie; "Sex in the City" was a successful television series which spawned two films; and lap-dancing and strip clubs are common around the towns of many Western Nations. Sex is used frequently in advertisements and women (and increasingly men)have been taught by the media to obsess about their bodies. Magazines for both men and women focus on sex and children are exposed to sex on films from an early age. What all of these examples have in common are

- Discussion/photographs of the female body
- Discussion/photographs of sex
- An underlying assumption that women like sexual abuse or being viewed as sexual objects
- An underlying assumption that women consent to these activities[387]

Sadly, for many women and men, consent to sex or other sexually based activities is a pipe-dream. From the examples of women and men raped by strangers to those raped by husbands, boyfriends and other family members, many people's decisions about sex are limited. This is also true for the three hundred thousand or so American children in the sex slavery business in the United States and for countless millions of sex slaves around the world. The dichotomy about sex is probably more obvious in Islamic culture where women are protected from sexual intercourse until marriage. This gives many men no outlet for their sexual feelings. In Shia culture the custom of temporary marriage is practiced.[388] The United States campaign "MissRepresentation" seeks to help women see themselves in terms of their jobs and roles as citizens rather than as sexual objects and there is a growing movement in western countries to de-objectify women and encourage them to be less obsessive about their looks – think fit not thin.[389]

---

[386] Jennifer Siebel Newsom, *Miss Representation* (Virgil Films and Entertainment, 2012).

[387] Samuel Vincent Jones, "HUMAN TRAFFICKING VICTIM IDENTIFICATION: SHOULD CONSENT MATTER?," *Indiana Law Review* 45, no. 2 (2012): 483–511.

[388]Post. Forced and child Marriage

[389] Newsom, *Miss Representation.*

The Prostitution Debate

> *"CONTRADICTORY AND CONFLICTING FEELINGS: 76% of interviewees stated that there is nothing wrong with having sex for money, but 85% said that they would not marry a prostitute, and 94% said they would not want their daughter to grow up to be a prostitute."*[390]

There is a long running and hard fought debate about prostitution.[391] What can probably be said is that the public view of prostitutes in the USA is extremely conflicted. A generation grew up with "Pretty Woman" and Lorena, from "Lonesome Dove" but few want that life for their children. Although the life of the Cantinera shown in Ruth Villatoro's film of the same name was forced upon her by her mother when she was aged twelve.[392] There seems little doubt that no child grows up wishing to become a Prostitute. Even children born into brothels would prefer a different life.[393]

An Example

Anita's story.

Anita was a young woman of twenty seven when she was trafficked. A mother of children and a wife she was forced to leave her home in Nepal after her husband took a second wife. After the arrival of the second wife her husband started to beat her. Eventually she decided to leave with her children. A strong woman, she went to farmers to buy vegetables and then sold them in the market. One day she was going about her work and accepted food from a passenger on her bus; she woke up in India after eating the food which had been drugged. Thereafter she was forced into prostitution and her children rendered highly vulnerable.[394]

Many people take strong positions. These range from

a. Prostitution allows sex slavery
b. Prostitution should be stamped out by effective policing
c. Attempts to stop prostitution drive it underground
d. Legalizing prostitution protects the women involved

---

[390] Rachel Durchslag and SAMIR GOSWAMI, "Deconstructing The Demand for Prostitution:Preliminary Insights From Interviews With Chicago Men Who Purchase Sex," *SA Promise*, 2012, http://www.sapromise.org/pdfs/deconstructing.pdf.

[391] Stephanie M. Berger, "NO END IN SIGHT: WHY THE 'END DEMAND' MOVEMENT IS THE WRONG FOCUS FOR EFFORTS TO ELIMINATE HUMAN TRAFFICKING," *Harvard Journal of Law & Gender.* 35, no. 2 (Summer 2012): 523–570.

[392] Ruth Villatoro, *La Cantinera* (Toro Films, 2012).

[393] Briski and Kauffman, *Born into Brothels.*

[394] Bales, Trodd, and Williamson, *Modern Slavery.*

e. Legalizing prostitution does nothing to protect the 'black market victims' who are children and sex slaves. In fact it makes them more difficult to find.
f. The Swedish model works best.[395] BUT....
Look at Swedish law - Swedish law on rape is also different and Swedish thinking – does one size fit all? Do Swedes think about women in a fundamentally different way than English or U.S, Arab, Japanese men?
g. Legalization makes victims easier to spot
h. Johns, not prostitutes, should be criminalized and the penalties should be increased for using a prostitute; others say this will drive the business underground and make it more dangerous for the prostitutes
i. Internet sites which offer 'adult services and massages' should be illegal. Others say that the demise of the adult services section of "Craig's List" just increased demand on other sites and these sites offers the Police the opportunity to find victims of trafficking.
j. Some say all prostitution is rape.

A recent report from ABT Associates looks at the effect of efforts to reduce demand for prostitution and sex slaves.[396] As has been seen where a child is a Minor they cannot consent to sex and so cannot be a prostitute.

An example

In RE: B.W. No. 08-1044 -- June 18, 2010

Earlier in the text the dissenting argument in this case was considered. In this case the Supreme Court of Texas considered the case of a mentally retarded young girl of thirteen years of age. She had been caught by an undercover police officer making money from offering sexual services on the streets. It turned out that she had a pimp with whom she was living; he was thirty one years old and she believed he was her boyfriend and she was making money for them as a 'couple'. The Police arrested her and, as she said she was nineteen, she appeared before an adult court charged with prostitution. At that hearing, charges were dismissed because of her age and then she was sent to juvenile court and charges were re-filed under the Family Code, which governs juvenile proceedings. (Tex. Fam.Code §§ 51.02(2), .04(a)) At this point she began the long road to justice which would take a couple of years. A state psychologist who examined BW was able to consider her problems which were listed as follows:

---

395 "Swedish Prostitution Law Attracts World Interest," *USA Today*, March 16, 2008, http://www.usatoday.com/news/world/2008-03-16-sweden-prostitution_N.htm.

396 Michael Shively et al., "A National Overview of Prostitution and Sex Trafficking Demand Reduction Efforts," *ABT Associates*, July 7, 2012, http://www.abtassociates.com/CMSPages/GetFile.aspx?guid=16b0e4c0-e5fe-46d9-9f0d-9aa29a880f1d.

a. history of sexual and physical abuse

b. untreated substance abuse and her report that she had been living, and having sex, with her thirty-two-year-old "boyfriend" for the last year and a half.

The psychologist reported "that B.W. was 'emotionally impoverished, discouraged and dependent.' However, the psychologist was also concerned about inconsistencies between probation reports for B.W. and her personal account. Whatever the truth, there seems little doubt that facing the identified issues set out above this 13 year old was in need of help.

When the matter came to trial, B.W. entered a plea of "true" to the charge that she had "knowingly agree[d] to engage in sexual conduct for a fee." The court found that she had engaged in delinquent conduct (Class B misdemeanor offense of prostitution : section 43.02 of the Penal Code). B.W. was sentenced to eighteen months of probation. The trial court refused to allow B.W. to have a new trial but allowed her to appeal. The Court of Appeals affirmed the lower court but the Supreme Court allowed the application for review of the judgment that she was delinquent because of the prostitution offence.

In the dissenting opinion of the Court it was argued that "the language of the prostitution statute includes thirteen-year-olds, and the Juvenile Justice Code makes them subject to juvenile delinquency proceedings for committing that offense" but the majority of the Court found that, as a matter of law, a thirteen year old should be considered a victim and not a criminal. It is interesting to note that the overarching Federal Trafficking Victims Protection Act (TVPA), as amended, provides that any child (defined as under eighteen) who is arrested or apprehended in a commercial sex act is legally defined as having been trafficked. A commercial sex act requires a payment to pass between user and slave.[397]

However, many nations have different ages at which a child can consent to sex and so where that age of consent is sixteen years, there is a tension between the CRC which states that a child is a child until eighteen and the child's ability to make an adult decision about his/her sexual behavior, perhaps a decision to enter into prostitution. In the United States of America, President Bush became involved in the debate about prostitution and human trafficking. In his National Security Presidential Directive 22, the issue of sex trafficking and prostitution were conflated:

> "Prostitution and related activities, which are inherently harmful and dehumanizing, contribute to the phenomenon of trafficking in persons, as does sex tourism, which is an estimated $1 billion per year business worldwide. The

[397] In Re: B.W. (Supreme Court of Texas 2010).

exposure of trafficked people to abuse, deprivation and disease, including HIV, is unconscionable."

This preamble was cited in the proposal of the End Demand for Sex Trafficking Act of 2005 (passed January 2006) and sponsored by Senator Cornyn of Texas and Representative Pryce of Ohio. The passing of this act was accompanied by much debate and controversy and review of the "Prostitution Debate" A short portion of the letters written to Congress about the Act can be read or the full congressional record is, of course available.

In 2010, Senator Cornyn addressed the issue of domestic child slavery again.[398] Together with Senator Ron Wyden (D-Ore.) he sponsored the Domestic Minor Sex Trafficking Deterrence and Victims Support Act, S. 596.[399] It passed the Senate on 9 December 2010. In the House it was HR 5575. The evidence given and submitted to the Subcommittee on Crime, Terrorism, and Homeland Security of the Committee on the Judiciary of the House of Representatives and given September 15, 2010, can be found on the web. The object of the Act was to set up a six-state pilot project to help law enforcement agencies to target pimps and traffickers whilst also creating shelters and programs to help the girls and boys caught up in the crime. Also, victims would have access to legal assistance.

During the briefing for the Bill, on March 16, 2011, a typical story was told by a former victim. Natasha Herzig told of how a woman in her late twenties had approached her when she was nineteen years old. Natasha was offered a job as a make-up artist. Sensibly she went to the head office of the company in San Francisco and met people there, including those who seemed to be learning the make-up trade. Her parents were suspicious, but Natasha thought that the job with good money and travel seemed what she wanted and the office had 'checked out'. On her first day she felt something was wrong and went to her car, there she was grabbed by the bosses and forced into prostitution. One of the coercive ways used by her pimp was to take her to the school which her younger brother attended and threaten to kill him if she stepped out of line. The make-up business was a front for a sex slavery ring.

Despite this evidence and the support of leading anti-trafficking voices, Representatives were unable to agree over mandatory sentences for possession of child pornography. They were paralyzed between their desire to help children and their ideological issues with mandatory sentencing. Sadly for the children, the latter won and the Bill received only forty votes which meant it could not pass on to the next stage. For further reading and the different perspectives look at the Coalition against Trafficking in Women, Project Protection, Equality Now and Planned Parenthood Federation of

---

[398] John Cornyn, *Domestic Minor Sex Trafficking Deterrence and Victims Support Act*, 2010, http://www.govtrack.us/congress/bills/112/s596/text.

[399] "Shared Hope International, Polaris Project, ECPAT Briefing Note," *Shared Hope International*, 2012, http://www.sharedhope.org/Portals/0/Documents/S596Summary.pdf.

America.[400] As was seen with the problems in the House about mandatory sentencing, a further aspect of this debate is that it is politically charged. When the politics of feminism, religion, liberalism, republicanism, abortion and contraception are introduced, some activists fear that that the debate about prostitution takes away focus and resources from trafficking.

The USA and Germany are the largest importers of slaves for sex. In an attempt to stem the tide, Germany legalized prostitution in 2002. The Trafficking In Persons (TIP) report from the State Department and the UN report that it remains a very high destination country for trafficked women. President G.W. Bush signed the original TVPA and President Obama's office has kept up the work on awareness and attempts to eradicate human trafficking. A list of, what the state department calls, 'accomplishments' is featured on the website of the US Department of State.[401]

---

[400] Megan Annitto, "Consent, Coercion, and Compassion: Emerging Legal Responses to the Commercial Sexual Exploitation of Minors," *Yale Law and Policy*, accessed April 12, 2012, http://yalelawandpolicy.org/sites/default/files/Annitto_30.pdf.

[401] Office To Monitor and Combat Trafficking in Persons, *Obama Administration Accomplishments on Combating Trafficking in Persons as of February 2012*.

Chapter 10

Sex Slavery

***"my family is just one of millions across the globe that were forged by sugar and slavery."*[402]**

> *"95% of victims experienced physical or sexual violence during trafficking (based on data from selected European countries)*
>
> *43% of victims are used for forced commercial sexual exploitation, of whom 98 per cent are women and girls*
>
> *32% of victims are used for forced economic exploitation, of whom 56 per cent are women and girls*
>
> *Many trafficking victims have at least middle-level education"*[403]
>
> *"Nobody wakes up and thinks: 'Gosh, I'd really like to sell myself today'." We have seen an increase in human trafficking in comparison with other illegal trades due to the 're-usability' of humans; she puts it like this: "where you only can sell a drug one time, you can sell a girl, or a boy, or a man or a women over and over and over again."*[404]

Whenever the words sex slavery are mentioned, images of women and girls come to the minds of most people. However, there is also a trade in boys for sexual purposes throughout the world. Boys are traded across borders and within nations. With the obvious exceptions of unwanted pregnancy, forced abortion, miscarriage and stillbirth, their sufferings are the same as the women and girls in this horrific trade.

An example:

In Afghanistan a practice outlawed by the Taliban has crept back into the commonplace and become accepted. It is the old Mujahidin practice of Bacha Bazi. During the time of the Russian war with the Mujahidin, commanders would take boys with them to war. The boys were their sexual companions and commanders obtained kudos from other commanders for the beauty and dancing ability of their "boy". It has been suggested that the rise to power of the Taliban was in part fueled by public

---

[402] Andrea Stuart, *Sugar in the Blood.* (Knopf/Jan, 2013).

[403] UNGIFT, "Human Trafficking - The Facts."

[404] *Truckers Against Trafficking Training Video*. Krista Melton, Assistant Criminal District Attorney in the Family Justice and Victim Protection Unit

anger against this practice. The penalty for sodomy under Islamic law is death and during the Taliban era, executions did take place. Now pre-pubescent boys are taken as Bachas and discarded when they develop manly traits, such as beards and the older man (owner) will find another young boy. The term owner is correctly descriptive of this practice where boys are seen as the property of the older man. These boys are traded with the particularly "beautiful" being extremely sought after and fetching in the tens of thousands of dollars. Unfortunately, the boys are generally from poor backgrounds and do not choose this work. They can be used for prostitution and for dancing at male-only parties.

Children are groomed for this role by their owners from an early age. A twenty two year old farmer interviewed by the Washington Post spoke about the nine year old he was grooming:

"'He is more handsome than anyone in the village,' …There was another important factor that made Waheed easy to take on as a bacha bazi, or a boy for pleasure: 'He doesn't have a father, so there is no one to stop this.'"[405]

An outstanding documentary about the abuse of these young boys was made by Frontline in 2010.[406]

In 2006 and onwards Canadian troops started to report this crime to their commanders. They were also concerned to find that the crime was prevalent amongst the soldiers and Police of the Afghan forces. They were told to ignore the crime.[407]

Wikileaks revealed unrest in the US government about the alleged practice of some employees of Dyncorp in the Kunduz region of using "Dancing Boys" for entertainment.[408]

Sex Slavery – Girls and Women

***"My bounty is as boundless as the sea, My love as deep; the more I give to thee, The more I have, for both are infinite."*[409]**

[405] Ernesto Londoño, "Afghanistan Sees Rise in 'dancing Boys' Exploitation," *The Washington Post*, August 10, 2012, sec. World, http://www.washingtonpost.com/world/asia_pacific/afganistans-dancing-boys-are-invisible-victims/2012/04/04/gIQAyreSwS_story.html.

[406] Najibullah Quraishi, "The Dancing Boys of Afghanistan," *PBS Frontline*, April 20, 2010, http://www.pbs.org/wgbh/pages/frontline/dancingboys/.

[407] Rick Westhead, "Don't Look , Don't Tell, Troops Told," *The Toronto Star*, June 16, 2008, http://www.thestar.com/news/2008/06/16/dont_look_dont_tell_troops_told.html.

[408] "US Embassy Cables: Afghan Government Asks US to Quash 'Dancing Boys' Scandal," *The Guardian*, December 2, 2010, http://www.theguardian.com/world/us-embassy-cables-documents/213720.

Love, romance, lust and greed. It is a sad fact that these four feelings are often intertwined to fuel the business of sex slavery. Women, in particular, but also some men, mistake lust and greed for love and romance. In the Western world, perhaps this is the fault of art, literature and history. Since Shakespeare started writing about young men and women who defied societal conventions for the sake of love we have seen this most powerful of adolescent emotions become the focus of female attention. Jane Austen told the world that "It is a truth universally acknowledged, that a single man in possession of a good fortune must be in want of a wife" and ever since, women have been thrilled by the marriage of the, 'unsuitable', Elizabeth Bennett to Mr. Darcy.[410] It is a marriage against societal conventions and against all odds. Nineteenth century readers had Thomas Hardy to follow in the "romance and love will win genre". Indeed, despite the terrible life and death of Tess of the D'Urbervilles, it was her love for Angel which shone above all else.[411] Even the destructive effect of the relationship of Heathcliff and Cathy on almost every other character in the book has been hailed as a huge love story.[412] Today young people are exposed to the notion that love is all and to be prized above family and society; see Bella in the Twilight series.[413] In the obverse, just as love and romance help sex slavery to thrive in the western world, for young people living outside the Western world the notion of compliance with societal norms is stronger and it is this which enables sex slavery to exist there. For some the cross-over between Western notions of love and non-western concepts of familial duty is fatal. Adulterous behavior is a stoning offence in Islamic societies, honor killings, mutilations and acid attacks can be seen where women are believed to have stepped outside the norms of behavior required by their society. But at the same time sexual slavery exists.

What are the guises of sexual slavery?

a. American teenagers labeled Prostitutes
b. American adults labeled Prostitutes
c. Islamic temporary marriage
d. Women and children in the porn industry
e. Sale of girls and boys into sex slavery

Enslavement of Americans:

Slavery in the United States of America was abolished in 1865. We know that there are foreign-born victims in the sex slave trade but fewer people are aware of the number of American children who are involved in what the media calls child prostitution, here it will be given its correct label as child sex slavery. As has been seen it is estimated that there are some three hundred thousand American children working as sex slaves.[414] The U.S. State

[409] William Shakespeare, *Romeo & Juliet* (Waxkeep Publishing, 2013).
[410] Jane Austen, *Pride and Prejudice*, 1 edition (CreateSpace Independent Publishing Platform, 2013).
[411] Thomas Hardy, *Tess of the d'Urbervilles* (CreateSpace Independent Publishing Platform, 2013).
[412] Emily Brontë, *Wuthering Heights* (Acheron Press, 2012).
[413] Stephenie Meyer, *Twilight* (New York: Little, Brown and Co., 2008).
[414] "Stop Child Trafficking Now."

Department puts a lower figure on the business; one hundred and fifty thousand. This is still a huge number. The majority of Human Trafficking cases in the United States are runaway and throwaway youth from the United States. The average age of introduction into trafficking for these children is twelve to thirteen years old. Where do they come from? Sadly, most have been in the child protective system or, missed being in it but have been abused in some way in their parental homes. They are intensely vulnerable as this statistic shows : one out of three runaways are picked up within forty eight hours of running away and lured into sex trafficking. There are abiding questions to ask here –

- How can they be lured into sex trafficking, don't they know that it is dangerous and wrong?
- Why don't they go to the authorities when they are tired, homeless and hungry?
- Why do they believe the people who they meet at bus stations across the country who offer them homes, jobs and food?

The answers are not hard to find. These children have often had disturbed childhoods without affection. They are hungry, scared and homeless. A person who offers them kindness, food and a bed for the night is seen as a rescuer. They want to be loved and cared for, they have been exposed to 'love stories' all their lives and they want it for themselves.[415] Love is a strong emotion, and one that they have often not felt themselves, or towards them[416]. The need for love is one that permeates all human beings, and one that stems from our earliest memories, when we lived in a society of small tribes, and depended on each other for protection. Therefore, when approached by someone offering even the smallest amount of affection, they are willing participants, until they realize the trap into which they have strayed. As for authority figures, they do not see them as a source which can be trusted, to help or to even listen. Often these children will have been in trouble with the police before, stemming from their homelessness, trouble at home, or hunger. They feel they are much less likely to be listened too, due to prejudice because of earlier transgressions.

A recent survey in the UK by Friends of the Elderly found that for every age group, including the eighteen to twenty four year old group, a lasting marriage was their principal aspiration.[417] This ranked above money and career success.

Perhaps it is not just women who buy into the idea of love but it is them who are most hurt and most exploited by it in the realm of sex slavery. Equally, the traffickers who supply and use the women and girls undoubtedly subscribe to the money first goal. But they are excellent at using the notions of love and romance to ensnare the women and girls

[415] Kristian Bryant Rose, "Looking for Love in All the Wrong Places: A Call to Reform State Law on Sex Trafficking.," *Oklahoma Law Review* 65, no. 2 (Winter 2013): 303–350.

[416] This is also seen in other countries – for example, see the autobiography of Somaly Mam

[417] Nigel Bunyan, "Young Spurn Wealth for Family Values," *Telegraph.co.uk*, May 28, 2012, sec. mother-tongue, http://www.telegraph.co.uk/women/mother-tongue/9293572/Young-spurn-wealth-for-family-values.html.

and keep them ensnared. The list of girls who have been and will be exploited by their desire for love and romance is endless.[418]

Often people ask, "how much do you have to pay for a sex slave?" The answer varies with the type of deal. If the sex slave is purchased from a parent or from another trafficker the figure will depend upon a number of variables.

These are some possible prices:

Thailand (Chiang Mai or Bangkok) - $750

Cambodia - $150[419]

USA (New York) - $3000.00

USA (Los Angeles) - $7500.00

Nepal - $450

Eastern Europe - $4800.00

India - $700.00

Western Europe - $4800.00[420]

One of the variables is the extent of the need of parents and the way in which they feel about their child. Many parents will give their children to traffickers having been convinced that they will be taken to a good job which will give them a better future.[421] They do not realize that they are sentencing their child to the life of a slave; they believe they are doing their best. Some will sell their child for the cost of an appliance like a color TV, some need the money for medical bills and other necessities. Women are less valued in the home in many countries than men and, in some religions and cultures, it is accepted that a daughter is the father's to deal with as he thinks fit.

This is a direct continuation of the African historical slave trade when women and girl slaves also had the most difficult of times. As domestic slaves they were subject to the sexual desires of their masters and, on the Middle passage, to the sexual desires of slavers. If they fell pregnant most had to work until delivery and then, on many plantations, the babies would be handed off to older women to rear so that the young women could return to hard-work. Even when the fathers were freemen the babies were often not acknowledged. This can be seen in the Code of Hammurabi and the records of Thomas Jefferson to take but two famous examples. This attachment of lack of value to female

---

[418] Lauterbach, *Flesh*.

[419] Half the Sky Turning oppression into opportunity for women worldwide. N.D. Kristoff and S WuDunn. Knopf. New York. 2009

[420] Siddharth Kara, *Sex Trafficking: Inside the Business of Modern Slavery* (New York: Columbia University Press, 2009).

[421] See the case of Sandra Beardon

slaves continued in the Americas even after the slave trade was abolished. Although they were required to produce the next generation of slaves their value would not rise as high as that of, for example, a groom or carpenter. Perhaps it is no wonder that female slaves suffered so because women generally were, and in many places remain, second class citizens. For example, in the Justinian Code they were not even allowed 'power over their own children'.

> *"Women, also, cannot adopt; for they have not even their own children in their power; but, by the indulgence of the emperor, as a comfort for the loss of their own children, they are allowed to adopt."*[422]

As will be seen, such powerlessness continues today as does the care women will automatically give to their children, even those born from rape by slave-owners and 'customers'. Just as, Andrea Stuart's family grew out of the demand of one of her ancestors for sex with her great-great- great grandmother, so too are lives started and affected by the modern slave trade.[423] The film Born into Brothels follows the lives of children born to the 'prostitutes' of India.[424] In 2011, in Austin, Texas, a young woman was rescued from a slave brothel, she was pregnant with a 'customers' child.[425]

Today, women and girls end up in slavery for much the same reasons as their ancestral cousins:

a. poverty;
b. sexual abuse at home;
c. forced marriage;
d. kidnappings – Toledo girls;[426]
e. fake offers of jobs;
f. lack of education;
g. economic need;
h. 'love';
i. trickery.

But however they start in slavery:

> *"their experiences of slavery are equally varied, ranging from blackmail, social isolation, thefts of their passports, and forced drug addiction, to beatings, torture, mock executions, private and public rapes, starvation, forced marriages, abortions, depression, enslaver's threats to kill their families, and multiple re-sales between different slaveholders"*[427]

Equally, the health problems from which they suffer, with the notable exception of HIV/AIDS, would be familiar to those who came before. These include, but are not

---

[422] "Justinian Code."
[423] Stuart, *Sugar in the Blood.*
[424] Briski and Kauffman, *Born into Brothels.*
[425] Supra - Introduction
[426] *Truckers Against Trafficking Training Video.*
[427] Bales, Trodd, and Williamson, *Modern Slavery.*

limited to, HPV leading to cancer, forced abortion and the results of non-medical abortions, torn vaginas and anuses, sexually transmitted diseases, septicemia from unhygienic and often forced tattooing, malnutrition, depression, post-traumatic stress disorder, infertility, cystitis, hepatitis B or C, and drug and other substance addiction.[428]

Poverty

As is seen throughout this book, poverty is one of the major causes of modern-day slavery and, in turn, modern-day slavery causes poverty. When a black market flourishes communities are deprived of taxes on the goods circulating in the black market and the growth of lawful commerce is impeded. This also happens where unfair trade barriers exist. An example of this is the subsidy paid by the US government to cotton farmers. This allows US cotton to be sold cheaply on the international market forcing some farmers in Asia to compete through the use of slave labor.[429]

Sexual Abuse at Home

This creates a 'triple whammy' for girls and boys. First, they want to run from the abuse which leads many of them into the arms of traffickers and second, the abuse probably continued for months, even years before the child runs away.[430] Therefore, the children have been conditioned to accept the secrecy, abuse and domination. Finally, they pluck up courage to run away only to find themselves in another form of living hell and so they learn to accept both their helplessness and hopelessness.

Forced Marriage

Forced marriage occurs throughout the world, even in Western societies with large Asian populations. In the UK, the government is debating a law which will make the arrangement of a marriage against the will of one party a criminal offence.[431] See the following Chapter on child brides and forced marriage.

Kidnappings

Around the world women and girls are kidnapped to serve as slaves. American citizens are always surprised that this applies equally to American girls who are kidnapped not just to feed the foreign desire for American slaves but also to feed the domestic sex market. The old notion of the 'white slave trade' is not fanciful. American girls find themselves enslaved in other countries, not least of which being Japan where blonde girls

---

[428] Alison Phinney, *Trafficking of Women and Children for Sexual Exploitation in the Americas" Alison Phinney* (Women, Health and Development Program Pan-American Health Organization, October 27, 2013), http://www.oas.org/en/cim/docs/Trafficking-Paper[EN].pdf.

[429] Pietra Rivoli, *The Travels of a T-Shirt in the Global Economy: An Economist Examines the Markets, Power, and Politics of World Trade* (Hoboken, N.J.: John Wiley, 2009).

[430] "Stop Child Trafficking Now."

[431] *Parliamentary Briefing Paper Sn 01003 - Forced Marriage (Civil Protection) Act 2007*, Parliamentary Briefing Paper, 2012, www.parliament.uk/briefing-papers/sn01003.pdf.

with blue eyes are especially sought after. The Japanese sex industry is worth some US$83 billion per year.

Example

In Bowling Green, Ohio, in January 2012, Darien McKinley was arrested, in Ohio, for trafficking two underage girls in his semi-trailer.[432] In April, 2013, he accepted a plea which led to him being incarcerated for three years. Interestingly, inmates from the prison in which he has been held volunteered to give eveidence of what he had said to him because they were so appalled by his behavior. They received no 'favor' for doing so. He accepted that he had kept the girls without food and otherwise abused them.[433]

Also, in Bowling Green, Ohio, in November 2013, Rose Marie Woolbright pled guilty to human trafficking and complicity in second-degree rape. She has sold her thirteen year old relative for sex. She has received twenty dollars and an additional five dollars for the thirteen 13year old. She was sentenced to eight and a half years in jail. Two men in the incident were sentenced to twenty years in jail.[434]

Example

In Toledo, USA, two young girls of fifteen and fourteen asked the mother of one of them if they could go to "Wendy's" in their town. As they were emerging from Wendy's they saw a Lincoln car pulling up. Before they could react, they had been pulled into the car and kidnapped. Their ordeal at the hands of traffickers who forced them into sex slavery is recounted by one of them in a video produced for training in the Trucking industry.[435] These girls were not introduced gently to the business of selling sex. They were beaten in front of one another and they were told that the other would be beaten if either did not cooperate[436]. They were locked up in a house in suburban Toledo and only allowed out to 'work'. Their work

---

[432] Tina Kaufmann, "Troopers Find Missing Kentucky Teen Girls, Charge Truck Driver with Kidnapping," *WEWS newsnet5*, October 29, 2013, http://www.newsnet5.com//dpp/news/local_news/troopers-find-missing-kentucky-teen-girls-charge-truck-driver-with-kidnapping.

[433] "Trucker Who Abducted Girls Gets Prison Term," accessed December 10, 2013, http://www.whio.com/news/news/crime-law/trucker-who-abducted-girls-gets-prison-term/nXKT2/.

[434] "BG Woman Pleads Guilty to Human Trafficking," *Bowling Green Daily News*, accessed December 10, 2013, http://www.bgdailynews.com/news/local/bg-woman-pleads-guilty-to-human-trafficking/article_fc0bd533-59e8-50eb-89e2-181171736218.html.

[435] *Truckers Against Trafficking Training Video.*

[436] Known as "seasoning" traffickers often use this beating and humiliation to break girls into the business of selling their bodies.

often consisted of being taken to truck stops where the traffickers made them offer their bodies to the truckers.[437] The psychological hold on the girls was such that they were unable to tell their 'customers' that they were not willingly offering their bodies for sex. Eventually, they were rescued because one trucker felt that what he saw, a group of young girls selling sex whilst being watched over by an adult, was not right. He called the Police and these girls returned to their lives. Of course, not without considerable help from professionals, family and friends.

In the film made of the Toldelo case for Truckers Against Trafficking one of the girls talks about her experiences and Evan Nicholas, FBI Supervisory Special Agent in the Crimes Against Children Unit comments that "the life expectancy of a child (after becoming) involved in prostitution is seven to nine years."[438]

Example

In December 2010 the body of twenty two year old Megan Waterman was found buried on Gilgo Beach, Long Island, New York. She was described in the press as a prostitute who had advertized escort services on Craigslist. Behind the bald facts of the case was a young mother doing what she had to in order to for her and her three year old daughter to survive. It is alleged that Megan only offered her body because if she refused her twenty year old boyfriend would beat her child. The money she earned was commandeered by her 'boyfriend' and relatives said she was unable to return home.

Megan's body, along with those of three other girls who had been selling sexual services on Craigslist, was found as part of a search for Shannon Gilbert. Shannon went missing after fleeing from a client's house near Oak Beach. She had been taken there by her driver Michael Pak. Why she left is not known. This was a simple house call for a girl who was selling her body and seemed no different to any other. Her pimp arranged the meeting through Craigslist and his driver took her there. Instead of returning to the driver, who was waiting for her, she ran. Not only did she run but also she called the Police for help. She was on the phone to the dispatcher for 23mins during which time she told them that "they are trying to kill me," also "there was also a struggle. You could hear her screaming" and then she disappeared.[439]

[437] Alicia Wilson, "Using Commercial Driver Licensing Authority to Combat Human Trafficking Related Crimes on America's Highways," *University of Memphs Law Review* 43, no. 4 (Summer 2013): 969–1012.
[438] *Truckers Against Trafficking Training Video*.
[439] *The Long Island Serial Killer*, CBS News, 2013, http://www.cbsnews.com/video/watch/?id=7392036n&tag=api.

However, during that time, she sought help from two residents who also called 911. One was Gus Colletti and the other was Mrs. Brennan. She asked both for help but seemed unable to be able to communicate with them properly above asking for help. Colletti notice a black SUV driven by an Asian man "coming a little bit and stopping". Whilst he was phoning 911, Shannon disappeared to hide under his boat and then seems to have fled on to Mrs. Brennan. Shannon's call for help to 911 was at 5.30pm, the Police arrived in the community, an exclusive area, at 6.20am by which time Shannon was long gone. Shannon's body was found December 2011. One of the identifying factors was the broken jaw she had received from her 'boyfriend', Alex Diaz, some years before which had to be mended with a metal plate.[440]

Essay: Dottie Laster believes that Megan and Shannon were human trafficking victims not voluntary prostitutes. Discuss.

Essay: Shannon Gilbert's family believe that the slow Police response to her 911 call was because she was identified as a prostitute. Is there any evidence of this being correct? Is there any evidence that calling a person a prostitute changes the way in which they are viewed by society?

How Are They Sold?

Escort Services.

As has been seen there are some escorts who are voluntary prostitutes and make very large sums of money. There are some escorts who live lives like Megan Waterman and Shannon Gilbert. Escort services can be found on the internet as well as by word of mouth and conventional advertising. It is portrayed as a world of parties and high life and may be an exciting inducement for girls who have nothing.

In 2011, it emerged that police in France were investigating the former head of the International Monetary Fund, Dominic Strauss-Kahn, on charges of allegedly supplying of prostitutes. When he was taken in for questioning his lawyer said that the sixty two year old had no idea the girls were prostitutes. "I challenge you to distinguish a naked prostitute from any other naked woman," Henri Leclerc told French television. In this case the police had already "arrested eight men on suspicion of organizing a prostitution ring and misusing corporate funds to pay for sex in a scandal known as the "Carlton affair" because

[440] Ibid.

of a Lille hotel where clients were allegedly supplied with call-girls."[441] On July 26, 2013, the New York Times reported that Mr. Strauss-Kahn would stand trial in Lille.[442] In France it is legal to consort with prostitutes but not to supply their services to others. The lavish parties and lifestyles described in books about escorts and film may be an indication of why girls think it would be ok to be an escort but find themselves in sex slavery which is a very different business. Indeed, from descriptions in the police report for the Judges in Lille there was little more than sex at these parties.[443]

Sexually Oriented Businesses and Massage Parlors

Strip Clubs, the euphemistically called Gentlemen's Clubs, lap-dancing clubs, massage parlors: these are all venues at which human trafficking victims ply their trade. Of course, as before, not all clubs have human trafficking victims working in them, but their existence helps to provide a cover for the illegitimate work of traffickers. Massage parlors can be legitimate, but again offer cover for those engaged in the illegal sex slave trade. Users of the website Rubmaps.com are invited to rate the sexual services offered by their masseuse and the cost. Many comment that the girl seemed to really enjoy the experience of having sex, or performing other sexual acts, with them. This adds to the complexity of whether the girl has a smile willingly or is coerced.

Cantinas and Bars

It is common to find women working against their will to encourage customer to drink, or pay for sex. Again it is difficult to tell the willing from the unwilling because of the consequences which befall the unwilling if they betray their feelings.[444]

An example

Mondragon case

In this case some one hundred and twenty girls were rescued; they were working in a cantina in Houston. The girls, who worked 6-7 days a week, had to encourage customers to buy them a certain amount of overpriced drinks (often beer) each night in exchange for their sexual favors or company. They had to produce the bottle tops from their beers or other proof of purchase at the end of the night to avoid being beaten. The women came from Central America, principally Honduras, El Salvador, Nicaragua and Guatemala. They were trafficked into the USA with the

---

[441] "Strauss-Kahn Held over 'Sex Ring,'" *BBC*, February 21, 2012, sec. Europe, http://www.bbc.co.uk/news/world-europe-17110618.

[442] Scott Sayare, "France Orders Strauss-Kahn to Stand Trial," *The New York Times*, July 26, 2013, sec. World / Europe, http://www.nytimes.com/2013/07/27/world/europe/trial-ordered-for-strauss-kahn-in-prostitution-case.html.

[443] "Dominique Strauss-Kahn Parties Were 'Sexual Carnage', Report Says," *TheAustralian*, October 27, 2013, http://www.theaustralian.com.au/news/world/dominique-strauss-kahn-parties-were-sexual-carnage-report-says/story-fnb64oi6-1226693324992.

[444] Villatoro, *La Cantinera*.

usual promise of good work. In the Cantina the chief of the trafficking ring, Mondragon, would force them to "pay off smuggling fees from eight to fifteen thousand U.S. dollars — as well as all living expenses".[445] Mondragon, who had been in the business for over a decade kept detailed notes of his business. These showed that he billed the victims for rent, clothes, transport, accommodation etc. Furthermore he kept detailed records of the backgrounds of the victims whose family he would threaten if they stepped out of line or to stop them trying to do so.

"Records show victims said he threatened to kill relatives or burn down family homes if they did not cooperate. "They were scared to death of him. ... They thought he was the devil," said Sgt. Michael Barnett of the Texas Alcoholic Beverage Commission's enforcement division in Houston."[446]

Sex Tourism

– see dedicated Chapter.

However, it is worth remembering that some foreign men come to the developed world for the purpose of using women and girls who are different from them. Human traffickers are ready to meet the need.

Via the Web

The Internet has increased the ways in which sex slaves can be sold and decreased the risks to the traffickers.[447] Again there are willing adults selling their bodies on internet websites such as:

- Backpage.com
- CityXguide.com
- Escortdater.com
- Adultsearch.com
- Localescortpages.com
- HushVIP.com
- Eccie.net
- Rubmaps.com

But they are also known to be used for the sale of human trafficking victims.

[445] "Crackdown on Houston Sex Ring Freed 120 Women," *Houston Chronicle*, October 27, 2013, http://www.chron.com/neighborhood/cyfair-news/article/Crackdown-on-Houston-sex-ring-freed-120-women-1790132.php#src=fb.
[446] Ibid.
[447] Herbert B. Dixon Jr, "Human Trafficking and the Internet (AND OTHER TECHNOLOGIES, TOO)," *Judge's Journal* 52, no. 1 (Winter 2013): 36–39.

Sex Slavery

Habbo Hotel (habbo.com) is a popular social networking site for teenagers. In June 2012, a Channel 4 documentary alleged the site was flooded with pornographic content.[448] The reporter, who posed as an eleven year old girl, described how she was immediately approached for cyber sex, known as cybering by boy cartoon characters who 'said' that they were feeling her 'boobs'. Additionally, they told her that they were following her into her bedroom and having sex with her. She had given no encouragement or permission for this behavior. The report explained how soon after the approaches turned into

> " ... *asking whether I would get naked on a webcam, or simply watch them masturbate. The requests were persistent and often forceful, making me feel pressured under the barrage.*[449]

Habbo Hotel is owned by Sulake, a Finnish company. The website has about ten million unique users a month. After this report they announced their intention to tighten security. One venture capital company withdrew its support following the allegations.

Other methods of selling sex slaves include:

- Flyers
- Marriage bureaus – see "Mail Order Brides"
- Social network sites
- Business cards – see "Introduction"
- Personal ads
- Brothels
- Truck stops – see supra
- Streets
- Strip clubs
- Lap dancing clubs
- Cantinas - see supra

> ESSAY - The mainstream media frequently features scenes set in strip and lap-dancing clubs, does this contribute to the plight of trafficking victims?

[448] Rachel Seifert, "Striptease and Cyber Sex: My Stay at Habbo Hotel," *4 News*, June 12, 2012, http://www.channel4.com/news/striptease-and-cyber-sex-my-stay-at-habbo-hotel.
[449] Ibid.

ESSAY – The Chief of Police in a seaside town, Newquay in Cornwall, UK opposed the opening of a lap-dancing club. He said that the club caused testosterone filled guys to commit crimes in the town, including an increase in rape which was outside the norm for the area. Discuss.[450]

An example - Sex slavery in Cambodia

"in a cage, with a snake"[451]

The quotation is taken from an interview which Somaly Mam gave to Tyra Banks in 2010. Somaly was describing her life as a teenage sex slave in Cambodia. Somaly Mam lost her mother when she was very young. At the age of about 10, she cannot be exact because she doesn't know when she was born, a man approached her and said he was her grandfather, he wanted to take her off the street. She believed him, or was desperate to believe him. Of course, it was a lie. After making her his domestic slave, he raped her. Later he introduced her to a man who became her husband. Her husband used and abused her most violently. When her husband disappeared, her 'Grandfather" reappeared and sold her on to a brothel. At this young age she was enslaved, expected to have sex with multiple partners without any choice and without any income. This is the fate of millions of women and children throughout S.E. Asia. The penalties for trying to run away vary around the world but usually include beatings, gang rapes and, in Somaly's brothel, being put in a cage with a snake.

It is well documented that sex slavery exists all over the world. In many cases it is fueled by poverty, but it can often be fueled by ignorance or cultural norms. Perhaps it is, or is becoming, a cultural norm for men in the United States of America to use prostitutes. Certainly the numbers of women and children trafficked into the USA for sex slavery are far higher per capita than, for example, those trafficked into the United Kingdom where agricultural slavery accounts for the greatest numbers.

These statistics show the number of men around the world who admit to using women they believed to be consenting prostitutes:

Europe

7% - Great Britain, (10% in 1990, 20% in 2000)

[450] "Lapdancing Clubs Encourage Rape and Sexual Assaults, Claims Police Chief," *Telegraph.co.uk*, May 23, 2012, sec. uknews, http://www.telegraph.co.uk/news/uknews/law-and-order/9284609/Lapdancing-clubs-encourage-rape-and-sexual-assaults-claims-police-chief.html.

[451] *Somaly Mam on the Tyra Banks Show (1 of 3)*, 2008.

10% - Russia

11% - Norway

13% - Finland, Sweden

14% - Netherlands

19% - Switzerland

39% - Spain

Asia

37% - Japan

73% - Thailand

USA

16% - At least once (ever)

.6% - Regularly

Norwegian Study (74 men who purchased sex acts)

10% < 3 times

50% 20-50 times

33 % > 50 times

U.S. Study

22 % 1-4 times

19% 5-10 times

14% 11-25 times

11% >100 times'"[452]

Thailand

Certainly it is a cultural norm for men in Thailand to use prostitutes, many of whom can be defined as sex slaves. The Thai girl is caught in a potent mix of traditional and modern attitudes to women and sex:

[452] Donna Hughes M., "Donna M. Hughes, PhD, January 17, 2007 Speech to Women in Federal Law Enforcement" (Powerpoint presentation presented at the Women in Federal Law Enforcement,, Washington, D.C, January 17, 2007), http://www.uri.edu/artsci/wms/hughes/reduce_demand.ppt.

- Culture
- Religion
- Prosperity
- The Western influence.

This section of the book is about the lives of girls and women enslaved in the sex trade in Thailand but the plight of boys and young men should not be forgotten. They, too, are enslaved in large number in Thailand, many for the gratification of sex tourists.[453]

Culture

In most Thai households a large picture of the King of Thailand will be displayed. The current King is monogamous but the traditions of his ancestors pervade Thai society. These traditions include the fact that the King kept 'minor wives'. It became a sign of wealth for men to keep minor wives as well as their first wife. Those who could not afford a minor wife used prostitutes. Thus, the use of prostitutes by men in Thailand became accepted by society, even by the wives. It was better for a wife if her husband used a prostitute because she would not be brought into the home nor produce children for which the family budget would have to be stretched.[454] Of course, with the massive spread of HIV/AIDS through the sex business in Thailand this is not such a good option for wives anymore but, it has become a cultural norm. As can be seen, seventy three percent of Thai men regularly use prostitutes. Indeed, it is culturally normal for sex with prostitutes to form part of a business deal and or be part of a night out drinking with the boys.

Religion

In Thailand, two factors combine to help enslave young women in Prostitution. The first is the fact that a woman cannot reach Nirvana and so her duty is to suffer patiently whatever life throws at her so that in her next life she may take a step up and become a man. The second is that Thai girls owe an overriding duty to their family. Thus, whatever the family wants her to do, a Thai girl must do, even if that includes sex slavery to help her family to pay the bills.[455]

Prosperity

The economic boom in Thailand increased the demand for the services of sex workers. This was not only from the increase in tourists to the area but also amongst Thai men. Those who could not afford Thai girls, who generally cost more for the traffickers to buy and whose services are sold at a higher cost, will have to content themselves with the use of cheaper girls. These girls come from different countries and, due to their ethnicity, do not command such a high price. Slavery is just as much at the mercy of the market

---

[453] See "Sex Tourism"

[454] Bales, *Disposable People, New Slavery in the Global Economy.*

[455] Ibid.

forces of supply and demand as any other business. As the demand went up traffickers had to find a supply of women to fulfill it.

The Western Influence

Thai business took on the western model. The natural resources of the country were rigorously exploited, forests were destroyed and the environment harmed. Along the way big profits were made, but for those laboring in the new industries health and safety was often disregarded. The girls of the sex slave are part of that expendable profit driven society. Bales says "Thailand is a country sick with an addiction to slavery…The situation is similar to that of the United States in the 1850s – with a significant part of the economy dependent on slavery, religion and culture are ready to explain why this is all for the best".[456]

Trafficking From Eastern Europe into the UK

Example:

During June and July 2012 the jury, at Isleworth Crown Court, heard a case of rape and trafficking which took place at the former home of the notorious serial killers, Fred and Rosemary West.[457] It was alleged that 36 year old Eddezider Herak 'seasoned' a twenty two year old Czech girl who had been trafficked into the UK. Whilst she was trying to sleep he raped her, repeating the rape a few days later. The victim was then repeatedly raped by another man, Magezi Clague, also involved in the trafficking ring. Then, his mother sold her to another man for one thousand G.B. pounds. Herak and his mother forced the victim into prostitution for which they received the money and the victim received food and cigarettes. This 'introduction' into sex slavery is all too familiar and both Herak and Clague faced other charges of rape committed against other girls. Additionally, this trafficking gang of seven people, male and female, was charged with conspiring to traffic women into the United Kingdom for sexual exploitation and for forced sham marriages. All defendants -Teodor Hunka, Zdeno Ssarissky, Herak, Ludmila Nistorova and Iveta Viragova admitted to forcing trafficked women into marrying foreign nationals and received sentences of imprisonment. Nistorova and Viragova received sentences of nine and eleven years respectively. The victims reported came from areas of Bosnia with high unemployment. [458]

---

[456] Ibid.

[457] R v Eddezider Herak and others (Isleworth Crown Court 2012).

[458] Clare Speak, "Czech Trafficking Gang Sentenced in London," *The Prague Post*, July 24, 2013, http://www.praguepost.com/opinion/16779-czech-trafficking-gang-sentenced-in-london.html.

Essay: Pimps and Pop Culture - 2006 "It's Hard Out Here for a Pimp" won the Academy Award. Consider the effect of the 'pimp culture' on the lives of sex trafficking victims.

1,000.-

Chapter 11

Slavery - Sex Tourism

When thinking about child sex tourism, or sex tourism generally, images of western men flying to sex tourism destinations in south eastern Asian and Central America come to mind. However, it is prevalent around the world, with people participating in sex tourism within their own countries or crossing borders to neighboring countries. Just as sex slavery occurs in Europe and the United States, so does sex tourism, particularly in areas where tourists normally visit, such as Las Vegas and Barcelona.

Definitions:

child sex tourism - travel to a place for the purpose of having commercial sex with a person under the age of 18. The Convention on the Rights of the Child protects children against this form of trafficking specifically in Articles 19, 34, 35, and 36.[459] There is also an Optional Protocol to the CRC on the sale of children, child prostitution and child pornography. Article 10 requires that signatories:

"*... take all necessary steps to strengthen international cooperation by multilateral, regional and bilateral arrangements for the prevention, detection, investigation, prosecution and punishment of those responsible for acts involving the sale of children, child prostitution, child pornography and child sex tourism. States Parties shall also promote international cooperation and coordination between their authorities, national and international non-governmental organisations and international organisations.*"[460]

Sex tourism - travel to a place for the purpose of having commercial sex with an adult

This is a case of trafficking were the victim does not move. Like the other transnational crimes, the growth of sex tourism reflects our increasingly globalized world and the economic disparities between rich and poor nations. Whereas, in the past, strong countries took advantage of weak countries; now strong individuals are able to take advantage of weak individuals around the world. No longer are people tied to their own locality where they are known and social inhibitors might prevent them from sexually abusing children. Equally, in a domestic setting there is a greater possibility of arrest and conviction than in many sex tourism destinations.

These are the countries in which sex tourism flourishes:

- Costa Rica
- Mexico

---

[459] Post

[460] UN, "Convention on the Rights of the Child."

- Columbia
- Kenya
- Nigeria
- Ghana
- Morocco
- The Gambia
- Cameroon
- South Africa
- Thailand
- Philippines
- India
- Indonesia
- Cambodia
- Brazil
- Dominican republic
- Romania
- Moldova

Sex tourism thrives where the combination of police corruption, poverty, urbanism, weak laws, Internet access, and easy travel exist.

Example

Costa Rica

The gangs "own" the people living in the slums which abut San Jose. At the weekends they load up buses with women and girls of the ages they wish to sell that weekend. These victims have no say in the matter because they fear reprisals. The women are taken to San Jose, some will be sent onto boats in the harbor 'to party' with tourists, others will be sent to high end hotels at which traffickers have rented whole floors for the 'parties'. When the 'partying' is over the girls are usually loaded up into the van but sometimes left to find their own way home. In one such case, victims found themselves re-victimized by police when they tried to get help to go home.[461]

In 2003, the USA moved to stop its citizens going abroad and committing sex crimes against children with impunity. The Protect Act of 2003 allows a US citizen to be prosecuted in the USA for child sex tourism abroad.[462] In the UK, the Sexual Offences

[461] Brooke Burns, "Sex Tourism in Costa Rica" (presented at the Human Trafficking Workshop, St. Edwards University, Austin, Texas, November 2010).

[462] "Protect Act - Fact Sheet" (US Department of Justice, April 30, 2003), http://www.justice.gov/opa/pr/2003/April/03_ag_266.htm.

Act 2003 allows prosecution of its citizens for sexual offences committed abroad.[463] Of course, implementation differs from country to country:

> *'While over thirty countries have implemented such extra-terrestrial laws, the requirements, effectiveness, and level of enforcement of such laws vary greatly. For example, in terms of enforcement, Japan has yet to prosecute anyone under its extraterritorial law,48 whereas the United States has charged at least twenty U.S. citizens under its most recent ET law. Canada recently convicted its first Canadian citizen under its revised criminal codes granting extraterritorial jurisdiction. In addition, ET laws also vary in their scope and requirements. The crimes for which nationals can be charged, as well as the age of protection vary from country to country.'*[464]

Thailand's Health System Research Institute reports that children in prostitution make up forty percent of sex worker in Thailand.[465] Chris Rodgers reported on BBC World about the growth of the child sex tourism industry in Brazil.

> *'Pia first started working as a prostitute at the age of seven, and UNICEF estimates there are 250,000 child prostitutes like her in Brazil. "I've been doing it for so long now, I don't even think about the dangers", Pia tells me. "Foreign guys just show up here. I've been with lots of them. They just show up like you."*[466]

Research shows that children involved in child sex tourism are between twelve and eighteen but the victims are often under twelve and can be as young three.[467] There is anecdotal evidence of babies being abused.

The perpetrators are categorized as

- **Situational** - these people will travel to another country and take the opportunity of sex with a child if it arises. They are usually on short holidays.
- **Preferential** – these people travel just to have sex with children, some will move to live in countries which offer this opportunity. Increasingly the preferential pattern is being seen with offenders posing as teachers, aid workers and in other positions which bring them into contact with children of the right age to abuse.

---

[463] "Sexual Offences Act 2003," Text, October 27, 2013, http://www.legislation.gov.uk/ukpga/2003/42/contents.

[464] Naomi Svensson L., "Extraterritorial Accountability: An Assessment of the Effectiveness of Child Sex Tourism Laws," *L.A. Int'l & Comp. L. Rev* 28, Loyola of Los Angeles International and Comparative Law Review (2006): 641.

[465] "About Health Systems Research Institute - Thailand," *Health Systems Research Institute*, accessed November 6, 2013, http://www.hsri.or.th/en.

[466] "Brazil's Sex Tourism Boom," *BBC*, July 30, 2010, sec. World, http://www.bbc.co.uk/news/world-10764371.

[467] Brittany Bacon, "Lost Innocence: Inside Child Sex Tourism," *ABC News*, July 17, 2007, http://abcnews.go.com/TheLaw/story?id=3385318&page=1.

Perpetrators are known to have a preferred age for the child against whom they will offend, and sixty one percent of the people caught were men looking for sex with boys; but they may just be more vulnerable to being caught because they have to make direct approaches.[468]

Women are traveling to West Africa and elsewhere to have sex with young males. The difference between female and male perpetrators is in the age of the victims, women choose older children.[469] On May 18, 2012, "Paradise: Love", the first part of a trilogy by director Ulrich Seidl premiered at the Cannes Film Festival. It explores the subject of sex tourism by rich, European white women.[470]

In 2004, a Code of Conduct for the protection of children from sexual commercial exploitation in travel and tourism was signed as a partnership of IGOs, NGOs and the travel industry. The object is to try to eradicate child sex tourism by raising awareness amongst tourists and those working in the tourism industry. In association with ECPAT, Air France shows anti child sex tourism videos on their flights.[471]

---

[468] Protection Project, *International Child Sex Tourism, Scope of the Problem and Comaparative Studies* (John Hopkins University, 2007), http://www.ecpat.nl/images/13/166.pdf.

[469] Anne Look, "Senegal Draws Tourists with Sun, Sea and Sex," *Global Post*, October 7, 2010, http://www.globalpost.com/dispatch/senegal/100428/senegal-news-sex-tourism.

[470] Ulrich Seidl, *Paradise: Love* (Ulrich Seidl Film Produktion GmbH, 2012).

[471] ECPAT, "ECPAT - Home," *ECPAT*, accessed November 6, 2013, http://www.ecpat.net/.

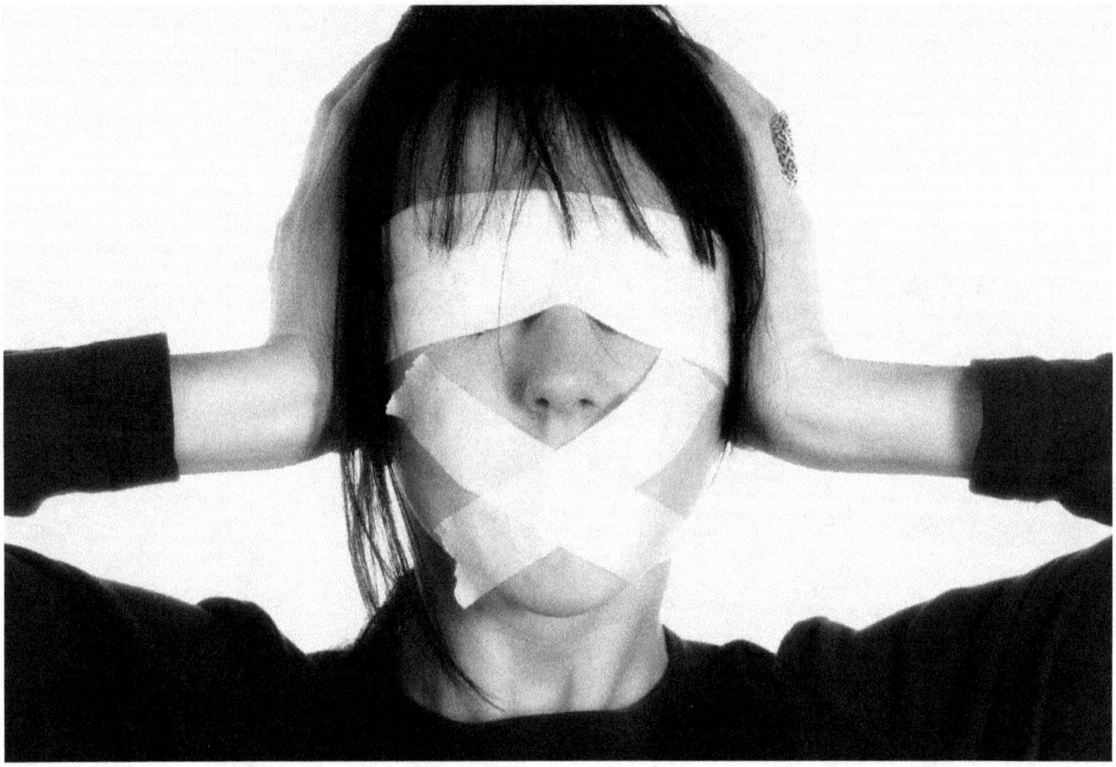

Chapter 12

Mail Order, Forced Marriage and Child Brides

"I knew my life is in danger and it will be over. I can read from his eyes."[472]

Mail Order Brides

A mail order bride comes to a Western country to be the wife of a Western man.[473] She is not a slave but may suffer abuse, intimidation and a lack of sexual self-determination common to slaves. The situation for mail order brides was deemed to be so bad in the USA that in 2004 International Marriage Broker Regulation Act 2005 (Subtitle D of Title VIII (Sec.831-834) of United States Public Law 109-162) was passed. This Act puts in place certain requirements for background checks before marriage visas can be issued. The law came into force partly because of the deaths of two foreign born wives of American citizens Susana Blackwell and Anastasia King.[474]

The presence of this law does not deter multiple internet mail order bride agencies from advertising. These women who advertise (or who are advertised) come from such diverse places as Russia, Asia and South America. The victim whose testimony is quoted at the top of this chapter came from Ethiopia. Mail order brides become the victims of human trafficking if they meet the criteria of the law against human trafficking which exists in the country into which they are married. For example, a woman brought into Great Britain as a mail order bride would be considered a trafficking victim if her circumstances breaches the Sexual Offences Act 2003.[475] Increasingly men from ethnic communities settled in the west are looking to 'order' brides from their home countries. Whilst the majority are simply traditional arranged marriages some can be more akin to the most abusive mail order marriage.

---

[472] *Evidence of a Victim to HEARING BEFORE THE SUBCOMMITTEE ON EAST ASIAN AND PACIFIC AFFAIRS* (Washington D.C., 2004), http://www.gpo.gov/fdsys/pkg/CHRG-108shrg96804/html/CHRG-108shrg96804.htm.

[473] Ryiah Lilith, "Buying a Wife but Saving a Child: A Deconstruction of Popular Rhetoric and Legal Analysis of Mail-Order Brides and Intercountry Adoptions," *Buffalo Women's Law Journal* 9 (October 10, 2000): 225.

[474] *Evidence of a Victim to HEARING BEFORE THE SUBCOMMITTEE ON EAST ASIAN AND PACIFIC AFFAIRS.*

[475] "Sexual Offences Act 2003."

Forced Marriage

Forced marriage is as a breach of the rights of the participants and can reduce the female participant to the status of a slave. The International Center for Research on Women claims that child marriages "undermine the achievement of each of the eight Millennium Development Goals and global targets to reduce poverty worldwide."[476] The United Nations Development Program adds that if child marriage were eliminated, countries could further the millennium development goals more swiftly.[477] As will be seen, child marriage brings with it a potent cocktail of abuse, slavery, termination of education (which, in turn prevents women from educating their children) and lack education in basic healthcare, such as the use of malaria nets, to help keep their children alive, possibility of premature death, orphans (from the mother's death in or after childbirth), HIV/AIDS and other sexually transmitted diseases (young wives often have no control over their reproductive health or use of condoms). There are links between female education and maternal mortality rates "female literacy rate and combined enrollment in educational programs are moderate predictors of maternal mortality rates".[478] Dead mothers are a predictor of poor outcomes for their children, many of whom die before five and those who live are vulnerable to slavery, abuse, living on the street and early death.

In some Western societies there has been a large scale immigration of people from Indian and Pakistan. Great Britain is a good example. Here we can see the tensions contained in the Universal Declaration of Human Rights and CEDAW. Both India and Pakistan are former colonies of the UK and members of the "Commonwealth". Until 1981 citizens of those countries were also citizens of the UK and many were encouraged to immigrate into the UK. It is common for large populations of immigrants to live in the same area for safely, kinship, religious, and other reasons. In the UK large populations of British-born Asians can be found. Here, then, are the tensions which now exist:

a. It is estimated that some eight thousand women in the UK, predominantly from Indian and Pakistani backgrounds, are forced into unwanted marriages each year.
b. Girls who do not want to enter into such marriages risk being beaten and worse by their families.[479] Also, they may ostracized by their community.[480]
c. Girls are commonly taken to India and Pakistan and forced into marriages, which have been arranged by their families, with unknown husbands.

---

[476] "Child Marriage," *INRW - International Center for Research on Women*, October 27, 2013, http://www.icrw.org/what-we-do/adolescents/child-marriage.

[477] "The Millennium Development Goals - Eight Goals for 2015" (United Nations Development Program, October 27, 2013), http://www.undp.org/content/undp/en/home/mdgoverview/.

[478] Chryssa McAlister and Thomas F. Baskett, "Female Education and Maternal Mortality: a Worldwide Survey," *Journal of Obstetrics and Gynecology* 28, no. 11 (November 2006): 983.

[479] "Shafilea Ahmed's Parents Found Guilty of Her Murder," *Channel 4 News*, August 3, 2012, http://www.channel4.com/news/shafilea-ahmeds-parents-found-guilty-of-her-murder.

[480] Jasvinder Sanghera, *Shame* (London: Hodder & Stoughton, 2007).

d. The girls have rights under Article 16 of UDHR to marry whomsoever they wish.
e. The girls have rights under Article 16 of CEDAW
f. The girls' parents have a right, under Article 18 UDHR to practice, freely, their religion and culture.
g. A child has the right to be protected from harm by its parents. CRC

So, who should have the right to decide upon a husband for the British Asian girl?

a. If she is under eighteen years of age, the parents because she is their child and children are supposed to do as their parents say. Under English law a child of "sufficient age and understanding" can apply to the Court to defy their parents, but they have to be aware of this right to exercise it.[481] If they apply then the English Court must weigh the "best interests" of the child. The cultural rights of the parents could be ignored in such circumstances.
b. The Forced Marriage (Civil Protection) Act 2007 is a civil law which allows women threatened with forced marriage to apply for an injunction to stop it occurring. Again the woman must be aware of her legal rights to exercise them. As only ten such orders have been made since 2008 it would seem that not many are aware. Again the making of a civil order breaches the culturally protected rights of the parents, and they would say of their daughter who should not be allowed to make her own decisions in the case of marriage.
c. Additionally, a British citizen is protected by the Human Rights Act 1998. This Act enables a woman to choose her own husband. Again, it could be argued that the cultural and religious rights of the parents are violated.[482]

These issues have been much debated by the British-Asian community and the general population of Britain in a government consultation document and the subject of legislation.[483] Some one thousand seven hundred people a year are reported as coming forward to voice concerns about being forced into arranged marriages by their families.[484] Critics of legislation have argued that "Victims will not be encouraged to report with the additional pressure that by reporting, their families will end up facing a prison sentence."[485]

---

[481] United Kingdom, "Children Act 1989."
[482] David Hodson, "CONSENT TO MARRY UNDER ENGLISH LAW," 6/10, http://www.davidhodson.com/assets/documents/consent_to_marry.pdf.
[483] *FORCED MARRIAGE – A CONSULTATION; SUMMARY OF RESPONSES* (UK Home Office, 6/12), https://www.gov.uk/government/uploads/system/uploads/attachment_data/file/157837/forced-marriage-response.pdf.
[484] John Bingham, "Forced Marriage Expected to Become a Crime," *Telegraph.co.uk*, June 7, 2012, sec. politics, http://www.telegraph.co.uk/news/politics/9315181/Forced-marriage-expected-to-become-a-crime.html.
[485] Deborah Kitson, "Marriage Reform, Comments from the Ann Craft Trust," *Family Law Week*, accessed November 4, 2013, http://www.familylawweek.co.uk/site.aspx?i=ed98339.

Of course, law does not cure a cultural problem, if this is acknowledged to be a "problem" at all. David Cameron, the UK Prime Minister, has said that people who had previously accepted forced marriage as a "cultural practice" could expect to face 'very very tough' sentences.[486] Clearly, he does not think that cultural practices which actually harm the human rights of one section of the community at the expense of another should be allowed. Whether a change in the law will force the practice underground will have to be seen. To ensure that the law is effective, young men and women have to be taught about the law. In many areas, children attend schools which represent their ethnicity and/or religion. How much room will the new law be given in such schools? Nevertheless, it can be posited that changes in the law do eventually change attitudes, for example, changes in segregation laws in the USA.

Forced marriages occur across the globe and the women and girls involved often suffer more violations than just not being able to choose their husband. Take, for example, the plight of Alisha.[487] Alisha was subjected to a forced marriage (aged 18) in Afghanistan. Alisha was used by her parents in payment of a debt under the old system of "Baad". She was enslaved in her husband's house. There she was expected to work long hours and was never allowed out or to have her own money. She couldn't complain to anyone. In her society religious rules required that she could not go out without the express permission of her husband or accompanied by a male family member. She was repeatedly beaten by her husband and his family and raped by him. Aged eighteen, she was finally so unhappy and desperate that she ran away to her parents. Her husband's family went to the village elders. Alisha, not the in-laws who had tortured her, was put on trial. For her crime of running away the following sentence was pronounced. Her husband should cut off her nose and her brother-in-law should cut off her ears. Sentence having been passed these appalling injuries were inflicted on her by the very people who had brutalized her in the first place. Fortunately, Alisha was able to get help from coalition forces stationed nearby. She did not bleed to death and has now had reconstructive surgery in the USA. When cultural practices exist which enable enslavement it is very hard to abolish slavery. Alisha's position in the family would not be viewed as enslavement, simply as the way of life for a wife in a small Afghan village.[488]

This case shows the tensions between the UDHR, which was, essentially, written by western powers following thoughts about human rights espoused in Europe, particularly in revolutionary France during the 18th century and the way others think. A tradition which goes hand in hand with some traditional practices which victimize women is honor killing.[489] Women who are seen to have done something outside the setting in which they are placed religiously can, and should, be killed or dishonored by the men in their family, or

[486] "England Moves to Ban Forced Marriages," *The Express Tribune*, August 6, 2012, http://tribune.com.pk/story/390976/england-moves-to-ban-forced-marriages/.

[487] Aryn Baker, "Afghan Women and the Return of the Taliban," *Time*, August 9, 2010.

[488] Andrew Anthony, "Afghanistan's Propaganda War Takes a New Twist," *The Guardian*, December 5, 2010, http://www.theguardian.com/world/2010/dec/05/bibi-aisha-afghanistan-disfigured-taliban.

[489] Mohammad Mazher Idreiss and Tahir Abbas, eds., *Honour, Violence, Women and Islam* (Abingdon: Routledge, 2010).

in the family which has been dishonored. Alisha had dishonored her husband by running away. A woman who is raped will be deemed to have dishonored her family and will often be offered the opportunity to kill herself (honor suicide) or be killed by a male relative. Acid attacks and other disfiguring of women can be used as 'honor punishment' and 'punishment rapes' are common in some societies.[490] In 2013, the Bernardo Kohler Center rescued a young woman who was living in an abusive marriage in the U.S. She had travelled to the U.S. to be the bride of someone her family had selected for her. When she left her father booked a flight to the U.S. with a view to avenging the dishonor she had done to his family by leaving her abusive husband.[491]

In Afghanistan the 2004 Constitution allows women the same rights as men, however, as Faranos Nazir, a thirty four year old woman in Kabul, stated "because of the Taliban, Afghanistan has become a jail for women. We haven't got any human rights. We haven't the right to go outside, to go to work, to look after our children."[492] Traditionalists do not believe in girls having education, and the result of that can be seen in the acid attacks on young girls as they go to school.[493] A list of things women are banned from doing or are punished for doing in Taliban society is set out below for consideration:

1. Complete ban on women's work outside the home, which also applies to female teachers, engineers and most professionals. Only a few female doctors and nurses are allowed to work in some hospitals in Kabul.
2. Complete ban on women's activities outside the home unless accompanied by a *mahram* (close male relative such as a father, brother or husband).
3. Ban on women dealing with male shopkeepers.
4. Ban on women being treated by male doctors.
5. Ban on women studying at schools, universities or any other educational institution. (Taliban have converted girls' schools into religious seminaries.)
6. Requirement that women wear a long veil (Burqa), which covers them from head to toe.
7. Whipping, beating and verbal abuse of women not clothed in accordance with Taliban rules, or of women unaccompanied by a mahram.
8. Whipping of women in public for having non-covered ankles.
9. Public stoning of women accused of having sex outside marriage. (This is not limited to Afghanistan: a number of lovers have stoned to death under this rule, for example "On 10 July 2012, Judge Imad Shamoun of Al-Nasir Criminal Court in Khartoum sentenced a twenty three year old woman to

---

[490] Niaz Muhammad et al., "Honor Killing in Pakistan: An Islamic Perspective.," *Asian Social Science* 8, no. 10 (August 2012): 180–195.
[491] Author interview with staff of the Bernado Kohler Center, 2013
[492] U.S. State Department, *Quotes By and About Women in Afghanistan, Report on the Taliban's War Against Women* (Bureau of Democracy, Human Rights and Labor, November 17, 2001), http://www.state.gov/j/drl/rls/6186.htm.
[493] Ibid.

death by stoning for adultery (Zina) under Article 146 of the Sudanese Penal Code 1991").[494]

10. Ban on the use of cosmetics. (Many women with painted nails have had fingers cut off).
11. Ban on women talking or shaking hands with non-*mahram* males.
12. Ban on women laughing loudly. (No stranger should hear a woman's voice).
13. Ban on women wearing high heel shoes, which would produce sound while walking. (A man must not hear a woman's footsteps.)
14. Ban on women riding in a taxi without a mahram.
15. Ban on women's presence in radio, television or public gatherings of any kind.
16. Ban on women playing sports or entering a sport center or club.
17. Ban on women riding bicycles or motorcycles, even with their *mahrams.*
18. Ban on women's wearing brightly colored clothes. In Taliban terms, these are "sexually attracting colors."
19. Ban on women gathering for festive occasions such as the Eids, or for any recreational purpose.
20. Ban on women washing clothes next to rivers or in a public place.
21. Modification of all place names including the word "women." For example, "women's garden" has been renamed "spring garden".
22. Ban on women appearing on the balconies of their apartments or houses.
23. Compulsory painting of all windows, so women can not be seen from outside their homes.
24. Ban on male tailors taking women's measurements or sewing women's clothes.
25. Ban on female public baths.
26. Ban on males and females traveling on the same bus. Public buses have now been designated "males only" (or "females only").
27. Ban on flared (wide) pant-legs, even under a burqa.
28. Ban on the photographing or filming of women.
29. Ban on women's pictures printed in newspapers and books, or hung on the walls of houses and shops.[495]

The Taliban are banned in Afghanistan but the Western powers are talking to them as part of the exit strategy and they have never been cleared out of remote parts of the country, such as Alisha's village. Nor too, do men have to be member of the Taliban to believe in a subservient role for women. Of course this portrays only one side of the Islamic tradition towards women.[496] The Prophet himself listened to advice from women

[494] "Sudanese Court Sentences Woman to Death By Stoning Over Adultery Claims," *Sudan Tribune*, July 15, 2012, http://allafrica.com/stories/201207160064.html.

[495] "Some of the Restrictions Imposed by Taliban on Women in Afghanistan" (Revolutionary Association of the Women of Afghanistan (RAWA), October 27, 2013), http://www.rawa.org/rules.htm.

[496] Myada Omar El-Sawi, "BEYOND THE 'TIERS' OF HUMAN TRAFFICKING VICTIMS: ISLAMIC LAW'S ABILITY TO PUSH THE MUSLIM WORLD TO THE TOP OF THE UNITED STATES TRAFFICKING TIER

and the adherents of the religion represent by many different aspects of the religion. Many scholars credit Fatima Al-Fihri, a Muslim woman, with the creation of the first University, Al-Qarawiyyin University, in 861CE. Jones-Pauly's book provides an interesting insight into the more liberal traditions of modern Islam.[497]

Child Marriage[498]

Under both the Universal Declaration of Human Rights and the Rights of the Child, child marriage is forbidden because it puts the, usually female, child at risk both physically and emotionally. In 1994, the UN Committee on the Convention on the Elimination of All Forms of Discrimination Against Women issued a nonbinding recommendation that countries put into effect a minimum age to marry of 18 for both sexes.

Article 16 of the U.N. Universal Declaration of Human Rights, *provides* –

> 1, "Men and women of full age, without any limitation due to race, nationality or religion, have the right to marry and to found a family. They are entitled to equal rights as to marriage, during marriage and at its dissolution,"
>
> 2, "Marriage shall be entered into only with the free and full consent of the intending spouses."

Domestic and international laws and treaties have attempted to address the issue without much success because, if the public refuses to accept them, enforcement is difficult. Child marriage can be found throughout the developing world, and in some developed nations. It continues through custom, culture, religion and sometimes as a result of economics. Some of the common reasons for child marriage are:

a. the importance of virginity of women,
b. women's inability to support themselves financially
c. women have a shorter biological reproductive life period.
d. women are valued only for what they can bring to a family by way of dowry
e. in some societies women can be used to pay off debts
f. women may be an economic burden to their birth family
g. the dowry which a husband pays for a bride belongs to the wife, but in the case of child brides, it is the property of the father of the bride because she is a minor. It is, therefore, possible to marry off a child bride years before having to pay the dowry which gives time to save up or obtain a dowry from the wife of one of your sons.

PLACEMENTS AND INTO COMPLIANCE WITH INTERNATIONAL LAW," *Georgia Journal of International & Comparative Law* 39, no. 2 (Winter 2011): 391–417.

[497] Christina Jones-Pauly, *Women under Islam: Gender, Justice and the Politics of Islamic Law* (London, U.K.: I.B. Tauris, 2011).

[498] *Ouagadougou Declaration on Child Marriages* (Ouagadougou: Forum on Marriage and the Rights of Women and Girls, October 2003), http://www.wluml.org/node/1211.

In many societies child marriage is simply a matter of custom which has grown out of balancing the books. If you have a son you need a wife for him. A wife for him will be more profitable for the family than keeping their daughter. The new wife will, in some cases, bring a dowry (even though it is outlawed in many countries). She will work in the family and will then have children who can also work. The daughter, however, is but one 'work unit'. After the thirty four day war with Israel in 2006 there were reports from Lebanon of an increase in "exchange marriages". This occurs "where a sister is given almost as a dowry in exchange for the sister of someone else."[499]

Child marriage is one of the things which has been measured by UNICEF as part of the Millennium Development Goals. Whilst there has been some impact in faster developing nations and amongst the middle class, poor women are still being forced into child marriages. Child marriage has a rightful place in a textbook about slavery because it involves the coercion of a girl into a marriage and a breach of her human rights. Even if it is through learned custom/religion, the child is often bought by the husband or his family, there is no escape from the marriage for the child and she loses her right to make alternative decisions for her adult life. A child bride loses her freedom, often, an education, friends and family and her childhood – a married women has no opportunity for play. Unfortunately, other abuses common to slavery occur in some child marriages with sexual abuse being the worst. UNICEF, categorizes this custom as "one of the most prevalent forms of sexual abuse and exploitation of girls."[500] According to UNICEF, worldwide, in 2010, thirty-six percent of women aged twenty to twenty four were married or in union before they reached eighteen years of age.

Child marriage can also be a death sentence for many girls. Just as sex slaves are forced to have sex without any control of their partner, so too are child brides. They do not chose when or how to have sex and thus, cannot choose whether to become pregnant. Like slaves, they are exposed to sexually transmitted disease and have no means of protecting themselves. Early pregnancy kills. Girls' bodies are not mature enough to safely deliver babies and young mothers die in huge numbers – it is estimated by UNICEF that fourteen million adolescents between fifteen and nineteen giving birth each year die - across the world simply because they are trying to have babies when they are children. One woman dies in child-birth every sixty seconds, girls of fifteen to nineteen years are twice as likely to die in childbirth than women in their twenties.[501] Sex with adult male partners can also kill. Take the case of Yemeni girl, Elham Assi.[502] She was just thirteen years old when her twenty three year old husband raped her, thereby rupturing her womb and causing her to bleed to death. This is not unusual in Yemen where "just under half of all girls…are

[499] "Child Marriages Make a Reappearance," *Beruit Online*, accessed November 2, 2013, http://beruit-online.net/portal/article.php?id=6058.

[500] "Child Protection Information Sheets - Child Marriage" (The Child Protection Section, UNICEF, May 2006), http://www.unicef.org/publications/files/Child_Protection_Information_Sheets.pdf.

[501] Ahmed Al-Haj, "Yemani Child Bride, 12, Dies in Labor," *CBS News*, September 13, 2009, http://www.cbsnews.com/2100-202_162-5307092.html.

[502] "Another Dead Child-Bride," *Nicholas D. Kristof Blog*, October 27, 2013, http://kristof.blogs.nytimes.com/2010/04/10/another-dead-child-bride/.

married before they are eighteen—classified as underage by the UN Convention on the Rights of the Child, to which Yemen is a signatory."[503]

In Yemen, despite the publicity surrounding the death of Elham Assi, and the actions of Nujood Ali, the ten year old Yemeni girl who went to court seeking a divorce from her husband, a man in his thirties, to whom she had been forced to marry, the practice continues as a representation of traditional Islamic faith.[504] The minimum age for marriage was set at seventeen prior to Yemen's unification in 1990, but after the north won, they established the age at fifteen; although, as has been seen, many children are married at much younger ages.[505] The Yemeni government did, in May 2010, raise the age of marriage for both sexes to seventeen but has not shown any political will to enforce the law.[506] In response, Sheikh Muhammed al-Hazmi, who had led the opposition movement to a change in the law setting a minimum age to marry, issued a fatwa warning against anyone supporting the "'anti-Islamic'" attempt to restrict marriage.[507]

The Islamic Sharia Codification Committee has considered the issue of child marriage and has refused to provide clarification by declaring an age for marriage.[508] Again, the tension between religious and cultural practices with the international law in the shape of the Convention on the Rights of the Child can be seen. The success of Nujood, despite the media attention surrounding it, should not be overestimated. There are only three recorded cases where child brides have successful divorced their husbands in Yemen. Sally, a ten year old girl, was forced to marry her twenty five year-old cousin; her case was successful against a backdrop of intense media interest.

In Afghanistan and Ethiopia girls, are often kidnapped and raped to ensure that their families will pay a dowry and consent to marriage.[509] A study from Tulane University looked at the mental health effects on child brides in Ethiopia finding a significant rise in suicidal thoughts amongst child brides.[510] In Iran, in 2012, the legal affairs committee ruled that nine years is the age when a girl reaches puberty and can marry. It asserted that to do otherwise would be un-Islamic and a challenge to the Prophet Muhammad, who married a

---

503 Hugh Macleod and Annasofie Flamand, "Sally's Story," *Al Jazeera*, October 27, 2013, http://www.aljazeera.com/photo_galleries/africa/2010831920332122.html.

504 Nujood Ali and Delphine Minoui, *I am Nujood, age 10 and divorced* (New York: Three Rivers Press, 2010).

505 Mohammad Jamjoom, "Vote on Child Marriage Law in Yemen Delayed," *CNN World*, October 4, 2010; Nadya Khalife, "Yemen Could Seize Moment to Ban Child Marriage," *Womens Enews*, December 16, 2011, http://womensenews.org/story/marriagedivorce/111215/yemen-could-seize-moment-ban-child-marriage#.Um1e5fnksXc.

506 The Media Line Staff, "New Yemen Marriage Law Needs Awareness Campaigns," *Yemen Post*, April 10, 2010, http://yemenpost.net/Detail123456789.aspx?ID=100&SubID=155&MainCat=10.

507 Macleod and Flamand, "Sally's Story."

508 Ibid.

509 Kristof and Wudunn, *Half the Sky*.

510 A.J. Gage, "Association of Child Marriage with Suicidal Thoughts and Attempts Among Adolescent Girls in Ethiopia," *The Journal Of Adolescent Health* 52, no. 5 (February 20, 2013): 654–6.

six year old and consummated the marriage when she was nine and would challenge Sharia Law.[511]

In India, the British government passed the Child Marriage Restraint Act as long ago as 1929. Nevertheless the tradition of child marriage (the girl will be the younger partner to the marriage) continues despite further legislation from the Indian government itself. In collaboration with the government of India, in 2007, UNICEF produced a "National Report on a World fit for Children" about the child bride issue.[512] Child marriage continues to be common amongst the rural poor. In 2006, the Prohibition of Child Marriage Act 2006 was passed to strengthen the law. However, the evils set out above which sustain child marriage persist in India and many other Asian countries. The Act regulates marriage making 18 the minimum legal age for women to marry and, for men twenty-one. The Act also sets out rules for punishing those who encourage child marriage:

> *when a man over 18 contracts a marriage with a child (under 18) he is liable to be punished by up to 2 years in prison or/and a fine of up to one lakh rupees*
>
> *Anyone who "performs, conducts, directs or abets" the marriage of a child is liable to be jailed for two years or/and a fine of one lakh rupees unless that person reasonably believed that the parties were not children.*
>
> *If there is a marriage of a child and the child's parent, guardian or anyone else who has lawful or unlawful care of the child who permits, negligently fails to prevent, or promotes the marriage is liable to a jail term of 2 years and/or a fine of up to one lakh rupees.*[513]

The Act also addresses issues relating to the children of these marriages. The Supreme Court of India felt that the 2006 Act did not go far enough and asked for the opinion of the Law Commission of India. They produced a report in 2007 offering suggestions to the Supreme Court and, in 2008, published the 205th report "Proposal to Amend the Prohibition of Child Marriage Act, 2006 and other allied Laws"[514] The Law Commission decided that the age of marriage should be eighteen for both sexes but that women were more vulnerable to early marriage than men. The Law Commission decided that the age for sexual consent should be sixteen for all young women.

As has been seen the passing of legislation is not a guarantee to successful change. The law must be enforced and the population made aware of it. The government seems to have been successful in some awareness raising because there was much media attention and Bollywood stars have joined in the work[515]. An example of what awareness raising can

---

[511] "Child Bride Practice Rising In Iran, Parliament Seeks To Lower Girl's Legal Marriage Age To 9," *International Business Times*, August 30, 2013.

[512] <http://www.unicef.org/worldfitforchildren/files/India_WFFC5_Report.pdf>

[513] "Prohibition of Child Marriage Act 2006" (The Gazette of India, January 11, 2007), http://wcd.nic.in/cma2006.pdf.

[514] *PROPOSAL TO AMEND THE PROHIBITION OF CHILD MARRIAGE ACT, 2006 AND OTHER ALLIED LAWS* (Law Commission of India, February 2008), http://lawcommissionofindia.nic.in/reports/report205.pdf.

[515] UNICEF < http://www.unicef.org/india/media_6408.htm>

achieve is the April 2012 annulment case brought by Laxmi Sargara. In "what is thought to be the first case of its kind"[516] Laxmi convinced the Court that her marriage, at aged one, to Rakesh, who was three, was unlawful even though her in-laws did not come to get her until she was legally able to marry at aged eighteen. However, as this article shows, change is slow.[517] According to UNICEF, child marriage remains on the increase amongst the very poor.[518]

In 2009, in Saudi Arabia, Judge Habib A. Al Habib was asked to allow a divorce.[519] Customary and religious rights needed to be balanced against Article 16 of the UN Universal Declaration of Human Rights. It is not reported whether the Judge considered the Declaration but it is unlikely because, as has been seen, Islamic countries have their own agreement on Human Rights.[520] Judge Habib ruled that the girl could file for divorce once she reached puberty. The Judgment has proved to be highly controversial. The applicant was an eight year old girl who was applying for a divorce from her husband who was in his late forties. Sentiment is split on the issue of child marriage in Saudi Arabia. The grand mufti supports the practice. The Prophet Muhammad married a nine year old girl and so that gives strict Muslims grounds to maintain the practice. More liberal thinkers, such as Amal Al Zahid contend that "allowing such crimes against childhood, we are incurring upon our own society…behavioral abnormalities and problems of which only Allah knows."[521] Again this shows the tensions between the CRC and religious practices. It has been seen that for children to bring issues to law they need to know of the law. In this case the girl knew of the law and had adult helpers but she was still unable to prevail.

Still other commentators on Sharia Law point to the fact that only where both parties consent to marriage is it legal.[522] Whereas it would be useful if this interpretation where to gain ground in Islamic countries, it is in those countries where forced and child marriages are particularly prevalent.

'In Lebanon, the phenomenon of early marriages is reappearing.'[523]

---

[516] Staff, "Indian Teenager Annuls Her Marriage," *BBC World News - India*, April 25, 2012, http://www.bbc.co.uk/news/world-asia-india-17838022.

[517] Kalpana Sharma, "The Other Half: When Children Marry," *The Hindu*, February 18, 2012, http://www.thehindu.com/opinion/columns/Kalpana_Sharma/article2906570.ece.

[518] UNICEF, *Executive Summary." The State of the World's Children 2011.*

[519] Caryle Murphy, "Child Marriage Case Showcases Deep Splits in Saudi Society," *Global Post*, May 30, 2010, http://www.globalpost.com/dispatch/saudi-arabia/090416/child-marriage-case-showcases-deep-splits-saudi-society.

[520] "Cairo Declaration on Human Rights in Islam."

[521] Murphy, "Child Marriage Case Showcases Deep Splits in Saudi Society."

[522] "Marriage: Rule 2379(v) of the Quran. 'The woman and the man should be willing to enter into a matrimonial alliance. If, however, the woman ostensibly displays hesitation while giving her consent, but it is known that in her heart, she is agreeable to the marriage, the marriage is in order.,'" *Al-Islam.org*, accessed November 3, 2013, http://www.al-islam.org/laws/marriage1.html#2421.

[523] Faten Sabah, "Child Marriages Make a Reappearance." at Development Action without Borders (Nabaa)

Of seventy seven women interviewed by Development Action without Borders seventy four percent said that family pressure had pushed them into early marriages and most 'expressed some regret.'"[524] Whilst Lebanon has signed up to the CRC, in some Muslim circles girls are being married at nine years old. It is the religious courts which govern marriage, divorce and other personal status issues. The early forced marriage issue also puts Lebanon in breach of its obligations under the Optional Protocol on the sale of children, child prostitution and child pornography to which it became a party in 2004.

The United States recognizes child marriage as a serious violation of human rights and, in 2009, Representative Betty McCollum (D-MN) introduced the International Protecting Girls by Preventing Child Marriage Act (H.R. 2103, S. 987). It was unanimously passed in the Senate but failed to pass in the House of Representatives the following year. It is interesting to consider why such a useful Act would not pass the House but, then both the 2012 re-authorization of the Violence Against Women Act and the TVPA were being hotly contested in the House, delaying necessary human rights legislation. The Act would have required the United States government to develop a strategy to prevent child marriage and would have provided aid, over a five year period, to support child marriage prevention programs in high incident countries.[525]

Many factors make it difficult to create change :

a. Traditional values
b. Religious values
c. Lack of documentation of the practice
d. Fear
e. Lack of law enforcement

When considering how change can be created it is worth looking at history where it has been shown that the imposition of Western values upon traditional societies does not work and many successful movements to re-shape cultural norms flourish because of local approval and 'buy-in'. The work done in the last century to bring an end to foot binding in China is a good example. In 1895, Mrs. Archibald Little, the wife of an English businessman, helped found the Natural Foot Society. A western resident in Shanghai she was appalled by the practice of foot-binding. She knew that her work was to stop the practice, but how? Seeing the success of the efforts of the Rev. John MacGowan who cooperated with Chinese women and Chinese scholars she followed his example and introduced local actors into the Society from the beginning before turning the society fully over to Chinese people in 1908. Some 300,000 Chinese people joined the Anti-Footbinding Society.[526]

---

[524] Ibid.

[525] "International Protecting Girls by Preventing Child Marriage Act of 2012 (2012H.R. 6087)," *GovTrack.us*, October 27, 2013, https://www.govtrack.us/congress/bills/112/hr6087.

[526] Kwame Anthony Appiah, "The Art of Social Change: Campaigns against Foot-Binding and Genital Mutilation.," *The New York Times*, October 22, 2010, sec. Magazine, http://www.nytimes.com/2010/10/24/magazine/24FOB-Footbinding-t.html.

Temporary Marriage

A focus on sexual promiscuity and the need to know the parentage of children underwrites many traditional customs which deny women rights or allow them to be abused. An example is the Shi'a practice of allowing a temporary marriage to take place so that sex can take place within a marriage.[527] There is a distinction seen between prostitution which is illegal in Islam and a temporary marriage. A temporary marriage should be concluded between the parties on mutually accepted terms and signed in front of a Mulla. Fathers of girls who fear that they may dishonor the family by engaging in sex outside marriage will agree a temporary marriage with a male friend of the family who can be trusted. Of course, this is forced marriage. The system is also designed to ensure that paternity of any child can be established, a woman must wait for forty five days between marriages but men may contract as many as they wish and as often as they wish. There is no divorce from a temporary marriage; it simply runs out on the terms agreed at the outset.[528] There are reports that this system is abused and is actually just a cover for prostitution where young women have inferior bargaining power and so they come out of the marriage with little or nothing, except maybe a mouth to feed. The reference is to the blog of an award winning Turkish journalist. There are substantial controls on Iranian speech and it is difficult to obtain verification.[529]

Religion and economics are drivers of these types of marriages which can also be seen in Bangladesh where, despite the Repression against Women and Children Act 2000, twenty percent of girls become wives before that age of fifteen.[530] In Bangladesh the NGO, Plan International, is trying a different approach to stop this form of slavery. They have recruited young men, like Oll Ahmed who is twelve-year-old, to work with other kids in his community to end child marriages. His group goes around his slum speaking to parents who may be considering an early marriage for their child to try to talk them out of the idea.[531] The program has been having good results and shows that there has been a reduction of child marriages where the program is in effect of up to fifty percent. Just as the work on foot-binding in China showed marked results from involving the community so too has this initiative. The International Center for research on Women has identified some ways to help in the fight against child marriage:

a. Giving girls information about alternatives to empower them
b. Giving girls skills and support networks

---

[527] Shahla Haeri, "Temporary Marriage and the State in Iran: An Islamic Discourse on Female Sexuality," *Social Research* 59, no. 1 (Spring 1992): 201–223.
[528] Ibid.
[529] RABİA ÖZDEN KAZAN, "Angels of Tehran," *Angels of Tehran*, accessed November 7, 2013, http://rabiaozdenkazan.blogspot.com/.
[530] "Child Marriages Blight Bangladesh," *BBC*, April 22, 2012, sec. Magazine, http://www.bbc.co.uk/news/magazine-17779413.
[531] Christine, "Case Example of Preventing Child Marriages in Bangladesh," *PACE International Law Review*, April 24, 2012, https://pilr.blogs.law.pace.edu/2012/04/24/case-example-of-preventing-child-marriages-in-bangladesh/.

c. Mobilizing parents and community members
d. Helping girls to go to school
e. Helping the girls and their families with economic resources
f. Having a good legal and policy framework in place

The most important of these have been raising awareness and proving skills and community networks for the girls. Lack of education for girls has been seen to impoverish communities which in turn causes forced and child marriage which starts the circle another time. However, again, change comes slowly and needs the support of the local officials.[532]

Female Genital Mutilation/Cutting[533]

The most common form of harmful cultural practice is female genital mutilation or cutting, with someone to one hundred and forty million girls and women affected worldwide. Traditionally the procedure is performed by excisors when the child is between four and twelve years of age. In some cases cutting takes place within a few days of birth and, in other cases, medical professionals will perform the procedure. This cutting is harmful on a number of levels:

a. Women die or suffer serious consequences from the procedure itself (In Sudan it is believed the one-third of women who have FGM die from the 'operation').[534]
b. "Long-Term Complications
   - Painful or blocked menses. In 1983,fifty five point four percent of women surveyed in Baydhaba, Somalia, reported abnormal menstruation.
   - Recurrent urinary tract infections. A 1983 study in the Sudan revealed that sixteen point four percent of women who had the operation experienced recurrent urinary tract infections.
   - Abscesses, dermoid cysts, and keloid scars(hardening of the scars).
   - Increased risk of maternal and child morbidity and mortality due to obstructed labor. Women who have undergone FGM are twice as likely to die during childbirth and are more likely to give birth to a stillborn child than other women. Obstructed labor can also cause brain damage to the infant and complications for the mother (including *fistula formation*, an abnormal opening between the vagina and the bladder or the vagina and the rectum, which can lead to incontinence). Among thirty three infibulated mothers followed at

[532] A. Erirajan, "Bangladesh Court Acts in Weekend Child Marriage Case," *BBC World News*, May 21, 2012, http://www.bbc.co.uk/news/world-asia-18152773.
[533] Fiona J. Green, "From Clitoridectomies to 'designer Vaginas': The Medical Construction of Heteronormative Female Bodies and Sexuality through Female Genital Cutting.," *Sexualities, Evolution & Gender.* 7, no. 2 (August 2005): 153–187.
[534] Laura Reymond, Asha Mohamud, and Nancy Ali, *Female Genital Mutilation – The Facts*, October 27, 2013, http://www.path.org/files/FGM-The-Facts.htm.

Somalia's Benadir Hospital in 1988, all required extensive episiotomies during childbirth. Their second-stage labor was five times longer than normal, five of their babies died, and twenty one suffered oxygen deprivation because of the long, obstructed labor.

- Infertility. In the Sudan, twenty to twenty five percent of female infertility has been linked to FGM complications.
- Some researchers describe the psychological effects of FGM as ranging from anxiety to severe depression and psychosomatic illnesses. Many children exhibit behavioral changes after FGM, but problems may not be evident until the child reaches adulthood. However, little research has been done on this subject.
- FGM is likely to increase the risk of HIV infection – often the same unsterilized instrument is used on several girls at a time, increasing the chance of spreading HIV or another communicable disease.

c. Loss or complete lack of sexual enjoyment. The 'operation destroys much or all of the vulval nerve endings and cuts, loss of skin elasticity, or development of neuroma (a tumor or mass growing from a nerve) can lead to painful intercourse. In a 1993 Sudanese study, five and a half percent of women interviewed experienced painful intercourse while nine point three percent of them reported having difficult or impossible penetration.
d. In a 2006 study by WHO, there was a link to the mutilation causing problems during childbirth and in some cases maternal deaths.[535]

There are twenty eight countries in Africa and just a few others in Asia and the Middle East that perform genital mutilation/cutting on woman and children as a cultural practice. The practice is found at all educational levels, in all social classes and in some religious groups. The frequency of these practices differs from country to country. In some areas of Somalia as many as ninety eight percent of women and girls have experienced FGM/C, but this is only one percent in Uganda.

Breast Ironing

In Cameroon at least thirty nine percent of women have undergone a much less commonly mentioned cultural practice: breast ironing also known as breast flattening. Indeed in the countries where it is practiced it is believed that one in four girls face the practice.[536] Those countries are:

a. Cameroon (all ethnic groups)
b. Chad
c. Benin

[535] "Female Genital Mutilation and Obstetric Outcome: WHO Collaborative Prospective Study in Six African Countries," *The Lancet* 367, no. 9525 (June 2006): 1835–1841, doi:10.1016/S0140-6736(06)68805-3.
[536] Staff, "Teenage Girls Undergo Breast Ironing in Cameroon," *Huffington Post*, July 23, 2010, http://www.huffingtonpost.com/2010/07/23/teenage-girls-undergo-bre_n_656965.html.

d. Ivory Coast
e. Togo
f. Kenya
g. Zimbabwe

In this traditional practice, which is believed to protect a woman from rape and early pregnancy, the immediately post-pubescent, girl will have her breast place on an, often, heated flat stone whilst another, usually a relative, pounds on the top of her breast with a hard club or stone. The practice, which is extremely painful, causes tissue damage, the formation of abscess, malformed breasts and may cause difficulty with breast feeding and depression.[537] RENATA is a non-profit working with girls in the Cameroon to help them understand the dangers of the practice as is the United Nations Populations Fund.[538]

Forced Marriage, Human Rights and International Criminal Law

The crime against humanity of forced marriage which was first articulated in the findings of the Appellate Court of Sierra Leone, and is a feature of the ongoing trials in the Extraordinary Chambers in the Courts of Cambodia.[539] In spite of the fact that it took until 2008 for forced marriage to be defined as a Crime against Humanity, as has been seen, the right to consent to marriage has been acknowledged as an international human right since 1948 and, in many countries, as a national right for longer.[540]

Historical Background - Marriage

The crime of forced marriage in, or arising from, war is well known, even among school students, but it is possible that most of them do not connect it with the common practice of forced marriage taking place around the world today, as custom or in war. An early historical account of forced marriage is found in the Rape of the Sabine Women. "It was in the fourth month after the founding of the city, as Fabius writes, that the rape of the Sabine women was perpetrated."[541] This story was memorialized in early writing of Fabius, Plutarch and Livy and immortalized in the paintings of Rubens and Poussin. The story continues with the heroic actions of Hersilia, daughter of Titus Tatius, leader of the Sabines, who was abducted and forced to become the wife of Romulus. In David's

[537] Rebecca Tapscott, "Understanding Breast 'Ironing' A Study of the Methods, Motivations, and Outcomes of Breast Flattening Practices in Cameroon.," *Feinstien International Center, Tufts University*, May 2012, hppt://sites.tufts.edu/Feinstein/2012/understanding-breast-ironing.

[538] Georgette TAKU ARREY, *Breast Ironing in Cameroon - Report under CEDAW and CRC*, UN Committee on CEDAW and CRC (U.N. Office of High Commissioner on Human Rights), accessed November 2, 2013, http://www.ohchr.org/Documents/HRBodies/CEDAW/HarmfulPractices/RENATA.pdf.

[539] M. E Hawkesworth, *Political Worlds of Women Activism, Advocacy, and Governance in the 21st Century* (Boulder, Colo.: Westview Press, 2012), http://site.ebrary.com/id/10542738.

[540] "The Universal Declarartion on Human Rights."

[541] Plutarch, John Dryden, and Arthur Hugh Clough, *Plutarch's Lives. the Dryden Translation, Edited with Preface by Arthur Hugh Clough□; Introduction by James Atlas. Volume I Volume I* (New York: Modern Library, 2001).

painting she is shown rushing between her husband and father to bring peace between the two tribes. The painting eloquently describes a continuing conundrum, that a woman should be glorified and protected but that rape and harm are by-products of war and male state-making. A key difference between this story and those of modern forced marriages is that, most often, today women suffer more. For them, there is little hope of recognition by her family, who may be dead or stigmatize her, or from her community. Nor is there help from her 'husband' or his family and community. This woman must bear her marriage alone and so must the children born from it. They do not grow to be soldiers and citizens of an Empire, their fate is less glorious.

Plutarch records that there are two stories which lie behind the rape of the Sabine women, which henceforth, will be defined in this paper in modern terms as the crime against humanity of forced marriage. The first is that the warlike Romulus "began unprovoked hostilities against the Sabines; for he did not take many maidens, but thirty only, since what he wanted was war rather than marriages."[542] However, Plutarch feels that the more likely reason was because his new city was a magnet for many unmarried men which was a recipe for problems. Romulus invited the Sabines to games and, upon his signal his followers "drew their swords, rushed in with shouts, and ravished away the daughters of the Sabines, but permitted and encouraged the men themselves to escape. Some say that only thirty maidens were seized, …but Valerius Antias puts the number at five hundred and twenty-seven, and Juba at six hundred and eighty-three, all maidens."[543] It is interesting that a marriage tradition exists today which comes from this forced marriage, "it continues to be a custom down to the present time that the bride shall not of herself cross the threshold into her new home, but be lifted up and carried in, because the Sabine women were carried in by force, and did not go in of their own accord."[544]

Whilst property was tied to marriage, even in advanced societies where slavery had been abolished women still had little choice about marriage. In the common law English system, prior to Hardwicke's Marriage Act 1753, marriages could be conducted in an irregular fashion, in that they didn't have to be recorded, or take place in a specific place or have any age for the participants. In this they were very similar to the ad hoc marriages created in Sierra Leone in the 1990s. The Act determined that marriages could not be performed unless the parties were aged fourteen (men) and twelve (women). Subsequently the age of marriage kept up with the age of consent, something which had not occurred in the past. Arranged marriages were common and the complex law around marriage settlements grew up to protect parties in such marriages; or at least the property in such marriages. In 1861, the Offences against the Person Act consolidated previous legislation on a range of sexual crimes against women and confirmed the age of consent for sex as twelve; this was increased to thirteen in 1875. By 1885, a press and public campaign lead to the passing of the Criminal Law Amendment Act which increased the age of consent to sixteen. In the colony of India, however, changes wrought by the British competed with the native demand for its customs to recognized. This led to a bizarre mismatch in

---

542 Ibid.
543 Ibid.
544 Ibid.

marriage law. A female could be married at ten but, by a change in the law in 1891, could not have lawful sexual intercourse until she was twelve.[545]

It was not until 1882 that married women were allowed to own, keep and dispose of their property after marriage in Britain.[546] In 1840, a court in Texas decided that "a married woman could make her own will, contract for family 'necessaries' (foods, clothing, and domestic supplies necessary in caring for a family), and exercise a veto power in the sale of her separate property or the family's homestead."[547] Additionally, the Texas law allowed a woman to enter into a martial contract and sue for divorce in her own right, together with being able to register a schedule of her own, separate, property.[548]

However, these burgeoning rights of women seem to have been forgotten in the negotiation of the Hague Convention in 1907 which was, on the whole, negotiated by men and paralyzed by the euphemisms which surrounded sexuality in the late 19th and early 20th centuries. Despite the ancestry of rape as a war crime in the Leiber Codes of 1863 the word itself disappeared from the language of the Hague Convention, 1907 - Article 46 states:

> "Family honour and rights, the lives of persons, and private property, as well as religious convictions and practice must be respected."

Similarly, when dealing with early human trafficking of women and girls the documents describes "the procuring of women or girls for immoral purposes."[549] International jurisprudence was slow to protect women who were often seen as 'the spoils of war' for a conquering army, perhaps the most notorious 20th century example being the behavior of the Red Army as it moved towards, and through, Germany. "Red Army soldiers don't believe in 'individual liaisons' with German women. Nine, ten, twelve men at a time – they rape them on a collective basis."[550] In fact, the Red army itself had a system akin to forced marriage. Stalin intervened to allow his soldiers to keep campaign wives, known as a "pokhodno-polevaya zhena'. These women were usually signalers clerks and medical orderlies, Musya Annenkova wrote of her 'husband', in the euphemisms of her day, "no sincere feelings, only short-lived passion or love with animal feelings."[551]

It can be seen from these examples that what was required was recognition of the crime against humanity of forced marriage. Placing the crime on record should reduce the

---

[545] *Indian Penal Code*, 1860.
[546] *Married Women's Property Act.*, 1882.
[547] Janet L Coryell, *Negotiating Boundaries of Southern Womanhood: Dealing with the Powers That Be* (Columbia, MO: University of Missouri Press, 2000).
[548] Ibid.
[549] *Art 1, International Agreement for the Suppression of the "White Slave Traffic" (entered into Force 07/18/1905)*, 1904.
[550] Antony Beevor, *Berlin the Downfall, 1945* (London: Viking, 2007), http://www.contentreserve.com/TitleInfo.asp?ID={B284B22D-FC2D-441E-A3E9-7C0ECF7A3E83}&Format=410. (from the diary of Zakhar Agranenko, 1945)
[551] Ibid. at 29

incidence because of the clear warning given to potential perpetrators. Crimes against women are more often than not exceptional for men.[552] However, as Beth Van Schaack says, "This line of cases reveals that so often, women's reality is not acknowledged until it is named."[553]

Naming the Crime against Humanity of Forced Marriage

Through the Geneva Protocols and the Special Tribunals of Rwanda and Yugoslavia it is possible to see the development of war crimes and crimes against humanity comprised by sexual violence. The Rome Statute of the International Criminal Court specifically prohibits forms of sexual violence both as war crimes and crimes against humanity (Articles 7 and 8). In the case of Prosecutor v. Brima, Kamara & Kanu the Appeals Chamber of the Special Court for Sierra Leone overturned the Trial Chamber's findings on forced marriage and declared "that no tribunal could reasonably have found that forced marriage was subsumed in the crime against humanity of sexual slavery. While forced marriage shares certain elements with sexual slavery such as non-consensual sex and deprivation of liberty, there are also distinguishing factors. First, forced marriage involves a perpetrator compelling a person by force or threat of force, through the words or conduct of the perpetrator or those associated with him, into a forced conjugal association with a another person resulting in great suffering, or serious physical or mental injury on the part of the victim. Second, unlike sexual slavery, forced marriage implies a relationship of exclusivity between the 'husband' and 'wife', which could lead to disciplinary consequences for breach of this exclusive arrangement. These distinctions imply that forced marriage is not predominantly a sexual crime."

In adding forced marriage as an "other inhumane act" the Court pointed out that a decision about whether an action can be elevated to the position of an "other inhumane act" must be made on a case by case basis. In making that decision the Court should consider, amongst other things the sex, health, age of the victim and the mental and physical effects of the alleged action upon the victim. The Court determined that interpretation should not be restrictive and, therefore, that the list of sexual crimes under Article 2.g did not preclude charging crimes with a sexual or gender issue within them under 'other inhumane acts'. This is interesting because it shows the willingness of the Appeal Chamber to elevate acceptance of gendered harms in war; a step forward for the female victims of way whose rights have so often been denied in the past. Thereby, the Appeals Chamber gave effect to most of the dissenting opinion of Trial Chamber Justice, Doherty, and "accurately recognized that the charge of sexual slavery alone fails to capture the full culpability of the accused and the total experience of the victim who finds herself

---

[552] Alexandra Stiglmayer, ed., *Rape, Genocide and Women's Human Rights (Catherine A. MacKinnon)*, Mass Rape: The War Against Women in Bosnia-Herzegovina (Omaha: University of Nebraska Press, 1994).

[553] Beth Van Schaack, "Introducing the Crime Against Humanity of Forced Marriage," *ASIL*, accessed November 2, 2013, http://www.asil.org/accountability/winter2009-10/winter2009-10_2.html.

trapped in a life not of her choosing, saddled with an irreversible conjugal status and innumerable 'conjugal duties'."[554]

Some questions arise from this judgment, most notably how forced marriage in war should be distinguished from the cultural practice of arranged marriage. In the Trial Chamber Justice Sebutinde made the distinction by refusing to find that the condition of the women amounted to any more than sexual slavery. The Defendant, Kanu, suggested, through his lawyers, that there was no difference.[555] As set out above, Justice Doherty, found in favor of creating the crime of forced marriage but against the defense put forward by Kanu.

Both the Trial Court and the Appeals Court received evidence from experts, Dr D. Thorsen for the Defense and from the Prosecution's expert, Zainab Bangura.[556] Ms Bangura argued that the difference between arranged or traditional marriage and forced marriage as a crime against humanity in this war was:

a. Lack of parental involvement, and thus protection for the 'wife'
b. No consent from the parents
c. No 'official' marriage

The important difference to be noted here is that the Trial Court was at pains to recognize that arranged marriage, accepted by many of the Judges as perhaps being created by coercion of the bride may be a breach of human rights under various human rights treaties but it is not a crime against humanity by virtue of being an 'other inhumane act'.[557] The Appeals Court, too, wished to draw a distinction whilst finding in favor of a crime of forced marriage in this war.[558]

---

[554] Ibid.

[555] Case 16: The Prosecutor vs. Brima, Kamara and Kanu (AFRC Case), accessed November 7, 2013.

[556] Since which time she has served as Sierra Leone Minister of Health and Sanitation and Foreign Minister in the government of President Ernest Bai Koroma of the All People's Congress Party. Since June 2012 she has acted as the United Nations Secretary-General's Special Representative on Sexual Violence in Conflict.

[557] Beth Van Schaack and Ronald Slye, *International Criminal Law and Its Enforcement: Cases and Materials* (New York, NY: Foundation Press: Thomson Reuters, 2010).

[558] Kirsty Champion et al., *Special Court for Sierra Leone - Forced* (Australian Red Cross, 2010), http://www.redcross.org.au/files/2010_Forced_Marriage_Sierra_Leone.pdf.

HELP
ME

Chapter 13

Street Children

In 2012, the Consortium for Street Children and the UN Committee for Human Rights identified street children as "children in and of the street". This gives a more comprehensive definition because it covers not only those children who live alone or in gangs of other children and have no home except the street but also those who work on the streets, for example begging, selling and providing services such as car screen washes and sex, and also children who live on an occasional basis with their families and those who live on the street with their families.

For many years it has been believed that there are an estimated one hundred to one hundred and twenty million street children in the world. However, in her report for the United Nations, Office of the High Commissioner on Human Rights, Sarah Thomas De Benitez suggested that this figure was an over-estimation.[559] Of course, just like slaves, children living on the street are difficult to count and their numbers change from day to day, indeed hour to hour if children who work on the streets but don't live on the streets are counted. Street children exist in every country but in some countries their numbers are growing rapidly, for example in China and India. This means that, because of lack of education and opportunity, there is a huge loss of structured labor amongst the nations which have large populations of street children. Even if the moral question about whether children should have to live on the street is ignored it could be said the world is wasting a vast supply of talent and these children are living out their, often, short lives, in poverty, fear and desperation.

Some of those are children are taken from the streets into a life of slavery. Street children are the most vulnerable population to the predations of traffickers. Be they runaways in the United States of America, or orphaned by AIDS in sub-Saharan Africa, or displaced by war, they are vulnerable because they want something better for themselves. This is coupled with a lack of understanding of the machinations of adults and, often, a need to be loved.[560] Additionally, as has been seen many children have not had their births registered and so are forced to live on the edge of society all of their, most often, short lives.[561]

---

[559] Sarah Thomas de Benítez and Consortium for Street Children, *State of the World's Street Children: Research* (London: Consortium for Street Children, 2011), http://www.streetchildren.org.uk/_uploads/publications/State_of_the_Worlds_Street_Children_Research_final_PDF_online.pdf.

[560] Somaly Mam and Ruth Marshall, *The Road of Lost Innocence* (New York: Spiegel & Grau, 2009).

[561] Bissell, "Children in Adversity."

Street Children Have Complex and Precarious Lives.

Example

In 2005, Zimbabwe launched 'operation Murambatsvina' (clean-up) of slum areas. This clean up was achieved by force and it is estimated that 223,000 children were left displaced and vulnerable.

The inability of children to access law is especially important where street children are concerned. They simply have no access to justice. They are too young to advocate for themselves and, without an adult protector, unable to access the system. Only through NGOs can street children be heard. Children who call the streets their home usually have disrupted relationships with their parents, just occasionally merely working on the streets and returning to an intact family. Usually they have lost contact with one or both parents and their extended family, or they have chosen to escape the extended family.

Example

A young man, we will call him William, was interviewed by the author in Cape Town in 2011. He said that his mother and father had left, he thought, to look for better work somewhere. He was left with his Aunt in the township of Langa on the outskirts of Cape Town. His aunt didn't like looking after him and he said he often had to sleep in the dog house. Desperate for education and love, he ran away to the streets. Fortunately for him he soon realized his mistake and turned himself into a Police station. At the Police station he pretended to be homeless and said he didn't have any family so that he would not be returned to his aunt. He was sent to a children's home and thanks to the care and love given to him was set to graduate high school and move on to technical school. Had he stayed on the streets his life would have been very different.[562]

Example

The life and near death of Judy Westwater , when she was living as a "Street Kid", is graphically told in her book of the same name.[563] In it she describes the problems of finding food, keeping clean and finding safe shelter from other children and adults who would have harmed her. In the harrowing account of being raped, we hear the story of countless young women who face this prospect on a daily basis. Perhaps it is little wonder that many street children come to believe they may as well sell their body to feed themselves than have someone

[562] Interview by author, Cape Town, 2011

[563] Judy Westwater and Wanda Carter, *Street Kid: One Child's Desperate Fight for Survival* ([Place of publication not identified]: Element, 2006).

rape them without payment. This form of prostitution may feed back into the Prostitution Debate.[564]

Example:

Perhaps the most outstanding example of street living children was found in Romania after the fall of its dictator, Nicolae Ceausescu in 1989. During the 1970-80s his communist regime required families to have at least five children and fined those who did not. Families were forced, by poverty, to give up some of these children and they were taken into the care of the Romanian state. In fact, this meant that they went into institutions where their care was minimal and abuse reigned. Some one hundred and seventy thousand children were in state care at the time of the fall of Ceausescu. Westerners who went into these orphanages were met by squalid scenes of under-stimulated children whose physical and mental health was damaged; for some totally beyond repair.[565] The children were living in military barracks and hunting lodges, some unfit for human habitation; indeed they lived anywhere that space could be found for these thousands of children who, it seemed nobody wanted to care for. Certainly none would have been able to fuel the economy in the way that Ceaucescu seemed to have hoped.

The children had little food or clothing and there was inadequate or no medical care available to them. The sharing of needles spread AIDS amongst these children, making Romania the worst affected country in Europe with some ten thousand children living in these orphanages infected.[566] When Bob Wylie visited in 1990, he found sixty three children sharing forty three beds. The potential, and actual, spread of disease in these conditions was huge. Even worse than the lack of heating and warm clothing for these children during winter, was the lack of nurturing which resulted in neglect and abuse. These children were seen to be head-banging and rocking from an early age. As Jack Shonkoff's studies with his team at Harvard show early deprivation will cause lifelong damage to the brain.[567] In 2000, filmmakers went to Bucharest to look at the problems for street children ten years on. What they found was that many were coping with the ordeal of having spent their early lives in care by self-medicating through illicit drugs. The film follows six children who live in a subway station.[568]

---

[564] supra

[565] "BBC Radio 4 - All in the Mind, Romanian Orphanage Babies: 21 Years On," *BBC*, October 29, 2013, http://www.bbc.co.uk/programmes/b015p62y.

[566] Bob Wylie, "In the Romanian 'Canyons of Horror,'" *BBC*, December 26, 2009, sec. Europe, http://news.bbc.co.uk/2/hi/europe/8428283.stm.

[567] "Dr. Jack Shonkoff on Brain Power: Why Early Learning Matters," *NBC Education Nation*, October 29, 2013, http://www.educationnation.com/index.cfm?objectid=E86C3CA6-E89A-11E0-B00E000C296BA163.

[568] Edet Belzberg, *Children Underground*, Documentary, 2003.

Chapter 14

How to Avoid Becoming a Victim of Human Trafficking

Don't Accept a Fake Offer of a Job

The Serious Organised Crimes Agency in the United Kingdom provided this advice:

> ***"How can I protect against the risk of becoming a victim of human trafficking?***
>
> *Any risk can be reduced by taking steps to ensure your own safety. Here are just a few pointers:*
>
> *If a job offer seems too good to be true, it probably is.*
>
> *Make your own independent enquiries about a company offering you a job. Don't rely on links or numbers which have been provided to you. These could be fraudulent sources set up by the traffickers.*
>
> *Make independent checks about local employment laws, pay scales, accommodation prices, transport etc. Don't rely only on what the people you are working for tell you.*
>
> *Check out the reputation of local authorities such as police forces or government offices. Traffickers often tell victims that the local police are corrupt or are likely to carry out worse abuse in order to create fear and control their victims more completely.*
>
> *Be aware that exploitation and control methods are often introduced very gradually. Keep asking yourself questions. Be alert to the use of relatively minor acts or events as leverage to threaten or justify more serious ones.*
>
> *Have a safety net. Leave details with family and have prearranged contact patterns and code words or phrases that can be given to family if you are under duress, without arousing suspicion if traffickers are listening.*
>
> *Stay alert to any use of threats, violence, gifts, declarations of love, or substances such as alcohol or drugs to get you to do something you don't want to do.*
>
> *If in doubt, bail out. If you suspect you are being, or are being prepared to be, trafficked get to a place of safety or raise the alarm as soon as is safely possible.*

> *In the UK, contact the local police. If this is not possible, use any of the other methods listed in this site. If you are not a UK national or language is a problem you may consider contacting your own police or embassy as another option."*

Of course, if a victim is in a desperate situation they may not have the leisure to analyze the job offer in this detail nor have any support network upon which they can rely. Where children are concerned their lack of judgment affects their ability to judge the offer multiples. Statistic produced by the Polaris Project in 2013 show that this form of recruitment is the third largest and tied to force and abduction.[569]

Seek Education and Look Before You Leap

Victims are more likely to be fooled when they have little or no education. Education empowers and also enhances the opportunity of a potential victim to obtain a job which is not, or is less, exploitative. However, even educated people can be duped. People who are, apparently, acting as a benefactors form the second largest method of recruitment.[570] Sandra Bearsden's story is relevant here.

Example

"A Lucrative Offer at the Mall"

…, young girls are unwittingly lured in to unwilling prostitution with promises of jobs, money, clothing and modeling.

That's what nineteen year old Miya said happened to her when she was working at a Phoenix mall selling sunglasses. Miya was working three jobs -- fourteen hours a day -- to pay off her bills and save for college.

One day when she was working, she was approached by a young woman and a well-dressed man. "He asked if it would be out of place if he said I was pretty," Miya said. "I was like, 'No.' I mean, it was a compliment."

The man was charming and had a flattering offer for Miya.

"He said that he was a model agent, [that] he was looking for new models in the area," she said. "It's not like something I've been wanting to do or anything, but, I mean, it was ... it seemed interesting."

Taken by the idea of modeling and making extra money, Miya agreed to meet the couple that night at a local restaurant.

"They said they were on their way to California to go back to their office and they were going to do some more photo shoots, and they wanted me to go along with them," Miya said. "He said that I could probably make about

569 "Big Data Stops Slavery," *Wired*, December 2013.

570 Ibid.

a thousand or more. ... He said I could try it for three days. ... And so I went with them."

The next morning Miya was thrilled when the couple took her to have her hair, makeup and nails done. At that point, she said she had no idea she was not being made over for a photo shoot but for a much more insidious reason. Later, when the couple began taking pictures, Miya said she became alarmed.

"They used just a cheap camera you can buy, the throwaway," she said. "And they said once we get to California that we would be at a photo shoot, and that they'd be using, uh, some really good equipment, they'd have makeup artists and stuff like that."

Miya said she didn't know what happened to those pictures until later, when she arrived in California with the couple. "He showed me a Web site that he put them up on," she said. "And it was an escort service site."[571]

Where Possible Ensure There is Someone Who Looks Out for You and Listen to What They Say

It is popular to think that parents are only there to spoil their children having fun. However, many victims would not be victims if they had trusted their parents or friends. Street children form gangs in the same way as fish school or birds flock in the hope of gaining protection from harm by numbers. Friends look out for friends.

An Example

One of the author's students went out on 6th Street in Austin, Texas for an evening with her friends. In a surprising lapse of common sense she let a stranger buy her a drink without watching it poured and brought to her. The drink was drugged and it wasn't long before she started to feel drowsy and ill. Fortunately, her friends were nearby and saw her. This was a young woman well acquainted with the problems of human trafficking but it could have taken only one lapse in judgment for her to be harmed.

Sometimes, even education and friends are not sufficient, however, the use of good judgment and double checking with parents, friends and others will help.

[571] "Teen Girls' Stories of Sex Trafficking in U.S.," *ABC News*, November 24, 2006, http://abcnews.go.com/Primetime/story?id=1596778&page=1.

Be Careful When Moving to a New Place

People are at their most vulnerable when they are migrating and lose their support networks. This may be as a result of war and famine or it may be to go to University or to find work.

Economic Need

Most migration, be it legal or illegal is as a result of economic need. This may be as basic as to prevent oneself starving or in search of a better way of life.

Protestations of Love

A massive fifty percent of all victims are recruited in this way.[572] Many young women, and some young men, who find themselves trafficked have low self-esteem, few friends and are willing to accept the first show of kindness a man offers to them. Sadly, traffickers and other sexual predators are brilliant at spotting that girl or boy.[573] The first stage of this predation is to show the victim a good time and to tell a number of lies which may include

a. if s/he is in conflict with his/her family, that s/he is misunderstood by them but s/he shouldn't worry about them because the 'trafficker' understands him/her. This is often a first stage in dividing him/her from his/her family so that s/he cannot go home for support and becomes more and more dependent on the trafficker.
b. s/he is so beautiful s/he could be a model, sometimes the trafficker will suggest that he could get a modeling contract for him/her.
c. s/he has qualities which only he sees and all the other people who know him/her are just mean.

Ignore the Lies

However a slave is lured into trafficking the outcome is usually the same. The offer of a good job is no good job at all but the traffickers play with the slave. They will continue to lie to them:

a. there will be a real job
b. you need to do this job (sex for money) to pay of the debts you have incurred to us for bringing you here.
c. we will send your money back to your family. In fact, this often happens because then the traffickers have another hold over the victims, a debt. These debts are usually inflated and for a girl who has been brought to the

[572] "Big Data Stops Slavery."
[573] Davis, *Cargo: Innocence Lost*.

United States may be as much as forty to sixty thousand U.S. dollars.[574] In Barcelona a report indicated that the traffickers were tattooing a woman's "debt" onto her wrist.[575]

d. if you leave you will be sent back to your own country (with the "T" Visa and "U" Visa system in the USA this should not happen). This is an effective lie because many victims do not want to be returned to their own country. This may be for multiple reasons, for example:
   - They fear stigma from their community and may be shunned. This is especially true for sex slaves returning to communities where a high price is put upon virginity and a woman's place (for example : Nepal and child soldiers).
   - They left their country illegally and fear repercussions.

e. In sex slavery, the good job may turn into being raped/performing sex acts up to four thousand times a year. Some children, aged twelve to fifteen, in the USA are known to have a daily quota and are required to earn the traffickers between five hundred and a thousand U.S. dollars per night.[576]

f. In sex slavery this is a common lie "I love you and once we get through the financial problems which are forcing me to ask you to be a sex slave things will be OK and we can stop". The emphasis is on the word "we". Often traffickers persuade sex slaves that they are in love.

A typical scenario can be seen acted out in the short trailer for the documentary "Flesh":

Step 1 : The trafficker finds a potential victim (see "what to look out for")
Step 2 : The trafficker talks to the victim and shows understanding and kindness for their difficulties. The object is to make the victim believe that s/he is a friend upon whom they can rely. Gradually, or swiftly, the trafficker drives a wedge between the victim and any sources of support s/he may have, the victim becomes reliant on the wonderful person s/he has met. His/her life becomes wonderful, the trafficker will buy presents, dinner etc but most of all will be caring and loving. This is known as 'grooming'.[577] Grooming is also a precursor to sexual abuse of children.[578] In some cases the trafficking will start with a 'holiday' which is in fact a kidnap, in others with a different sort of lie
Step 3 : I am a little short of money can you earn some for us. "It won't be long before we are on our feet." Or, "Try this (drug) it will be fun, what are you scared

[574] Bales, Trodd, and Williamson, *Modern Slavery*.
[575] Daley, "Women Enslaved by Spain's Brothel Tourism Boom."
[576] Bales and Soodalter, *The Slave next Door Human Trafficking and Slavery in America Today*, 2009.
[577] David Shannon, "Online Sexual Grooming in Sweden—Online and Offline Sex Offences against Children as Described in Swedish Police Data," *Journal of Scandinavian Studies in Criminology and Crime Prevention* 9, no. 2 (2008): 160–180, doi:10.1080/14043850802450120.
[578] Samantha Craven, Sarah Brown, and Elizabeth Gilcrest, "Sexual Grooming of Children: Review of Literature and Theoretical Considerations.," *Journal of Sexual Aggression* 12, no. 3 (November 2006): 287–299.

of, you …" Or "Do it for me/us". Of course, in some this step is skipped. It is always skipped when there has been a kidnap[579] of victims.

Step 4 : the victim begins to work in the sex industry a few times a week. At this point the traffickers may be becoming violent with the victim or getting them addicted to drugs or alcohol. If the victim is not willing, or if s/he becomes unwilling the trafficker will 'season' the victim. This occurs when the victim is subjected to a series of rapes, some by gangs, and often, also beaten. The effect is to break the victims' will, making them too frightened to run, tell the authorities or befriend customers.[580]

Step 5 : a modern slave has been created.[581]

Trickery

Traffickers often seem to have an innate ability to pick a victim based on circumstance but also on non-verbal communication. Scholars of communication say that non-verbal communication "is a primary tool for conveying our feelings and attitudes and for detecting the emotional states of others."[582] The work of Albert Mehrabian shows that fifty five percent of our emotional meaning comes from facial expressions whilst thirty eight percent of our emotional meaning comes from vocal cues. This means that a huge ninety three percent of emotional meaning in human beings is conveyed non-verbally.[583] As has seen many victims believe themselves to be in love and/or loved even after the abuse has started. They have often been targeted because of their low self-esteem which works in favor of the traffickers. Victims will convince themselves that if they work harder or better, their 'lover' will return. Alternatively, that they deserve to be beaten/raped/abused because they are worthless.

In a case in the UK, Gheeta, from India, was trafficked into forced labor in England by a family friend based in the UK, where she was terrorized for four years.

> *"He expected me to do all the housework for him as well as cook for him everyday. He would shout at me if I made mistakes. Before long he started to hit me too."*
>
> *She was forced to work at a local shop for 80 hours a week and give all her earnings to her trafficker. "Things got really bad though after I found out my father had died. He told me that he could do anything he wanted to me now because there was no one to look after me. That's when he started raping me. I tried to fight back but he threatened to stab me with a knife. Once when I tried to stop him he said he would kill me, chop me up and send the pieces to the family."*

---

[579] See definition of "Kidnap"

[580] For more information on why slaves do not leave see post

[581] Lauterbach, *Flesh*.

[582] Steven A. Beebe, Susan J. Beebe, and Diana K. Ivy, *Communication: Principles for a Lifetime, 4th Edition*, 4th edition (Pearson, n.d.).

[583] Ibid.

> *Gheeta was not recognised as trafficked – the arguments in her refusal letter (from immigration services) said they doubted her claim to be coerced or exploited because she didn't try and escape even though she had a television in the flat, held the key to the flat, went out for grocery shopping once every two months and was allowed to leave the flat to work.*
>
> *The refusal letter also said that while her frequent rape was "extremely unpleasant" it did not amount to trafficking because it was "triggered by your father's death", after which time they accepted that the trafficker felt he could then act with impunity.'*[584]

Three problems for victims can be seen from Gheeta's story:

a. The unwillingness of authorities to see victims as victims.
b. A lack of understanding of the coercion techniques used by traffickers, just because Gheeta was allowed out, it didn't mean see could escape. This lack of understanding is not just unfortunate but incomprehensible. There have been multiple studies about how victimization, for example in domestic and child violence situations, prevents the victim from being able to leave the abuser.[585]
c. The unwillingness to recognize that rape is a crime whoever it is committed by or against and there is no excuse for such a crime.

Locations from which Victims are recruited

The largest numbers of victims are recruited in a 'social setting'. This is closely followed by recruitment from a public place. The third largest recruiting ground is the internet with bars/clubs and residences/shelters coming fourth. A significant number of victims are recruited elsewhere and so it is important to be aware of other things too.[586]

Other Things to Look Out For

a. Men who are much older than the girls, for example, men of thirty who befriend girls in their teens via the internet. This is especially true of girls who have discussed being sad, alienated from family or friends, depressed, alone, suicidal or truanting.
b. Offers of modeling or show business contracts
c. Declarations of love from men about whom little, or in some case nothing, is known by the girls, her family or friends.

---

[584] "BACKGROUND: HUMAN TRAFFICKING IN THE UK," *Anti-Slavery Campaign*, accessed November 7, 2013, http://www.antislavery.org/english/campaigns/background_on_trafficking_for_forced_labour_in_the_uk.aspx.

[585] Dorchen A. Leidholdt, "HUMAN TRAFFICKING AND DOMESTIC VIOLENCE A Primer for Judges," *Judge's Journal* 52, no. 1 (Winter 2013): 16–21.

[586] "Big Data Stops Slavery."

d. Offers of jobs.

Example:

A young Romanian girl from a good family accepted the offer of a job in the UK from an outwardly respectable firm. She was taken to Totnes, a small seaside town on the South West coast of the UK. There she was raped by 10 men before being set to work as a prostitute. A week later, her traffickers thought that she had been subdued sufficiently to take her out to a Pub (bar). Fortunately for her, she was brave enough to stand up and scream. When the traffickers tried to force her from the Pub other customers protected her until the Police came. She was sent to a safe house and, after the Police had thoroughly checked out her family to ensure it was safe for her to return she was reunited with them.

Why Don't the Victims Just Leave?

Fear:

a. Children disappeared from Kent Social Services probably because of fear of aging out of care and being deported.
b. Traffickers threaten to kill or maim their family (Mondragon)
c. Traffickers threaten to destroy the property of their family (Mondragon)
d. They have nowhere to go (for example families often will not take them back after sex work.) Thus, as Kristoff and Wu Dunn say "Rescuing girls from brothels is the easy part, however. The challenge is keeping them from returning. The stigma that the girls feel in their communities after being freed, coupled with drug dependencies or threats from pimps, often lead them to return to the red-light districts."[587]
e. They have been forced to use drugs which make them addicts.
f. They are too frightened of their pimps
g. They have been conditioned into thinking that there is nothing more for them in life and this is their fate.
h. They believe they are in love, this also accounts for the fact that women too become pimps and traffickers. They are often former sex slaves who have bettered their situation by obedience and thus can be trusted with the other slaves.
i. They believe things will get better.
j. They don't speak the language
k. They fear the authorities
l. Voodoo[588]

---

[587] Kristof and Wudunn, *Half the Sky*.

[588] Musikilu Mojeed, *Nigeria - Voodoo Aids Human Trafficking*, October 24, 2008, http://lastradainternational.org/lsidocs/Nigeria.pdf.

The Human Trafficking Industry

In some countries communities either do not understand the problem or positively embrace it as a way of making money. The example of Long Mei is quite shocking.[589]

The Long Mei Model

Long Mei is a small village of approximately eighty households with five hundred people, located in Nanping Township, Guangnan County, Wenshan Prefecture, south of Yunnan Province. It gained notoriety some years ago because of its involvement in trafficking babies.

According to official sources, seventy per cent of the villagers in Long Mei, mostly women, were involved in trafficking, both directly and indirectly. Initially, forty five people were arrested for reportedly trafficking one hundred and four infants. Soon afterwards, the authorities, Women's Federation (WF), and Public Security Bureau (PSB) started finding ways to address the problem.

In 2000, the Guangnan County WF, PSB, and the government cooperated with Save the Children UK (China) to support community prevention work to eliminate trafficking.

Below are its key activities:

Training: Building on the practical experiences of women, various trainings on women's rights, marriage rights, trafficking-related laws, women's role in managing public affairs, protecting the rights of children, and eliminating trafficking in women and children were conducted.

Protection network: The villages formed a protection network and established rules and regulations consistent with the Public Security Bureau guidelines.

Transformation into a 'civilized village:' The transformation of Long Mei into a model 'civilized village' started to gain momentum on December 2001 with the increase in co-operation and collaboration of various government departments. Villagers define 'civilized village' as a place where people are healthy, respectful, helpful, and look after old people; where women and children's rights are respected, children go to school, and villagers acquire knowledge and technology; where there are no crimes such as trafficking, discrimination and domestic violence; and where there is good infrastructure.

---

[589] *Community-Based Initiatives Against Trafficking in Children in the Mekong Sub-Region 2003-2006* (Save the Children UK, October 27, 2013), http://www.streetchildrenresources.org/wp-content/uploads/2013/01/project-report-trafficking-mekong.pdf.

Subsequently, Long Mei received full support from the government, WF and PSB, hastening its transformation into 'civilized village'. The support it received consisted of twenty four thousand Yuan for building a community center; forty four thousand Yuan to build a drinking water pool; renovation of fish pond and provision of fish seedlings; provision of training on science and technology to improve farming and livestock including cattle raising; improvement in electricity and installation of telephone lines.

The Long Mei Model was initially intended to be replicated in eight villages—one in each of the eight counties. Now the plan is to replicate it in thirty eight out of the one hundred and twenty eight counties in Yunnan Province

"Long Mei" Model

- "professional trafficking village"
- Trade/ produce babies for sale
- Participatory livelihood analysis – poverty, poor access to water, lack of job opportunities
- Partnership with Women's Federation (WF), Public Security Bureau (PSB) and local authorities
- Support water resources; technology/ material for farming/livestock; train/ promote women's rights/ children's rights; mobilize women's participation & leadership

Three years later :

- Produce/ average income risen two-fold
- No more trafficking
- Approved to be replicated to thirty eight other areas

Chapter 15

The Impact of Attitudes Toward Immigration

"If civilization is to survive we must cultivate the science of human relationships – the ability of all peoples, of all kinds, to live together, in the same world at peace."[590]

The important misunderstanding is that, although the victims may have chosen to move to the country in which they become enslaved, not one of them, to borrow from Col. T Collins, woke up and decided that they wished to be enslaved in the country to which they move.[591] Thus, as has been seen, when American Immigration and Customs Officers ask victims the question "Did you want to come to America" many will answer "yes". What they did not want to do was come to America to work long hours for no reward or little reward and never be allowed to find alternative employment.[592]

It is certainly true that, for example, in the USA, modern slaves start life as illegal immigrants.[593] This confuses the issue in the US, especially in strong anti-immigrant states. Often, a slave in America will have chosen to enter the US illegally. They will have paid to be smuggled across the border. What happens is that once over the border the 'coyotes' who brought them across the border assess their customers. Those illegal immigrants who have family or friends or others north of the border go on their way but those with no one are 'gifts' to the 'coyotes'. On these people, they can make extra money by selling them into slavery. Therefore, such slaves are illegal immigrants but go on to suffer the tortures of being enslaved. At what point do they transfer from being criminals to being victims?

There are essential difference between victims of human trafficking and illegal immigrants:

a. The trafficked person is forced to remain working for their master whereas the illegal immigrant is able to move freely from job to job.

[590] "PRESIDENT ROOSEVELT'S UNDELIVERED JEFFERSON DAY ADDRESS," April 13, 1945.
[591] Dave Beckett, "Colonel Tim Collins' Speech," *Journalblog*, March 2003, http://journal.dajobe.org/journal/2003/03/collins/.
[592] Sharron FitzGerald, "Vulnerable Bodies, Vulnerable Borders: Extraterritoriality and Human Trafficking," *Feminist Legal Theory* 20, no. 3 (2012): 227–244.
[593] Britta S. Loftus, "COORDINATING U.S. LAW ON IMMIGRATION AND HUMAN TRAFFICKING: LIFTING THE LAMP TO VICTIMS," *Columbia Human Rights Law Review* 43, no. 1 (Fall 2011): 143–214.

b. More often than not the trafficked person gets no pay beyond that which they have to pay back to their master for food and lodging.
c. The trafficked person is a victim of criminal activity whereas the illegal immigrant is a criminal.
d. The illegal immigrant has to cross an international border but the trafficking victim does not have to be moved and does not have to be foreign. The crime of human trafficking is a crime against the 'person' of the victim. The illegal immigrant commits a crime by crossing an international border. The trafficked victim may cross a border but does not consent to being enslaved.
e. The trafficked victim has been the subject of fraud, force, or coercion whereas the illegal immigrant is a volunteer.
f. The trafficked victim is exploited in forced labor following the arrival in the destination country. The illegal immigrant may also be exploited, in that s/he earns less money than a legal worker but has the choice of which work is performed.

Why Do People in Western Societies Use Slaves?

Slavery is, and always has been, caused by economics, or, more pejoratively, fueled by greed. However, if the demand does not exist then the supply would not occur. Historically it is easy to see how slaves were needed. They improved the productivity of the country and the exploitation of the agricultural and natural resources of the Americas could simply not have happened, at least at the rate it did, without slavery.

However, it is more difficult to see why people living in Western countries choose to have slaves. Certainly, it comes back to greed on the part of the slave-traders. At a Panel of Human Trafficking Experts held in Austin Texas on November 30, the head of Austin Police Department Human Trafficking unit said that, in his city, one enslaved girl in the sex industry would earn her captor approximately two hundred thousand U.S. dollars per annum. In his book, "Sex Trafficking : Inside the Business of Modern Slavery", Siddhartha Kara has re-constructed the budgets of brothels in Queens, New York and Italy.[594] There is little doubt that large sums of money are made from enslaving girls in the sex trade. But why are people 'employing' these victims? As has been seen, perhaps the people who use sex slaves don't know they are sex slaves, haven't heard about sex slavery, pretend that the men or women slaves are enjoying sex or, simply, don't care?

In some countries of the world, traditional slavery endures, for example, debt bondage in Asia and traditional slavery in Mauritania. However, why would an "ordinary" person living in a Western country today, where the ownership of slaves is outlawed and socially unacceptable, choose to own a domestic slave? There is little evidence that people enjoy enslaving others per se, however, they do enjoy the benefits of owning a slave. If a cleaner is paid as much as ten U.S. dollars per hour the actual amount saved over a year by having a slave is small. However, perhaps it is because by having a slave you have

[594] Kara, *Sex Trafficking.*

something which you cannot legitimately pay for from one person: twenty four hour service and total domination over another human being.

Example:

Sandra Beardon was a, seemingly normal, young suburban housewife, a citizen of Mexico married to an America called Warren. In 2001, she decided to recruit a domestic worker to help her look after her small, four year old, child. It appears, from her trial, that she decided to recruit a young Mexican girl for this work. Sandra crossed the border; she lived in Laredo, Texas, and went to Vera Cruz. There, she convinced a family to part with their twelve year old daughter, Maria.

This is the twenty first century and African Chiefs no longer sell their prisoners and people to slave-traders, so how does a twenty six year old housewife persuade a family to part with their child? At this point a common recruitment strategy comes into play. The nice young woman from America promises the family something of which they can only dream. In this case, that their daughter would be educated in America in exchange for light household and nannying duties. The American Dream is within the reach of their child. What parents do not want a better life for their child? In fact, it is that basic human desire – "I want my child to have a better life than I did" which becomes one of the ways in which trafficking is fueled around the world.

What happened when Sandra Beardon took the child home is, sadly, typical of the descent into abuse of power which is common amongst slave owners. What is interesting is that Sandra had been born in Mexico too and so she chose to destroy the hopes and dreams of a child who is the same as her. Of course, by this time, Sandra has grown well away from her roots. It may be that she intended for the child to go to school, but she never sent her, instead she "used violence and terror to squeeze work and obedience from the child".[595] At work, the child had to cook and clean. When judged not to be working hard enough or if she had fallen asleep exhausted, Sandra used pepper spray in Maria's eyes by way of punishment. Additional punishments included breaking a bottle over her head, a broom over her back and vaginally raping her with a garden tool. Amazingly, on her days off Maria suffered even more. These were days she spent chained up, her arms behind her back and her legs chained in the backyard without food and water behind an 8ft concrete fence. Sometimes, before chaining her, Sandra would amuse herself by making Maria eat dog feces.

Maria would probably have died had not luck stepped up to help her. The Bearden's neighbor had to do repairs on his roof. He climbed his ladder

[595] Bales and Soodalter, *The Slave next Door Human Trafficking and Slavery in America Today*, 2009.

and was horrified to find that he was living next door to a family who had a child chained up in the back-garden. He called 911. At this point it is to be hoped everyone would call 911, but many people who see trafficking either don't notice it or don't want to "be wrong and cause a fuss" and, therefore, don't report it. "Images entered as evidence show the girl emaciated in a dirty red cotton dress leaning against a tire, with a steel chain wrapped around her waist, arms locked behind her with a padlock. Her bare feet were held together with a similar length of chain with two padlocks.

"The white of one eye was bloodied and appeared infected. Scars and cuts covered her face. Other photos showed thick welts and cuts on the girl's arms and legs where the steel chains had cut into her flesh."[596]

The Police Officer who found her said "This is the worst case I've ever seen, worse than murder. It's tragic all the way round". Sandra Beardon went to jail for life. Sandra's small son lost his mother which may have a profound effect on him. But let us pause and think about Maria. She has been physically, sexually and mentally abused. How can she ever trust again, how can she come anywhere near to having a 'normal life'? Few can know what she has suffered and, however good the therapy she receives she has been irrevocably harmed.

Essay : Did Sandra Beardon receive a fitting sentence? The answer will depend upon the readers' view of capital punishment, which exists in Texas. Had Maria died would Sandra Beardon have faced the death penalty? Consider these statements:

Sandra Beardon, with malice aforethought took everything that makes a human being human from Maria except her soul. How do we define life, is it just the fact of life or is it something more? The rights set out in the Universal Declaration of Human Rights suggest that life for a human being is more than just being alive. If a person deliberately strips their humanity from another human being, is that worse for the human being than being murdered? The murder victim feels nothing after death. Maria will live with her pain forever.

What happened to Maria, the sad fact is that we don't know. The Mexican government paid for her parents to come to Laredo and take her home. Her father said "We made a decision that we thought would be good for our child, and look what happened. I made a mistake, truly, and this is all my fault."[597] So here we find more victims, the parents who thought they were doing the best thing for their daughter. They took her home; she was just thirteen years old. Did she have therapy? Did she have the

[596] "Women Sentenced to Life in Prison for Torturing Maid," *Lubbock Online*, October 19, 2001, http://lubbockonline.com/stories/101901/upd_075-4746.shtml.
[597] Roma Khanna, "Girl Reunited with Parents," *Laredo Morning Times*, May 17, 2001.

specialist care that someone who has been so victimized should receive? We don't know. Maria was entitled to a T-Visa. Maria is a example of the question often asked about slaves; why didn't s/he run away? Here we see ways in which slave owners are clever. Sandra kept Maria in a state of pain, exhaustion, fear and hopelessness which bred helplessness in Maria. But, looked at logically, there were other factors which kept her from running, and are typical of slaves: disorientation and fear of the authorities.

Example:

Two domestic slaves were found on Long Island in New York. They had been brought into America from Indonesia. Their owners, Varsha Mahender Sabhnani, and Mahender Murlidhar Sabhnani, were wealthy and respected business people. One of the slaves was interviewed by Police when she was found, her face bruised, wandering clad in only a towel and pants. She was helped by shop workers at Dunkin Donuts who called the Police after she had mimed being slapped and said the word 'master'. The second slave, Nona, was found in a closet under the stairs when the Police raided the Sabhnani's home. Both women told of long working hours, little food, sleeping on mats on the floor, hiding when their owners had visitors and frequent beatings of Samirah by Mrs Sabhnani. The contract which the slaves believed they had would have paid them three hundred U.S. dollars per month each but the one hundred U.S. dollars which was paid was sent to Samirah's daughter in Indonesia, Samirah received nothing. Mrs Sabhnani was also charged with cutting Samirah with a knife, burning her with cigarettes and forcing her to eat a lot of hot chili peppers. On conviction, Mahender Sabhnani was sentenced to forty months imprisonment, to be followed by a three-year term of supervised release. "He was also ordered to pay a twelve and a half thousand U.S. dollar fine and a special assessment of twelve hundred U.S. dollars. Varsha Sabhnani was sentenced to one hundred and thirty two months' imprisonment, followed by a three-year term of supervised release, and was ordered to pay a fine of 25 thousand U.S. dollars and a special assessment of twelve hundred U.S. dollars. The court also required both defendants to pay the sum of nine hundred and thirty six thousand five hundred and forty six U.S. dollars and twenty two cents in restitution to their victims, and ordered both defendants to forfeit their ownership interest in their home, where their victims had been held."[598] Mahender appealed his conviction but only the restitution part of the sentence was amended.

The injuries to Samirah were photographed and appear in this article about the case.[599]

---

[598] U.S. v. SABHNANI (U.S. Court of Appeals, 2nd Cir. 2010).

[599] "Muslim Housekeepers Treated as Slaves in U.S.," *The Islamic Workplace*, October 27, 2013, http://theislamicworkplace.com/2007/12/17/muslim-housekeepers-treated-as-slaves-in-us/.

Essay: Samariah's owners received custodial sentences. Where they sufficient to meet the crime?

Many developed countries are involved in discussions about immigration. In the UK, during the Premiership of Tony Blair, a liberalization of immigration laws lead to thousands of legal immigrants from Eastern Europe moving to the UK, which added nought point twenty five percent growth to the UK annual economy. In 2012, with the economy still trying to recover from the world recession many started a re-assessment of the situation discussing the role of the immigrant in preventing British workers from getting jobs. In London, in June 2012, the leader of the Labour Party, Ed Milliband spoke about the fact that immigration laws needed to be changed to protect the working classes of Britain. In the past, speaking out against immigration has been termed racist, Mr. Milliband said he was not racist because he was trying to protect the working class Britain.

"Worrying about immigration, talking about immigration, thinking about immigration, does not make them (his constituents) bigots. They are anxious about the future" he said.[600]

This amounts to a considerable volte face for the Labour Party bringing it in line with what some Conservatives have been saying for many years.

In the USA the debate about immigration has also been going on for many years. In 2012, the number of people of Hispanic origin living in Texas was larger than the number of all other ethnic backgrounds together. In Arizona, in 2010, the State passed legislation on immigration issues, some of which were struck down as unconstitutional by the Supreme Court on 25th June 2012. In many areas it is believed that immigrants take the work of Americans. However, in America it is not legal migration which is the problem. The US has such strong immigration rules that few are permitted to immigrate legally. Thus, those who wish to work in the USA have to do so as illegal immigrants. This increases the level of hostility towards them, especially if they are perceived to be 'taking our jobs', and, there is a consequential increase in vulnerability for the illegal immigrant.[601] However, it is known that protection of immigrants protects them from human trafficking.[602]

Into this potent cocktail falls the trafficking victim. In the UK, it is the job of the Border Agency to decide if a person is an illegal immigrant or a human trafficking victim. In the USA, that job is very often performed by Immigration and Customs Executive.

[600] "Ed Miliband Was Right to Acknowledge Immigration Concerns," *The Guardian*, June 22, 2012, http://www.theguardian.com/politics/blog/2012/jun/22/ed-miliband-right-immigration-concerns.
[601] *Colbert Stays in Character at Congressional Hearing*, 2010, http://www.youtube.com/watch?v=ewPburLEZyY&feature=youtube_gdata_player.
[602] Sovereign Hager, "FARM WORKERS AND FORCED LABOR: WHY INCLUDING AGRICULTURAL GUEST WORKERS IN THE MIGRANT AND SEASONAL WORKER PROTECTION ACT PREVENTS HUMAN TRAFFICKING," *Syracuse Journal of International Law & Commerce* 38, no. 1 (Fall 2010): 173–199.

However, the victim in the US is better off because s/he can also be identified through court proceedings and by other law enforcement agencies and non-profits which can bring them into the "T" or "U" visa system. However, where there is an ingrained dislike or distrust of the illegal immigrant it is often found that the trafficking victim falls between the cracks. A common threat to foreign born victims is that they will be deported or imprisoned because they are illegal immigrants or the law officers will return them to the traffickers. Only part of this sentence is a lie; often slaves are seen as illegal and imprisoned until they are deported. Unfortunately this happens regularly. Victims are deported because they are not identified as trafficking victims, see Gheeta's story.[603] They fear deportation because of

a. Face saving.
b. Their family needs money.
c. Threats of being killed by their traffickers' friends if they return. This is a major concern for victims. Where traffickers are harvesting a village or area which is uneducated as to their schemes the last thing they want is someone coming to explode their cover.
d. Threats that their family will be killed.
e. Stigmatization on their return; many foreign communities are unforgiving of a woman who has lost her virginity even when it has been through rape, trafficking into sex slavery often makes it impossible for these victims to return to their homes. Even where victims could return they fear stigmatization.[604]

The consequence of this is that, as seen in Bought and Sold, some women do not leave the sex slavery into which they were trafficked.[605] Some women take on business roles in the brothels or sex businesses in which they were enslaved, even recruiting others and some victims, fearing deportation even once they are saved, leave protection to take their chances on the illegal immigrant market which makes them vulnerable once again to being caught up in trafficking. A particularly sad case of the fear victims feel was seen in the UK in 2011 when twenty five children, aged twelve to seventeen who were

> *"...suspected of being trafficked into the UK this year through Kent's channel ports have gone missing from care... Anti-trafficking campaigners believe the children from Afghanistan, Vietnam, Algeria, Morocco, India, Albania and Palestine are likely to have fallen back into the hands of the international criminal networks who trafficked them into Britain."*[606]

---

[603] Supra

[604] Gillian Caldwell, *Bought and Sold, an Investigative Documentary about the International Trade in Women 2009* (Global Survivor Network, 1999), http://humantrafficking.unc.edu/2011/05/01/bought-and-sold-an-investigative-documentary-about-the-international-trade-in-women-multimedia-resource-gillian-caldwell-global-survivor-network-1999/.

[605] Ibid.

[606] Robert Booth, "Children Lost from Care in Human Trafficking Cases, Says Council," *The Guardian*, October 18, 2011, http://www.theguardian.com/law/2011/oct/18/children-lost-human-trafficking.

The children had been in children's homes and foster homes with the Kent County Council but, as a spokesperson said, it is impossible to prevent the children from running away without incarcerating them.[607]

Immigration Considerations

T-Visa

In passing The Trafficking Victims Protection Act (TVPA) the US Federal Government recognized that returning a trafficked victim to his or her native country may not be in their best interest, and that victims may need the opportunity to rebuild their lives without fear of deportation. The TVPA was the beginning of an enhanced effort to address human trafficking through a unique approach – combining the principles of protection, prevention, and prosecution to combat the crime. On the protection end, there is the T-Visa

What is it? – A "T-visa" is a temporary visa that is issued to victims of "severe trafficking" (severe Trafficking is defined by statute as using force, fraud, or coercion for sex and/or labor trafficking), that enable them to remain in the country up to four years. It also enables them to obtain an Employment Authorization Document (EAD) that enables them to work legally in the U.S. After applying for and receiving T non-immigrant status from the US Citizenship and Immigration Services, the individual may apply for Legal Permanent Resident (LPR) status after a period of continuous physical presence in the United States.

Additional Resources–A T-visa enables a victim to become eligible for certification to receive benefits and services (health care, housing, etc.) under State and Federal programs to the same extent as a refugee.

NOTE: A minor does not need to be "certified" to obtain benefits.

"U-Visa"

Another option available for non-citizen victims of human trafficking is the "U-Visa". It serves the same function of allowing them to temporarily remain in the United States for purposes of rebuilding and establishing Legal Permanent Residence.

What is it? - A "U-visa" is another temporary visa that is issued to individuals who have suffered a great amount of physical or mental abuse from a US citizen as a result of

[607] "Unless we keep [children] under lock and key we can't guarantee they won't go missing and go into a horrendous life of trafficking . We will do everything possible to encourage these children to speak with us and build a relationship of trust." Jenny Whittle, Kent county council's cabinet member for specialist children's services.

being the victim of certain specified crimes that includes sexual exploitation, involuntary servitude, etc.[608]

Additional Resources – There are not as many resources available to the victim under this type of temporary visa.

Continued Presence

Immigration and Customs Enforcement (ICE) grants "Continued Presence" upon request from a Federal Law Enforcement officer for a victim of "severe trafficking" who is a potential witness. This allows them to remain in the country for one year during the course of the investigation or prosecution, and also to obtain an EAD to work legally.

[608] *For objection to extension of "U" Visa system to illegal immigrants see* "Administration Moves Ahead on Three More Little Amnesties," *Center for Immigration Studies*, May 3, 2012, Administration Moves Ahead on Three More Little Amnesties.

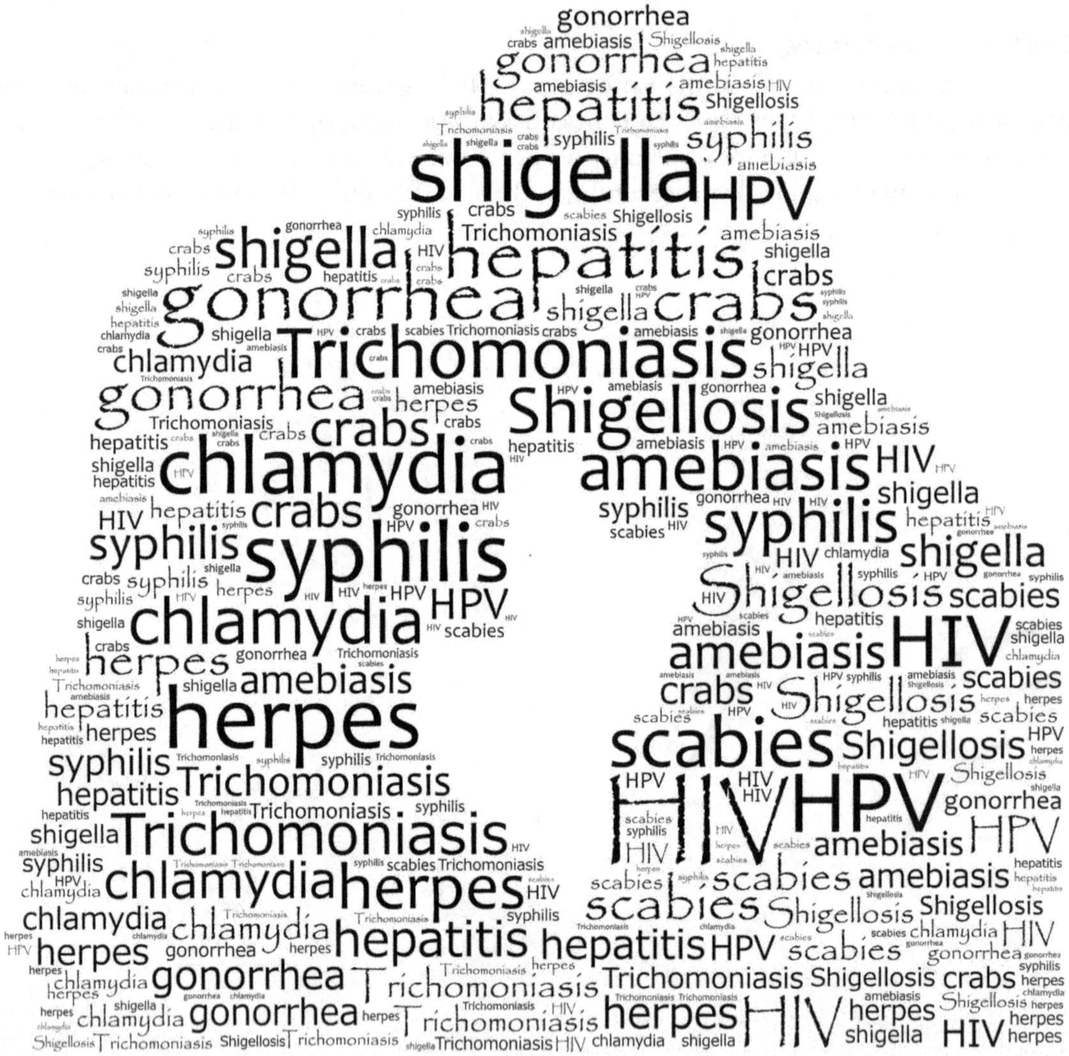
gonorrhea
hepatitis
shigella
HPV
syphilis
Trichomoniasis
crabs
Shigellosis
chlamydia
amebiasis
herpes
scabies
HIV

Chapter 16

Health Risks

The horrors of the Middle Passage where slaves were chained up in conditions which did not allow them to stand, and in some cases even turn when lying are embedded in the minds of most readers. As has been seen the plight of the slaves taken in Arab Dowls was also awful. Unfortunately, this is another way in which modern slavery emulates its predecessor. People still die on their way into slavery. Many slaves cross the desert to get into the USA and women trafficked from Eastern Europe into the Middle East often find themselves travelling the old slave routes through the Sahara desert. In 2008, fifty four Burmese victims died on their way to Thailand.[609] There are many stories of slave victims dying and being injured on their journeys. In one case a couple, who were holidaying in Cancun, Mexico, were kidnapped and forced to walk through the desert into the USA. During that forced march the woman miscarried her baby. Eventually, once they had raised a sufficient ransom, they were allowed to go free, but irrevocably scarred.

Sex Slaves:

What do you do with yourself following a life which includes some, maybe all, of the following health problems? Physical and sexual assault, forced terminations, exhaustion, torture, malnutrition, diseases (including vaginal illnesses – cystitis), sterility, sexually transmitted diseases, HIV/AIDS, TB, hepatitis, emotional and mental health problems (including PTSD, depression, substance abuse, self-loathing, helplessness) and permanent removal from ones family. Veterans returning from war zones where they have witnessed murders, torture and been in fear of the lives sometimes suffer PTSD for which they, rightly, receive high levels of care. This is rarely available to the victims of trafficking and hardly ever available for the length of time required to help a victim.[610]

Adolescents are more likely to catch HIV than older women. They have thinner skin in the vagina and are less able to accommodate an adult penis, however HIV infection rates across all ages are high for sex slaves.[611] For example, forty percent of a sample of three hundred women repatriated in Nepal during 1997-2002 had HIV. Of those forced into sex slavery under fifteen years old, the prevalence was four times higher than those

---

[609] Ian MacKinnon in Bangkok, "54 Burmese Migrants Suffocate in Packed Lorry," *The Guardian*, April 11, 2008, http://www.theguardian.com/world/2008/apr/11/burma.thailand.

[610] Lisa R. Muftic and Mary A. Finn, "Health Outcomes Among Women Trafficked for Sex in the United States: A Closer Look.," *Journal of Interpersonal Violence* 28, no. 9 (Jun2013): 1859–1885, doi:10.1177/0886260512469102.

[611] Minsoo Yung, "Associations of Physical and Sexual Health with Suicide Attempts Among Female Sex Workers in South Korea," *Sexuality & Disability* 31, no. 3 (September 2013): 275–286.

trafficked at eighteen years plus.[612] Things are made worse by douching with astringent solutions. These make the vagina feel 'tighter' for clients but dry it leaving it more prone to tearing.[613] When menstruation occurs most women are more susceptible to infections. Sex at this time increases such risks and the risk of being beaten if the client finds that the victim has her period. Victims are usually told to keep rooms dark to avoid 'clients' finding out, but darkness is not always a perfect cover. Male sex slaves have similar issues regarding HIV.[614]

Condom use: client's are willing to take the obvious risk of contracting HIV or an STD from a sex slave and many refuse to wear condoms. This not only increases their chances of illness but dramatically increases the risks for the victims who may be seeing up to forty clients a day. It also increases the demand for virgins who are disease free. This increases risks to young victims of being repeatedly stitched to 'fake' virginity. In many areas of S.E. Asia men believe that sex with a virgin will cure HIV and other STDs. Where condoms are used, they may be charged to the victim – simply increasing the debt she owes. Even condoms do not necessarily protect against HIV because repeated use of the condom in the vagina can cause bleeding abrasions. Unprotected sex brings further suffering for young girls because ninety percent of them will fall pregnant within a year of enslavement in a brothel.[615] In 2007, over sixty six thousand deaths worldwide were thought to come from botched abortions.[616] Sex slaves only have access to illegal abortions and death is a frequent side effect of pregnancy for these girls.

Additionally, sex slaves run the risk of frequent beatings from their owners but also from their clients. Nowhere is this trafficking worse than it is in Moldova where experts estimate that since the fall of the Soviet Union between two hundred thousand to four hundred thousand women have been sold into prostitution, perhaps up to ten percent of the female population.[617]

Labor Slaves

Imagine living a life where you do back-breaking work, or stand for long hours or repeatedly make a particular item, or make charcoal in the Amazon rainforest. You will probably suffer physical injuries which may be torture, malnutrition, diseases (for example TB, hepatitis), cuts, amputations, burns, back problems, repetitive strain, exhaustion and

---

612 Silverman JG et al., "HIV Prevalence and Predictors of Infection in Sex-Trafficked Nepalese Girls and Women," *JAMA* 298, no. 5 (August 1, 2007): 536–542, doi:10.1001/jama.298.5.536.

613 Bales, Trodd, and Williamson, *Modern Slavery*.

614 William C.W. Wong, Phil W.S. Leung, and C. W. Li, "HIV Behavioural Risks and the Role of Work Environment among Chinese Male Sex Workers in Hong Kong," *AIDS Care* 24, no. 3 (March 2012): 340–347.

615 Bales, Trodd, and Williamson, *Modern Slavery*.

616 Andrew Cole, "Botched Abortions Kill More than 66 000 Women Each Year," *BMJ* 335, no. 7625 (October 27, 2007): 845–845, doi:10.1136/bmj.39374.628171.DB1.

617 Preston Mendenhall msnbc.com, "Infiltrating Europe's Shameful Trade in Human Beings," *Msnbc.com*, October 27, 2013, http://www.nbcnews.com/id/3071965/ns/us_news-only/t/infiltrating-europes-shameful-trade-human-beings/.

physical assault. As other slaves you will have emotional and mental health problems, including PTSD, depression, substance abuse, self-loathing helplessness, and, often permanent removal from ones family. Some women in labor slavery, particularly as domestic slaves also suffer sexual abuse, forced terminations, diseases (including vaginal illnesses – cystitis, sterility, sexually transmitted diseases, HIV/AIDS). The case of Beardon shows that victims can also suffer dehydration and sunstroke/exposure.

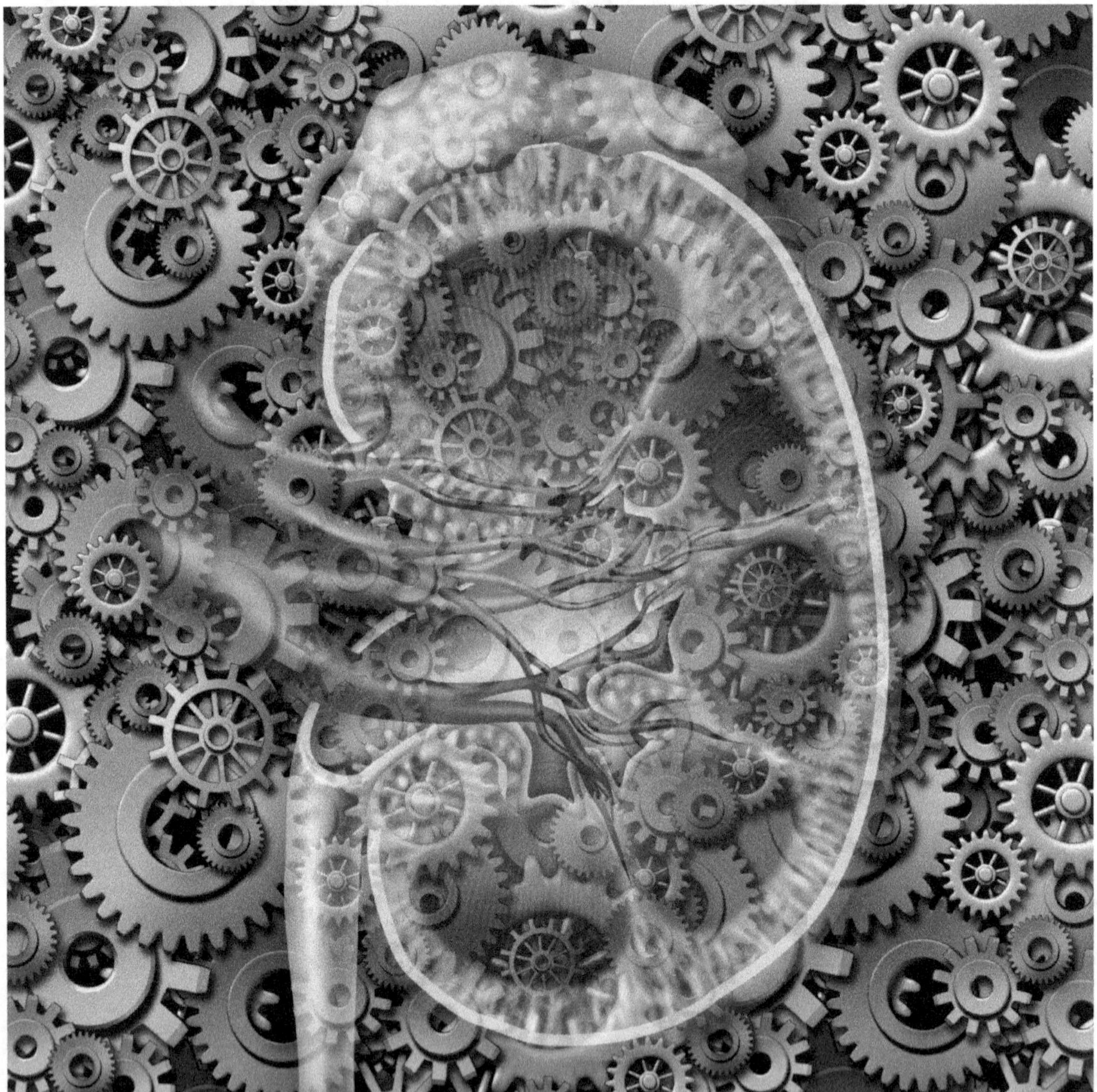

Chapter 17

Organ Trafficking

"the growing insufficiency of available human material for transplantation to meet patient needs"[618]

In Peter Bent Brigham Hospital, Boston on December 23, 1954 the first successful transplant of a kidney took place. Dr Christian Barnard continued transplantation work, eventually, in 1967 performing the first heart transplant in Cape Town, South Africa. Since then transplantation of body parts has come a long way. Now it is possible to transplant

- Liver
- Heart
- Lung
- Kidney
- Pancreas
- Corneal
- Heart valve
- Dural matter
- Bone & Joint
- Tissue
- Skin
- Fat & other

In 2004, the World Health Assembly expressed concern about the shortage of supply of human material for transplant.[619] These shortages have a number of causes: Increasing numbers of people needing transplants due to diet and lifestyle, new types of transplants becoming successful, acceptance of patients who are sicker than the patients previously selected, more re-transplantation and aging populations with longer life expectancy.[620]

The USA looked at this issue in the Organ Trafficking Prohibition Act 2009. In 1984, the USA introduced the National Organ Transportation Act which made buying and

[618] *Human Organ and Tissue Transplantation*, Fifty-Seventh World Health Assembly (World Health Organization, May 22, 2004), http://apps.who.int/gb/ebwha/pdf_files/WHA57/A57_R18-en.pdf.
[619] Ibid.
[620] "Trafficking in Persons for Organ Removal: Prevention Of Trafficking in Persons, Chapter 9" (United Nations Office of Drugs and Crime), accessed January 11, 2013, https://www.unodc.org/documents/human-trafficking/Toolkit-files/08-58296_tool_9-19.pdf.

selling of organs illegal. The offence could be punished by a sentence of up to five years in prison and fifty thousand U.S dollar fine.

Although it is illegal to buy organs in many western countries, the desire to have transplants is strong amongst the population in the west.[621] This is because the waiting time to receive organs is so long. Typically organs come from bodies, they will be removed at death and protected from deterioration until transplant. In organ trafficking, the donor is typically still alive. The two areas where donors are dead are in the People's Republic of China and Singapore, where the organs of executed prisoners are harvested for transplant. There are reports of these being sold to wealthy recipients from abroad.

In some cases organs can be transplanted in the USA illegally, despite the National Organ Transplant Act of 1984. However, the people receiving organs are usually wealthy enough to pay such fines. Interestingly, it takes a lot of people to be complicit for organ trafficking to take place, these include

a. the organ brokers;
b. donor;
c. recipient;
d. surgeons - they have to work together on the donor and the recipient;
e. nursing staff from start of procedure to post op; sometimes also for the donor;
f. lab technicians for matching purposes;
g. hospital administrators;
h. sometimes, medical insurance companies;
i. some patient advocacy or other groups concerned for the recipient; and
j. nephrologists
k. and lawyers, if they get caught

It is surprising then that cases take place in the USA; but it seems even the finest private hospitals work on a "don't ask don't tell" basis.[622]

Example

Levy Izhak Rosenbaum was a resident of Brooklyn. In July 2009 he was arrested for being a "matchmaker" for organ transplants where the recipient of the organ had to buy it from the donor. He was finding matches in Israel for wealthy people in the USA. The charge was about one hundred and fifty thousand U.S. dollars per kidney. The transplants were being done in the USA but the matching was done in Israel. There were also

---

[621] Leonard Territo and Matteson, eds., *The International Trafficking of Human Organs⍰: A Multidisciplinary Perspective* (Boca Raton, Florida: Taylor Francis, 2012).

[622] Nancy Scheper-Hughes, "Organ Trafficking" (presented at the Transplantation in the USA: The Shortage of available organs and public policy, New York, NY, April 19, 2010), http://transplantusa.kidneyurology.org/.

suggestions that donors came from Eastern Europe (see below) but, because he had entered a guilty plea the reports are limited. Having been on bail under house arrest since 2009, he entered his guilty plea in 2011. He was supposed to be sentenced on 2 February 2012, but the sentencing date was postponed. He agreed to forfeit his capital, four hundred and twenty thousand U.S. dollars and on July 11, 2012 was sentenced to two and a half years in jail. Once he has served his time he may be deported to Israel. At the sentencing hearing, those who had received kidneys called Levy Izhak Rosenbaum a hero but the prosecuting Attorney spoke for those poor and vulnerable people who had lost a kidney in the process.

In fact, Dr. Scheper-Hughes asserts that she told the authorities about Rosenblum some seven years before the arrest.

As might be expected the source countries for live organ donations are:

- India
- People's Republic of China
- Singapore
- Pakistan
- Iraq
- Iran
- Moldova
- Russian Federation
- Philippines
- Brazil
- Columbia
- Bolivia
- Egypt
- Israel
- Peru
- Romania[623]
- Turkey
- Nigeria
- Cambodia
- Indonesia
- Laos
- Vietnam
- Georgia

Hub countries:

[623] Carminola Ionescu, "Donor Charged in Romania's First Organ Trafficking Trial," *Lancet* 365, no. 9475 (June 4, 2005): 1918, doi:10.1016/S0140-6736(05)66644-5.

These are places where organ tourism is prevalent

- South Africa[624]
- Columbia[625]
- Turkey
- Kosovo[626]

Home countries of recipients

- Western European countries[627]
- U.S.A.
- Canada
- Israel
- Saudi Arabia
- UAE
- Hong Kong
- China
- Korea
- Japan
- Malaysia
- Philippines
- Singapore
- Kuwait
- Oman
- Bahrain

Are organs donated with full disclosure?

This is the profile of a typical organ donor in India. He or she will be young, poor, and in desperate need of money for their family. If the choice is food or a kidney, it is possible to posit that it is not a choice at all. Many young women in India are required, by their family, to give an organ. They may have to do so to raise money for their dowry or they may be required to do so by their husband or father to finance the family. There are few alternatives for a poor and uneducated woman in India but to obey the men in her family. In some cases they can be rescued by NGOs but those are few and far between. In

[624] Elaine Pearson, *Coercion in the Kidney Trade? A Background Study on Trafficking in Human Organs Worldwide* (Deutsche Gesellschaft für Technische Zusammenarbeit (GTZ) GmbH, April 2004), https://www.giz.de/Themen/en/dokumente/en-organ-trafficking-2004.pdf.

[625] Charles Channon, "Transplant Tourism in Colombia," *The Blog of the Institute for the Elimination of Global Organ Trafficking (IEGOT)*, February 19, 2007, http://organtrade.blogspot.com/2007/02/transplant-tourism-in-columbia.html.

[626] *Committee on Legal Affairs and Human Rights Inhuman Treatment of People and Illicit Trafficking in Human Organs in Kosovo* (Council of Europe, December 12, 2010).

[627] European Parliament, Starsbourg, *Additional Protocol to the Convention on Human Rights and Biomedicine Concerning Transplantation of Organs and Tissues of Human Origin*, 2002.

a study in Tamil Nadu, a province in India, of three hundred and five donors seventy one percent were women.[628] Also, in Nigeria, kidney sellers are poor young women.

Often donors and recipients do not have the same quality of care; nor do they get the same reward. Recipients receive the best care money can buy and a new lease of good quality life in lovely surroundings. Donors receive, on average, two and a half to three thousand U.S. dollars for a kidney, often poor or limited post-operative care and find they cannot do the jobs they used to do, forcing them into greater poverty than they had experienced. This loss of money often causes a loss of health.

Cases:

Dorin Razlog lives in pain in an abandoned van in Moldova after selling a kidney.

Vladimir Diminetz, died at the age of twenty five in Moldova after selling a kidney. Vasile Diminetz says he wishes he'd stopped his late son from selling his kidney.[629]

How Much Does a Liver Cost?

Despite the illegality of buying organs in the West, a number of websites cater to westerners looking for replacement organs. A liver will cost between one hundred and two hundred thousand U.S. dollars including the transplant surgeons, hospital etc. What will the donor receive? It depends upon where the recipient lives and the supply and demand statistics at the time. Jerome Feldman used to run a website "Liver4you" from his home in the Philippines. In 2011, having been deported to the USA he was convicted and sentenced for advertising the sale of liver transplants.[630]

The World Health Organization (WHO) estimates ten thousand black market operations involving human organs take place each year. "Kidneys make up seventy five per cent of the global illicit trade in organs".[631] Rising rates of diabetes, high blood pressure and heart problems are causing demand for kidneys to far outstrip supply. Data from the WHO shows that of the one hundred and six thousand eight hundred and seventy nine

---

[628] Pearson, *Coercion in the Kidney Trade? A Background Study on Trafficking in Human Organs Worldwide*.

[629] Michael Smith, Daryna Krasnolutska, and David Glovin, "Organ Gangs Force Poor to Sell Kidneys for Desperate Israelis," *Bloomberg*, October 27, 2013, http://www.bloomberg.com/news/2011-11-01/organ-gangs-force-poor-to-sell-kidneys-for-desperate-israelis.html.

[630] Steven Meyerowitz, "Liver4you Health Care Fraud Leads To 'Mass-Marketing' Sentencing Enhancement," *Financial Fraud Law*, August 3, 2011, http://www.financialfraudlaw.com/lawblog/liver4you-health-care-fraud-leads-%E2%80%98mass-marketing%E2%80%99-sentencing-enhancement/2631.

[631] Denis Campbell and Nicola Davison, "Illegal Kidney Trade Booms as New Organ Is 'Sold Every Hour,'" *The Guardian*, May 27, 2012, http://www.theguardian.com/world/2012/may/27/kidney-trade-illegal-operations-who.

solid organs known to have been transplanted in ninety five member states in 2010 (legally and illegally), about seventy three thousand one hundred and seventy nine (sixty eight and a half percent) were kidneys. But those one hundred and six thousand eight hundred and seventy nine operations satisfied just ten percent of the global need.[632]

Involuntary Donation

Case: Laudiceia da Silva

In 1997 Ms da Silva needed to have an ovarian cyst removed. Later, her Doctor found that the surgeons in her hospital in Sao Paulo, Brazil, had also removed one of her kidneys.[633]

Case: Hu Jie

In 2012 Hu Jie, a twenty five year old Chinese migrant worker, agreed to sell his kidney but then changed his mind. Unfortunately, the traffickers said he could not escape surgery once he had signed for it.[634]

Case: Yafimau

Aged thrity and from the Ukraine, Yafimau found himself locked in a hotel room for a month in Quito, Ecuador, waiting for surgeons to cut out an organ. Roini Shimshilashvili, a former kickboxer, was holding him on behalf of an international organ-trafficking ring, when Yafimau pleaded with Shimshilashvili to let him get out of the deal and go home, the big man sliced the air with Thai-boxing moves and threatened him. “He said if I didn’t go through with it, he would leave me in Ecuador and kill my family,” Yafimau says.[635]

In Nigeria, just as in Long Mei, there is a market for small babies. Sometimes the women consent to be impregnated and live in hospitals until the babies are born. On other occasions, poor young women who cannot afford to have a baby are lured into a hospital for what they think is an abortion and kept incarcerated, until they have their baby. They may be offered a token payment before release. They are frightened to talk and fear Police corruption. The babies are most often adopted but there is a market for body parts in Nigeria for voodoo ceremonies.[636]

---

[632] Ibid.

[633] Albert Huebner, “Organ Snatchers 5/04,” *Toward Freedom*, June 23, 2005, http://towardfreedom.com/special-reports/454-organ-snatchers-504.

[634] Campbell and Davison, “Illegal Kidney Trade Booms as New Organ Is ‘Sold Every Hour.’”

[635] Smith, Krasnolutska, and Glovin, “Organ Gangs Force Poor to Sell Kidneys for Desperate Israelis.”

[636] Staff, “Babies Bred for Sale in Nigeria,” *Mail & Guardian, South Africa*, November 9, 2008, http://mg.co.za/article/2008-11-09-babies-bred-for-sale-in-nigeria.

Questions:

Would you have an organ transplant bought from a non-family donor?

What are the ethical issues for participants, including Doctors and medical staff in this trade?

What would stop westerners from using organ transplants?

Do you consider the people who are so sick that they need a new organ in order to live, or live normal lives, in the same category as the traffickers who buy and sell human beings for profit?

Significant progress has been made in the re-growth of organs and tissue. Ian Goldin anticipates that the special Olympic will die out by 2040 because of this research progress. Perhaps the end of organ trafficking is also not far away?[637]

[637] Ted Talks, *Ian Goldin: Navigating Our Global Future*, TED Talks (Oxford, U.K., 2009).

Sex

Chapter 18

Internet - Friend or Foe

"The problem is exacerbated by "social networking sites and easy access to pornography. In one case, boys aged 14 and 15 were 'summoned' via Blackberry message to the gang rape of a 'very, very young girl' which lasted several days"[638]

On June 12, 2012, Sue Berelowitz, the UK Deputy Children's Commissioner reported to the Home Office Select Committee that children are being exploited in every "town, village and hamlet".[639] Peter Davies, chief executive of Child Exploitation and Online Protection, believes that group and gang related child sexual exploitation is far more widespread than people like to imagine.[640]

The evidence came soon after a case in which Asian men in Rochdale, England, had groomed, drugged and intoxicated girls before passing them around for sex.[641] After that case there was much media attention focused on the British Asian community but the deputy commissioner told the committee that the increased evidence of sexual abuse was not related to color or race but more to boys trying to copy what they see on pornography sites. She recounted one case, which she said illustrated the problem, where a girl had been contacted via the internet by someone she thought she knew through the internet as a friend. The girl went to meet this 'friend' only to find a gang of eight boys who raped her before letting another gang do the same. Further she spoke of cases where boys are using their phones to call their friends to rapes. "Boys were being called while some were raping the girl to say 'come, come, come, you can join in too' and they were arriving and elbowing each other out of the way to rape her".[642] Blaming online pornography for making things worse, including the filming of rapes and other sexual assaults she said "We've had boys say to us 'It was like being in a porn movie'... It (online pornography) has definitely affected children's thresholds of what they think is normal"[643] The Children's

---

[638] *Child Sexual Exploitation and the Response to Localised Grooming.*
[639] Ibid.
[640] Ibid.
[641] Nigel Bunyan, "Rochdale Grooming Trial: How the Case Unfolded," *Telegraph.co.uk*, June 21, 2012, sec. uknews, http://www.telegraph.co.uk/news/uknews/crime/9347305/Rochdale-grooming-trial-how-the-case-unfolded.html.
[642] *Child Sexual Exploitation and the Response to Localised Grooming.*
[643] Ibid.

Commissioner created a full report on this matter including all the scholarly studies done around the world.[644]

Does Access to Porn Online cause the Breakdown of Societal Norms Allowing the Use of Victims of Human Trafficking?

In May 2012, a fourteen year old, who had been twelve years old at the time of the offence, appeared before the High Court in Edinburgh to plead guilty to the rape of a nine year old girl. In his defense the boy's lawyer, Sean Templeton said

> *"There is a real risk that young people of the current generation are growing up with a skewed view of what sex is and sexual activity. This was an emulation of an adult act witnessed by him at an early age. He was afforded unfettered access to the internet and it has become apparent that from a very young age, the age of 12, he was accessing hard-core pornography."*

In sentencing him, Lady Smith, the Judge, said

> *"You should not and must not regard pornography as any guide at all as to how to behave sexually. You should not have engaged in sexual activity of any sort with a nine year old girl or indeed any other young girl who, under our law, is not able to consent to it.'*[645]

As has been seen in these cases the viewing of (child) pornography online helps the offenders to 'validate' their actions. It also introduces them to other who think like them and have similar appetites which continues the 'normalization' process. It is difficult for the authorities to stop online pornography and arrest and convict perpetrators. Equally, stopping traffickers forcing children to work in the porn industry is problematic. Despite misgivings by law enforcement a non-profit called Perverted Justice traps perpetrators through chat room activity and goes on to seek convictions.[646] The issue of self-produced child pornography and sexting is also a growing problem and differing views have been offered as to the correct response of society.[647] Professor Smith offered a different viewpoint to that expressed by Professor Leary, especially after the actions of the District

---

[644] Miranda, A.H. Horvath et al., *Basically Porn Is Everywhere* (Children's Commissioner, June 2013), http://www.childrenscommissioner.gov.uk/force_download.php?fp=%2Fclient_assets%2Fcp%2Fpublication%2F680%2FBasically_porn_is_everywhere_cyp_version.pdf.

[645] Simon Johnson, "A Generation Is Growing up Skewed by Internet Pornography, Court Hears, as 12-Year-Old Who Raped a Schoolgirl Is Spared Jail," *The Telegraph*, May 31, 2012, http://www.telegraph.co.uk/news/uknews/crime/9303598/A-generation-is-growing-up-skewed-by-internet-pornography-court-hears-as-12-year-old-who-raped-a-schoolgirl-is-spared-jail.html.

[646] Perverted Justice < http://www.perverted-justice.com/>

[647] Mary Graw Leary, ", Self-Produced Child Pornography: The Appropriate Societal Response to Juvenile Self-Sexual Exploitation," *VA J. Soc. Policy & L.* 15, no. 1 (2007).

Attorney of Wyoming, Pennsylvania.[648] In 2008, he offered sexting teens a choice; attend an education course or be charged with child pornography. The Circuit Court ruled that such a scheme was likely to be unconstitutional.

In a study in June 2012, conducted by the Chartered Institute for Marketing in the United Kingdom one thousand parents were polled of whom forty four percent supported the enactment of new legislation to stop the commercialization and sexualization of children. Parents reported concerns about the use of sexual images in advertising to children. The British government has set up "ParentPort", which is run by British media regulators, and has been looking at taking measures to introduce new filters for online pornography. The government has been reluctant to use legislation preferring a 'social responsibility' route.

The British government spent the spring of 2012 debating what to do about children being able to access porn online. A report of MPs was produced in which the MPs called for an 'opt-in' system.[649] This automatically blocks adult material on any new purchase of a computer, smartphone or on signing up for broadband. The user then needs to deactivate the 'opt-in' system to use such content. Andy Flanagan CEO of NSPCC said "Long term we back the next step which is the introduction of an opt-in filtering system for all internet accounts in the UK. This will mean all new internet accounts will default automatically to a setting that blocks access to adult content.[650] However, the vendors of broadband all developed 'active choice' which allowed users to choose controls rather than the automatic imposition. The government itself favored this system. The matter became very controversial when it was thought that the government was saying one thing and doing another but the 'active choice +' system was eventually agreed. Dr Katherine Rake CEO of Family and Parenting Institute remains concerned about what protection will be given to children whose parents already have electronic devices and broadband.

Here we see an untidy confluence of ideas and problems. Those who wish to ensure freedom of speech and those who would like to see curtailment of online pornography sites to protect children. Child pornography is big business which means that those who suffer are the child victims making the porn, the children who view it and the children, as in the above cases, who are abused because of it.

In the U.S. the Courts have been trying to find a way between the protection of the child and maintaining the constitutional rights of the citizen. The following cases are presented to give the reader some idea of the complexities:

---

[648] Stephen F. Smith, "Jail for Juvenile Child Pronographers?:a Reply to Professor Leary," *15VA. J. Soc. Pol'y & L.* (2008): 505.

[649] *Independent Parliamentary Inquiry into Online Child Protection- Findings and Recommendations* (UK Parliament, April 17, 2012), http://www.claireperry.org.uk/downloads/independent-parliamentary-inquiry-into-online-child-protection.pdf.

[650] John Bingham, "Online Pornography: Opt-in System Planned to Protect Children," *Telegraph.co.uk*, June 28, 2012, sec. news, http://www.telegraph.co.uk/technology/news/9359848/Online-pornography-opt-in-system-planned-to-protect-children.html.

U. S. Case Law

United States v Michael Timothy Arnold[651]

In July 2005 Arnold returned from a trip to the Philippines. At the airport in Los Angeles he was stopped by Border Control. In his luggage the officer found a number of digital items including a laptop computer. She asked him to switch on the computer which reviewed two folders on the desktop; 'Kodak Pictures' and 'Kodak memories'. The customs officer opened the file which showed two photographs of naked women. The officers questioned Arnold and investigated his computer on which they found images they believed showed child pornography. It has long been the law that Border Control can search 'closed containers' such as "purses, wallets and pockets", indeed, with reasonable suspicion they may search a person's alimentary canal.[652] The Supreme Court held that the laptop was no different from a closed box and, thus, could be subjected to a 'suspicionless' search. They refused Arnold's argument to privacy distinguishing between privacy at home or in the office and privacy crossing territorial borders.

As has been seen the scope of this problem is huge and the Courts have been developing child pornography as a separate category of prohibited 'speech'. Of course, the problem with the internet is that, unlike 'closed containers' at the border the 'border' are blurry and this is a truly transnational problem.[653] As Mary Graw Leary explains, the number of enquires for child pornography (one hundred and sixteen thousand daily from one website) and the number of photographs being loaded onto the internet (twenty thousand per week) show an exponential growth in abuse.[654]

The principle federal statute is the Child Pornography Prevention Act of 1996 U.S. Title 18 §2252A. A number of cases have been tried under these provisions and show the evolution of the law. They start with the obscenity case of Miller.[655] In New York v Paul Ira Ferber 458 U.S. 747 (1982) the Court decided that pornographic images could only be banned if they were obscene but child pornography could be banned whether or not the images are obscene. The mere possession of child pornography was deemed illegal in Clyde Osborne v Ohio 495 U.S. 103 (1990). The Supreme Court in John D. Ashcroft v The Free Speech Coalition 535 U.S. 234 (2002) considered whether the Child Pornography Prevention Act of 1996 abridges freedom of speech. Specifically whether images which use new technology to create images which look like child pornography but do not feature children fell within the ambit of the Act. In the opinion of the Court, delivered by Justice Kennedy, the act was unconstitutional in so far as it sought to enable the government to suggest that virtual images designed to look like children but which were not children were child pornography. Justice Thomas pointed out that no Defendant had successfully been

---

[651] 523 F.3d 941 (9th Cir. 2008)

[652] United States v. Montoya de Hernandez, 473 U.S. 531, 541 (1985)

[653] U.S. Department of Justice, *The National Strategy for Child Exploitation and Interdiction: A Report to Congress 2-3* (U.S. Congress, 2010).

[654] Graw Leary, ", Self-Produced Child Pornography: The Appropriate Societal Response to Juvenile Self-Sexual Exploitation."

[655] Marvin Miller v California, 413 U.S. 15 (1973)

able to claim the images for which s/he was being tried were virtual images which were not actually children. He did allow for the fact that the Government may have to enact new law as technology advanced in this area.

Distribution and Possession of Child Pornography

In Navrestadt the Court held that it was not distribution of child pornography to send a hyperlink to Yahoo! Briefcase during a 'chat', whereas in Dodd, the Court decided that placing child pornography in a Person to person file share folder was distribution. [656] Three cases illustrate the development of the law of possession. First, is Romm; in this case he was held to have 'exercised dominion and control' over the pictures because he has enlarged them and the saved them for five minutes after which he deleted them.[657] In Bass the Court decided that evidence of the Defendant having used "History Kill" and "Window Washer" to rid a computer of child pornography was sufficient evidence for a jury to conclude that he had known child pornography was automatically saved to his mother's computer, which he had been using.[658] The Defendant in Mercer had repeatedly searched for a term related to child pornography and was found to 'be aware' that he was 'controlling the request' for child pornography to be sent. Further when the Defendant was on a child pornography website and browsing the images he had control of those images – he could decide what to look at and what to reject – therefore, he possessed the images.[659]

---

[656] United States v. Joshua P. Navrestad, 66 M.J. 202 (C.A.A.F. 2008) and United States v. William Ralph Dodd 598 F.3d 449 (8th Cir. 2010)
[657] United States v. Stuart Romm, 455 F.3d 990 (9th Cir. 2006)
[658] United States v. Brian Bass 411 F.3d 1198 (10th Cir. 2005)
[659] State v Benjamin W. Mercer, 782 N.W.2d 125 (Wis. Ct. App. 2010)

Chapter 19

Conclusion

What Can Be Done?

Prosecutions

> *"In 2006 there were only 5,808 prosecutions and 3,160 convictions throughout the world. This means that for every 800 people trafficked, only one person was convicted in 2006."*[660]

What Questions Should you Ask of Yourself?

- Am I willing to help
- How can I help
- How can I help and be safe (your safety is of paramount concern, traffickers are criminals and many of them are violent - do not put yourself in danger).

Readers of this book do an important thing to help: they become aware. The next step is to make other people aware by talking about the book and the problems about which you have read. Then know where your products come from and who made them. The Anti-Slavery Society (the modern descendent of Wilberforce's society) has a website called "Products of Slavery" through which you can inform yourself.[661] In the Annex there is a list of websites which offer slave free items. There is an app for phones called Free2Work which helps consumers to check that items they are buying are slave labor free. Also check out your slave footprint at Slavery Footprint.Org (http://slaveryfootprint.org/)

Join one of the many organizations which are dedicated to abolish modern slavery and volunteer for them. Like the trucker who saved the girls in Toledo don't be afraid to make a call. The authorities would rather investigate a wrong lead than miss helping victims. In the United States use these numbers:

- National Human Trafficking Resource Center (24 hours) will assist in connecting victims to services they may be eligible to receive. (Polaris Project sponsored by DHHS) **1-888-373-7888**

---

[660] Department Of State. The Office of Website Management, "Trafficking in Persons Report 2007."
[661] "Products of Slavery," *Anti-Slavery Campaign*, accessed November 7, 2013, www.productsofslavery.org.

- National Center for Missing and Exploited Children (NCMEC) Family Service Liaison **1-800-THE-LOST (1-800-843-5678)**
- Email Dottie Laster at Bernardo Kohler Center (http://bernardokohler.org/)
- **But for the quickest action call the local Police and ask for their Human Trafficking Department.**

Read the Appendix in which W. J. Sifuentes (Retired) Austin Police Department HTD, Texas, talks about what they do and what needs to be done. Consider what you want your neighborhood to look and feel like. It was seen that the comments of the Police Chief enabled authorities to refuse permission for a lap-dancing club in Newquay, Cornwall, UK. Remember that in the United States Police Chiefs prioritize their work based on electors wishes, make a noise!

Phone your Senator and Representative about what they are doing to support anti-human trafficking initiatives. You can make them keep the issue on their radar. Look at local actions which can be taken. In 1994, Nassau County had an initiative to close down massage parlors. They chose to look at violations of building codes and other issues involving the owners of buildings let to massage parlors. This resulted in all known illegal county massage parlors being closed or vacated.[662]

Stay informed, there are lots of websites dedicated to this problem. Google can be set so that it sends alerts of articles which may be good to read. If you are a fan of a celebrity bring the information you know to his or her attention. Write to chat show hosts and raise the issue at political meetings you attend. Give informal talks about trafficking at your Church, Mosque, Synagogue, Temple and to Clubs at which you are a member etc.

If you are worried about someone you meet, perhaps at a nail salon, here are some

Questions to Ask

- How did you get here?
- Do you know where you are?
- Where do you live, eat, and sleep?
- Are you working to pay a debt?
- Where is your passport or ID?
- Has someone threatened your family?
- Are you being abused?
- Can you leave if you want to?
- Are you afraid of someone?
- Are you doing this of your own free will?
- Are you truanting? Why?

---

[662] Hughes, "Donna M. Hughes, PhD, January 17, 2007 Speech to Women in Federal Law Enforcement."

- Have you runaway?
- Who do you live with? How are they related?
- Where do you come from?
- If appropriate ask about any tattoos

As has been seen victims may not be as you expect – many don't want to get away or, if they do, are too frightened. Plan to help them by involving the authorities, they have more tools available to them and you shouldn't place yourself in a dangerous position. Never take a victim home. There are some brothel outreach organizations. For example, Redeem Ministries operate brothel outreach in Austin and Houston in Texas. There may be something similar in your city.

Whatever you do remember your safety must be paramount. The authorities have many more tools available to them than you do – make that call…

A Few Success Stories:

On the radio

The indefatigable soldier against human trafficking, Dottie Laster, hosted a radio show called 'Trafficked' on 'Hear Women Talk'. One day she received an email which contained a photograph of a female victim's arm into which she had carved the words "Save Me".

Dottie has certainly not "seen it all" because what she and many people working in this area will say is that just when you think there can be nothing worse along it comes, however Dottie didn't break stride in her efforts to help. She made contact with the young American slave who had done this to her arm and, this lady (and her cat) were rescued by Dottie.

Groundbreaking sentence increase for human trafficker

04/29/2004

The Attorney General in the UK is permitted to take criminal cases to the Court of Appeal if the sentences are thought to be too low (Criminal Justice Act 1988). In 2004 the Court of Appeal more than doubled the sentence of Luan Plakici, an Albanian living in London, from ten to twenty three years. Plakici had been convicted, after a trial lasting four months, in December 2003, of fifteen counts of assisting unlawful immigration, living on prostitution, kidnapping, procuring a girl to have unlawful sexual intercourse and incitement to rape.

In addition to the longer sentence detectives continued work on trying to seize the assets, two hundred thousand G.B pounds, amassed in under two and half years and a Ferrari and a BMW.

The case came to light when a girl ran from a house in Palmers Green, London, she went to the local police and had the courage to tell them that she was an illegal immigrant. She was seventeen years old and had been held there against her will with her twenty year old sister. It was October 2002, when she had first met the defendant, Plakici, in Romania. He told them that he could get them work in a Bar in the UK and that he would get them entry into the country. Unfortunately, when they arrived he enslaved them in the sex industry and they were kept with two other girls in the Palmers Green house. If they refused Plakici's commands they were raped and beaten.

During investigations the Metropolitan Police discovered the normal tools of the traffickers trade "a sophisticated network with ready access to false documents, money, accommodation and transport."[663] When the case came to trail seven victims, all aged between seventeen to twenty four told the court of their time in captivity. They came from Romania (four) and Moldova (three) and told of their journeys through the Czech Republic, Italy and France.

Baby Face

In this case, reported by Nicholas Kristoff in the New York Times, the young slave had obviously not been sufficiently traumatized by her trafficker or perhaps, was so terrified that, she was utterly desperate.[664] The girl, called 'Baby Face' by Kristoff, was in sexual slavery. In November 2011, she had been taken by her trafficker to an apartment building in Brooklyn, New York.

She was sent into the building by her pimp to provide sexual services to a customer who had 'ordered' her. 'Baby Face' chose this small opportunity of not being supervised to seek help. She banged on a door she passed and was fortunate enough to get help from the inhabitants of the apartment.

The Future?

There are many things which need to be done in order to resolve this social injustice. Throughout the book examples of improvements to laws, health and education have been mentioned. This short-list is meant to gather ideas together for the reader which can be used for thinking more deeply about solutions:

[663] "Groundbreaking Sentence Increase for Human Trafficker" (Crown Prosecution Service, April 29, 2004), http://www.cps.gov.uk/news/latest_news/118_04/.

[664] Nicholas D. Kristof, "How Pimps Use the Web to Sell Girls," *The New York Times*, January 25, 2012, sec. Opinion, http://www.nytimes.com/2012/01/26/opinion/how-pimps-use-the-web-to-sell-girls.html.

What Can Be Done?

- More effective criminal laws[665]
- Changes to State and Federal Law in the United States[666]
- Re-thinking policy[667]
- A change in employment laws[668]
- More effective international cooperation in policing and border control
- Better education of law enforcement personnel
- Better care for Victims[669]
- Better Education (Access for all and quality) [670]
- Healthcare, specifically for women and girls
- Social Responsibility amongst producers[671] and consumers[672]
- Increased enforcement of labor regulations nationally and internationally[673]
- Better global policy decisions[674]

It is to be hoped that many of the things which have been discussed in this book may have a mere historical context as the world turns. Already we have seen robots replacing child slaves as jockeys in the United Arab Emirates.[675] Advances in robotic technology may reduce costs of robotic workers so rendering the use of slave labor less profitable. Where the business can generate a larger profit without slave labor the trade may end. Of course, it is difficult to see when that may come but only a few years ago self-driving cars where an idea of the future but with Google successfully test driving them in 2012 in California and

---

[665] Siddharth Kara, "Designing More Effective Laws Against Human Trafficking.," *Journal of International Human Rights* 9, no. 2 (Spring 2011): 123–147; Scott Davidson Dyle, "Beginning to Seize the Instrumentalities of Human Trafficking: Chapter 514 Allows Criminal Forfeiture of Property Used to Facilitate the Sex Trafficking of Minors.," *McGeorge Law Review* 44, no. 3 (April 2013): 575–582; Scott Davidson Dyle, "Chapter 515: Combating Human Trafficking by Enhancing Awareness Through Public Postings," *McGeorge Law Review* 44, no. 3 (April 2013): 583–590.

[666] Tiffanie N. Choate, "Protecting the Lydias, Linas, and Tinas from Sex Trafficking: A Call to Eliminate Ambiguities of 18 U.S.C. § 1591," *Oklahoma Law Review; Summer2013, Vol. 65 Issue 4, p665-716* 65, no. 4 (Summer 2013): 665–716.

[667] Elizete D. Velado, "SHIFTING GEARS: IMPROVING ANTI-TRAFFICKING EFFORTS THROUGH A SHIFT IN POLICY FOCUS," *Journal of Transnational Law & Policy* 22 (January 1, 2012): 187.

[668] Hila Shamir, "A Labor Paradigm for Human Trafficking," *UCLA Law Review* 60, no. 1 (October 2012): 76–136.

[669] Mary P. Van Hook, "Modern Day Slavery: Trafficking of Persons in Rural America," *Rural Mental Health* (Summer 2004).

[670] Sugata Mitra and Ritu Dangwal, "Limits to Self-Organising Systems of Learning: The Kalikuppam Experiment.," *British Journal of Educational Technology* 41, no. 5 (September 2010): 672–68.

[671] Naomi Jiyoung Bang, "American Geographical Society's Focus on Geography. Summer2013, Vol. 56 Issue 2, p54-65," *Houston Journal of International Law* 35, no. 2 (Spring 2013): 255–322.

[672] Anna Williams Shavers, "HUMAN TRAFFICKING, THE RULE OF LAW, AND CORPORATE SOCIAL RESPONSIBILITY.," *South Carolina Journal of International Law & Business* 9, no. 1 (Fall 2012): 39–88.

[673] Beate Andrees, *Forced Labour and Human Trafficking: Handbook for Labour Inspectors* (Geneva: International Labour Office, 2008).

[674] Roza Pati, "Trading in Humans: A New Haven Perspective," *Asia Pacific Law Review* 20, no. 2 (2012): 135–166.

[675] *Robot Replace Children as Camel Jockeys in the UAE.*

many auto manufacturers proposing production of increasingly automatic cars within the next few years.[676] The 'future' may be closer than expected.[677] In 2012, two scientists from New Zealand posited that robotic 'prostitutes' would be in wide use by 2050.[678] Professors Henrik Sharfe and Hiroshi Ishiguro have been working with their robotic 'clones' for years.[679]

Of course, it could be that population changes will simply make the people currently vulnerable to human trafficking more desirable and so less vulnerable. In this context the evidence which shows population coffins within the Western world is important. As Ian Goldin says, the xenophobic concerns of today may disappear as we need to recruit workers at all levels to help to hold up the excessive number of retirees in the West where birth rate has failed to keep up with need.[680] Likewise in China it is widely agreed that the high number of workers fueled the 'economic miracle'.[681] However, these workers have been, largely, limited to having one child per couple since 1979. This one child policy has created a number of generations of single, extremely spoilt, children.[682] The Chinese government has had to enact laws to require them to look after their parents and grandparents, emotionally and physically. If the 'miracle' is not to fail, China may have to import workers from other countries which would fundamentally change the ethnicity of the country. As has been seen, foreign slaves in China are considered to be ethnically inferior. Would a mass immigration create more or fewer divisions?

In 2013, Time magazine feature the following on its cover: "Can Google Solve Death? The Search Giant is launching a venture to extend the human life span. That would be crazy – if it weren't Google."[683] Such hyperbole is merely reflective of some of the long-term thinking being done in the technology industries. For example, Google employed Ray Kurtzweil in 2012; he has long been a proponent of extending human life through

---

[676] Google, "Self-Driving Car Test: Steve Mahan," *Google*, accessed November 10, 2013, http://www.google.com/about/jobs/lifeatgoogle/self-driving-car-test-steve-mahan.html; Andrew English, "Toyota's Driverless Car," *Telegraph.co.uk*, October 25, 2013, sec. car-manufacturers, http://www.telegraph.co.uk/motoring/car-manufacturers/toyota/10404575/Toyotas-driverless-car.html.

[677] Oxford Martin School and University of Oxford, "Oxford Martin School | University of Oxford," *The Oxford Martin School*, accessed November 10, 2013, http://www.oxfordmartin.ox.ac.uk/; "Singularity University," accessed November 10, 2013, http://singularityu.org; "Singularity Hub," accessed November 10, 2013, http://singularityhub.com.

[678] Ian Yeoman and Michelle Mars, "Robots, Men and Sex Tourism," *Science Direct* Futures Volume 44, no. 4 (May 2012): 365–371.

[679] TED, *TEDx Brussels 2011 - Henrik Sharfe - DK Geminoid* (Brussels, Belgium, 2011), http://www.youtube.com/watch?v=oiyviOdF_ac.

[680] Ted Talks, *Ian Goldin: Navigating Our Global Future*.

[681] Sheying Chen and Jason L. Powel, eds., *Aging in China: Implications to Social Policy of a Changing Economic State* (New York, NY: Springer, 2012).

[682] L. Cameron et al., "Little Emperors: Behavioral Impacts of China's One-Child Policy.," *Science* 339, no. 6122 (February 22, 2013): 953–7.

[683] Harry McCracken and Lev Grossman, "Can Google Solve Death? The Search Giant Is Launching a Venture to Extend the Human Life Span. That Would Be Crazy – If It Weren't Google," *Time*, 2013.

technology.[684] In May 2013, National Geographic featured this on its cover: "This Baby will live to be 120 (It's not just hype. New Science could lead to very long lives)."[685] As Ian Goldin and many others ask, is this a new eugenics or a genuine step forward for ALL of the human race. In either case the ramifications for human rights are enormous.

A final thought...

It is often said that the debate about prostitution does not help human trafficking victims because it obscures the issues of the trafficked victim in rhetoric around the morality and consent concerning prostitution. Furthermore, it has long been said that prostitution cannot be eradicated; it is the 'oldest profession', or maybe the second oldest after slavery. It is also said that anti-trafficking campaigns are anti-prostitution. This is true in so far as they seek to stop people working against their will rather than as willing participants.[686] Countries with liberal views have tried to limit the damage to men women and children in the 'profession' by legalizing prostitution or, as in the case of Sweden, only making the user of prostitutes a criminal. However, it is posited that this interpretation only masks the social problems that cause prostitution. Likewise, the social problems which create human trafficking victims can also create unwilling prostitutes. Where the line is drawn is a major point for discussion. The solution to those social problems of, for example, poverty and lack of education which lead to a lack of real choice as to work would take a sea change in society. The question then arises as to whether society has to change fundamentally for prostitution to be considered so dangerous to the majority of its workers that it becomes as socially unacceptable as victimizing the LGBT community or racism. To achieve that does not require a great change; young people have to be socially aware and concerned, awareness needs to be raised and the patriarchal society defused by the elevation of women within society. Never, in the past, has any major country in the world been non-patriarchal but with a future in which 60% of undergraduates in the U.S. are women that change should come.[687] Will it bring a feminist view which applauds the liberation of the sex worker who can sell her body or, as has been the theme of this book, an understanding that the bulk of prostitution involves unwilling workers who would like a better life outside their 'profession' or perhaps that there is room for both without exploitation of the latter.

---

[684] Ray Kurzweil, *The Singularity Is Near: When Humans Transcend Biology* (New York, NY: Penguin Group, 2005).

[685] Stephen S. Hall, "'This Baby Will Live to Be 120 (It's Not Just Hype. New Science Could Lead to Very Long Lives).,'" *National Geographic Magazine*, May 2013.

[686] Janie A. Chuang, "RESCUING TRAFFICKING FROM IDEOLOGICAL CAPTURE: PROSTITUTION REFORM AND ANTI-TRAFFICKING LAW AND POLICY," *University of Pennsylvania Law Review* 158, no. 6 (May 2010): 1655–1728.

[687] Alex Williams, "The New Math on Campus," *The New York Times*, February 5, 2010, sec. Fashion & Style, http://www.nytimes.com/2010/02/07/fashion/07campus.html.

Glossary

APD:HTD – Austin Police Department Human Trafficking Division

BKC – Bernardo Kohler Center

CRC – Convention on the Rights of the Child 1989

CRPD – Convention on the Rights of Persons with Disabilities and Optional Protocol 2006

CEDAW – Convention on the Elimination of all forms of Discrimination Against Women 1979

CEOP – Child Exploitation and Online Protection

DRC – Democratic Republic of the Congo

ECPAT – End Child Prostitution, Child Pornography, and Trafficking of Children for Sexual Purposes

HT – Human Trafficking

ICE – Immigration and Customs Enforcement Agency (USA)

ILO – International Labor Organization

NSPCC – National Society for the Prevention of Cruelty to Children (UK)

TVPA – Victims of Trafficking and Violence Protection Act 2000 as amended and reauthorized in 2003, 2005 and 2008

UDHR – Universal Declaration of Human Rights 1948

UK – United Kingdom

UNGIFT – United Nations Global Initiative to Fight Human Trafficking

UNICEF – United Nations Children's Fund

UNODC – United Nations Office on Drugs and Crime

WHO – World Health Organization

Appendix 1:
Suggested Questions for Human Trafficking Interview Used by Austin Police Department, Texas (which questions are used is at the discretion of the interviewing officer)

Appendix 1:

Suggested Questions for Human Trafficking Interview Used by Austin Police Department, Texas (which questions are used is at the discretion of the interviewing officer)

Consider using some of the following key questions provided in your interview to determine whether someone is a victim of human trafficking.

Background

- Name: Have the victim write his or her name.
- Ask for the victim's real name, not the name the defendants may have given him/her.
- Where were you born?
- How old are you?
- Where did you grow up?
- Do you have a mother and father?
- How many siblings do you have?
- How many years of school have you completed?
- What was your profession?
- In former jobs, were you free to come and go as you wished?
- Did your former employer ever force you to work?
- Were you ever abused by a former employer?
- Were you ever threatened by a former employer?
- Do you have possession of your identification and immigration papers?

Recruitment

- How did you learn about the job under investigation?
- Where?
- From whom?
- What type of work did you think you would be doing?
- How did the person who recruited you convince you to take the job?
- Were any promises made to you about wages?

Appendix 1:
Suggested Questions for Human Trafficking Interview Used by Austin Police Department, Texas (which questions are used is at the discretion of the interviewing officer)

- Were any promises made to you about work hours/days off/vacations?
- Were you shown any photographs (i.e., pictures of happy workers or parties)?
- How many meetings did you have to discuss the job being offered?
- Who was with you when you were talking about the job?
- Where did the meeting take place?
- Describe what was said and promised at each meeting.
- Were you told that you would owe them money after you started work?
- If so, how much?
- How would the money be paid back?
- Were you told that you would have to pay money up front?
- If so, where did you get that money?

Transportation

- Where are you from?
- How did you arrive in New Mexico?
- Conditions of travel (If not by common carrier)
- Truck? If so, where did you ride in the truck?
- Food and water?
- Rest stops?
- What was the treatment of men and women in the truck?
- Was there overcrowding in the truck?
- Did anyone meet you at the airport (if transportation was by plane)?
- Who paid for the airline ticket?
- Did the person who paid for the ticket use cash or a credit card?
- Who met you at the airport?
- Where did you go from the airport?
- In what type of vehicle did you travel in?
- Who drove?
- Where did you sit in the vehicle?

Arrival at Workplace

- How did you get to the place of work?
- Who met you at the workplace?
- Who told you the 'rules of the house?'
- What were the rules?

Appendix 1:
Suggested Questions for Human Trafficking Interview Used by Austin Police Department, Texas (which questions are used is at the discretion of the interviewing officer)

- Were you told anything about where you were not allowed to go?
- What were you told would happen if you left without permission?
- Were you told who the boss was?
- Who was the boss?
- Were you physically abused, beaten, or raped on arrival?

Fraud/Financial Coercion

- Were you forced to do different work than what was promised?
- Who forced you into doing different work than what was promised?
- Was there some sort of work contract signed?
- Were you getting paid to do your job?
- Did you actually receive payment or is your money being held for you?
- Did you owe your employer money?
- What, if anything, did you think would happen back home about the debt?
- Are there records or receipts of what is owed to your employer/recruiter?
- Are there records/receipts of what was earned/paid to you?
- How were financial transactions handled?
- Are you in possession of your own legal (I.D.) documents? If not, why?
- Were you provided false documents or identification?
- Are you being made to do things that you do not want to do?
- Were you told a story that you and others should tell if you were picked up by police?

Physical Abuse

- Did any of the owners ever say things to try and keep you/others from leaving?
- What was said?
- Who said them?
- Were people afraid to leave?
- Why?
- Did anyone say what would happen if people tried to leave?
- Were you ever threatened with harm if you tried to leave?
- Did you ever witness any threats or abuse against other people if they tried to leave?
- Has your family been threatened?
- Do you know about any other person's family ever being threatened?

Appendix 1:
Suggested Questions for Human Trafficking Interview Used by Austin Police Department, Texas (which questions are used is at the discretion of the interviewing officer)

- Were you ever physically abused, or did you ever witness abuse against another person?
- What type of physical abuse did you witness?
- Was anyone ever hit or threatened for doing bad work or for working too slowly?
- Did you ever hear about anyone being killed?
- Were there any objects or weapons used in the physical abuse?
- Where are these objects or weapons located?
- Was knowledge of this abuse ever communicated to a person outside of this situation (e.g., police reports, domestic violence reports, hospital records, social service records)?
- Did you receive a tattoo or brand from your pimp/boyfriend?

Psychological Coercion

- Who are you afraid of?
- Why are you afraid of them?
- What would you like to see happen to the people who hurt you (e.g., jail, deportation)?
- How do you feel about the police? Why?
- Did they ever say anything bad about the police?

Work

- What type of work did you do?
- What were your hours of work?
- Did you have any breaks? When did they occur?
- What were your days off?
- What was your pay?
- Average per month? Per week?
- Were you given any record of your pay?
- Did your boss take anything out of your pay?
- How much?
- What for?
- Were you given any records which reflected the deductions?
- Describe conditions of the workplace.
- Where was the workplace located?

Appendix 1:
Suggested Questions for Human Trafficking Interview Used by Austin Police Department, Texas (which questions are used is at the discretion of the interviewing officer)

- How many people worked there?
- Was the workplace crowded?
- Did you travel for work? Where? How often?
- Who supervised your work?
- How did the supervisor treat the workers?
- Did the supervisor say mean things to the workers?
- What specifically was said?
- Were people ever forced to work when they did not want to?
- What would happen if you told your boss that you did not want to work that day?

Other Living Conditions

- Sleeping arrangements
- Where did you sleep?
- Did you live and work in the same place?
- Did you sleep on the bed or on the floor?
- What time did you go to bed? What time did you you wake up?
- Were you allowed to sleep late if you wanted to?
- What would happen if you happened to sleep late on a workday?
- Did you have to pay for lodging?
- Where did the alleged perpetrators live/eat/sleep?
- Clothing
- How many changes of clothing did you have?
- Was any clothing taken away from you?
- Were you allowed to buy your own clothing?
- Did your boss add the cost of your clothing to any debt you owed?
- Food
- How many meals did you eat each day?
- What times did you eat?
- Could you eat at anytime you wanted?
- Was the food locked up?
- Did you have to pay for your food?
- Could you buy it from anyone other than the boss?
- Did they charge money for the food or did they deduct it from your pay?
- Did this make your debt grow?
- Were you ever hungry?

Appendix 1:
Suggested Questions for Human Trafficking Interview Used by Austin Police Department, Texas (which questions are used is at the discretion of the interviewing officer)

- Did you have permission to eat?
- Who did you have to ask for permission to eat?
- What would happen if someone ate without asking permission?
- Did you ever sneak any food? Did you ever smuggle any food?
- Did anyone ever give you food secretly?
- • Medical Treatment
- Did you or anyone else ever get sick?
- Was anyone ever required to keep working even if they were sick?
- Did you ever see a doctor?
- Who took you to see the doctor?
- How long after you asked to see a doctor were you taken?
- What is the name and location of the doctor?
- Were you allowed to see the doctor alone?
- Who paid for the doctor's visit?
- Freedom of Movement
- Was your freedom of movement restricted?
- What were the conditions under which you were left unattended?
- Were there instances of physical restriction through locks, chains, etc.?
- Where are the locks used and who has the keys to them?
- How was movement in public places handled (e.g., car, van, bus, subway)?
- Who supervised your movement in public places?
- How was the purchase of private goods and services handled (e.g., medicines, prescriptions)?
- What forms of media or telecommunication did you have access to (e.g., television, radio, newspapers, magazines, telephone, the Internet)?
- Were you allowed to have relationships outside of your living and work places?
- Physical Barriers
- Were there any bars or locks on the windows?
- Were the locks changed on any doors?
- Did doors lock from inside or outside?
- Did you have a key?
- Were doors kept opened or closed?
- Who locked you in?

Appendix 1:
Suggested Questions for Human Trafficking Interview Used by Austin Police Department, Texas
(which questions are used is at the discretion of the interviewing officer)

Escapes

- Did you ever think about trying to leave?
- Why didn't you try to leave?
- What were you afraid of that kept you from leaving?
- Did you ever ask to stop working there?
- Why?
- Did anyone else ever try to leave but was unable to?
- What happened?
- Do you know where those individuals are now?
- What are their names?
- Did anyone every say anything about whether it was safe outside?
- Did you or others ever talk about wanting to leave?

Family Threats

- Did anyone ever threaten anyone's family members?
- Did anyone ever threaten to do anything to the family members' homes?

Guards

- Was there anyone responsible for watching the workers to make sure that they did not escape or leave?
- Who?
- Did these people ever accompany you or others to the store or when you would leave from where you lived/worked?
- Did these people ever carry any weapons?
- If so, what type?
- Did they ever threaten anyone with their weapons?
- Did they ever fire their guns?
- Did they ever fire their guns at anyone?

Rescue/Escape

If already out of situation:

- How did you get away?
- Whom did you contact?
- Did you ever try to get help before?

Appendix 1:
Suggested Questions for Human Trafficking Interview Used by Austin Police Department, Texas (which questions are used is at the discretion of the interviewing officer)

- If so, what happened?
- What made you leave when you did?
- Was there any particular event that happened that day or close to that time?
- Tell the story of how you got out of the situation. What happened that day?
- Have the people you escaped from tried to find you at all?
- Do you ever hear from or have any contact with anyone still there?

Appendix 2: Interview, by Author, of W.J. Sifuentes Austin Police Department, Human Trafficking Division, Texas, U.S.A. (Retired)

Q. Please explain the creation of the Human Trafficking Unit and how you became involved:

A. The department experienced its first Human Trafficking case in 2003. It was not handled very well, not because of the people involved, but because NGOs were not involved. We had no support structure for the three trafficking victims at the time. It was then that our dept and Texas Refugees Services got together and applied for a dual grant, one for Legal Enforcement and the other for the NGO. In 2004 the grant was awarded for both. I joined the unit which comprised a Sergeant, and three detectives, in July 2005. Our mission was not totally clear, and neither was our unit name. We were known as the Immigrant Protection Team, and it seemed like every immigrant victim of a crime came our way which interfered with our real mission which was to rescue trafficking victims. Because I knew the department and the police culture it was an easy fit. I had been retired for eight years already and this seemed like something I would be a contributor to. But Law Enforcement is just a small part of our victims because it is with the NGOs that they have the hope of restoring their lives. APD has enjoyed a tremendous relationship with Texas Refuge Services.

Q. Tell me a little about cases in which APR have been involved?

A. The most dangerous and active case we had we called El Tio. The case involved a 15 yr old grand niece and her mother, the niece of the trafficker. The child and her mother were smuggled from Honduras to the USA, paid by the Tio (uncle). Once here he enslaved the 15 year old and separated the family under threat of death if they called the police or saw each other. She was forced to conduct cocaine deals, carry his cocaine into bars and be touched by the Tio's customers. She also carried his gun. The danger of this was he was family, and knew where the 15 yr olds brother and other relatives lived. We decided to get him on drug and gun charges due to his lengthy criminal record here before he became a trafficker. This was for the safety of the victims, and so she would not have to testify. He is in prison for many years, and the family reunited is living somewhere in California.

Q. What is the make-up of the Unit?

A. Commander (oversees all the units in the Organized Crime Division, OCD)

Lieutenant (oversees other units assigned to him in OCD)

Sergeant (HT and VICE supervisor)

Appendix 2: Interview, by Author, of W.J. Sifuentes Austin Police Department, Human Trafficking Division, Texas, U.S.A. (Retired)

Seven Detectives

The mission and investigations of human trafficking take a leading role in the unit. VICE operations are second when we have an active and on-going trafficking case. All the detectives work assigned cases, which include trafficking and VICE. There is not tension between wearing the 'twin hats of trafficking and VICE" the detectives know that their role here is to save and rescue trafficking victims.

Q. Can you give me an example of great cooperation with ICE or FBI?

A. In 2008, we were developing a case with the FBI that was referred to us by the FBI field office in Houston. The case involved an outcry made by a Guatemalan female who was put into sex trafficking by a family that was working out of Staples, Texas, outside San Marcos. She was very good witness. The case involved ICE and FBI , but we were the lead agency. This investigation lead to identifying numerous individuals including the leader a woman named Rosalinda Alvarez Trevino. The organized group were professional smugglers who turned into traffickers. The case ended with a raided on a stash house where 27 immigrants were found. Twenty six individuals were indicted and all went to prison. The victim is leaving in Tennessee.

Q. Can you give me numbers of trafficking arrests in Austin – even if they haven't led to successful prosecutions but have saved victims. Do you think that the lack of prosecutions and convictions masks the great job forces do and do you see this as a problem for funding and the whole anti-Human Trafficking (HT) movement?

A. Although in Austin we have not seen cooperation from federal and state prosecutors on actual HT charges we do see the state accepting charges such as Compelling Prostitution, Promotion of Prostitution. But for the most part is has been a thorn on our side. After all we want to hit the trafficker with the heavy hammer using both the federal TVPA and state legislation but it is still up to the prosecutors to wield that hammer. As in anything when public funds are used in any project there is an expectation of forward motion or success. The lack of numbers could certainly prevent funds coming into the units or departments where Law Enforcement is very active but yet lacks the support of the federal or state prosecutors.

Appendix 2: Interview, by Author, of W.J. Sifuentes Austin Police Department, Human Trafficking Division, Texas, U.S.A. (Retired)

Human Trafficking Task Force Metrics

Agency reporting: Austin Police Department (put your agency name here, TCSO, FBI, etc)

Agency contact person/phone number:		***1/1/05 - 6/30/05***	***7/1/05 - 12/31/05***	***1/1/06 - 6/30/06***	***7/1/06 - 12/31/06***	***1/1/07 - 6/30/07***	***7/1/07 - 12/31/07***	***1/1/2008 - 6/30/2008***	***7/1/2008- 12/31/08***	***1/1/09- 6/30/09***	***7/1/09- 12/31/09***	***1/1/10- 6/30/10***	***7/1/10- 12/31/10***	***1/1/11- 6/30/2011***	***07/01/11- 12/31/12***	***01/01/12- 06/30/12***	***Final***
	Progress Report Period #	**1st**	**2nd**	**3rd**	**4rd**		**5th**	**6th**	**7th**								
Performance Metrics																	
1. Number of individuals identified as potential victims of human trafficking. *Please note the case number and address associated with each of the potential victims of human trafficking. We should be include those individuals that we reasonably believed could be victims of*		4	14	16	9	12	12	2	12	12	21	6	5	5	1		131

human trafficking even if after further investigation, were identified as being involved in smuggling or hostage taking. ***Please attach a brief description of each case (name of subjects/ potential victims; date; location and general description of the case)***																
2. Number of applications made to DHS for victims to obtain continued presence in the U. S. *Please include name of each victim and an associated case number.*	0	3	1	5	1	3	2	3	0	0	0	0	0	1		19
3. Number of																

Appendix 2: Interview, by Author, of W.J. Sifuentes Austin Police Department, Human Trafficking Division, Texas, U.S.A. (Retired)

law enforcement officers and other person receiving training in the identification of trafficking victims. *Please include a brief description of the training, who attended, date held and number of attendees.*	151	173	467	250	***146**	180	60	472	501	340	77	102	380	571		3724
4. Number of sessions held for training in the identification of trafficking victims. *Please include a brief description of the training, who attended, date held and number of attendees.*	5	7	3	5	3	16	2	9	12	11	3	2	9	10		97
5. Number of trafficking awareness presentati	63	16	7	3	0	16	3	3	1	3	5	8	5	2		135

ons made to the public. *Please include a brief description of the event, who attended, date held and number of attendees.*																	
6. Number of service providers identified and collaborative agreements entered into before and after project implementation. (This measure is for the nonprofit Coalition partners, will be reported by APD Liaison or Kathi West as a Coalition rep)	*Before*	20	20									27					
	Currently	20	20	20	23	23	23	25	27	27	27	27	27	27	27		27
7. Number of community support groups identified and	*Before*	8															

collaborative agreements entered into before and after project implementation. This measure is for the nonprofit Coalition partners, will be reported by APD Liaison or Kathi West as a Coalition rep)	*Currently*	8	8	8	9	9	9	10	11	11	11	11	12	27	27		11
8. Number of community education entities identified and collaborative agreements entered into before and after project implementation. (This measure is for the nonprofit Coalition partners, will be reported by APD Liaison or Kathi West as a Coalition	*Before*	8															
	Currently	8	8	8	8	8	9	8	8	8	8	8	8	8	8		8

Appendix 2: Interview, by Author, of W.J. Sifuentes Austin Police Department, Human Trafficking Division, Texas, U.S.A. (Retired)

rep)															

Appendix 2: Interview, by Author, of W.J. Sifuentes Austin Police Department, Human Trafficking Division, Texas, U.S.A. (Retired)

Q. How do you think the law/ law enforcement needs changing so we save more victims?

A. Law Enforcement will always be the first to encounter victims. Training and awareness must be the cornerstone to strengthen our ability to recognize the crime. Across the USA training must become a mandatory topic when Law Enforcement is doing in-service training and within the academy lesson plans. After 12 yrs why are we still not finding more victims? The lack of wiliness from policy makers to provide training is one big reason.

Q. How do you think the law/enforcement needs changing so that we achieve more successful prosecutions?

A. Unfortunately, it will take mandates and laws to encourage prosecutors to file HT charges and not reduce them to misdemeanors. Last year Texas began taking that step.

Q. In the UK the abolition of slavery in the 19th century mainly came about because of the work of the anti-slavery society in raising awareness amongst the general public and riding a wave of public outrage. Is this what is needed to stop modern slavery in the US? Or are we now just so used to having cheap goods that we are happy to close our eyes to the way in which they are produced?

A. I believe that, sadly we are a country that has no moral compass when our companies go overseas. Yesterday an article in the Yahoo page reported that child labor continues to be a major problem in India. I think as long as it stays over there people here will not involve themselves to stop trafficking of any kind. But I have seen a change in the sex slave industry and how we see it, but only because, lately, we have seen more news and programs about the domestic victims, the American girl or boy.

Q. There were some public service announcements about trafficking – do you see these as an effective way to go?

A. Several years ago everyone thought PSAs were the way to go, so we saw numerous NGO spent precious dollars to a campaign with good intentions. I think it was not money well spent. APD and the CTCAHT also ran a PSA. To my knowledge we did not get one single victim from it. PSA, billboards and radio announcement do work for certain products and ideas, but if you look around those messages are produced by professionals who are thinking with their minds and not hearts. Again it all comes down to resources, and most NGOs or departments do not have those types of funds.

Q. Has there been any success with a victim safe house?

A. Freedom Place, in Houston has just been opened serving victims in the Houston area. There are no others in Texas. I think we are behind the times for these shelters because we have relied on places like Safe Place. Now, we see the victim of trafficking is a different person, and needs a lot more. We also see the trafficking victim is in need of a longer time in a shelter. So now we see ourselves trying to catch up. And, by the way, where are we sheltering our minors?

Q. All around us agencies working in this area are losing their grants for HT, including you yourself, – do you see this as the end of concern about HT? What I am thinking is that 'causes' tend to have a limited shelf-life with public, media and politicians. So many people still know little or nothing about HT. Is it going out of fashion or, is it because of the lack of successful prosecutions that politicians are saying they are not getting value for money. What do you think?

A. In reality, I do not believe this crime has been front center for many NGOs and Law Enforcement departments. I understand that everything has an end, including funds for these crimes. I don't think enough as been done, however. If you will remember how we treated family violence in the 70's and earlier 80's, and how, now, it is a standalone in courts, treatments, shelters and advocates. HT should be like that, it should be a continuous program until it can stand alone.

Q. I remember you talking about looking for victims on Backpage – can you remind me of your work on this? In my class we have been looking at Rubmaps – why don't you and officers around the country raid these places and save the victims – I imagine the answer is funding – the trafficker make loads of money but you don't have enough to fight back but it may be deeper than that?

A. Backpage.com has been in media eyes recently because Law Enforcement have found many trafficking victims in that media. Backpage is protected under our constitution, as are the businesses listed in the pages of Rubmaps. I think most Law Enforcement departments prioritize investigations when it comes to VICE issues. Also, in some communities VICE is not a major concern so that also dictates how Law Enforcement resources are spent. But we are slowly turning the page. We are trying to hit the business in a different manner. One that does not require us to establish probable cause; that is inspections based on the city ordinances and health laws. At the same time we can also interviews the women in these establishments. It has been a great success in other parts of the country.

Q. What do you think about the efficacy of 'John' schools?

A. John schools have been a proven success in other cities, the main objective, however, has been to educate the men on the dangers of sex for hire. I don't think sex slavery has been given much time in the lesson plans. But if the man does not return then that trafficking victim has suffered one less rape. I just want to see the lesson plan which includes a woman who was a slave, not just a willing participate like it is now in most schools.

Q. You suggested that Police officers need more HT training, what is missing at present?

A. The bottom line is if police officers will not move to self-educate themselves, well we should take it to them.

I believe that it is important for the media to stop using names like 'child prostitutes' but instead child victims…any comment?

I think that through more education and exposure, descriptive terms we are accustom to using to describe people or businesses will change. Take, for example, my own training, long ago I used the word prostitute to describe our victims. Then I realized that was so wrong. Also, I change phases like "having sex with the john" to "being raped". I think in time and with work we will see changes.

Appendix 3: Increasing Awareness and Engagement: Strengthening the National Response to Human Trafficking"[688]

This is the title of the 2011 Annual Report of the Polaris Project. The project runs a hotline number for victims and others to report trafficking. In its press release of June 12, 2012 which disseminated the full report, the Project drew attention to the following:

"In 2011, call volume increased by 64 percent over the previous year. Call Specialists answered 19,427 calls, and 2,945 victims of human trafficking were connected to services and support. Calls from self-identifying victims increased by 61% in 2011…New approaches that help to identify and reach more victims of human trafficking are desperately needed, said Sarah Jakiel, Deputy Director of Polaris Project."

Key 2011 NHTRC Hotline Statistics

- Calls to the hotline by self-identifying victims of human trafficking increased nearly 61% over 2010.
- Sex trafficking was reported in 52% of cases, and labor trafficking or exploitation in 48% of cases.
- U.S. citizens made up 391 cases (46%), and 306 cases (just under 36%) involved foreign nationals.
- The NHTRC hotline received calls from all 50 states and the District of Columbia. The states where potential human trafficking was most frequently reported were California, Texas, Florida, and New York.
- The NHTRC received 578 crisis calls 4% of the total calls to the hotline -- where there was a threat of imminent danger or harm to a victim of human trafficking and an immediate response was required.
- Approximately 15% of calls were tips about a potential human trafficking situation, and 12% were at-risk calls that referenced related forms of abuse and exploitation, including labor exploitation, domestic violence, sexual assault, and more."

[688] The full report can be found at <http://www.polarisproject.org/resources/hotline-statistics>

Appendix 4: Some Links to Slave Free Goods

Sweat Free Purchasing Consortium

http://buysweatfree.org/about

Free 2 Work

www.free2work.org

Better World Shopper

www.betterworldshopper.com

Change

www.change.org

(human trafficking, fair trade)

Slave Free Chocolate

www.slavefreechocolate.org

Bibliography

"Abolition of Slavery." *Morning Chronicle*. January 24, 2013.

"About Health Systems Research Institute - Thailand." *Health Systems Research Institute*. Accessed November 6, 2013. http://www.hsri.or.th/en.

Abu-Zidan, Dr Fikri M. "Prevention of Child Camel Jockey Injuries: A Success Story From The UAE." *Clin J Sport Med.* 22(6) (2012): 467.

Adams, Cherish. "RE-TRAFFICKED VICTIMS: HOW A HUMAN RIGHTS APPROACH CAN STOP THE CYCLE OF RE-VICTIMIZATION OF SEX TRAFFICKING VICTIMS." *George Washington International Law Review* 43, no. 1 (2011): 201–234.

"Additional Protocol to the Convention on Human Rights and Biomedicine Concerning Transplantation of Organs and Tissues of Human Origin." Council of Europe, January 24, 2002. http://conventions.coe.int/Treaty/Commun/QueVoulezVous.asp?NT=186&CL=ENG.

"Administration Moves Ahead on Three More Little Amnesties." *Center for Immigration Studies*, May 3, 2012. Administration Moves Ahead on Three More Little Amnesties.

Addo, Michael, K. *The Legal Nature of International Human Rights*. !st. Leiden, The Netherlands: Martinus Nijhoff Publishers, 2010. http://www.brill.com/legal-nature-international-human-rights.

Aiken, M, R.M. Moran, and M.J. Berry. "Child Abuse Material and the Internet: Cyberpsychology of Online Child Related Sex Offending." Lyons, France, 2011. http://www.interpol.int/Crime-areas/Crimes-against-children/Internet-crimes.

Al-Haj, Ahmed. "Yemani Child Bride, 12, Dies in Labor." *CBS News*, September 13, 2009. http://www.cbsnews.com/2100-202_162-5307092.html.

Ali, Nujood, and Delphine Minoui. *I am Nujood, age 10 and divorced.* New York: Three Rivers Press, 2010.

Alien's Action For Tort. 28 USC 1350. Accessed October 20, 2013. http://www.law.cornell.edu/uscode/text/28/1350.

"All in the Mind□: Romanian Orphanage Babies 21 Years on." BBC Radio 4. Accessed November 4, 2013. http://www.bbc.co.uk/programmes/b015p62y.

"An Act for the Abolition of the Slave Trade 1807." London, U.K., March 25, 1807. http://www.pdavis.nl/Legis_06.htm.

Andersson, Hilary. "Marange Diamond Field: Zimbabwe Torture Camp Discovered." *BBC; Panorama*, August 8, 2011. http://www.bbc.co.uk/news/world-africa-14377215.

Andrees, Beate. *Forced Labour and Human Trafficking□: Handbook for Labour Inspectors*. Geneva: International Labour Office, 2008.

Andrew Anthony. "Afghanistan's Propaganda War Takes a New Twist." *The Guardian*, December 5, 2010. http://www.theguardian.com/world/2010/dec/05/bibi-aisha-afghanistan-disfigured-taliban.

Annitto, Megan. "Consent, Coercion, and Compassion: Emerging Legal Responses to the Commercial Sexual Exploitation of Minors." *Yale Law and Policy*. Accessed April 12, 2012. http://yalelawandpolicy.org/sites/default/files/Annitto_30.pdf.

"Another Dead Child-Bride." *Nicholas D. Kristof Blog*, 17:50:55. http://kristof.blogs.nytimes.com/2010/04/10/another-dead-child-bride/.

Anthony, Andrew. "Afghans Propoganda War Takes a New Twist." *The Guardian*, December 4, 2010. http://www.guardian.co.uk/world/2010/dec/05/bibi-aisha-afghanistan-disfigured-taliban.

"Anti-Charcoal Operation Needs Funding!" *Gorilla CD. Virunga National Park, D.R.C.* Accessed November 7, 2013. http://gorillacd.org/2011/07/19/anti-charcoal-operation-needs-funding/.

"Anti-Slavery Campaign." *Coalition of Immokalee Workers*, July 7, 2012. http://ciw-online.org/slavery.html.

Anti-Slavery Campaign. "Bonded Labour." *Anti-Slavery Campaign*. Accessed November 5, 2013. http://www.antislavery.org/includes/documents/cm_docs/2009/b/bonded_labour.pdf.

Appiah, Kwame Anthony. "The Art of Social Change: Campaigns against Foot-Binding and Genital Mutilation." *The New York Times*, October 22, 2010, sec. Magazine. http://www.nytimes.com/2010/10/24/magazine/24FOB-Footbinding-t.html.

Apted, Michael. *Amazing Grace*. 20th Century Fox, 2007.

Aristotle, and Benjamin Jowett. *Politics*. Mineola, NY: Dover Publications, 2000.

Armitage, Jim. *The Independent*. July 30, 2013. http://www.independent.co.uk/life-style/gadgets-and-tech/even-worse-than-foxconn-apple-rocked-by-child-labour-claims-8736504.html.

Art 1, International Agreement for the Suppression of the "White Slave Traffic" (entered into Force 07/18/1905), 1904.

Association, Press. "Rochdale Paedophile Ringleader Is Named." *The Guardian*, June 21, 2013. http://www.guardian.co.uk/uk/2012/jun/21/ringleader-rochdale-paedophiles-named.

Austen, Jane; Austin Dobson, introduction, and Charles E. Brock. *Pride and Prejudice*. Reprint edition. Macmillan, n.d.

Austin Police Department Human Trafficking Division, William J. Sifuentes. *Business Cards - Human Trafficking*, n.d.

Austin Police Department, Human Trafficking Division, William J. Sifuentes. *Teddy Bear - Human Trafficking Evidence*, 2010.

"BACKGROUND: HUMAN TRAFFICKING IN THE UK." *Anti-Slavery Campaign*. Accessed November 7, 2013. http://www.antislavery.org/english/campaigns/background_on_trafficking_for_forced_labour_in_the_uk.aspx.

Bacon, Brittany. "Lost Innocence: Inside Child Sex Tourism." *ABC News*, July 17, 2007. http://abcnews.go.com/TheLaw/story?id=3385318&page=1.

Baker, Aryn. "Afghan Women and the Return of the Taliban." *Time*, August 9, 2010.

Baker, Carrie, N. "CRIME & PUNISHMENT: THE MODERN DEVELOPMENT OF HOMEGROWN CREATIVE JUSTICE: THE INFLUENCE OF INTERNATIONAL HUMAN TRAFFICKING ON UNITED STATES PROSTITUTION LAWS: THE CASE OF EXPUNGEMENT LAWS." *Syracuse Law Review* 62 (January 1, 2012): 171.

Bales, Kevin. *Disposable People, New Slavery in the Global Economy*. 1st ed. Berkeley, CA: University of California Press, 1999.

Bales, Kevin, and Ron Soodalter. *The Slave next Door Human Trafficking and Slavery in America Today*. Berkeley: University of California Press, 2009.

———. *The Slave next Door Human Trafficking and Slavery in America Today*. Berkeley: University of California Press, 2009.

———. *The Slave next Door Human Trafficking and Slavery in America Today*. Berkeley: University of California Press, 2009.

Bales, Kevin, and Peter T. Robbins. "No One Shall Be Held in Slavery or Servitude: A Critical Analysis of International Slavery Conventions." *Human Rights Review* 2, no. 2 (2001): 18–45.

Bales, Kevin, Zoe Trodd, and Alex Kent Williamson. *Modern Slavery: The Secret World of 27 Million People*. Oxford: Oneworld, 2009.

Bangkok, Ian MacKinnon in. "54 Burmese Migrants Suffocate in Packed Lorry." *The Guardian*, April 11, 2008. http://www.theguardian.com/world/2008/apr/11/burma.thailand.

"Bangladesh Child Wedding Dispute." *BBC*, May 21, 2012, sec. Asia. http://www.bbc.co.uk/news/world-asia-18152773.

"Bangladesh Factory Fire Kills at Least 20." *N.Y. Times*, December 14, 2010. http://www.nytimes.com/2010/12/15/world/asia/15bangladesh.html?_r=0.

Barry, Ellen, and Mansi Choksi. "In Mumbai Case, a Group of Assault Suspects Had Little Fear of the Law." *The New York Times*, October 26, 2013, sec. World / Asia Pacific. http://www.nytimes.com/2013/10/27/world/asia/gang-rape-in-india-routine-and-invisible.html.

Basler, Roy, P., ed. *Letter to Albert G. Hodges (April 4. 1864*. Vol. VII. The Collected Works of Abraham Lincoln. New Brunswick, NJ: Rutgers University Press, 1953.

"BBC Radio 4 - All in the Mind, Romanian Orphanage Babies: 21 Years On." *BBC*, 01:28:57. http://www.bbc.co.uk/programmes/b015p62y.

Beckett, Dave. "Colonel Tim Collins' Speech." *Journalblog*, March 2003. http://journal.dajobe.org/journal/2003/03/collins/.

Beckford, Martin. "Paedophile Spared Extradition to US on Human Rights Grounds." *The Telegraph*. June 28, 2012. http://www.telegraph.co.uk/news/uknews/crime/9362298/Paedophile-spared-extradition-to-US-on-human-rights-grounds.html.

Beebe, Steven A., Susan J. Beebe, and Diana K. Ivy. *Communication: Principles for a Lifetime, 4th Edition*. 4th edition. Pearson, n.d.

Beevor, Antony. *Berlin the Downfall, 1945*. London: Viking, 2007. http://www.contentreserve.com/TitleInfo.asp?ID={B284B22D-FC2D-441E-A3E9-7C0ECF7A3E83}&Format=410.

Belmaker, Gideon. "New York City: Point of Entry for Human Trafficking in US." *Epoch Times*, March 23, 2011. http://www.theepochtimes.com/n2/united-states/new-york-city-point-of-entry-for-human-trafficking-in-us-53388.html.

Belzberg, Edet. *Children Underground*. Documentary, 2003.

Berger, Stephanie, M. "NO END IN SIGHT: WHY THE 'END DEMAND' MOVEMENT IS THE WRONG FOCUS FOR EFFORTS TO ELIMINATE HUMAN TRAFFICKING." *Harvard Journal of Law & Gender*. 35, no. 2 (Summer 2012): 523–570.

"Big Data Stops Slavery." *Wired*, December 2013.

Bingham, John. "Forced Marriage Expected to Become a Crime." *Telegraph.co.uk*, June 7, 2012, sec. politics. http://www.telegraph.co.uk/news/politics/9315181/Forced-marriage-expected-to-become-a-crime.html.

———. "Online Pornography: Opt-in System Planned to Protect Children." *Telegraph.co.uk*, June 28, 2012, sec. news. http://www.telegraph.co.uk/technology/news/9359848/Online-pornography-opt-in-system-planned-to-protect-children.html.

"Biography – THORPE, ROBERT – Volume VII (1836-1850) – Dictionary of Canadian Biography." Accessed October 27, 2013. http://www.biographi.ca/en/bio.php?id_nbr=3696.

Bissell, Susan. "Children in Adversity." USAID, Washington D.C., 2011.

Black, Robert, E, Linsay H. Allen, Zulfiqar A. Bhutta, Louisa E. Caufield, Mercedes De Onis, Majid Ezzoti, Colin Mathers, and Juan Rivera. *Maternal and Child Undernutricion: Global and Regional Exposures and Health Consquences*. Maternal and Child Undernutrician. John Hopkins University and World Health Organization, January 17, 2010. http://www.who.int/nutrition/topics/Lancetseries_Undernutrition1.pdf.

Blackstone, William. *Blackstone's Commentaries on the Laws of England*. Accessed October 20, 2013. http://avalon.law.yale.edu/subject_menus/blackstone.asp.

Bollinger, Kate, and Kim McQuay. "Human Trafficking Rampant in Thailand's Deep-Sea Fishing Industry." *The Asia Foundation*, October 27, 2013. http://asiafoundation.org/in-asia/2012/02/08/human-trafficking-rampant-in-thailands-deep-sea-fishing-industry/.

"Bollywood Actress Priyanka Chopra Becomes UNICEF National Ambassador." Unicef, August 10, 2010. http://www.unicef.org/india/media_6408.htm.

"BONDED LABOUR." *Anti*, October 27, 2013. http://www.antislavery.org/english/slavery_today/bonded_labour.aspx.

Booker, Christopher. *Legal Miracle Then Business as Usual*, n.d.

Booler, Christopher. "Legal Miracle Then Business as Usual." *The Telegraph*. June 23, 2012. http://www.telegraph.co.uk/comment/9350679/A-legal-miracle-then-business-as-usual.html.

Booth, Robert. "Children Lost from Care in Human Trafficking Cases, Says Council." *The Guardian*, October 18, 2011. http://www.theguardian.com/law/2011/oct/18/children-lost-human-trafficking.

Bose, K S, and R H Sarma. "Delineation of the Intimate Details of the Backbone Conformation of Pyridine Nucleotide Coenzymes in Aqueous Solution." *Biochemical and Biophysical Research Communications* 66, no. 4 (October 27, 1975): 1173–1179.

Boston Dynamics. *Darpa PetMan Robot - Complete Info*, 2013. http://www.youtube.com/watch?v=5S4ZPvr6ry4.

Bradford, Henry. "10 Most Viiolent States in the US: The Institute for Economics and Peace." *The Huffington Post*, April 13, 2011.

"Brazil's Sex Tourism Boom." *BBC*, July 30, 2010, sec. World. http://www.bbc.co.uk/news/world-10764371.

Briski, Zana, and Ross Kauffman. *Born into Brothels*, 2004. http://www.imdb.com/title/tt0388789/.

Brontë, Emily. *Wuthering Heights*. Acheron Press, 2012.

Bryan Mealer. *All Things Must Fight to Liv*. New York, NY: Bloomsbury, 01/08/20111.

Bryant Rose, Kristian. "Looking for Love in All the Wrong Places: A Call to Reform State Law on Sex Trafficking." *Oklahoma Law Review* 65, no. 2 (Winter 2013): 303–350.

Bunyan, Nigel. "Rochdale Grooming Trial: How the Case Unfolded." *Telegraph.co.uk*, June 21, 2012, sec. uknews. http://www.telegraph.co.uk/news/uknews/crime/9347305/Rochdale-grooming-trial-how-the-case-unfolded.html.

———. "Young Spurn Wealth for Family Values." *Telegraph.co.uk*, May 28, 2012, sec. mother-tongue. http://www.telegraph.co.uk/women/mother-tongue/9293572/Young-spurn-wealth-for-family-values.html.

"Bureau of Justice Statistics." *Bureau of Justice Statistics*, September 16, 2011. http://www.state.gov/r/pa/ei/biog/124083.htm.

Burke, Alicia, and Stefania Ducci. *Trafficking in Minors for Commercial Sexual Exploitation - Thailand.* United Nations Interregional Crime and Justice Research Institute, October 27, 2013. http://www.unicri.it/topics/trafficking_exploitation/archive/minors/countries_partners/dr_thailand.pdf.

Burke, Laura. "Ivory Coast's Child Labor behind Chocolate." *Global Post*, January 28, 2012. http://www.globalpost.com/dispatch/news/regions/africa/120116/ivory-coast-child-labor-chocolate.

Burns, Brooke. "Sex Tourism in Costa Rica." presented at the Human Trafficking Workshop, St. Edwards University, Austin, Texas, November 2010.

Byerly, Robin, T. "Combating Modern Slavery: What Can Business Do?" *Journal of Leadership, Accountability & Ethics.* 9, no. 5 (November 2012): 25–34.

C.W. Wong, William, Phil W.S. Leung, and C. W. Li. "HIV Behavioural Risks and the Role of Work Environment among Chinese Male Sex Workers in Hong Kong." *AIDS Care* 24, no. 3 (March 2012): 340–347.

"Cairo Declaration on Human Rights in Islam." United Nations document. U.N. GAOR, World Conf. on Hum. Rts., 4th Sess., August 5, 1990. http://www1.umn.edu/humanrts/instree/cairodeclaration.html.

"Cairo Declaration on Human Rights in Islam," August 5, 1990. http://www1.umn.edu/humanrts/instree/cairodeclaration.html.

Caldwell, Gillian. *Bought and Sold, an Investigative Documentary about the International Trade in Women 2009.* Global Survivor Network, 1999. http://humantrafficking.unc.edu/2011/05/01/bought-and-sold-an-investigative-documentary-about-the-international-trade-in-women-multimedia-resource-gillian-caldwell-global-survivor-network-1999/.

Camastra, Emily. "Hazardous Child Labor as a Crime against Humanity: An Investigation into the Potential Role of the International Criminal Court in Prosecuting Hazardous Child Labor as Slavery." *Georgetown Journal on Poverty Law & Policy* 15 (July 1, 2008): 335.

Cameron, L., N. Erkal, L. Gangadharan, and X. Meng. "Little Emperors: Behavioral Impacts of China's One-Child Policy." *Science* 339, no. 6122 (February 22, 2013): 953–7.

Campbell. "A Growing Concern: Modern Slavery and Agricultural Production in Brazil and South Asia" (n.d.).

Campbell, Denis, and Nicola Davison. "Illegal Kidney Trade Booms as New Organ Is 'Sold Every Hour.'" *The Guardian*, May 27, 2012. http://www.theguardian.com/world/2012/may/27/kidney-trade-illegal-operations-who.

Campbell, Justin. "A Growing Concern: Modern Slavery and Agricultural Production in Brazil and South Asia." *Topical Research Digest: Human Rights and Contemporary Slavery. University of Denver, Colorado, USA* (2008): 131–141.

Canada, Government of. *An Act to Amend the Immigration and Refugee Protection Act, the Balanced Refugee Reform Act, the Marine Transportation Security Act and the Department of Citizenship and Immigration Act*, 2013. https://openparliament.ca/bills/41-1/C-31/.

Carole S., Vance. "States of Contradiction: Twelve Ways to Do Nothing about Trafficking While Pretending To." *Social Research* 78, no. 3 (Fall 2011): 933–948.

Carroll Sager, Rebecca. "An Anomaly of the Law: Insufficient State Laws Fail to Protect Minor Victims of Sex Trafficking." *New England Journal on Criminal & Civil Confinement* 38, no. 2 (Summer 2012): 359–378.

Cartwright 1569, Historical Collections J. Rushworth 468 (n.d.).

Casas, Bartolomé de las. *History of the Indies.* New York: Harper Torchbooks, Harper & Row, 1971.

Case 16: The Prosecutor vs. Brima, Kamara and Kanu (AFRC Case). Accessed November 7, 2013.

Center for History and New Media. "Zotero Quick Start Guide," n.d. http://zotero.org/support/quick_start_guide.

Champion, Kirsty, Emma Lee, Melanie Hyde, Kate Trumbell, and Mallesons Stephen Jaques. *Special Court for Sierra Leone - Forced.* Australian Red Cross, 2010. http://www.redcross.org.au/files/2010_Forced_Marriage_Sierra_Leone.pdf.

Channon, Charles. "Transplant Tourism in Colombia." *The Blog of the Institute for the Elimination of Global Organ Trafficking (IEGOT)*, February 19, 2007. http://organtrade.blogspot.com/2007/02/transplant-tourism-in-columbia.html.

Chen, Sheying, and Jason L. Powel, eds. *Aging in China□: Implications to Social Policy of a Changing Economic State.* New York, NY: Springer, 2012.

Cheung, K.C., Ming H. Wong, Anna O.W. Leung, and Nurdan S. Duzgoren-Aydin. "Heavy Metals Concentrations of Surface Dust from E-Waste Recycling and Its Human Health Implications in Southeast China." *Environmental Science and Technology*. American Chemical Society (2008).

"Child Bride Practice Rising In Iran, Parliament Seeks To Lower Girl's Legal Marriage Age To 9." *International Business Times*, August 30, 2013.

"Child Marriage." *INRW - International Center for Research on Women*, October 27, 2013. http://www.icrw.org/what-we-do/adolescents/child-marriage.

"Child Marriage." *International Center for Research on Women.* Accessed November 6, 2013. http://www.icrw.org/what-we-do/adolescents/child-marriage.

"Child Marriages Blight Bangladesh." *BBC*, April 22, 2012, sec. Magazine. http://www.bbc.co.uk/news/magazine-17779413.

"Child Marriages Make a Reappearance." *Beruit Online.* Accessed November 2, 2013. http://beruit-online.net/portal/article.php?id=6058.

"Child Protection Information Sheets - Child Marriage." The Child Protection Section, UNICEF, May 2006. http://www.unicef.org/publications/files/Child_Protection_Information_Sheets.pdf.

Child Sexual Exploitation and the Response to Localised Grooming. House of Commons Home Affairs Committee. London, U.K., 2014 2013. http://www.publications.parliament.uk/pa/cm201314/cmselect/cmhaff/68/68ii.pdf.

Child Trafficking Update. U.K. Home Office. Accessed November 7, 2013. http://ceop.police.uk/Documents/ceopdocs/child_trafficking_update_2011.pdf.

Children and Young Persons Act 1963, 1963. http://www.legislation.gov.uk/ukpga/1963/37.

Choate, Tiffanie, N. "Protecting the Lydias, Linas, and Tinas from Sex Trafficking: A Call to Eliminate Ambiguities of 18 U.S.C. § 1591." *Oklahoma Law Review; Summer2013, Vol. 65 Issue 4, p665-716* 65, no. 4 (Summer 2013): 665–716.

Chocolate The Bitter Truth 1 of 5 Child Trafficking BBC Panorama Investigation, 2011. http://www.youtube.com/watch?v=LD85fPzLUjo&feature=youtube_gdata_player.

Christine. "Case Example of Preventing Child Marriages in Bangladesh." *PACE International Law Review*, April 24, 2012. https://pilr.blogs.law.pace.edu/2012/04/24/case-example-of-preventing-child-marriages-in-bangladesh/.

Chuang, Janie, A. "RESCUING TRAFFICKING FROM IDEOLOGICAL CAPTURE: PROSTITUTION REFORM AND ANTI-TRAFFICKING LAW AND POLICY." *University of Pennsylvania Law Review* 158, no. 6 (May 2010): 1655–1728.

Clawson, Heather, J, Nicole M. Dutch, Amy Salomon, and Lisa Goldblatt Grace. *Study of HHS Programs Serving Human Trafficking Victims□: Final Report*, December 2009. http://aspe.hhs.gov/hsp/07/humantrafficking/final/index.shtml.

Coalition of Immokalee Workers. "About." Accessed November 4, 2013. http://ciw-online.org/.

Coercion in the Kidney Trade? A Background Study on Trafficking in Human Organs Worldwide. Deutsche Gesellschaft für Technische Zusammenarbeit (GTZ) GmbH, April 2004.

Colbert Stays in Character at Congressional Hearing, 2010. http://www.youtube.com/watch?v=ewPburLEZyY&feature=youtube_gdata_player.

Cole, Andrew. "Botched Abortions Kill More than 66 000 Women Each Year." *BMJ* 335, no. 7625 (October 27, 2007): 845–845. doi:10.1136/bmj.39374.628171.DB1.

Coleman, Clive. *UK Inmates Lose Right to Vote Ruling.* Journal Article. London: BBC, October 16, 2013. http://www.bbc.co.uk/news/uk-24545294.

Committee of Ministers, The. *Recommendation CM/Rec(2012)2 of the Committee of Ministers to Member States on the Participation of Children and Young People under the Age of 18*. Human Rights and Rule of Law. Council of Europe, March 28, 2012. http://www.coe.int/t/dg3/children/participation/Newdefault_en.asp.

Committee on Legal Affairs and Human Rights Inhuman Treatment of People and Illicit Trafficking in Human Organs in Kosovo. Council of Europe, December 12, 2010.

Community-Based Initiatives Against Trafficking in Children in the Mekong Sub-Region 2003-2006. Save the Children UK, October 27, 2013. http://www.streetchildrenresources.org/wp-content/uploads/2013/01/project-report-trafficking-mekong.pdf.

Condie, Steven. *Simon Schama's Rough Crossings*. BBC Home Entertainment, 2009.

"Convention on Consent to Marriage, Minimum Age for Marriage and Registration of Marriages." United Nations, November 7, 1962. http://www.ohchr.org/EN/ProfessionalInterest/Pages/MinimumAgeForMarriage.aspx.

"Convention on the Elimination of All Forms of Discrimination against Women." Copenhagen, July 17, 1980. http://www.un.org/womenwatch/daw/cedaw/text/econvention.htm.

"Convention on the Nationality of Married Women." 1957, n.d. http://treaties.un.org/doc/Treaties/1958/08/19580811%2001-34%20AM/Ch_XVI_2p.pdf.

"Convention on the Political Rights of Women 1952," 1952. http://www.un.org/womenwatch/directory/convention_political_rights_of_women_10741.htm.

Cornyn, John. *Domestic Minor Sex Trafficking Deterrence and Victims Support Act*, 2010. http://www.govtrack.us/congress/bills/112/s596/text.

Coryell, Janet L. *Negotiating Boundaries of Southern Womanhood: Dealing with the Powers That Be*. Columbia, MO: University of Missouri Press, 2000.

———. , ed. *Negotiating the Boundaries of Southern Womanhood: Dealing with the Powers That Be*. Kansas City: Unversity of Missouri Press, 2000.

Council of Europe. "European Convention on Human Rights." Strasbourg, 1950. http://www.echr.coe.int/Documents/Convention_ENG.pdf.

———. "High Level Conference on the Future of the European Court of Human Rights: Brighton Declaration." Brighton U.K., 2012. http://www.echr.coe.int/Documents/2012_Brighton_FinalDeclaration_ENG.pdf.

Cowper-Coles, Sherard. *Cables from Kabul: The inside Story of the West's Afghanistan Campaign*. London: HarperPress, 2012.

"Crackdown on Houston Sex Ring Freed 120 Women." *Houston Chronicle*, 20:46:04. http://www.chron.com/neighborhood/cyfair-news/article/Crackdown-on-Houston-sex-ring-freed-120-women-1790132.php#src=fb.

Crane, Andrew. "MODERN SLAVERY AS A MANAGEMENT PRACTICE: EXPLORING THE CONDITIONS AND CAPABILITIES FOR HUMAN EXPLOITATION." *Academy of Management Review*. 38, no. 1 (January 2013): 49–69.

Craven, Samantha, Sarah Brown, and Elizabeth Gilcrest. "Sexual Grooming of Children: Review of Literature and Theoretical Considerations." *Journal of Sexual Aggression* 12, no. 3 (November 2006): 287–299.

Cross, Allison. "Slipping Through the Cracks: The Dual Victimization of Human-Trafficking Survivors." *McGeorge Law Review* 44, no. 2 (January 2013): 395–422.

Custer. "Kidnapped and Sold: Inside the Dark World of Child Trafficking in China." *The Atlantic*, July 25, 2913. http://www.theatlantic.com/china/archive/2013/07/kidnapped-and-sold-inside-the-dark-world-of-child-trafficking-in-china/278107/.

"D.R. Congo War Deaths Exaggerated." *BBC News*. Accessed November 3, 2013. http://news.bbc.co.uk/2/hi/africa/8471147.stm.

Dagistanil, Selda, and Sanja Milivojevic. "Appropriating the Rights of Women: Moral Panics, Victims and Exclusionary Agendas in Domestic and Cross-Borders Sex Crimes." *Womens Studies International Forum* 40 (October 2013): 230–242.

Daley, Suzanne. "Women Enslaved by Spain's Brothel Tourism Boom." *The New York Times*, April 6, 2012, sec. World / Europe. http://www.nytimes.com/2012/04/07/world/europe/young-men-flock-to-spain-for-sex-with-trafficked-prostitutes.html.

———. "Women Enslaved by Spain's Brothel Tourism Boom." *The New York Times*, April 6, 2012, sec. World / Europe. http://www.nytimes.com/2012/04/07/world/europe/young-men-flock-to-spain-for-sex-with-trafficked-prostitutes.html.

Davidson Dyle, Scott. "Beginning to Seize the Instrumentalities of Human Trafficking: Chapter 514 Allows Criminal Forfeiture of Property Used to Facilitate the Sex Trafficking of Minors." *McGeorge Law Review* 44, no. 3 (April 2013): 575–582.

———. "Chapter 515: Combating Human Trafficking by Enhancing Awareness Through Public Postings." *McGeorge Law Review* 44, no. 3 (April 2013): 583–590.

Davis, David Brion. *DAVIS PROB SLAVERY REV 1770-1823 C.* Oxford University Press, 1999.

Davis, Michael, C. *Cargo: Innocence Lost.* The Journey Film Group, 2008. http://http://www.cargoinnocencelost.com/.

———. *Cargo: Innocence Lost*, 2008. http://www.cargoinnocencelost.com/.

De Montmorency, Mathieu. "The Rights of Man and Citizen." Paris, France, 1789.

Deane, Tameshnie. "Cross-Border Trafficking in Nepal and India-Violating Women's Rights." *Human Rights Review* 11, no. 4 (December 2010): 491–513.

Department Of State. The Office of Website Management, Bureau of Public Affairs. *II Quotes By and About Women in Afghanistan.* Report. Department Of State. The Office of Website Management, Bureau of Public Affairs., January 1, 2004. Afghanistan|. http://www.state.gov/j/drl/rls/6186.htm.

———. "Trafficking in Persons Report 2007," June 12, 2007. http://www.state.gov/j/tip/rls/tiprpt/2007/.

Dess, Melissa. "WALKING THE FREEDOM TRAIL: AN ANALYSIS OF THE MASSACHUSETTS HUMAN TRAFFICKING STATUTE AND ITS POTENTIAL TO COMBAT CHILD SEX TRAFFICKING." *Boston College Journal of Law & Social Justice* 33, no. 1 (Winter 2013): 147–182.

DeStefano, Anthony M. *The War on Human Trafficking: U.S. Policy Assessed.* New Brunswick, N.J.: Rutgers University Press, 2008.

Diderot, D. and J d'Alembert, ed. "Natural Law." *French Encyclopedia*, 1755. http://quod.lib.umich.edu/d/did/.

Dixon Jr, Herbert, B. "Human Trafficking and the Internet (AND OTHER TECHNOLOGIES, TOO)." *Judge's Journal* 52, no. 1 (Winter 2013): 36–39.

Dillon, Justin. *Call and Response*, 2010. http://www.callandresponse.com/cast_detail.php?e=west.

Dirrian, Garath. "150 Afghan Schoolgirls Seriously Ill after Being Poisoned in Anti-Education Attack by Muslim Extremists." *The Mail*, April 18, 2013. http://www.dailymail.co.uk/news/article-2131526/Afghan-schoolgirls-poisoned-contaminated-water--Radicals-blamed.html#ixzz1uDMtawjx http://www.malala-yousafzai.com/.

Disposable People: New Slavery in the Global Economy. Updated with a New Preface edition. University of California Press, 2012.

"Dominique Strauss-Kahn Parties Were 'Sexual Carnage', Report Says." *TheAustralian*, 20:47:18. http://www.theaustralian.com.au/news/world/dominique-strauss-kahn-parties-were-sexual-carnage-report-says/story-fnb64oi6-1226693324992.

Dorchen, Leidholdt, A.. "HUMAN TRAFFICKING AND DOMESTIC VIOLENCE A Primer for Judges." *Judge's Journal* 52, no. 1 (Winter 2013): 16–21.

Dorothy, Nicole. *Eglantine Jebb Saves the Children.* London, U.K.: Blue Hills, 2010.

"Dr. Jack Shonkoff on Brain Power: Why Early Learning Matters." *NBC Education Nation*, 01:27:56. http://www.educationnation.com/index.cfm?objectid=E86C3CA6-E89A-11E0-B00E000C296BA163.

Draper, Robert. "Opium Wars." *National Geographic Magazine*, February 2011. http://ngm.nationalgeographic.com/2011/02/opium-wars/draper-text.

"DrugScope Reveals Child Victims of UK Cannabis Farm Boom." *Drugscope*, September 6, 2007. http://www.drugscope.org.uk/Media/Press+office/pressreleases/Cannabis-farms-trafficked-children.

Durchslag, Rachel, and SAMIR GOSWAMI. "Deconstructing The Demand for Prostitution:Preliminary Insights From Interviews With Chicago Men Who Purchase Sex." *SA Promise*, 2012. http://www.sapromise.org/pdfs/deconstructing.pdf.

Dysart, Tessa, L. "THE PROTECTED INNOCENCE INITIATIVE: BUILDING PROTECTIVE STATE LAW REGIMES FOR AMERICA'S SEX-TRAFFICKED CHILDREN." *Columbia Human Rights Review* 44, no. 3 (Spring 2013): 619–695.

"Eat Traffick Free Chocolate." *Stop the Traffick*. Accessed October 25, 2013. http://www.stopthetraffik.org/campaign/chocolate.
ECPAT. "ECPAT - Home." *ECPAT*. Accessed November 6, 2013. http://www.ecpat.net/.
"Ed Miliband Was Right to Acknowledge Immigration Concerns." *The Guardian*, June 22, 2012. http://www.theguardian.com/politics/blog/2012/jun/22/ed-miliband-right-immigration-concerns.
Editorial. "Unpacking the Sex Trafficking Panic." *Contemporary Sexuality* 47, no. 2 (. Mar2013): 1–6.
Edwards, Bernard. *Royal Navy versus the Slave Traders: Enforcing Abolition at Sea 1808-1898*. Barnsley: Pen & Sword Maritime, 2007.
Elizete D. Velado. "SHIFTING GEARS: IMPROVING ANTI-TRAFFICKING EFFORTS THROUGH A SHIFT IN POLICY FOCUS." *Journal of Transnational Law & Policy* 22 (January 1, 2012): 187.
"England Moves to Ban Forced Marriages." *The Express Tribune*, August 6, 2012. http://tribune.com.pk/story/390976/england-moves-to-ban-forced-marriages/.
English, Andrew. "Toyota's Driverless Car." *Telegraph.co.uk*, October 25, 2013, sec. car-manufacturers. http://www.telegraph.co.uk/motoring/car-manufacturers/toyota/10404575/Toyotas-driverless-car.html.
Erirajan, A. "Bangladesh Court Acts in Weekend Child Marriage Case." *BBC World News*, May 21, 2012. http://www.bbc.co.uk/news/world-asia-18152773.
European Parliament, Starsbourg. *Additional Protocol to the Convention on Human Rights and Biomedicine Concerning Transplantation of Organs and Tissues of Human Origin*, 2002.
Evidence of a Victim to HEARING BEFORE THE SUBCOMMITTEE ON EAST ASIAN AND PACIFIC AFFAIRS. Washington D.C., 2004. http://www.gpo.gov/fdsys/pkg/CHRG-108shrg96804/html/CHRG-108shrg96804.htm.
EXECUTIVE OFFICE OF THE PRESIDENT, OFFICE OF NATIONAL DRUG CONTROL POLICY. *National Drug Control Budget - FY 2012 Funding Highlights*. Washington D.C., 2012. http://www.whitehouse.gov/sites/default/files/ondcp/policy-and-research/fy12highlight_exec_sum.pdf.
"Experiential Learning – Eating as a Farmer in Debt Bondage." *Allies against Slavery*, August 19, 2010. http://alliesctx.wordpress.com/2010/08/19/147/>.
F. Sunter, Andrew. "The Harm of Drug Trafficking: Is There Room for Serious Debate?" *The Manitoba Law Journal* 32 (January 1, 2007): 174.
Faber, Marion. *Mass Rape: The War against Women in Bosnia-Herzegovina*. Lincoln [u.a.: Univ. of Nebraska Press, 1994.
Farris, Michael. "Protecting Children By Empowering Parents." *Parental Rights.org*. Accessed October 27, 2013. http://www.parentalrights.org/index.asp?SEC={CE4F4C7A-F6ED-4732-8FA5-677F0649AF8D}&Type=B_BASIC.
"Father Was 'Last to See Shafilea.'" *BBC*, July 19, 2012, sec. Manchester. http://www.bbc.co.uk/news/uk-england-manchester-18911508.
Feasley, Ashley. "TIME FOR A TUNE-UP: RETOOLING THE 2012 TIP REPORT IN ORDER TO BETTER MEET INTERNATIONAL LEGAL RESEARCH STANDARDS." *Florida Journal of International Law* 25, no. 1 (April 2013): 5–26.
"Federal Bureau of Investigation." *Federal Bureau of Investigation*. Accessed November 4, 2013. http://www.fbi.gov/about-us/investigate/civilrights/human_trafficking/initiatives.
"Female Genital Mutilation and Obstetric Outcome: WHO Collaborative Prospective Study in Six African Countries." *The Lancet* 367, no. 9525 (June 2006): 1835–1841. doi:10.1016/S0140-6736(06)68805-3.
"Ferrero Sets Date to End Cocoa Slavery." *CNN Freedom Project Ending Modern Slavery*, April 20, 2012. http://thecnnfreedomproject.blogs.cnn.com/2012/04/20/ferrero-sets-date-to-end-cocoa.
Firth-Butterfield, Kay. *Human Trafficking and Human Rights*. [S.l.]: Kendall Hunt, 2012.
Firth-Butterfield, Kay, and Tina Miranda. *Laws on Human Trafficking*. [S.l.]: Kendall Hunt, 2012.
FitzGerald, Sharron. "Vulnerable Bodies, Vulnerable Borders: Extraterritoriality and Human Trafficking." *Feminist Legal Theory* 20, no. 3 (2012): 227–244.
Flomo v. Firestone Natural Rubber Co LLC, Boimah FLOMO, et al., Plaintiffs–Appellants, v. Firestone Natural Rubber Co., LLC (United States Court of Appeals, Seventh Circuit 2011).
"'Flores Settlement' Flores v. Meece Agreement," January 1, 1997. http://www.aclu.org/files/pdfs/immigrants/flores_v_meese_agreement.pdf.
"For a World Without Slavery." *Polaris Project*. Accessed November 2, 2013. http://www.polarisproject.org/.

FORCED MARRIAGE – A CONSULTATION; SUMMARY OF RESPONSES. UK Home Office, 6/12. https://www.gov.uk/government/uploads/system/uploads/attachment_data/file/157837/forced-marriage-response.pdf.

"Forced Marriage to Become a Criminal Offence, Announces the Government." *Family Law Week*, October 27, 2013. http://www.familylawweek.co.uk/site.aspx?i=ed98339.

Fox, William. *Address to the People of Great Britain on the Utility of Refraining from the Use of West India Sugar and Rum*. London, U.K.: M. Gurney and W. Darton and Co, 1791. https://ia600508.us.archive.org/6/items/addresstopeopleo1791foxw/addresstopeopleo1791foxw.pdf.

Frankle, R T. "Nutrition Education in the Medical School Curriculum: A Proposal for Action: A Curriculum Design." *The American Journal of Clinical Nutrition* 29, no. 1 (January 1976): 105–109.

Free England: Or, Old Stories of the English Parliament, by H.E.B., 1884.

"Free the Slaves." *Free the Slaves*. Accessed November 5, 2013. www.freetheslaves.net/.

Gage, A.J. "Association of Child Marriage with Suicidal Thoughts and Attempts among Adolescent Girls in Ethiopia." *The Journal Of Adolescent Health* 52, no. 5 (February 20, 2013): 654–6.

Gallagher, Anne. "Improving the Effectiveness of the International Law of Human Trafficking: A Vision for the Future of the US Trafficking in Persons Reports." *Human Rights Review* 12, no. 3 (September 2011): 381–400.

Gentleman, Amelia. "Katya's Story: Trafficked to the UK, Sent Home to Torture." *The Guardian*. April 18, 2011. http://www.guardian.co.uk/law/2011/apr/19/sex-trafficking-uk-legal-reform.

George, Shelly. "THE STRONG ARM OF THE LAW IS WEAK: HOW THE TRAFFICKING VICTIMS PROTECTION ACT FAILS TO ASSIST EFFECTIVELY VICTIMS OF THE SEX TRADE." *Creighton Law Review* 45, no. 3 (April 2012): 563–580.

"Global Chocolate, Cocoa Beans, Lecithin, Sugar and Vanilla Market By Market Share, Trade, Prices, Geography Trend and Forecast (2011-2016)." *MarketsandMarkets.com*, September 2011. http://www.marketsandmarkets.com/Market-Reports/global-chocolate-market-164.html.

Google. "Self-Driving Car Test: Steve Mahan." *Google*. Accessed November 10, 2013. http://www.google.com/about/jobs/lifeatgoogle/self-driving-car-test-steve-mahan.html.

Government of France. "Victor Schoelcher (1804-1893), A Life, a Century, Slavery Past and Present." *Senat*. Accessed October 23, 2013. http://translate.google.com/translate?hl=en&ie=UTF8&prev=_t&sl=fr&tl=en&u=http://www.senat.fr/evenement/victor_schoelcher/abolitions.html&sandbox=0&usg=ALkJrhg_szTHJcaTzukJqjc_hB6OgVkFcg.

Graw Leary, Mary. ", Self-Produced Child Pornography: The Appropriate Societal Response to Juvenile Self-Sexual Exploitation." *VA J. Soc. Policy & L.* 15, no. 1 (2007).

Gray, Todd. *Devon and the Slave Trade: Documents on African Enslavement, Abolition and Emancipation from 1562 to 1867*. Exeter: Mint Press, 2007.

Greeley, Horace. *A History of the Struggle for Slavery Extension or Restriction in the United States from the Declaration of Independence to the Present Day*, 1856.

Green, Fiona, J. "From Clitoridectomies to 'designer Vaginas': The Medical Construction of Heteronormative Female Bodies and Sexuality through Female Genital Cutting." *Sexualities, Evolution & Gender.* 7, no. 2 (August 2005): 153–187.

Greenpeace. *Driving Destruction in the Amazon*, 2012. http://www.greenpeace.org/international/Global/international/publications/forests/2012/Amazon/423-Driving-Destruction-in-the-Amazon.pdf.

Gregson v. Gilbert, 3 Doug 232 (Court of Appeal, Engand and Wales 1783).

Grotius, Hugo, and A. C. Campbell. *The Rights of War and Peace*. Evergreen Review, Inc., 2009.

"Groundbreaking Sentence Increase for Human Trafficker." Crown Prosecution Service, April 29, 2004. http://www.cps.gov.uk/news/latest_news/118_04/.

Gurd, Amy, and Erin O'Brien. "Californian 'John Schools' and the Social Construction of Prostitution." *Sexuality Research & Social Policy: Journal of NSRC* 10, no. 2 (June 2013): 149–158.

Haeri, Shahla. "Temporary Marriage and the State in Iran: An Islamic Discourse on Female Sexuality." *Social Research* 59, no. 1 (Spring 1992): 201–223.

Hager, Sovereign. "FARM WORKERS AND FORCED LABOR: WHY INCLUDING AGRICULTURAL GUEST WORKERS IN THE MIGRANT AND SEASONAL WORKER PROTECTION ACT

PREVENTS HUMAN TRAFFICKING." *Syracuse Journal of International Law & Commerce* 38, no. 1 (Fall 2010): 173–199.

Hague, William. *William Wilberforce: The Life of the Great Anti-Slave Trade Campaigner.* Orlando: Harcourt, 2007.

Hall, Stephen, S. "'This Baby Will Live to Be 120 (It's Not Just Hype. New Science Could Lead to Very Long Lives).'" *National Geographic Magazine*, May 2013.

Hallett, Robin. *The Penetration of Africa: European Enterprise and Exploration Principally in Northern and Western Africa Up to 1830.* Routledge & Kegan Paul, 1965.

Hallett, Robin {Ed }. *Records of the African Association 1788-1831.* 1St Edition edition. Thomas Nelson & Sons,Ltd., n.d.

Hamilton, Keith, and Patrick Salmon. *Slavery, Diplomacy and Empire: Britain and the Suppression of the Slave Trade, 1807-1975.* Sussex Academic Press, 2009.

Hammadi, Saad, and Matthew Taylor. "At Least 27 Die and More than 100 Are Injured in Blaze at Bangladesh Manufacturing Plant." *The Guardian*, December 14, 2010. http://www.theguardian.com/world/2010/dec/14/bangladesh-clothes-factory-workers-jump-to-death.

Hardy, Thomas. *Tess of the d'Urbervilles.* CreateSpace Independent Publishing Platform, 2013.

Hargrave, Francis, James Sommersett, Great Britain. Court of King's Bench, and Miscellaneous Pamphlet Collection (Library of Congress) DLC. *An Argument in the Case of James Sommersett, a Negro, Lately Determined by the Court of King's Bench□: Wherein It Is Attempted to Demonstrate the Present Unlawfulness of Domestic Slavery in England□: To Which Is Prefixed a State of the Case.* London□: Printed for the author□: And sold by W. Otridge ..., 1772. http://archive.org/details/anargumentincas00harggoog.

"Harkin-Engel Protocol." Responsible Chocloate. Accessed October 20, 2013. < http://responsiblecocoa.com/about-us/the-harkin-engel-protocol/.

Hawkesworth, M. E. *Political Worlds of Women Activism, Advocacy, and Governance in the 21st Century.* Boulder, Colo.: Westview Press, 2012. http://site.ebrary.com/id/10542738.

Hawksley, Humphrey. "Ivory Coast Cocoa Farms Child Labour: Little Change," October 20, 2011. http://www.bbc.co.uk/news/world-africa-15681986.

Healy Vardaman, Samantha, and Christine Raino. "Prosecuting Demand as a Crime of Human Trafficking: The Eighth Circuit Decision in United States v. Jungers." *University of Memphis Law Review* 43, no. 4 (summer 2013): 917–967.

Heinrich, Kelly, and Kavitha Sreeharsha. "The State of State Human-Trafficking Laws." *Judge's Journal* 52, no. 1 (Winter 2013): 28–31.

Helfman, Tara. "Court of Vice Admiralty at Sierra Leone and the Abolition of the West African Slave Trade, The." *Yale LJ* 115 (2005): 1122.

Hodson, David. "CONSENT TO MARRY UNDER ENGLISH LAW," 6/10. http://www.davidhodson.com/assets/documents/consent_to_marry.pdf.

Hoganson, D A, and D P Stahly. "Regulation of Dihydrodipicolinate Synthase during Growth and Sporulation of Bacillus Cereus." *Journal of Bacteriology* 124, no. 3 (December 1975): 1344–1350.

Holmes, Leslie. *Trafficking and Human Rights□: European and Asia-Pacific Perspectives.* Cheltenham: Edward Elgar Publishing, 2010.

Homeland Security Act 2002. USC, 2002. http://www.law.cornell.edu/uscode/text/6/111.

Horvath, Miranda, A.H., Llian Alys, Kristina Massey, Afroditi Pina, Mia Scally, and Joanna Adler R. *Basically Porn Is Everywhere.* Chidren's Commissioner, June 2013. http://www.childrenscommissioner.gov.uk/force_download.php?fp=%2Fclient_assets%2Fcp%2Fpublication%2F680%2FBasically_porn_is_everywhere_cyp_version.pdf.

House of Commons. "Papers Relating to the West Indies, Viz. Correspondence Between the Earl of Liverpool and Governor Elliot: In Reference to the Trial and Execution of Arthur Hodge, for the Murder of A Negro Slave, Ordered to Be Printed. No. 254." London, U.K., June 26, 1811.

Hua, Julietta. *Trafficking Women's Human Rights.* Minneapolis: University of Minnistota Press, n.d.

Huebner, Albert. "Organ Snatchers 5/04." *Toward Freedom*, June 23, 2005. http://towardfreedom.com/special-reports/454-organ-snatchers-504.

Hughes, Donna, M. "Donna M. Hughes, PhD, January 17, 2007 Speech to Women in Federal Law Enforcement." Powerpoint presentation presented at the Women in Federal Law Enforcement,, Washington, D.C, January 17, 2007. http://www.uri.edu/artsci/wms/hughes/reduce_demand.ppt.

Human Organ and Tissue Transplantation. Fifty-Seventh World Health Assembly. World Health Organization, May 22, 2004. http://apps.who.int/gb/ebwha/pdf_files/WHA57/A57_R18-en.pdf.

"Human Organ and Tissue Transplantation." World Health Organisation, May 22, 2004. http://www.who.int/ethics/en/A57_R18-en.pdf.

Human Trafficking - the Facts. United Nations - Global Initiative to Fight Human Trafficking, October 27, 2013. http://www.unglobalcompact.org/docs/issues_doc/labour/Forced_labour/HUMAN_TRAFFICKING_-_THE_FACTS_-_final.pdf.

"Human Trafficking in the UK." *Anti Slavery*, October 27, 2013. http://www.antislavery.org/english/campaigns/background_on_trafficking_for_forced_labour_in_the_uk.aspx.

Human Trafficking: Mail Order Bride Abuse. Government Prtint Office, 2004. http://www.gpo.gov/fdsys/pkg/CHRG-108shrg96804/html/CHRG-108shrg96804.htm.

Hunt, Lynn. *The French Revolution and Human Rights: A Brief Documentary History.* Boston: Bedford Books of St. Martin's Press, 1996.

Iloegbunam, Chuks. "The Death of a Writer." *The Guardian*, November 10, 2006. http://www.theguardian.com/theguardian/1995/nov/11/fromthearchive.

"Immigration to Texas." Accessed April 20, 2013. http://www.usimmigrationsupport.org/texas.html.

In Re: B.W. (Supreme Court of Texas 2010).

In Rememberance - Ken Saro-Wiwa, Part I, 2009. http://www.youtube.com/watch?v=qkFEhnnwfWI&feature=youtube_gdata_player.

Independent Parliamentary Inquiry into Online Child Protection- Findings and Recommendations. London, U.K., April 2012. http://www.claireperry.org.uk/downloads/independent-parliamentary-inquiry-into-online-child-protection.pdf.

Independent Parliamentary Inquiry into Online Child Protection- Findings and Recommendations. UK Parliament, April 17, 2012. http://www.claireperry.org.uk/downloads/independent-parliamentary-inquiry-into-online-child-protection.pdf.

"India Girl Ends Child 'Marriage.'" *BBC*, April 25, 2012, sec. India. http://www.bbc.co.uk/news/world-asia-india-17838022.

Indian Penal Code, 1860.

Intelligence Reform and Terrorism Prevention Act, 2004.

International Labour Organisation. "Questions and Answers on Forced Labour." *Forced Labour.* Accessed October 28, 2013. http://www.ilo.org/global/about-the-ilo/newsroom/comment-analysis/WCMS_181922/lang--en/index.htm.

———. "State of Child Labour 2000." Accessed October 20, 2013. http://www.childlaborphotoproject.org/childlabor.html.

International Labour Organization. *Report of the Commission Appointed under Article 26 of the Constitution of the International Labour Organisation to Examme the Complaint Filed by the Government of Portugal Concerning the Observance by the Government of Liberia of the Forced Labour Convention, 1930.* International Labour Organisation, April 1963. https://www.ilo.org/dyn/normlex/en/f?p=1000:50012:0::NO:50012:P50012_COMPLAINT_PROCEDURE_ID,P50012_LANG_CODE:2508364,en:NO.

"International Labour Standards on Forced Labour." *International Labour Organization*, October 27, 2013. http://www.ilo.org/global/standards/subjects-covered-by-international-labour-standards/forced-labour/lang--en/index.htm.

International Programme on the Elimination of Child Labour, and International Labour Organization. *Children in Hazardous Work What We Know, What We Need to Do.* Geneva: International Labour Office, 2011. http://site.ebrary.com/id/10512167.

"International Protecting Girls by Preventing Child Marriage Act of 2012 (2012H.R. 6087)." *GovTrack.us*, 18:30:49. https://www.govtrack.us/congress/bills/112/hr6087.

Ionescu, Carminola. "Donor Charged in Romania's First Organ Trafficking Trial." *Lancet* 365, no. 9475 (June 4, 2005): 1918. doi:10.1016/S0140-6736(05)66644-5.
Islam, Joseph, A. "NIKAAH AL-MUT'AH - Temporary Marriage." *The Quran and Its Message*, November 23, 2011. http://quransmessage.com/pdfs/Mut-ah.pdf.
Jain, Tarun. "Child Marriage in India: Policy Changes Proposed by the Law Commission of India." *Law-in-Perspective*, February 18, 2008. http://legalperspectives.blogspot.com/2008/02/child-marriage-in-india-policy-changes.html.
Jamasmie, Cecilia. "Diamonds Are Now Your Washings Best Friend." *Mining*, June 26, 2012. www.mining.com.
Jamieson, Dave, and Emran Hossain. "Bangladesh Factory Fire Victim Calls O Walmart to Pay Compensation." *The Huffington Post*, April 12, 2013. http://www.huffingtonpost.com/2013/04/12/bangladesh-factory-fire-walmart_n_3071974.html.
Jamjoom, Mohammad. "Vote on Child Marriage Law in Yemen Delayed." *CNN World*, October 4, 2010.
Jennings, Judith. *The Business of Abolishing the British Slave Trade: 1783 - 1807*. London [u.a.: Cass, 1997.
Jenson, Cari, B. "Child Slavery and the Fish Processing Industry in Bangladesh." *American Geographical Society's Focus on Geography* 56, no. 2 (Summr 2013): 54–65.
Jiyoung Bang, Naomi. "American Geographical Society's Focus on Geography. Summer2013, Vol. 56 Issue 2, p54-65." *Houston Journal of International Law* 35, no. 2 (Spring 2013): 255–322.
"John Schools." *John Schools*. PBS, May 30, 2008. http://www.pbs.org/now/shows/422/prostitution.html.
Johnson, Simon. "A Generation Is Growing up Skewed by Internet Pornography, Court Hears, as 12-Year-Old Who Raped a Schoolgirl Is Spared Jail." *The Telegraph*, May 31, 2012. http://www.telegraph.co.uk/news/uknews/crime/9303598/A-generation-is-growing-up-skewed-by-internet-pornography-court-hears-as-12-year-old-who-raped-a-schoolgirl-is-spared-jail.html.
Jones-Pauly, Christina. *Women under Islam□: Gender, Justice and the Politics of Islamic Law*. London, U.K.: I.B. Tauris, 2011.
"Justinian Code," 534. http://www.fordham.edu/halsall/basis/535institutes.asp.
Kara, Siddharth. *Bonded Labor: Tackling the System of Slavery in South Asia*. 1st ed. Columbia University Press, 2012.
———. "Designing More Effective Laws Against Human Trafficking." *Journal of International Human Rights* 9, no. 2 (Spring 2011): 123–147.
———. *Sex Trafficking: Inside the Business of Modern Slavery*. New York: Columbia University Press, 2009.
———. *Sex Trafficking: Inside the Business of Modern Slavery*. New York: Columbia University Press, 2009.
Kaufmann, Chaim D, and Robert A. Pape. "Explaining Costly International Moral Action: Britain's Sixty-Year Campaign Against the Atlantic Slave Trade." *International Organization* 53, no. 4 (Autumn 1999): 631–668.
Kaufmann, Tina. "Troopers Find Missing Kentucky Teen Girls, Charge Truck Driver with Kidnapping." *WEWS newsnet5*, 00:28:21. http://www.newsnet5.com//dpp/news/local_news/troopers-find-missing-kentucky-teen-girls-charge-truck-driver-with-kidnapping.
Keene, Edward. "A Case Study of the Construction of International Hierarchy: British Treaty-Making Against the Slave Trade in the Early Nineteenth Century." *International Organization* 61, no. 2 (Spring 2007): 311–339.
Kendall, Virginia. *Child Exploitation and Trafficking□: Examining the Global Challenges and U.S. Responses*. Lanham: Rowman & Littlefield Publishers, 2012.
Kenny A v Sonny Perdue (UNITED STATES DISTRICT COURT FOR THE NORTHERN DISTRICT OF GEORGIA ATLANTA DIVISION 2006).
Khalife, Nadya. "Yemen Could Seize Moment to Ban Child Marriage." *Womens Enews*, December 16, 2011. http://womensenews.org/story/marriagedivorce/111215/yemen-could-seize-moment-ban-child-marriage#.Um1e5fnksXc.
———. "Yemen Could Seize the Moment to Ban Child Marriage." *Women's E News*, December 16, 2011.
Khanna, Roma. "Girl Reunited with Parents." *Laredo Morning Times*, May 17, 2001.
"Kidnapping - False Imprisonment:Offences against the Person: Sentencing Manual: Legal Guidance: The Crown Prosecution Service." Accessed October 27, 2013. http://www.cps.gov.uk/legal/s_to_u/sentencing_manual/kidnapping_false_imprisonment/.
Kidron, Beeban. "Devadasi Practice in India." *Every Child*. Accessed October 27, 2013. http://www.everychild.org.uk/devadasi.

King, L.W., trans. "The Code of Hammurabi. The Prologue and Rules (1760BCE)." Accessed October 20, 2013. http://avalon.law.yale.edu/ancient/hamframe.asp.
Kingsbury, Kathleen. "Immigration: No Correlation With Crime." *Time*, 20:27:41. http://content.time.com/time/nation/article/0,8599,1717575,00.html.
"Kiobel v Royal Dutch Petroleum." *SCOTUSblog*. Accessed October 20, 2013. http://www.scotusblog.com/case-files/cases/kiobel-v-royal-dutch-petroleum/?wpmp_switcher=desktop.
Kitson, Deborah. "Marriage Reform, Comments from the Ann Craft Trust." *Family Law Week*. Accessed November 4, 2013. http://www.familylawweek.co.uk/site.aspx?i=ed98339>.
Kloer, Amanda. "Your Tomato's Possible Ties to Slavery." *CNN Freedom Project*. Accessed November 28, 2013. http://thecnnfreedomproject.blogs.cnn.com/2011/04/21/your-tomato-possible-ties-to-slavery/.
Koerner, Brendan, I. "How Do I Figure out How Many Non-Bot Twitter Followers I Have?," June 22, 2012. http://www.wired.com/opinion/2012/06/st_kia_twitter_followers/.
Kontorovich, Eugene. "THE CONSTITUTIONALITY OF INTERNATIONAL COURTS: THE FORGOTTEN PRECEDENT OF SLAVE-TRADE TRIBUNALS." *University of Pennsylvania Law Review* 158, no. 1 (December 2009): 39–115.
Krieg, Sarah, H. "Trafficking in Human Beings: The EU Approach between Border Control, Law Enforcement and Human Rights." *European Law Journal* 15, no. 6 (November 2009): 775–790.
Kristof, Nicholas D, and Sheryl WuDunn. *Half the Sky: Turning Oppression into Opportunity for Women Worldwide.* WuDunn. New York: Vintage Books, 2010.
Kristof, Nicholas D. "How Pimps Use the Web to Sell Girls." *The New York Times*, January 25, 2012, sec. Opinion. http://www.nytimes.com/2012/01/26/opinion/how-pimps-use-the-web-to-sell-girls.html.
———. "She Has a Pimp's Name Etched on Her." *The New York Times*, May 23, 2012, sec. Opinion. http://www.nytimes.com/2012/05/24/opinion/kristof-she-has-a-pimps-name-etched-on-her.html.
———. ""Stories of Survival and Courage from the Fight to End Human Trafficking."" Speecch. Austin, Texas, February 13, 2012. http://ddce.utexas.edu/news/2012/02/09/feb-13-pulitzer-prize-winning-columnist-to-speak-about-human-trafficking/.
Kristof, Nicholas D., and Sheryl Wudunn. *Half the Sky*. 1 edition. Vintage, 2009.
Kruger, H B.., and H Oosthuizen. "SOUTH AFRICA - SAFE HAVEN FOR HUMAN TRAFFICKERS? EMPLOYING THE ARSENAL OF EXISTING LAW TO COMBAT HUMAN TRAFFICKING." *Potchefstroom Electronic Law Journal* 15, no. 1 (2012): 282–343.
Kumar, R, and M Tao. "Multiple Forms of Casein Kinase from Rabbit Erythrocytes." *Biochimica et Biophysica Acta* 410, no. 1 (November 20, 1975): 87–98.
Kurzweil, Ray. *The Singularity Is Near□: When Huamns Transcend Biology*. New York, NY: Penguin Group, 2005.
"L CdeBaca." *U.S. Department of State*. Accessed October 20, 2013. http://www.state.gov/r/pa/ei/biog/124083.htm.
Labour Organisation, International. "CONVENTION CONCERNING THE PROHIBITION AND IMMEDIATE ACTION FOR THE ELIMINATION OF THE WORST FORMS OF CHILD LABOUR (Convention 182)." International Labour Organization, June 17, 1999. http://www.ilo.org/public/english/standards/relm/ilc/ilc87/com-chic.htm.
"Lapdancing Clubs Encourage Rape and Sexual Assaults, Claims Police Chief." *Telegraph.co.uk*, May 23, 2012, sec. uknews. http://www.telegraph.co.uk/news/uknews/law-and-order/9284609/Lapdancing-clubs-encourage-rape-and-sexual-assaults-claims-police-chief.html.
Lauterbach, Kristin, Ross. *Flesh*, 2010. http://www.fleshthemovie.org/.
Law, US Public. "Victims of Trafficking and Violence Protection Act of 2000." *Public Law* 106 (2000): 386.
Le Breton, Binka. *Trapped□: Modern-Day Slavery in the Brazilian Amazon*. Bloomfield, CT□: Kumarian Press, 2003.
Lenora C., Babb. "UTAH'S MISGUIDED APPROACH TO THE PROBLEM OF SEX TRAFFICKING: A CALL FOR REFORM." *Journal of Law & Family Studies*. 14, no. 2 (2012): 277–298.
Leo Africanus. *The History and Description of Africa: And of the Notable Things Therein Contained.* Edited by Robert Brown. Translated by John Pory. Cambridge Library Collection Hakluyt First Series. Cambridge University Press, 2010.
Levine, Andrew. *The Day My God Died.* Independent Lens, 2004. http://www.pbs.org/independentlens/daymygoddied/film.html.

Liberia. *An Act to Amend the Labor Practices Law in Relation to the Rights and Duties of Labor Organizations and the Members There Of.*, 1962. http://dlxs.library.cornell.edu/l/liberian/.
Liberia, International Commission of Inquiry into the Existence of Slavery and Forced Labor in the Republic of, and Cuthbert Christy. *Report of the International Commission of Inquiry into the Existence of Slavery and Forced Labor in the Republic of Liberia. Monrovia, Liberia, September 8, 1930.* U.S. Govt. print. off., 1931.
Lilith, Ryiah. "Buying a Wife but Saving a Child: A Deconstruction of Popular Rhetoric and Legal Analysis of Mail-Order Brides and Intercountry Adoptions." *Buffalo Women's Law Journal* 9 (October 10, 2000): 225.
Locke, John. *Two Treatises of Government.* [Whitefish, Mont.]: Kessinger Publishing, 1988.
Loftus, Britta, S. "COORDINATING U.S. LAW ON IMMIGRATION AND HUMAN TRAFFICKING: LIFTING THE LAMP TO VICTIMS." *Columbia Human Rights Law Review* 43, no. 1 (Fall 2011): 143–214.
LoGerfo, James, W. "Sir William Dolben and 'The Cause of Humanity': The Passage of the Slave Trade Regulations Act of 1788." *Eigtheenth-Century Studies* 6, no. 4 (Summer 1973): 431–451.
Londoño, Ernesto. "Afghanistan Sees Rise in 'dancing Boys' Exploitation." *The Washington Post,* August 10, 2012, sec. World. http://www.washingtonpost.com/world/asia_pacific/afganistans-dancing-boys-are-invisible-victims/2012/04/04/gIQAyreSwS_story.html.
Look, Anne. "Senegal Draws Tourists with Sun, Sea and Sex." *Global Post,* October 7, 2010. http://www.globalpost.com/dispatch/senegal/100428/senegal-news-sex-tourism.
Macdonell, Sir John, and Sir John Edward Power Wallis. *Reports of State Trials: New Series... 1820 to [1858]...* H.M. Stationery Office, 1889.
Mackie, Gerry. "Ending Footbinding and Infibulation: A Convention Account." *American Sociological Review* 61, no. 6 (December 1996): 999–1017. doi:10.2307/2096305.
Macleod, Hugh, and Annasofie Flamand. "Sally's Story." *Al Jazeera,* October 27, 2013. http://www.aljazeera.com/photo_galleries/africa/2010831920332122.html.
"Malala Yousafzai." *Malala Yousafzai.* Accessed October 27, 2013. http://www.malala-yousafzai.com/.
Malik, Preeti. "HONOUR-BASED VIOLENCE WITH SPECIAL REFERENCE TO 'KHAP PANCHAYAT' IN HARYANA AND THE INDIAN PANEL CODE." *Indian Streams Research Journal* 3, no. 5 (June 2013): 1–4.
———. "KILLING IN THE NAME OF HONOUR AND TRADITION." *Golden Research Thoughts* 2, no. 12 (June 2013): 1–3.
Mam, Somaly, and Ruth Marshall. *The Road of Lost Innocence.* New York: Spiegel & Grau, 2009.
———. *The Road of Lost Innocence.* New York: Spiegel & Grau, 2009.
———. *The Road of Lost Innocence.* New York: Spiegel & Grau, 2009.
"Manhattan DA: Father, Son's Prostitution Business Busted; Men Branded Victims With Tattoos." *Huffington Post,* April 24, 1920. http://www.huffingtonpost.com/2012/04/24/manhattan-da-father-sons-prostitution-ring-busted_n_1449107.html.
"Marriage (Part I of II)." *Al-Islam.org,* 18:31:40. http://www.al-islam.org/islamic-laws-ayatullah-al-uzma-sayyid-ali-al-husaini-seestani/marriage-part-i-ii.
"Marriage: Rule 2379(v) of the Quran. 'The woman and the man should be willing to enter into a matrimonial alliance. If, however, the woman ostensibly displays hesitation while giving her consent, but it is known that in her heart, she is agreeable to the marriage, the marriage is in order.'" *Al-Islam.org.* Accessed November 3, 2013. http://www.al-islam.org/laws/marriage1.html#2421.
Married Women's Property Act., 1882.
Martinez, Jenny, S. *The Slave Trade and the Origins of International Human Rights Law.* Oxford: Oxford University Press, 2011.
Mason, Matthew. "Keeping Up Appearances: The International Politics of Slave Trade Abolition in the Nineteenth-Century Atlantic World." *William & Mary Quarterly* 66, no. 4 (October 2009): 809–832.
Mazher Idreiss, Mohammad, and Tahir Abbas, eds. *Honour, Violence, Women and Islam.* Abingdon: Routledge, 2010.
McAlister, Chryssa, and Thomas F. Baskett. "Female Education and Maternal Mortality: A Worldwide Survey." . " *Journal of Obstetrics and Gynecology* 28, no. 11 (November 2006): 983.
McCracken, Harry, and Lev Grossman. "Can Google Solve Death? The Search Giant Is Launching a Venture to Extend the Human Life Span. That Would Be Crazy – If It Weren't Google." *Time,* 2013.

Melillo, Edward, D. "The First Green Revolution: Debt Peonage and the Making of the Nitrogen Fertilizer Trade, 1840–1930." *American Historical Review* 117, no. 4 (October 2012): 1028–1060.
Meyer, Stephenie. *Twilight.* New York: Little, Brown and Co., 2008.
Meyerowitz, Steven. "Liver4you Health Care Fraud Leads To 'Mass-Marketing' Sentencing Enhancement." *Financial Fraud Law*, August 3, 2011. http://www.financialfraudlaw.com/lawblog/liver4you-health-care-fraud-leads-%E2%80%98mass-marketing%E2%80%99-sentencing-enhancement/2631.
"Minutes of the First Meeting of the Committe for the Abolition of the Slave Trade." Accessed October 20, 2013. http://www.bl.uk/onlinegallery/takingliberties/staritems/66minutesofcommitteeabolition.html.
Mistrati, Miki, and Robin Romano. *The Shady Side of Chocolate*, 2012.
Mitra, Sugata, and Ritu Dangwal. "Limits to Self-Organising Systems of Learning: The Kalikuppam Experiment." *British Journal of Educational Technology* 41, no. 5 (September 2010): 672–68.
Mojeed, Musikilu. *Nigeria - Voodoo Aids Human Trafficking*, October 24, 2008. http://lastradainternational.org/lsidocs/Nigeria.pdf.
"Mr. Know-It-All: Twitter Followers, Language Learning, Cell-Phone Bloodshed | Wired Opinion | Wired.com." *Wired Opinion*, 01:36:38. http://www.wired.com/opinion/2012/06/st_kia_twitter_followers/.
msnbc.com, Preston Mendenhall. "Infiltrating Europe's Shameful Trade in Human Beings." *Msnbc.com*, 20:01:03. http://www.nbcnews.com/id/3071965/ns/us_news-only/t/infiltrating-europes-shameful-trade-human-beings/.
Muhammad, Niaz, Mufti M. M. Ahmed, Fazie Omer, and Naqeeb Hussain Shah. "Honor Killing in Pakistan: An Islamic Perspective." *Asian Social Science* 8, no. 10 (August 2012): 180–195.
Muftic, Lisa, R., and Mary A. Finn. "Health Outcomes Among Women Trafficked for Sex in the United States: A Closer Look." *Journal of Interpersonal Violence* 28, no. 9 (Jun2013): 1859–1885. doi:10.1177/0886260512469102.
Murphy, Caryle. "Caryle Murphy, Child Marriage Case Showcases Deep Splits in Saudi Society." *Global Post*, May 30, 2010. http://www.globalpost.com/dispatch/saudi-arabia/090416/child-marriage-case-showcases-deep-splits-saudi-society.
"Muslim Housekeepers Treated as Slaves in U.S." *The Islamic Workplace*, 20:18:30. http://theislamicworkplace.com/2007/12/17/muslim-housekeepers-treated-as-slaves-in-us/.
"Muslim Housekeepers Treated as Slaves in U.S." *The Islamic Workplace Enabling Muslims and Non-Muslims To Work More Effectively and Harmoniously Together*, December 7, 2007. http://theislamicworkplace.com/2007/12/17/muslim-housekeepers-treated-as-slaves-in-us/.
Nack, Marisa. "THE NEXT STEP: THE FUTURE OF NEW YORK STATE'S HUMAN TRAFFICKING LAW." *Journal of Law & Policy* 18, no. 2 (2010): 817–853.
Napier, Sir William Francis Patrick. *History of General Sir Charles Napier's Administration of Scinde: And Campaign in the Cutchee Hills.* Chapman and Hall, 1851.
National Report on "A World Fit for Children." Ministry of Women and Child Development, Government of India, 2007. http://www.unicef.org/worldfitforchildren/files/India_WFFC5_Report.pdf.
Nations, United. *Convention on the Political Rights of Women*, 1952.
———. "Gender Equality (Goal 3)." *Millenium Development Goals*, n.d.
———. *Protocol to Prevent, Suppress and Punish Trafficking in Persons Especially Women and Children, Supplementing the United Nations Convention against Transnational Organized Crime*, 2000. http://www2.ohchr.org/english/law/protocoltraffic.htm.
———. *Violence Against Children.* United Nations, Office of the Secretary General, 2006. http://www.unviolencestudy.org.
"New Yemen Marriage Law Needs Awareness Campaigns." *Yemen Post*, April 10, 2010. http://yemenpost.net/Detail123456789.aspx?ID=100&SubID=155&MainCat=10.
New York Penal Code. Accessed November 4, 2013. http://codes.lp.findlaw.com/nycode/PEN.
Newsom, Jennifer Siebel. *Miss Representation.* Virgil Films and Entertainment, 2012.
Ngwe, Job Elom, and O Oko Elechi. "HUMAN TRAFFICKING: THE MODERN DAY SLAVERY OF THE 21ST CENTURY." *African Journal of Criminology & Justice Studies; Nov2012, Vol. 6 Issue 1/2, p103-119* 6, no. 1/2 (November 2012): 103–119.
Nielsen, Michael. "The Politics of Corporate Responsibility and Child Labour in the Bangladeshi Garment Industry." *International Affairs* no. 81.3 (2005): 559–580.

"Nigeria: Country Urged to Show Commitment On Child Lead Poisoning." *All Africa*, May 6, 2012. http://allafrica.com/stories/201205071058.html.

Nossiter, Adam. "Mauritania Confronts Long Legacy of Slavery." *New York Times*. November 11, 2013. http://www.nytimes.com/2013/11/12/world/africa/mauritania-confronts-long-legacy-of-slavery.html?_r=0.

Notes. "COUNTERACTING THE BIAS: THE DEPARTMENT OF LABOR'S UNIQUE OPPORTUNITY TO COMBAT HUMAN TRAFFICKING." *Harvard Law Review* 126, no. 4 (January 1, 2013): 1012–1033.

Obama, President. "Remarks." New York, 2012. http://www.whitehouse.gov/the-press-office/2012/09/25/remarks-president-clinton-global-initiative.

———. "REMARKS BY THE PRESIDENT ON A NEW BEGINNING." *The White House*, June 4, 2099. http://www.whitehouse.gov/the_press_office/Remarks-by-the-President-at-Cairo-University-6-04-09.

Office To Monitor and Combat Trafficking in Persons. *Obama Administration Accomplishments on Combating Trafficking in Persons as of February 2012*. President's Interagency Task Force & Senior Policy Operating Group, March 15, 2012. http://www.state.gov/j/tip/rls/reports/2012/184881.htm.

Olaudah Equiano. *The Life of Olaudah Equiano*. Dover Thrift Editions. Dover Publications, 2012.

Omar El-Sawi, Myada. "BEYOND THE 'TIERS' OF HUMAN TRAFFICKING VICTIMS: ISLAMIC LAW'S ABILITY TO PUSH THE MUSLIM WORLD TO THE TOP OF THE UNITED STATES TRAFFICKING TIER PLACEMENTS AND INTO COMPLIANCE WITH INTERNATIONAL LAW." *Georgia Journal of International & Comparative Law* 39, no. 2 (Winter 2011): 391–417.

"Opium Brides." *FRONTLINE*, 01:09:14. http://www.pbs.org/wgbh/pages/frontline/opium-brides/.

Ouagadougou Declaration on Child Marriages. Ouagadougou: Forum on Marriage and the Rights of Women and Girls, October 2003. http://www.wluml.org/node/1211.

Oversight of Public and Private Incentives to Eliminate the Worst Forms of Child Labor in the Cocoa Sector in the Cote De Ivoire and Ghana. Tulane University. Accessed October 15, 2013. http://www.childlabor-payson.org/Tulane%20Final%20Report.pdf.

"Overview." *Global Slavery Index 2013*, October 27, 2013. http://www.globalslaveryindex.org/findings/#overview.

"Overview." *Global Slavery Index*. Accessed October 27, 2013. http://www.globalslaveryindex.org/findings/#overview.

ÖZDEN KAZAN, RABİA. "Angels of Tehran." *Angels of Tehran*. Accessed November 7, 2013. http://rabiaozdenkazan.blogspot.com/.

Palermo Protocol. Unitied Nations, October 27, 2013. http://www.unodc.org/documents/treaties/UNTOC/Publications/TOC%20Convention/TOCebook-e.pdf.

Parliamentary Brefing Paper Sn 01003 - Forced Marriage (Civil Protection) Act 2007. Parliamentary Briefing Paper, 2012. www.parliament.uk/briefing-papers/sn01003.pdf.

Pati, Roza. "Trading in Humans□: A New Haven Perspective." *Asia Pacific Law Review* 20, no. 2 (2012): 135–166.

Patterson, Pete. "Revealed: Qatar's World Cup 'Slaves.'" *The Guardian*, September 25, 2013. http://www.theguardian.com/world/2013/sep/25/revealed-qatars-world-cup-slaves.

Peabody, Sue. *There Are No Slaves in France: The Political Culture of Race and Slavery in the Ancien Régime*. New York: Oxford University Press, 1996.

Pearson, Elaine. *Coercion in the Kidney Trade? A Background Study on Trafficking in Human Organs Worldwide*. Deutsche Gesellschaft für Technische Zusammenarbeit (GTZ) GmbH, April 2004. https://www.giz.de/Themen/en/dokumente/en-organ-trafficking-2004.pdf.

"Perverted Justice." *Perverted Justice*. Accessed November 7, 2013. http://www.perverted-justice.com/.

Peters, Alicia, W. "'Things That Involve Sex Are Just Different': US Anti-Trafficking Law and Policy on the Books, in Their Minds, and in Action." *Anthropological Quarterly* 86, no. 1 (Winter 2013): 221–256.

Phinney, Alison. *Trafficking of Women and Children for Sexual Exploitation in the Americas" Alison Phinney*. Women, Health and Development Program Pan-American Health Organization, October 27, 2013. http://www.oas.org/en/cim/docs/Trafficking-Paper[EN].pdf.

Pierce, Alexandrra. "American Indian Adolescent Girls: Vulnerability to Sex Trafficking, Intervention Strategies." *American Indian and Alaska Native Mental Health Research: The Journal of the National Center* 9 (2012): 37–56.

Pierre Morel. *Taken*, 2009.

Plutarch, John Dryden, and Arthur Hugh Clough. *Plutarch's Lives. the Dryden Translation, Edited with Preface by Arthur Hugh Clough□; Introduction by James Atlas. Volume I Volume I.* New York: Modern Library, 2001.
Polaris Project. *National Human Trafficking Resource Center Call Data 2009 Executive Summary*, 2009.
Policy Coalition, Latino. "Latino Policy Coalition Files United Nations Human Rights Complaint Against the United States of America for Removal of Children From Undocumented Immigrant Parents." *PRneswire.* Accessed October 27, 2013. http://www.prnewswire.com/news-releases/latino-policy-coalition-files-united-nations-human-rights-complaint-against-the-united-states-of-america-for-removal-of-children-from-undocumented-immigrant-parents-147840825.html.
"PRESIDENT ROOSEVELT'S UNDELIVERED JEFFERSON DAY ADDRESS." April 13, 1945.
"Press Release: Kimberley Process." *Global Witness*, December 5, 2011. http://www.globalwitness.org/library/global-witness-leaves-kimberley-process-calls-diamond-trade-be-held-accountable.
"Products of Slavery." *Anti-Slavery Campaign.* Accessed November 7, 2013. www.productsofslavery.org.
"Professor Goes on 'Slave Diet.'" *Free the Slaves BLOG*, 01:24:17. http://ftsblog.net/2010/08/06/professor-goes-on-slave-diet/.
"Prohibition of Child Marriage Act 2006." The Gazette of India, January 11, 2007. http://wcd.nic.in/cma2006.pdf.
PROPOSAL TO AMEND THE PROHIBITION OF CHILD MARRIAGE ACT, 2006 AND OTHER ALLIED LAWS. Law Commission of India, February 2008. http://lawcommissionofindia.nic.in/reports/report205.pdf.
"Protect Act - Fact Sheet." US Department of Justice, April 30, 2003. http://www.justice.gov/opa/pr/2003/April/03_ag_266.htm.
Protection Project. *International Child Sex Tourism, Scope of the Problem and Comaparative Studies.* John Hopkins University, 2007. http://www.ecpat.nl/images/13/166.pdf.
Quraishi, Najibullah. "The Dancing Boys of Afghanistan." *PBS Frontline*, April 20, 2010. http://www.pbs.org/wgbh/pages/frontline/dancingboys/.
R v Eddezider Herak and others (Isleworth Crown Court 2012).
"R v Samo and Others, Two Letters of the Slave Trade." Sierra Leone, 1812. http://www.recoveredhistories.org/pamphlet1.php?page=1&orderby=MaxID&catid=50.
R v Stapleton, 8 Cox, C.C. 69 (n.d.).
Rachel Lloyd. *Girls Like Us: Fighting for a World Where Girls Are Not for Sale: A Memoi.* Harper Perennial, 2012.
Re: J (A Child) [2012] EWCA Civ 720, Samantha Bangham. Accessed October 20, 2013.
Refugees Center, Women's. *Forced from Home: The Lost Boys and Girls of Central America.* New York, NY, October 2012. http://www.youthtoday.org/hotdocs/Forced%20From%20Home1.pdf.
"Refworld | Afghan Girls Suffer for Sins of Male Relatives." *Refworld*, 01:08:36. http://www.refworld.org/cgi-bin/texis/vtx/rwmain?docid=49dc4b201c.
"Refworld | Afghan Girls Suffer for Sins of Male Relatives." *Refworld*, July 14, 2012. http://www.refworld.org/docid/49dc4b201c.html.
Reymond, Laura, Asha Mohamud, and Nancy Ali. *Female Genital Mutilation – The Facts*, October 27, 2013. http://www.path.org/files/FGM-The-Facts.htm.
Rights Council, Human. *Report of the Independent Expert on Minority Rights. Mission to Bulgaria.* United Nations General Assembly, July 11, 2013. <http://www2.ohchr.org/english/bodies/hrcouncil/19session/reports.htm.
Riley, Brad. *Truckers against Trafficking*, 2013. http://www.truckersagainsttrafficking.com.
Ris, M M, R A Deitrich, and J P Von Wartburg. "Inhibition of Aldehyde Reductase Isoenzymes in Human and Rat Brain." *Biochemical Pharmacology* 24, no. 20 (October 15, 1975): 1865–1869.
Rivoli, Pietra. *The Travels of a T-Shirt in the Global Economy: An Economist Examines the Markets, Power, and Politics of World Trade.* Hoboken, N.J.: John Wiley, 2009.
Robot Replace Children as Camel Jockeys in the UAE. IRINFILMS, 2007. https://www.youtube.com/watch?v=b0aEtNH1NyY.
Rocha, Pricilla, A. "OUR BACKYARD SLAVE TRADE: THE RESULT OF OHIO'S FAILURE TO ENACT COMPREHENSIVE STATE-LEVEL HUMAN-SEX-TRAFFICKING LEGISLATION." *Journal of Law & Health* 25, no. 2 (2012): 381–417.
"Safe Horizon." Accessed November 4, 2013. http://www.safehorizon.org/.

Salmon, David, W. "A New System of Peonage--A Challenge to Industrial Relations." *Labor Law Journal* 24, no. 8 (August 1973): 558–564.

Sanghera, Jasvinder. *Shame.* London: Hodder & Stoughton, 2007.

Satre, Lowell, J. *Chocolate on Trial□: Slavery, Politics, and the Ethics of Business.* Athens, OH: Ohio University Press, 2005.

Sattin, Anthony. *The Gates of Africa: Death, Discovery and the Search for Timbuktu.* London: Harper Perennial, 2004.

"Save the Children." Accessed October 20, 2013. http://www.savethechildren.org/site/c.8rKLIXMGIpI4E/b.6115947/k.8D6E/Official_Site.htm.

Sayare, Scott. "France Orders Strauss-Kahn to Stand Trial." *The New York Times*, July 26, 2013, sec. World / Europe. http://www.nytimes.com/2013/07/27/world/europe/trial-ordered-for-strauss-kahn-in-prostitution-case.html.

Scelle, Foundation. "La Prostitution par pays." Accessed November 4, 2013. http://www.fondationscelles.org/index.php?option=com_content&view=article&id=2&Itemid=140.

Schackle, Samira. "Slavery on Britain's Cannabis Farms." *New Statesman*, November 26, 2008. http://www.newstatesman.com/law-and-reform/2008/11/cannabis-farms-children.

Scheper-Hughes, Nancy. "Organ Trafficking." presented at the Transplantation in the USA: The Shortage of available organs and public policy, New York, NY, April 19, 2010. http://transplantusa.kidneyurology.org/.

School, Oxford Martin, and University of Oxford. "Oxford Martin School | University of Oxford." *The Oxford Martin School.* Accessed November 10, 2013. http://www.oxfordmartin.ox.ac.uk/.

Seidl, Ulrich. *Paradise□: Love.* Ulrich Seidl Film Produktion GmbH, 2012.

Seifert, Rachel. "Striptease and Cyber Sex: My Stay at Habbo Hotel." *4 News*, June 12, 2012. http://www.channel4.com/news/striptease-and-cyber-sex-my-stay-at-habbo-hotel.

"Sexual Offences Act 2003." Text, 19:41:33. http://www.legislation.gov.uk/ukpga/2003/42/contents.

Shackle, Samira. "Slavery on Britain's Cannabis Farms." *The New Statesman*, November 26, 2008.

"Shafilea Ahmed's Parents Found Guilty of Her Murder." *Channel 4 News*, August 3, 2012. http://www.channel4.com/news/shafilea-ahmeds-parents-found-guilty-of-her-murder.

Shakespeare, William. *Romeo & Juliet.* Waxkeep Publishing, 2013.

Shamir, Hila. "A Labor Paradigm for Human Trafficking." *UCLA Law Review* 60, no. 1 (October 2012): 76–136.

Shannon, David. "Online Sexual Grooming in Sweden—Online and Offline Sex Offences against Children as Described in Swedish Police Data." *Journal of Scandinavian Studies in Criminology and Crime Prevention* 9, no. 2 (2008): 160–180. doi:10.1080/14043850802450120.

Shapiro, Harry, and David Guttenfelder. *Politics of the Poppy.* Druglink, November 2011. http://www.drugscope.org.uk/Resources/Drugscope/Documents/PDF/Publications/politics_of_the_poppy.pdf.

"Shared Hope International, Polaris Project, ECPAT Brriefing Note." *Shared Hope International*, 2012. http://www.sharedhope.org/Portals/0/Documents/S596Summary.pdf.

Sharma, Kalpana. "The Other Half: When Children Marry." *The Hindu*, February 18, 2012. http://www.thehindu.com/opinion/columns/Kalpana_Sharma/article2906570.ece.

Sharpe, Glanville. "The Plan for Sierra Leone 1786," 1786. http://assets.cambridge.org/97805216/62345/excerpt/9780521662345_excerpt.pdf.

Shively, Michael, Kristina Kliorys, Kristin WHEELER, and Dana Hunt. "A National Overview of Prostitution and Sex Trafficking Demand Reduction Efforts." *ABT Associates*, July 7, 2012. http://www.abtassociates.com/CMSPages/GetFile.aspx?guid=16b0e4c0-e5fe-46d9-9f0d-9aa29a880f1d.

Shoaps, Laura, L. "ROOM FOR IMPROVEMENT: PALERMO PROTOCOL AND THE TRAFFICKING VICTIMS PROTECTION ACT." *Lewis & Clark Law Review* 17, no. 3 (2013): 931–972.

Siebel Newsom, Jennifer. *MissRepresentation*, n.d.

Sifuentes, William, J. "Human Trafficking in Austin, Texas," 2010.

Silverman JG, Decker MR, Gupta J, Maheshwari A, Willis BM, and Raj A. "HIV Prevalence and Predictors of Infection in Sex-Trafficked Nepalese Girls and Women." *JAMA* 298, no. 5 (August 1, 2007): 536–542. doi:10.1001/jama.298.5.536.

"Singularity Hub." Accessed November 10, 2013. http://singularityhub.com.

"Singularity University." Accessed November 10, 2013. http://singularityu.org.

Skinner, E. Benjamin. "Slaves Put Squid on Dining Tables From South Pacific." *Bloomberg*, 01:03:32. http://www.bloomberg.com/news/2012-02-23/slaves-put-squid-on-u-s-dining-tables-from-south-pacific-catch.html.

———. "How U.S. Budget Cuts Prolong Global Slavery." *Time*, June 28, 2011.

"Slavery Today." *Free the Slaves*. Accessed October 29, 2013. http://www.freetheslaves.net/page.aspx?pid=301.

Smith, Christopher. *Trafficking Victims Protection Reauthorization Act of 2011. HR 3589*, n.d.

Smith, Heather. "Sex Trafficking: Trends, Challenges, and the Limitations of International Law." *Human Rights Review* 12, no. 3 (September 2012): 271–286.

Smith Kendal, Nicole. "HUMAN TRAFFICKING AND RICO: A NEW PROSECUTORIAL HAMMER IN THE WAR ON MODERN DAY SLAVERY." *George Mason Law Review* 18 (April 1, 2011): 759.

Smith, Michael, Daryna Krasnolutska, and David Glovin. "Organ Gangs Force Poor to Sell Kidneys for Desperate Israelis." *Bloomberg*, 19:44:30. http://www.bloomberg.com/news/2011-11-01/organ-gangs-force-poor-to-sell-kidneys-for-desperate-israelis.html.

Smith, Stephen, F. "Jail for Juvenile Child Pronographers?:a Reply to Professor Leary." *15 VA. J. Soc. Pol'y & L.* (2008): 505.

Society for Effecting the Abolition of the Slave Trade. *Stowage of the British Slave Ship "Brookes" under the Regulated Slave Trade of 1788*, 1788. Library of Congress. http://www.loc.gov/rr/rarebook/guide/ra023002.html.

Somaly Mam on the Tyra Banks Show (1 of 3), 2008. http://www.youtube.com/watch?v=YlpjTc8iJqo&feature=youtube_gdata_player.

Somaly Mam on the Tyra Banks Show (1 of 3), 2008. http://www.youtube.com/watch?v=YlpjTc8iJqo&feature=youtube_gdata_player.

"Some of the Restrictions Imposed by Taliban on Women in Afghanistan." Revolutionary Association of the Women of Afghanistan (RAWA), October 27, 2013. http://www.rawa.org/rules.htm.

Somersett v Sharpe, Lofft 1 (English Court of Appeal 1772).

Sooldalter, Ron. "In Our Own Backyard: Child Prostitution and Sex Trafficking in the United States." Austin: Kozmetsky Center, 2010.

"SOWC_2011_Executive_Summary_EN_01122011[1].pdf," n.d.

Speak, Clare. "Czech Trafficking Gang Sentenced in London." *The Prague Post*, July 24, 2013. http://www.praguepost.com/opinion/16779-czech-trafficking-gang-sentenced-in-london.html.

Staff. "Babies Bred for Sale in Nigeria." *Mail & Guardian, South Africa*, November 9, 2008. http://mg.co.za/article/2008-11-09-babies-bred-for-sale-in-nigeria.

———. "Indian Teen Annuls Her Marriage." *BBC World News - India*, April 25, 2012. http://www.bbc.co.uk/news/world-asia-india-17838022.

———. "Teenage Girls Undergo Breast Ironing in Cameroon." *Huffington Post*, July 23, 2010. http://www.huffingtonpost.com/2010/07/23/teenage-girls-undergo-bre_n_656965.html.

Stiglmayer, Alexandrra, ed. *Rape, Genocide and Women;s Human Rights (Catherine A. MacKinnon).* Mass Rape: The War against Women in Bosnia-Herzegovina. Omaha: University of Nebraska Press, 1994.

"Stop Child Trafficking Now." *Stop Child Trafficking Now*. Accessed November 2, 2013. http://www.sctnow.org.

Stoughton, John. *William Wilberforce*. London□: Hodder and Stoughton, 1880. http://archive.org/details/williamwilberfor00stou.

"Strauss-Kahn Held over 'Sex Ring.'" *BBC*, February 21, 2012, sec. Europe. http://www.bbc.co.uk/news/world-europe-17110618.

Strickland, Pat. "Forced Marriage." UK House of Commons Library, September 16, 2013. http://http://www.parliament.uk/briefing-papers/sn01003.pdf.

Stuart, Andrea. *Sugar in the Blood.* Knopf/Jan, 2013.

"Sudanese Court Sentences Woman to Death By Stoning Over Adultery Claims." *Sudan Tribune*, July 15, 2012. http://allafrica.com/stories/201207160064.html.

Svensson, Naomi, L. "Extraterritorial Accountability: An Assessment of the Effectiveness of Child Sex Tourism Laws." *L.A. Int'l & Comp. L. Rev* 28. Loyola of Los Angeles International and Comparative Law Review (2006): 641.

Swartz, Mimi. "The Lost Girls." *Texas Monthly*, April 2010.

"Swedish Prostitution Law Attracts World Interest." *USA Today*, March 16, 2008. http://www.usatoday.com/news/world/2008-03-16-sweden-prostitution_N.htm.
TAKU ARREY, Georgette. *Breast Ironing in Cameroon - Report under CEDAW and CRC.* UN Committee on CEDAW and CRC. U.N. Office of High Commissioner on Human Rights. Accessed November 2, 2013. http://www.ohchr.org/Documents/HRBodies/CEDAW/HarmfulPractices/RENATA.pdf.
Tapscott, Rebecca. "Understanding Breast 'Ironing' A Study of the Methods, Motivations, and Outcomes of Breast Flattening Practices in Cameroon." *Feinstien International Center, Tufts University*, Mat 2012. hppt://sites.tufts.edu/Feinstein/2012/understanding-breast-ironing.
"Target 3.A: Eliminate Gender Disparity in Primary and Secondary Education, Preferably by 2005, and in All Levels of Education No Later than 2015." United Nations. Accessed October 25, 2013. http://www.un.org/millenniumgoals/gender.shtml.
Taylor, Jerome, and Paul Peachey. "Cannabis: Britain's Growth Industry." *The Independent*, 01:13:21. http://www.independent.co.uk/news/uk/crime/cannabis-britains-growth-industry-7704330.html.
TED. *TEDx Brussels 2011 - Henrik Sharfe - DK Geminoid.* Brussels, Belgium, 2011. http://www.youtube.com/watch?v=oiyviOdF_ac.
Ted Talks. *Ian Goldin: Navigating Our Global Future.* TED Talks. Oxford, U.K., 2009.
"Teen Girls' Stories of Sex Trafficking in U.S." *ABC News*, November 24, 2006. http://abcnews.go.com/Primetime/story?id=1596778&page=1.
Territo, Leonard, and Matteson, eds. *The International Trafficking of Human Organs□: A Multidisciplinary Perspective.* Boca Raton, Florida: Taylor Francis, 2012.
Texas. *Code of Criminal Procedure*, 2010.
———. *Family Code*, 2010.
"Texas Attorney General." *Texas Attorney General*, July 21, 2011. https://www.oag.state.tx.us/oagnews/release.php?id=3807.
Texas Penal Code, 2010.
"Thai Fishing and Slavery." *Ethical Consumer*, January 6, 2011. http://www.ethicalconsumer.org/latestnews/tabid/62/entryid/703/thai-fishing-and-slavery.aspx.
The Associated Press. "Slave Labor Camp Raided in East Palatka." *The Gainsville Sun.* June 7, 2005.
The Better Angels of Our Nature Why Violence Has Declined. Brilliance Audio, 2012.
"The Children's Commissioner." *The Children's Commissioner.* Accessed October 20, 2013. http://www.childrenscommissioner.gov.uk/info/about_us.
The Long Island Serial Killer. CBS News, 20:49:17. http://www.cbsnews.com/video/watch/?id=7392036n&tag=api.
The Media Line Staff. "New Yemen Marriage Law Needs Awareness Campaigns." *Yemen Post*, April 10, 2010. http://yemenpost.net/Detail123456789.aspx?ID=100&SubID=155&MainCat=10.
"The Millennium Development Goals - Eight Goals for 2015." United Nations Development Program, October 27, 2013. http://www.undp.org/content/undp/en/home/mdgoverview/.
"The Universal Declarartion on Human Rights." UN Treaty, 1948. http://www.un.org/en/documents/udhr/.
Thomas De Benitez, Sarah. *State of the World's Street Children – Violence.* Consortium for Street Children, October 20, 2007. http://www.amazon.com/State-Worlds-Street-Children-Violence/dp/0954788656.
Thomas de Benítez, Sarah, and Consortium for Street Children. *State of the World's Street Children: Research.* London: Consortium for Street Children, 2011. http://www.streetchildren.org.uk/_uploads/publications/State_of_the_Worlds_Street_Children_Research_final_PDF_online.pdf.
Thomas, Gwenda. "Welsh Government Makes Children's Rights a Priority." *Western Mail, Wales Online*, May 7, 2012. http://www.walesonline.co.uk/news/health-news/2012/05/07/welsh-government-makes-children-s-rights-a-priority-91466-30914333/.
"Thomas Jefferson and Sally Hemings: A Brief Account." *The Jefferson Monticello*, n.d. http://www.monticello.org/site/plantation-and-slavery/thomas-jefferson-and-sally-hemings-brief-account.
Tofan, C., and W. van der Wolf. *The Extraordinary Chambers in the Courts of Cambodia: Case I Volume I Kaing Guek Eav.* International Courts Association, 2010.
Tomita, Toko. "Fighting Slavery Today." Anti-Slavery Campaign. Accessed October 28, 2013. http://www.anti-slaverysociety.addr.com/media.htm.

Tomkins, Stephen. *William Wilberforce: A Biography*. Michigan: William B. Eerdmans Publishing Company, 2007.
"Trafficking." *Bernardo Kohler Center*. Accessed October 26, 2013. http://www.bernardokohler.org/Trafficking.htm.
"Trafficking in Persons for Organ Removal: Prevention of Trafficking in Persons, Chapter 9." United Nations Office of Drugs and Crime. Accessed January 11, 2013. https://www.unodc.org/documents/human-trafficking/Toolkit-files/08-58296_tool_9-19.pdf.
"Trafficking of Persons Especially Women and Children: USA Route." The Future Group, 2002. http://www.thefuturegroup.org/id20.html.
Truckers Against Trafficking Training Video. Truckers Against Trafficking. Accessed October 27, 2013. http://truckersagainsttrafficking.org/.
Trust, National. "Get Your Free Soho Stories Here." Accessed October 20, 2013. http://www.nationaltrust.org.uk/article-1356398419972/.
Truth and Reconciliation Commission Report For the Children of Sierra Leone. UNICEF Sierra Leone, 2004. http://www.unicef.org/infobycountry/files/TRCCF9SeptFINAL.pdf.
"U Visa for Immigrants Who Are Victims of Crimes." *US Immigration Support*, October 27, 2013. http://www.usimmigrationsupport.org/visa-u.html.
U.S. Department of Justice. *The National Strategy for Child Exploitation and Interdiction: A Report to Congress 2-3*. U.S. Congress, 2010.
U.S. Dept of State. "Tier Placements." Accessed October 23, 2013. http://www.state.gov/j/tip/rls/tiprpt/2012/192363.htm.
U.S. Dept. of Health and Human Services. *Results from the 2010 National Survey on Drug Use and Health: Summary of National Findings*, 2010. http://www.oas.samhsa.gov/NSDUH/2k10NSDUH/2k10Results.htm.
U.S. Dept. of State. "Trafficking in Persons." *State Government Trafficking in Persons*. Accessed October 30, 2013. http://www.state.gov/j/tip/laws/.
U.S. Government. United States v Justin Evans, Government Notice of Filing,. Accessed October 20, 2013.
U.S. State Department. *Quotes By and About Women in Afghanistan, Report on the Taliban's War Against Women*. Bureau of Democracy, Human Rights and Labor, November 17, 2001. http://www.state.gov/j/drl/rls/6186.htm.
U.S. v. SABHNANI (U.S. Court of Appeals, 2nd Cir. 2010).
"UK 'Breaches Human Rights Laws' over Youth Sentencing." *Channel 4 News*, March 15, 2012. http://www.channel4.com/news/uk-breaches-human-rights-laws-over-youth-sentencing.
UN. "Convention on the Rights of the Child," 1989. http://www.ohchr.org/en/professionalinterest/pages/crc.aspx.
"Unam Sanctum Catholicam." Accessed October 23, 2013. http://unamsanctamcatholicam.blogspot.com/2011/02/dum-diversas-english-translation.htm.
UNGIFT. *About*. UNGIFT. Accessed October 20, 2013. http://www.ungift.org/.
———. "Human Trafficking - The Fact," 2007. http://www.unglobalcompact.org/docs/issues_doc/labour/Forced_labour/HUMAN_TRAFFICKING_-_THE_FACTS_-_final.pdf.
UNICEF. "Child Protection from Violence, Exploitation and abuseChild Protection from Violence, Exploitation and Abuse - Child Labour." *UNICEF*. Accessed October 27, 2013. http://www.unicef.org/protection/57929_58009.html.
———. *Executive Summary." The State of the World's Children 2011*. UNICEF, 2011. http://www.unicef.org/publications/files/SOWC_2011_Executive_Summary_EN_01122011.pdf.
United Kingdom. "An Act for the Abolition of Slavery throughout the British Colonies; for Promoting the Industry of the Manumitted Slaves; and for Compensating the Persons Hitherto Entitled to the Services of Such Slaves. 1833." Act of Parliament. London, U.K., 1833. http://www.pdavis.nl/Legis_07.htm.
———. "Children Act 1989," 1989. http://www.legislation.gov.uk/ukpga/1989/41/contents.
———. "Human Rights Act," 1998. http://www.legislation.gov.uk/ukpga/1998/42/contents.
United Nations. "Convention for the Suppression of the Traffic in Persons and of the Exploitation of the Prostitution of Others," 1949. http://treaties.un.org/Pages/ViewDetails.aspx?src=IND&mtdsg_no=VII-11-a&chapter=7&lang=en.
———. "Convention on the Rights of Persons with Disabilities," 2006. http://www.un.org/disabilities/convention/conventionfull.shtml.

United Nations Convention Against Transnational Organized Crime and Protocols Thereto (Palermo Protocol). United Nations. Accessed October 26, 2013. http://www.unodc.org/documents/treaties/UNTOC/Publications/TOC%20Convention/TOCebook-e.pdf.

United States v Justin Evans, 476 F.3d 1176 (11th Cir. 2007), 1177-78, Justia (11th Cir. 2007).

United States v. Elnora Calimlim, 129 S. Ct. 2237 2244 (Supreme Court 2009).

United States v. Eric A. Olson (7th Cir. 2008).

United States v. Kendal Ray Williams, 291 F.3d 1180 (9th Cir. 2002).

United States v. Michael Wayne Thomas (10th Cir. 2005).

"US Embassy Cables: Afghan Government Asks US to Quash 'Dancing Boys' Scandal." *The Guardian*, December 2, 2010. http://www.theguardian.com/world/us-embassy-cables-documents/213720.

US v. Jacobo Dominguez Vazquez and Others (District Court Wyoming 2007).

Vafa, Yasmin. "Bishops and House Republicans Seeking to Deny Essential Services to Victims of Sex Trafficking." *Human Rights Project for Giirls*. Accessed April 18, 2012. http://www.rights4girls.org/.

Van Hook, Mary, P. "Modern Day Slavery: Trafficking of Persons in Rural America." *Rural Mental Health* (Summer 2004).

Van Schaack, Beth. "Introducing the Crime Against Humanity of Forced Marriage." *ASIL*. Accessed November 2, 2013. http://www.asil.org/accountability/winter2009-10/winter2009-10_2.html.

Van Schaack, Beth, and Ronald Slye. *International Criminal Law and Its Enforcement: Cases and Materials*. New York, NY: Foundation Press□: Thomson Reuters, 2010.

Veash, Nicole. "Violent Death Claims Survivors of Brazils Child Massacres." *The Guardian*, September 9, 2000.

Victims of Trafficking and Violence Protection Act of 2000, 2000. http://www.state.gov/documents/organization/10492.pdf.

"VICTORY! Philips Accepts Recycling Responsibility." *Greenpeace*, February 26, 2009. http://www.greenpeace.org/international/en/news/features/victory-philips260209/.

Villatoro, Ruth. *La Cantinera*. Toro Films, 2012.

Vincent Jones, Samuel. "HUMAN TRAFFICKING VICTIM IDENTIFICATION: SHOULD CONSENT MATTER?" *Indiana Law Review* 45, no. 2 (2012): 483–511.

Violence Against Women and Department of Justice Reauthorization Act of 2005. Accessed October 25, 2013. http://usaimmigrationattorney.com/images/IMBRA2005.pdf.

"Vote on Child Marriage Law in Yemen Delayed - CNN.com," 18:45:27. http://www.cnn.com/2010/WORLD/meast/10/04/yemen.child.marriage.law/.

Walshe, Sadhbh. "New Court Helps New York's Human Trafficking Victims." *Al Jazeera*, October 31, 2013. http://america.aljazeera.com/articles/2013/10/31/new-court-systemhelpsvictimsofhumantraffickinginnewyork.html.

Westhead, Rick. "Don't Look , Don't Tell, Troops Told." *The Toronto Star*, June 16, 2008. http://www.thestar.com/news/2008/06/16/dont_look_dont_tell_troops_told.html.

Westwater, Judy, and Wanda Carter. *Street Kid: One Child's Desperate Fight for Survival*. [Place of publication not identified]: Element, 2006.

"What Is the Red Thread Movement." *The Red Thread Movement*. Accessed October 26, 2013. http://www.gogirlsmusic.com/rtm_band.pdf.

Whitegead, Tom. "Age of Criminal Responsibility Should Be Raised, Says Leading Barrister." *The Telegraph*, October 7, 2010. http://www.telegraph.co.uk/news/uknews/law-and-order/7804238/Age-of-criminal-responsibility-should-be-raised-says-leading-barrister.html.

WHO. "Why Do so Many Women Still Die in Pregnancy or Childbirth?," August 21, 2013. http://www.who.int/features/qa/12/en/.

"Wife Charged with Grooming Sex Slave." *UPI*, 20:33:13. http://www.upi.com/Top_News/US/2011/03/31/Wife-charged-with-grooming-sex-slave/UPI-95431301608012/.

Wilberforce, Robert Isaac, and Samuel Wilberforce. *The Life of William Wilberforce*. John Murray, 1838.

William Wilberforce Trafficking Victims Protection Reauthorization Act of 2008. USC, 2013.

Williams, Alex. "The New Math on Campus." *The New York Times*, February 5, 2010, sec. Fashion & Style. http://www.nytimes.com/2010/02/07/fashion/07campus.html.
Williams Shavers, Anna. "HUMAN TRAFFICKING, THE RULE OF LAW, AND CORPORATE SOCIAL RESPONSIBILITY." *South Carolina Journal of International Law & Business* 9, no. 1 (Fall 2012): 39–88.
Wilson, Alicia. "Using Commercial Driver Licensing Authority to Combat Human Trafficking Related Crimes on America's Highways." *University of Memphs Law Review* 43, no. 4 (Summer 2013): 969–1012.
"Women Sentenced to Life in Prison for Torturing Maid." *Lubbock Online*, October 19, 2001. http://lubbockonline.com/stories/101901/upd_075-4746.shtml.
"World Vision Child Slavery." *Orld Vision*. Accessed October 23, 2013. http://www.worldvision.org/our-impact/child-protection?campaign=11935146&gclid=CLP41byLvLoCFenm7AoduVwAVA.
Wylie, Bob. "In the Romanian 'Canyons of Horror.'" *BBC*, December 26, 2009, sec. Europe. http://news.bbc.co.uk/2/hi/europe/8428283.stm.
"Yemeni Child Bride, 12, Dies in Labor." *CBS News*, 18:49:46. http://www.cbsnews.com/8301-202_162-5307092.html.
Yeoman, Ian, and Michelle Mars. "Robots, Men and Sex Tourism." *Science Direct* Futures Volume 44, no. 4 (May 2012): 365–371.
Youngbee, Dale. "Cote D'Ivoire and Ivorian Government: Leader in Child Labor, Abuse and Trafficking." *The Wasshington Post.* March 18, 2012. http://communities.washingtontimes.com/neighborhood/rights-so-divine/2012/mar/18/real-trafficker-chocolate-slavery/.
"Your Tomato's Possible Ties to Slavery," 01:05:41. http://thecnnfreedomproject.blogs.cnn.com/2011/04/21/your-tomato-possible-ties-to-slavery/.
Yung, Minsoo. "Associations of Physical and Sexual Health with Suicide Attempts Among Female Sex Workers in South Korea." *Sexuality & Disability* 31, no. 3 (September 2013): 275–286.
"Zimbabwe: End Repression in Marange Diamond Fields." *Human Rights Watch*, June 26, 2009. http://www.hrw.org/news/2009/06/26/zimbabwe-end-repression-marange-diamond-fields.
Zucconi-Grassi, G, and V Grassi. "[Internal chemoreceptors. Chemical regulation of respiration]." *Recenti progressi in medicina* 58, no. 6 (June 1975): 605–642.
Zwick, Edward. *Blood Diamond.* Warner Bros., 2006.

Index

A

B

C

D

E

F

G

H

I

J

S

T

U

V

W

Y

Z

Awareness and/or Fund Raising Campaign

You will be placed in groups and asked to create a campaign to raise awareness of human trafficking and/or fund-raise for human trafficking victims. This will take half of the semester and will include a presentation of your campaign in class. The class will vote on which campaign the whole class wishes to work on for the rest of the semester. The class will then work on that idea in order to carry out the project at the end of the semester.

You will need

- A slogan/tag line
- A logo
- An advertisement
- An advertising strategy
- Strategy for bringing the campaign to the widest audience

Example 1

Coasters – on one side of the coasters there is a deliberately blurred photo of a slave with the line "Can you see me?" On the other side the slave's story is told. They are placed in coffee/tea and bars around the town in the expectation that customers will be curious enough to read them.

Example 2

Sale – many victims make things to sell. The money from sales supports them and other rescue efforts. An example of a non-profit which brings such items together is eternal threads based in Abilene, Texas. They ship the goods out on a sale or return basis to Universities, schools, Churches etc. Such sales raise money and awareness.

Templates to be used for Group Meetings:

Groups work much better where you have assigned roles and agendas. In your first meeting you should appoint individuals to specific roles.

The *facilitator* should ensure that the meeting runs smoothly and that everyone has a chance to participate fully. Don't let one or two hijack meetings. This person should also circulate and agenda for each meeting a couple of days ahead of a meeting so that others can think creatively. S/he should record it below

The *Note-taker* should keep a full note (recorded below) of the important suggestions made and issues discussed at the meeting. Attribute the ideas and discussions to group members. Also, note who will be responsible for which actions.

The *Time-keeper* should liaise with other group members to arrange meeting times, book rooms and, during the meeting ensure that time is not wasted. You are all busy people and you need to have efficient meetings. A tip for this is to arrange for people to come 5mins early. This enables them to get 'social talking' out of the way so that when the meeting starts you can concentrate on the matter at hand.

Other members of the group should use the following templates to record all the information set out therein. You will hand in one template for each meeting at the end of the semester to inform part of your participation grade.

As a group you may find that you need to assign other jobs e.g. project coordinator but all three of the above are required.

Template 1

Facilitator: ______________________________

Note-taker ______________________________

Time-keeper ______________________________

Title of Project ______________________________

Agenda:

Notes of the meeting:

Before the next meeting I must DO:

Decisions made in the meeting:

Peer grade (letter) assigned to each of the group members for this meeting and any work done between meetings – explain in a couple of sentences why you awarded the grade.

Template 2

Facilitator: ______________________________

Note-taker ______________________________

Time-keeper ______________________________

Title of Project ______________________________

Agenda:

Notes of the meeting:

Before the next meeting I must DO:

Decisions made in the meeting:

Peer grade (letter) assigned to each of the group members for this meeting and any work done between meetings – explain in a couple of sentences why you awarded the grade.

Template 3

Facilitator: ______________________________

Note-taker ______________________________

Time-keeper ______________________________

Title of Project ______________________________

Agenda:

Notes of the meeting:

Before the next meeting I must DO:

Decisions made in the meeting:

Peer grade (letter) assigned to each of the group members for this meeting and any work done between meetings – explain in a couple of sentences why you awarded the grade.

Template 4

Facilitator: ____________________

Note-taker ____________________

Time-keeper ____________________

Title of Project ____________________

Agenda:

Notes of the meeting:

Before the next meeting I must DO:

Decisions made in the meeting:

Peer grade (letter) assigned to each of the group members for this meeting and any work done between meetings – explain in a couple of sentences why you awarded the grade.

Template 5

Facilitator: ____

Note-taker ____

Time-keeper ____

Title of Project ____

Agenda:

Notes of the meeting:

Before the next meeting I must DO:

Decisions made in the meeting:

Peer grade (letter) assigned to each of the group members for this meeting and any work done between meetings – explain in a couple of sentences why you awarded the grade.

Template 6

Facilitator: ____________________

Note-taker ____________________

Time-keeper ____________________

Title of Project ____________________

Agenda:

Notes of the meeting:

Before the next meeting I must DO:

Decisions made in the meeting:

Peer grade (letter) assigned to each of the group members for this meeting and any work done between meetings – explain in a couple of sentences why you awarded the grade.

Template 7

Facilitator: ______________________________

Note-taker ______________________________

Time-keeper ______________________________

Title of Project ______________________________

Agenda:

Notes of the meeting:

Before the next meeting I must DO:

Decisions made in the meeting:

Peer grade (letter) assigned to each of the group members for this meeting and any work done between meetings – explain in a couple of sentences why you awarded the grade.

Template 8

Facilitator: ______________________________

Note-taker ______________________________

Time-keeper ______________________________

Title of Project ______________________________

Agenda:

Notes of the meeting:

Before the next meeting I must DO:

Decisions made in the meeting:

Peer grade (letter) assigned to each of the group members for this meeting and any work done between meetings – explain in a couple of sentences why you awarded the grade.

SOLUTIONS WORKSHEET
(SEMESTER AND SOLUTIONS CLASS)

Student Name:..Section.......................

Use this worksheet to keep a note of ideas for Solutions that we discuss in class or which occur to you during the semester.

Solutions Homework:

Write down **TWO** workable Solutions – these should be local, regional or international. You should reality test them:

Example: There should be an International Court for Human Traffickers – Reality testing

a. Would the U.S. sign up?
b. What would it take to encourage the U.S. to sign up?
c. What problems do the U.S. have about other Human Rights based Treaties? And more....
d. Would it matter if the U.S. didn't sign up
e. Test the idea against other International Courts for efficacy

Solution One

Reality Test:

Positive Points

Negative Points

Solution Two

Reality Test:

Positive Points

Negative Points

Solutions Class

You will be placed in a group and given time in class to discuss your two options with others. From the ideas which you bring to the discussion write down below the **THREE** best solution ideas which come from your group. You will be asked to share them with the rest of the class and then turn in this worksheet. (If you run out of room add a sheet of paper).

Solution One

___

Reality Test:

Positive Points

___

___

___

___

Negative Points

___

___

___

___

Solution Two

___

Reality Test:

Positive Points

___

___

___

___

Negative Points

___

___

___

___

Solution Three

Reality Test:

Positive Points

Negative Points